# THE EARLY COINS OF AMERICA.

# PLATE I.

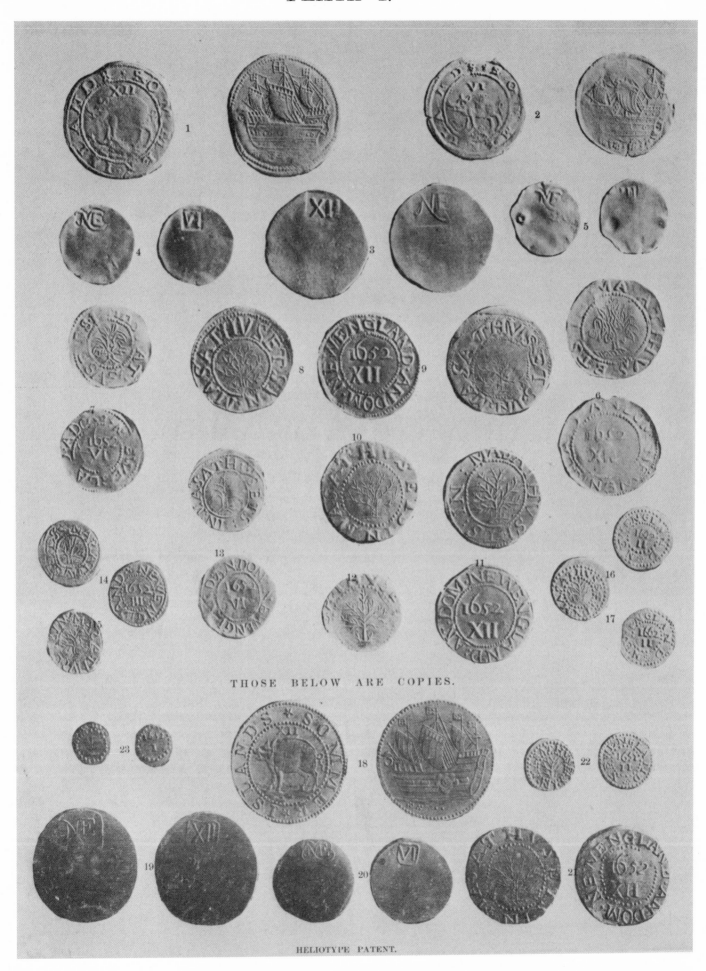

THOSE BELOW ARE COPIES.

HELIOTYPE PATENT.

THE

# Early Coins of America;

AND THE

LAWS GOVERNING THEIR ISSUE.

COMPRISING ALSO DESCRIPTIONS OF

THE WASHINGTON PIECES, THE ANGLO-AMERICAN TOKENS,

MANY PIECES OF UNKNOWN ORIGIN,

OF THE SEVENTEENTH AND EIGHTEENTH CENTURIES,

AND THE

FIRST PATTERNS OF THE UNITED STATES MINT.

By SYLVESTER S. CROSBY.

**Sanford J. Durst**
Numismatic Publications
**New York, N.Y.**

Copyright

©

1983

Sanford J. Durst
29-28 41st Avenue
Long Island City, N.Y. 11101

ISBN No. 0-942666-24-0
LC No. 83-71431

Originally published

by

The Author
Boston - 1875

This is a reprint

# INTRODUCTION.

————▶•◀————

In view of the great interest in the study of Numismatology, and the many recent discoveries of local coins not heretofore described, as well as the numerous errors (perhaps unavoidable at their time,) into which writers upon the subject of American coins have fallen, it was deemed expedient, a few years since, by the NEW ENGLAND NUMISMATIC AND ARCHÆO-LOGICAL SOCIETY, at the suggestion of their then Vice President, (Mr. CHARLES CHAPLIN,) to publish a work which should contain full and correct descriptions of those coins known among American collectors as "Colonials." A committee, consisting of Messrs. SYLVESTER S. CROSBY, DUDLEY R. CHILD, CHAS. CHAPLIN, CHAS. S. FELLOWS, T. EDWARD BOND, and JAS. E. ROOT, was thereupon appointed to prepare the work for publication.

When it became known that such a work was contemplated, many friends, in whose judgment the greatest confidence was reposed, advised that it should be made to include also copies of the laws by authority of which such coins were issued, as well as of acts and proposals, or petitions, having in view the establishment of a coinage, which were presented to or passed by those States which took action upon this subject. This advice was accepted, though not without much hesitation, in consequence of the magnitude of the work which such a plan would necessitate, and the time requisite for the study and research which should be devoted to the subject to insure reliability.

Circumstances having relieved the Committee to whom the work was entrusted, from their labor, the duty of preparing this volume most unexpectedly devolved upon myself, originally the Chairman of the Committee. Having constantly in view the plan adopted, I have therefore personally inspected and copied nearly all the records and documents relating to coinage which the strictest search could discover in the archives of the several States; and of most of those not examined by me, certified copies have been procured. Of some documents I have been compelled to obtain copies from the State Paper Office in England, where they were made for me with great care, and carefully revised. Among these may be mentioned some papers referring to the coinage of New England, to that of Lord Baltimore, and to the patents of William Wood.

When this work was undertaken, it was with the feeling that there was little to be found not already known to most of those who are interested in this science; but my labors have been rewarded with more success than I had reason to expect, and I think I can say with truth, that this work contains much information never before published, and several important papers heretofore entirely unknown.

My intention has been to give all the trustworthy information at my command relative to those coins, or the tokens which were intended to serve as coins, which were either struck in those parts of America which now constitute the United States, or were intended for use therein. Some coins are treated upon herein which perhaps are not strictly comprised within the above limits, but which, being of interest from their connection with the early history of our country, or from association therewith, are eagerly sought by collectors of American coins. The most noticeable instance of this kind is the coin of the Sommer Islands; in reference to these I have quoted much from Smith's History of those islands which was thought to be of interest in this connection, as it contains the only early reference to these coins that has come to my knowledge, as well as some other passages of numismatic interest.

I would here express my obligation to many numismatists who have materially aided me in my undertaking: To WILLIAM S. APPLETON, A. M., of Boston, for great assistance in descriptions, particularly upon points of heraldry, as well as for facilities for illustrating many pieces in his extensive collection; to Hon. CHARLES H. BELL, of Exeter, New Hampshire, for copies of the Act, and drawings of the designs of coins for that State; to J. CARSON BREVOORT, Esq., of Brooklyn, N. Y., for assistance in the tabulation of State coins, and the loan of many coins required for illustration; to CHARLES I. BUSHNELL, Esq., of New York, so well known as an indefatigable student and collector, not only of coins, but also of their history, for much of the result of his labors; to CHARLES CLAY, M. D., of Manchester, England, for impressions of many coins in his collection, then in England; to JEREMIAH COLBURN, A. M., of Boston, for many important favors; to ROBERT C. DAVIS, Ph. G., and EDWARD MARIS, M. D., of Philadelphia, for many new varieties of coins, and for copies of papers not otherwise attainable; to Hon. CHARLES J. HOADLY, of Hartford, Conn., for copies of papers unknown to us except through him; to Messrs. LORIN G. PARMELEE, of Boston, the present, and GEORGE F. SEAVEY, of Cambridge, the former owner of the "Seavey Collection," for the use of any specimens in that collection that would facilitate my object; to MATTHEW A. STICKNEY, Esq., of Salem, Mass., for the use of several specimens, unknown except in his Cabinet, as well as for other assistance ; to Messrs. HENRY S. ADAMS, SAMUEL A. GREEN, M. D., and Dr. W. ELLIOT WOODWARD, of Boston, Messrs. BENJAMIN BETTS, EDWARD COGAN, COLIN LIGHTBODY and WILLIAM H. STROBRIDGE, of Brooklyn, N. Y., ISAAC FRANCIS WOOD, Esq., of New York, WILLIAM FEWSMITH, A. M., of Philadelphia, AUGUSTINE SHURTLEFF, M. D., of Brookline, Mass., and to many others, who have rendered me valuable assistance.

The subscribers, who have the sincere thanks of the author for their assistance and forbearance, will call to mind, some with impatience, and many with regret, but none with the sorrow of the author, the many occasions of delay in the issue of the several parts. These delays were unavoidable, but have, beyond a doubt, contributed to the completeness of the work, as the interest awakened by it, and the time allowed for the exercise of that interest, have been the means of bringing to light several new and important pieces, and some information of value, which would otherwise have remained unavailable in this connection.

I intend no exaggeration in stating that I have long anticipated the day that should witness the completion of my labors, as a day that would bring me relief from the greatest care with which I have been burdened; a care I would never have accepted had I entertained the most remote idea that the whole labor and responsibility would devolve upon me, as has proved to be the case. And although my labors in this undertaking have brought me many pleasant correspondents, acquaintances and friends, yet the frequent, long, and often vexatious delays, and the absence of expected assistance, have rendered them, at times, extremely arduous.

I now send forth this volume, in the hope that I have fallen into no more grievous errors than has been the fortune of earlier numismatic writers; that my labors have not been fruitless in obtaining material for some addition to the amount of knowledge upon a subject which has been too much neglected; and, as the study of Numismatics is a valuable adjunct to the study of History, I trust that my work may not prove to be without value in an historical point of view.

S. S. CROSBY.

BOSTON, JULY 1, 1875.

In commencing this work, it was thought that a book might be produced free from typographical errors, if not from errors of statement; but the force of the old couplet, —

"Whoever thinks a faultless piece to see
Thinks what ne'er was, nor is, nor e'er will be,"

is realized, and attention must be called to the following corrections.

Page 16, twelfth line, for Felget. read Felgat.

Page 82, seventh line, for ꝑ read p

Page 98, last line, for John Addington, read Is$^a$ Addington.

Page 106, last line, for p̄ces, read p̄ies.

Page 121, first line, for 1605, read 1705.

Page 162, tenth line, for 14, read 24.

Page 180, cuts No. 29 and 30, should be transposed.

Page 249, the lower brace in the dash column of the table of reverses, should include F.

Page 290, twenty-sixth line, for March 5th, read March 3d.

Page 347, seventh line, $\frac{i}{v}$, should be $\frac{I}{V}$

# MARKS AND CONTRACTIONS.

A Dash (–) over a letter, indicates the omission of a letter, usually a repetition, following the one marked.

A Curved Line ~ indicates the omission of one or more letters after the one marked.

Superior Letters, usually indicate the omission of contiguous letters, either preceding or following them, though they are sometimes used where the word is written full.

Some doubtful words are placed between brackets [ ].

Repetitions in the original records are printed in Italics, as are also some parts which in the original were erased.

The following characters are used in the manner indicated:—

ã, — treãr, treasurer.
õ͠, — tio, — acõ͠n, action.
m̄, — mm, — com̄on, common.
m̃, — settlem̃ᵗᵗ, settlement.
n̄, — nn, año, anno.
ñ, — restraiññg, restraining.
õ, — amõᵗᵗ, amount.
p̃, — par, por, — p̃t, part ; p̃tion, portion.
p, — per, — pform, perform.
ꝑ, — pro, — ꝑvide, provide.
p̄, — pre, — p̄face, preface.
s̃, — s̃d, said.
t̃, — capt̃, captain.
ũ, — goũeʳ, governor.

## DIRECTIONS TO THE BINDER.

—oo:o:oo—

# CONTENTS.

# SOMMER ISLANDS.

———— ‹•••› ————

As the coinage for the Bermuda or Sommer Islands was doubtless the first ever struck for the English colonies in America, that first claims attention in the development of our plan.

These islands, although now having no political connection with the United States, were claimed by the Virginia Company as included in their grant, until their claim was sold, about 1612.

The following sketch of the history of their settlement, as given by Capt. John Smith, in "The Generall Historie of Virginia New-England and the Summer Isles," published in London in 1624, may not be without interest, aside from the numismatic information it furnishes.

In excuse for quoting so much which is apparently irrelevant to the subject, the reader is referred to the first sentence of these extracts, in which he may make the alterations necessary to suit it for the purpose; for, as Geography has an intimate connection with History, so also has Numismatology a relation hardly less intimate or less important. Captain Smith writes :

"Before we present you the matters of fact, it is fit to offer to your view the Stage whereon they were acted, for as Geography without History seemeth a carkasse without motion, so History without Geography, wandreth as a Vagrant without a certaine habitation. Those Ilands lie in the huge maine Ocean, and two hundred leagues from any continent, situated in 32. degrees and 25. minutes, of Northerly latitude, and distant from England West South-West, about 3300. miles, some twenty miles in length, and not past two miles and a halfe in breadth, enuironed with Rocks, which to the North-ward, West-ward, and South-East, extend further then they haue bin yet well discouered : by reason of those Rocks the Country is naturally very strong, for there is but two places, and scare two, vnlesse to them who know them well, where shipping may safely come in, and those now are exceeding well fortified, but within is roome to entertaine a royall Fleet : the Rocks in most places appeare at a low water, neither are they much couered at a high, for it ebbs and flowes not past fiue foot."

"How these Iles came by the name of Bermudas, or the infinite number of blacke Hogs, or so fearefull to the world, that many called them the Ile of Deuils, that all men did shun as Hell and perdition ; I will not expostulate, nor trouble your patiences with those vncertaine antiquities further then thus ; our men found divers crosses, peeces of Spanish monies here and there. Two or three wracks also they found, by certaine inscriptions to bee some Spanish, some Dutch, some French ; but the greatest rumour is, that a Spanish ship called Bermudas was there cast away, carrying Hogges to the West-Indies that swam a shore, and there increased : how the Spaniards escaped is vncertaine : but they say, from that ship those Iles were first called Bermudas, which till then for six thousand yeares had beene namelesse. But the first English-man that was euer in them, was one Henry May, a worthy Mariner that went with Captaine Lancaster to the East-Indies 1591," who, on their return, were, on the seventeenth of the following December, "cast away vpon the North-west of the Bermudas."

"You haue heard, that when Captaine Smith was Gouernor of Virginia, there were nine ships sent with Sir Thomas Gates, and Sir George Somers, and Captaine Nuport with fiue hundred people, to take in the old Commission, and rectifie a new gouernment : they set saile in May, and in the height of thirty degrees of Northerly latitude, they were taken with an extreme storme, or rather a part of Hericano, vpon the fiue and twentieth of Iuly, which as they write, did not onely separate them from the Fleet, but with the violent working of the Seas, their ship became so shaken, torne and leake, she receiued so much water as couered two tire of Hogsheads aboue the ballace, that they stood vp to the middles, with Buckets, Baricos, and Kettles, to baile out the water. Thus bailing and pumping three daies and three nights without intermission, and yet the water seemed rather to increase then diminish. * * That Sir George Somers all this time sitting vpon the poupe, scarce taking leisure to eat nor sleepe, couing the ship to keepe her as vpright as he could, otherwaies she must long ere that needs haue foundered, most wishedly and happily descried land ; * * not long it was before they strucke vpon a rocke, till a surge of the sea cast her from thence, and so from one to another, till most luckily at last so vpright betwixt two, as if she had beene in the stocks; * * they vnshipped all their goods, victuall, and persons into their Boats, and with extreme ioy, euen almost to amazednesse, arriued in safetie, though more then a league from the shore, without the losse of a man ; yet were they in all one hundred and fiftie: * * and they found it the richest, healthfullest and pleasantest they euer saw, as is formerly said."

"At their first hunting for hogs they found such abundance, they killed 32 and this hunting and fishing was appointed to Captaine Robert Walsingham, and Mr. Henry Shelly for the company in general : they report they killed at least 500 besides Pigs, and that many were killed by diuers others; for the birds in their seasons, the facility to make their cabens of Palmeta leaues, caused many of them vtterly forget or desire euer to returne from thence, they liued in such plenty, peace and ease." Captain Smith jocosely says, " You may plainly see no place knowne hath better walls nor a broader ditch."

"But hauing finished and rigged their two new Cedar ships with such prouisions they saued from the Sea-aduenturer they left amongst the Rocks, they called the one the Patience, the other the Deliuerance, * * they set saile the tenth of May 1610, onely leauing two men behinde them."

"Lord Laware * * vnderstanding what plenty there was of hogs and other good things in the Bermudas, was desirous to send thither to supply his necessary occasions ; whereupon Sir George Summers, the best acquainted with the place, whose noble minde euer regarded a generall good more then his owne ends, though aboue threescore yeeres of age, and had meanes in England sutable to his ranke, offered himselfe by Gods helpe to performe this dangerous voyage againe for the Bermudas, which was kindly accepted, so vpon the 19. of Iune he imbarked in his Cedar ship, about the burthen of thirty tunnes, and so set saile."

"Much foule and crosse weather he had, and was forced to the North parts of Virginia, where refreshing himselfe vpon this vnknowne coast, he could not bee diuerted from the search of the Bermudas, where at last with his company he safely arriued : * * In that very place which we now call Saint Georges towne, this noble Knight died, whereof the place taketh the name. But his men * * embalmed his body and set saile for England, being the first that euer went to seeke those Ilands, which haue beene euer since called Summers Iles, in honour of his worthy memory. * * This Cedar ship at last with his dead body arriued at Whit-Church in Dorsetshire, where by his friends he was honourably buried, with many vollies of shot, and the rites of a Souldier, and vpon his tombe was bestowed this Epitaph. In English thus :

"*Alas* Virginia's *Summer so soone past,*
*Autumne succeeds and stormy* Winters *blast,*
Yet Englands *ioyfull Spring with ioyfull showers,*
O Florida, *shall bring thy sweetest flowers.*"

"Now you are to vnderstand, that Captaine Matthew Somers, Nephew and heire to Sir George, that returned with his dead body, though both he and his Company did their vtmost in relating all those passages to their Countrey-men and aduenturers, their relations were beleeued but as trauellers tales, till it came to be apprehended by some of the Virginia Company, how beneficiall it might be, and helpfull to the Plantation in Virginia, so that some one hundred and twentie of them bought the pretended right of all the Company, and had sent this ship to make a triall ; but first they had obtained Letters Patents of the Kings most excellent Maiestie. Sir Thomas Smith was elected Treasurer and Gouernour heere, and Master Richard More to be Gouernour of the Iles and Colony there."

"Master More * * so presently landed his goods and sixty persons towards the beginning of Iuly 1612, vpon the South side of Smiths Ile."

Governor More was succeeded in 1615, according to Smith, by six Governors, who were to rule one month each, alternately, although but four are named by him as having occupied that position, viz : Charles Caldicot, John Mansfield, Christopher Carter, and Miles Kendall.

"The next newes that happened in this time of ease, was, that a merry fellow hauing found some few Dollars against the Flemish wracke, the bruit went currant the treasure was found, and they all made men. Much adoe there was to preuent the purloining of it, before they had it : vvhere after they had tyred themselues vvith searching, that they found, amounted not to aboue twenty pounds starling, vvhich is not vnlike but to be the remainder of some greater store, washed from some wracke not farre from the shore."

After many troubles under the rule of the several Governors, choice was made of "Master Daniel Tuckar, that a long time had bin a planter in Virginia in the gouernment of Captaine Smith."

"About the mistd of May (1616) arriued this Gouernor, where finding the Inhabitants both abhorring all exacted labour, as also in a manner disdaining and grudging much to be commanded by him ; it could not but passionate any man liuing. But at last according to the Virginia order, hee set euery one was with him at Saint Georges, to his taske, to cleere grounds, fell trees, set corne, square timber, plant vines and other fruits brought out of England. These by their taske Masters by breake a day repaired to the wharfe, from thence to be imployed to the place of their imployment, till nine of the clocke, and then in the after-noone from three till Sunne-set. Beside meat, drinke and cloaths, they had for a time a certaine kinde of brasse money with a hogge on the one side, in memory of the abundance of hogges was found at their first landing."

Richard Sanders, with four others, having built a boat of three tons, in which to make their escape from the tyranny of the Governor, after several weeks of buffeting among the waves, and having nearly destroyed their little vessel for firewood, finally landed in Ireland. In the words of Smith, " This fortunate Sanders going to the East Indies, in the rifling some ships there tooke, it was his chance to buy an old chest, for three or foure shillings, but because it wanted a key hee repented his bargaine, and would gladly haue sold it againe for lesse. A certaine time it lay tossed to and fro as a thing hee little regarded, but at last hauing little to doe, hee broke it open, where he found a thousand pounds starling, or so much gold as bought him in England a good estate, which leauing with his wife he returned againe to the East Indies."

Governor Tuckar being much disliked, and much trouble arising there-from, he returned to England, leaving Miles Kendall in authority as his deputy. Kendall seems to have been much liked, but he was, in October, 1619, succeeded by Captain Nathaniel Butler, who arrived on the twentieth day of that month, — a very energetic Governor. Captain Smith writes that he "Finding accidentally a little crosse erected in a by place, amongst a many of bushes, vnderstanding there was buried the heart and intrailes of Sir George Summers, hee resolued to haue a better memory for so worthy a Souldier, then that. So finding also a great Marble stone brought out of England, hee caused it by Masons to bee wrought handsomely and laid ouer the place, which hee inuironed with a square wall of hewen stone, Tombe like ; wherein he caused to bee grauen this Epitaph he had composed, and fixed it vpon the Marble stone ; and thus it was,

*In the yeere  1  6  1  1,*
*Noble Sir George Summers went hence to heauen ;*
*Whose well tri'd worth that held him still imploid,*
*Gaue him the knowledge of the world so wide.*
*Hence 'twas by heauens decree, that to this place·*
*He brought new guests, and name to mutuall grace.*
*At last his soule and body being to part,*
*He here bequeath'd his entrails and his heart."*

At the expiration of his rule, in 1621, Gov. Butler left the government of these islands in charge of Captains Felget and Stokes, and Masters Hewes, Nedom, and Ginner. In 1622 John Bernard arrived, who lived only six weeks, when both he and his wife died so nearly at the same time that both were buried in one grave and on the same day.

Master John Harrison was then chosen as Governor until orders should come from England. He was ruling in 1623, at which time Captain Smith thus dismisses the subject : "It is too true, in the absence of the noble Treasurer, Sir Edward Sackvill, now Earle of Dorset, there haue beene such complaints betwixt the Planters and the Company, that by command the Lords appointed Sir Thomas Smith againe Treasurer, that since then according to their order of Court he is also elected, where now we must leaue them all to their good fortune and successe, till we hear further of their fortunate proceedings."

It is to these islands that we are indebted for the earliest coinage which can be considered as intended for America.

History has preserved for us but the most meagre account of this first coinage struck in Europe for her possessions in the New World, — one only, and that simply Smith's passing notice of the former use and partial description of this coin, can we glean from her pages ; and the all-devouring tooth of Time has spared us but few specimens from which to determine with what legends and devices it was embellished.

Three of the Shillings and one Sixpence are all now known to the numismatic world of the coinage struck for the "Sommer Islands ;" and no records exist for our instruction as to its precise date, by whom coined, or the circumstances under which it was issued or obtained a currency.

Smith informs us that "Master Daniel Tuckar" arrived at the islands about the middle of May, 1616 ; and he leaves it to be inferred that it was under the rule of this Governor that "Beside meat, drinke and cloaths, they had for a time a certaine kinde of brasse money with a hogge on the one side, in memory of the abundance of hogges was found at their first landing."

Governor Tuckar's rule was for about two years ; thus, if the inference be correct, the currency of these coins must have commenced between May, 1616, and 1619, and it could not have been of long continuance, as in 1624 it is recorded as an event of the past.

These coins have been considered as medals, struck in commemoration of some event of interest relating to these islands ; but the recent discovery of a similar coin, of half the size and value of those before known, sets at rest all speculation upon that point, and is sufficient, even in the absence of Capt. Smith's assertion that they were "money," to prove that they were intended to serve the purposes of coin, even though they may have been issued without the authority requisite to legalize their currency, and thus entitle them to be denominated coins.

## SHILLING.

Obv. a hog, standing, facing left, above which are the Roman numerals XII, the whole surrounded by a beaded circle. Legend : SOMMER ✶ ISLANDS ✶ around which is a circle similar to that enclosing the device.

Rev. A full-rigged ship, under sail, to the left, with a flag flying from each of her four masts. The circle around it is composed of larger beads than those upon the obverse.

Copper ; size 19 ; weight, 177 grains.

[Plate I, Fig. 1.]

But two of these pieces are known to us, one of which is in the collection of William S. Appleton, Esq., of Boston, and the other has recently come into the possession of the writer. The latter piece was found, a few years since, in a bag of old coppers considered as of very little value, and bought, without knowledge of its rarity, by a junk dealer in New York ; but, being discovered by a collector, was quickly rescued from its obscurity, and has now found its way to its present resting-place.

## SIXPENCE.

The design of the Sixpence is similar to that of the Shilling, but has the numerals VI over the hog.    Legend : SOM MER ✠ ILA NDS ✠ Size 17.

[Plate I, Fig. 2.]

The only known specimen of the Sixpence was found, some twenty years since, in a garden upon one of the Bermuda Islands, (the island of St. George, if we mistake not,) and is now owned by Benjamin Betts, Esq., of Brooklyn, N. Y., through whose kindness our illustration of it is obtained.

These coins have been supposed to be made of brass, because of the term "brasse money," applied to them by Capt. Smith, who used that expression in accordance with the custom, common in early days, of giving that name to copper, or its alloys, without proper discrimination.

In illustration of this use of the word, we find written in the Scripture, "A land whose stones are iron, and out of whose hills thou mayest dig brass;" "Provide neither gold, nor silver, nor brass in your purses."

A fact pertinent to this subject is that the Roman copper coins are still known as "first brass," "second brass," or "third brass," according to their sizes.

# VIRGINIA.

Although in the charter granted by King James to Virginia, April 10th, 1606, the right of coining money was specified as one of the privileges conveyed thereby, this privilege does not appear to have been taken advantage of by the colonists, and no disposition to exercise that right seems to have been manifested until the passage of the act of November, 1645, which will be given in its proper place.

Section X of the charter referred to runs thus[1]: "And that they shall, or lawfully may, establish and cause to be made a coin, to pass current there between the people of those several colonies, for the more ease of traffic and bargaining between and amongst them and the natives there, of such metal, and in such manner and form, as the said several Councils there shall limit and appoint."

In relation to the financial condition of Virginia, during the early years of her colonial existence, we can furnish no information more reliable than that contained in the "Sketch of the Early Currency in Maryland and Virginia,"[2] by S. F. Streeter, read before the Historical Society of Maryland. He says :

"At the time of the settlement of Maryland, the Virginians had already begun to feel the inconvenience of thus relying upon an article of fluctuating and diminishing value as currency ; and in August, 1633, the assembly of

---

[1]Lucas's Charters of the Old English Colonies, p. 5.    [2]Historical Magazine, vol. ii. p. 42.

that Colony passed a law requiring all contracts, bargains, pleas, and judgments to be made in money, and not in tobacco, since the exclusive use of the latter 'had bred many inconveniences in trade, and occasioned many troubles, as well to the merchants as the planters and inhabitants among themselves.'

"In January, 1640, 'tobacco, by reason of excessive quantities made,' had become so cheap, that it was decided to burn all the bad and half the good tobacco in the country; require all creditors to take forty pounds in the hundred, and to demand for all tobacco made during the year one shilling per pound, and two shillings for the next year's crop. These measures, however, do not appear to have increased the quantity of specie in circulation, for the next year a law was passed making money debts not recoverable or pleadable, on account of the 'manie and great inconveniences which do dayly arise by dealing for monie.' In March, 1643, 'for the encouragement of the owners of horses, mares, or sheepe,' an exception was made in their favor, and they were allowed to require and receive cash for the sale of those animals.

"At the same session was confirmed an agreement which had been made with the Governor of Maryland, on the third of June, 1642, allowing the people of the two colonies to trade or barter for all kinds of commodities raised within their respective territories, (servants and goods imported, and horses, mares, and sheep excepted,) provided tobacco was not used as a medium of exchange; yet the last act of this assembly brought the circulating medium nearer to that appropriate for a primitive condition of society than had been recognized since the establishment of the colony. The troubles in England between Charles the First and his Parliament had cut off the supplies of Sir William Berkeley, his majesty's Governor, and a levy was therefore made of two shillings a head on every tithable person in the colony, to be paid in provisions, at fixed rates. Among these were 'corn at 10s. per barrel; wheat at 4s. per bushel; beef at 3½d. per lb.; good hens at 12d.; capons at 1s. 6d.; calves at six weeks old, 25s.; butter at 8d. per lb.; good weather goats at 20s.; piggs to roast at three weeks old, at 3s. per pigg; cheese at 6d. per lb.; and geese, turkeys, and kidds at 5s. per peece.' These articles were deposited at places appointed, and transported in boats to James City, where they were deposited in the Governor's grand larder or treasury. About the same period tavern-keepers were by law forbidden to take more than ten pounds of tobacco for a meal, and to sell any wines or strong liquor, excepting strong beer, for which they were allowed to charge 'eight lbs. of tobacco per gallon, and no more; and ratably for smaller quantities.' The tonnage duties upon vessels arriving at this time were payable in powder and shot, 'one halfe pound of powder per every tunne burthen, and three pound of leaden shott, or lead.'"

Thus feeling the necessity of some more convenient medium of exchange, the following act[1] was passed at a session begun in James City, November 20, 1645 :

"ACT. XX. The Governor, Council and Burgesses of this present Grand Assembly having maturely weighed & considered how advantageous a quoine current would be to this collony, and the great wants and miseries which do daily happen vnto it by the sole dependency vpon tob'o, *have at length resolved and enacted, and be it by the authoritie aforesaid enacted* as the onely way to procure the said quoine and prevent the further miseries, That all peeces of Eight in Spanish money be valued and taken in payment, att the rate of sixe shillings and all other Spanish silver quoines proportionably which shall be brought into the collony : And whereas it is conceived that the said quoine will not continue with vs vnless we have a leger quoine, Therefore serious consideration had of the many wayes tending to that effect, It was at length generally allowed, That a quoine of copper would be the most beneficial to, and with most ease procured by the collony, And that after proclamation made by the Governour and Council that all person or persons within this collony whether merchants or others do desist or leave off tradeing for tob'o, vpon the penaltie and forfeiture of the thing so bought or sold, The one moyetie whereof shall be and come to the informer, and the other to the benefit of the state.

"The quoine to be erected after this manner, 10000 lb. of copper to be bought by the publique at the rate of 18d per lb. which amounts to £750 sterl. which to be paid in tob'o. at the rate of 1d. 1-2 per lb. 120000 of tob'o. which being collected per pole accounting 5000 persons in this collony it comes to 24 lb. of tob'o per pole every pound of copper to make 20s. and to allow for the mintage 12d. per pound soe there will remaine £9.500 sterl. The mintage allowed and deducted. The stocke to be Equallie divided amongst the adventurers to be quoined in two pences, three pences, sixe pences and nine pences. And if it shall happen at any time hereafter that the aforesaid

---

[1]The original of this Act is in the Library of Congress, Washington, D. C., and we are indebted to C. I. Bushnell, Esq., for our copy of it.

quoine be called in and become not currant, Yet the republique shall make good the quantity of so much (vizt.) £10000 to be levied per pole, And that it may be provided that this quoine may not be counterfeited and brought in, Besides the inflicting of capitall punishment vpon these who shall be found delinquents therein, That vppon every peece of coyne there be two rings, The one for the motto, The other to receave a new impression which shall be stamped yearly with some new ffigure, by one appointed for that purpose in each county, And that the hon'ble, Sir William Berkeley, Knt. Gov'r, shall have the disposall and placing of such and soe manie officers as shall be necessarilye required for performing and finishing the aforesaid service, Onely Capt. John Upton is hereby confirmed Mint Master Generall : Wee reposing much confidence in his care, ability and trust for the performance of the said office."

This act probably was never put in execution, as, had it been, we should doubtless have some of its results preserved among our numismatic treasures. Mr. Streeter remarks upon it :

"Whether it was ever carried into effect we are not informed ; but if it was, the conflicting legislation, the various expedients, and the depressed condition of the colony in after years, show that the new issue neither supplied the place of tobacco, nor met all the wants of the community for purposes of convenience and traffic."

"The legislature of Virginia [in 1645] prohibited dealing by barter, and established the Spanish piece of eight at six shillings, as the standard of currency for that colony."[1]

In 1655 "the Virginian legislature changed the Spanish piece of eight from six shillings, and established it at five shillings sterling, as the standard of its currency."[2]

Oldmixon, in his History,[3] says of trade in Virginia, "Tho the common way of Traffick there is by Barter or Exchange of one Commodity for another, or of any for Tobacco ; yet there is some Silver Coins, English and Spanish, and were much more, till the lowering of the Value tempted People to export the Coin to the other Plantations, where it went for more than it did in *Virginia*.

"The Chief of their Coins are either Gold of the Stamp of *Arabia*, or Silver and Gold of the Stamp of *Spanish America*, or English Money. There's very little of either kind to be seen in this Country for the Reasons abovemention'd.

---

[1]Holmes's American Annals, vol. i., p. 336.     [2]Ibid, p. 366.     [3]Oldmixon, vol. i., p. 315.

"The Government, round about it, often raising the Value of the Coin, is the Cause that *Virginia* is drain'd of the little it has. And 'tis impossible to prevent this Inconvenience, unless all the Colonies on the Continent were oblig'd to have one and the same Standard for their Coin, which there have lately been some attempts made to effect, tho without the Success that was expected and desir'd.

"The Scarcity of Money is such in this Plantation, that Gentlemen can hardly get enough for Travelling Charges, or to pay Labourers and Tradesmens Wages. It occasions also the commencing many vexatious Suits for Debt, which by this means are contracted.

"The Value of the several Coins that are there, is as follows :

|  | £ | s. | d. |
|---|---|---|---|
| The Spanish Double Doublon, | 03 | 10 | 00 |
| The Doublon, consequently, | 01 | 15 | 00 |
| The Pistole, | 00 | 17 | 06 |
| *Arabian* Chequins, | 00 | 10 | 00 |
| Pieces of Eight, (except of *Peru*,) weighing 16 penny Weight, | 00 | 05 | 00 |
| French Crowns, | 00 | 05 | 00 |
| *Peru* Pieces of Eight, and Dutch Dollars, | 00 | 04 | 00 |

And all English Coin as it goes in *England*."

Oldmixon[1] further informs us that in 1679 "The Assembly taking into Consideration their Loss by lowering their Coin, which had occasion'd the Country's being almost drain'd of it by Exportion to Places where it past for more than it did in *Virginia*, order'd a Bill to be brought in for raising it.

"The Governour interposing in the matter, told them, it was the King's Prerogative to alter the Value of the Coin, and the Prerogative being intrusted with him, he wou'd do it by Proclamation. The Assembly durst not oppose such an Argument. Those were not times to dispute the Prerogative Royal; so the Governour's Reasons were allow'd and the Act dropt.

"His Lordship (Colpepper,) having gain'd his Point, privately bought up all the light Pieces of Eight he could get, at 5 s. the Piece ; and then put forth a Proclamation, to raise the Value of them to 6 Shillings : He soon after produc'd an Order to pay and disband the Regiment that had been sent

---

[1]Vol. i., p. 259.

over by Sir *John Berry;* and accordingly he paid them off with those Pieces at 6 s. a piece ; and they were forc'd to take them at that rate.

"This Lord however found very great Inconveniencies by his raising the Coin, as well on account of his own Sallary, his Duty on Ships, as of the King's Taxes, which were paid in Pieces of Eight at 6 s. a piece : The loss was like to be more than his Gain, by injuring the poor Soldiers."

# MASSACHUSETTS.

## SILVER CURRENCY.

Before entering upon the records of the laws for the establishment and government of the silver mint of Massachusetts, it may not be unprofitable briefly to consider the straits to which the colonists were reduced for want of a convenient medium of exchange, and the laws passed by them, for the regulation of such as appeared to them most available, amongst the many materials which were presented for their consideration.

The use of furs, grain, and fish[1] for purposes of exchange, and the payment of private debts, as well as taxes, had existed from the first settlement of the country ; but the earliest attempt made to establish a currency, if we may except the fixing of a certain value, by the General Court, upon these, as well as cattle and some other commodities, which may in some measure entitle them to the name of currency, they being current by legal enactment, was the adoption of the shell money, or wampum, of the Indians, which was

---

[1] In Marblehead, some time ago, while Signor Blitz was giving performances, a large number of people who were short of quarters paid for their admission in fish. The receipts in this currency, on one occasion, amounted to twenty dollars. In some parts of Mexico pieces of soap pass in exchange for merchandise, as a substitute for a better currency. In Iowa territory, in 1840, the marriage fee was three goat skins or four bushels of sweet potatoes. In the back settlements of Oregon the only money consisted of live stock currency. A hog was one dollar ; a sheep, fifty cents ; turkeys twenty-five cents each ; and a pup, twelve-and-a-half cents ; so if A owed B four dollars and ninepence he sent him five hogs, and received as change one sheep, one turkey, and a pup.

first brought by the Dutch from Manhadoes, in 1627, and the regulation of the trade therein, and of its value, which, as well as that of the various other materials serving the same purpose, was changed from time to time, as the demands of trade seemed to indicate a necessity therefor.

Although wampum may be said to have been the first adopted, the first legislation upon the subject of a small currency was that of March 4th, $16\frac{34}{35}$,[1] here following : " It is ordered that hereafter farthings shall not passe for currant pay.—

" It is likewise ordered, that muskett bulletts of a full boare shall passe currantly for a farthing apeece, provided that noe man be compelled to take above xii$^d$ att a tyme in them."

The purpose of this order may have been to compel a more thorough distribution of the munitions of war, which, at that time, were liable to be called into requisition at a moment's warning, rather than a desire to drive from circulation the small brass or copper coins of English origin, which must have formed a much more agreeable medium of exchange than the bulky and inconvenient substitute here authorized.

The first record we find relating to the value of wampum is dated November 15th, 1637,[2] " It was ordered that Wampampege should passe at 6 a penny for any sume vnder 12$^d$:"  On the 7th of October, 1640,[3] " It is ordered that white Wampampege shall passe at 4 a penny & blewe at 2 a penny, & not above 12$^d$ at a time except the receiver desire more."  June 2d, 1641,[4] " It is ordered that Wampampege shall passe currant at 6 a penny for any sume under 10$^l$ for debts heareafter to bee made."  On the 27th of September 1642,[5] " It was ordered that for the payment of the rate (w$^{ch}$ is to bee paid the nynth month) wheate, & barley shall passe at 4 sh$^s$ the bushell, rye, & pease at 3$^s$ 4$^d$ the bushell ; indian corne at 2$^s$ 6$^d$ the bushell in these at these prices, or in beaver money, or wampam pay is to bee made."

The following fragment of an order, changing the amount as fixed by that last copied, is at the foot of page 36, volume ii, the lower part of which is worn off, with the most important part of the order : Oct. 17, 1643, " Whereas by a former order, men were ordered in debts to accept Wampam to the

---

[1]Massachusetts Records, vol. i., p. 138.  The quotations from these Records are from the originals, but the corresponding pages can be found in the printed Records by the starred page numbers on their margins.

[2]Mass. Records, i. 204 ; [3]i. 287 ; [4]i. 308 ; [5]ii. 22.

valewe of 10¹, it is now ordered it shall passe: but to the value of"——— the remainder is missing.

On the 27th of October, 1648,¹ "It is voted for tryall, untill the next Coʳte that all pasable or payable peage henceforth shalbe intire wᵗʰout breaches, both the white, & black, wᵗʰout deforming spots͘ sutably strung, in eight knowne p̃cels the penny 3ᵈ. 12ᵈ 5ˢ in white the 2ᵈ. 6ᵈ 2½ˢ & 10ˢ in black." Under the same date an act was passed by both Houses, conferring upon ferrymen certain privileges. We here give the record of the vote of the House of Deputies:² "Vppon the petition of ffrauncis Hudson & James Heydon farmours of Charlstowne ferry wherein they expresse there desirs that some Course may be taken to p̃vent passengers disorderly pressinge into Boats & escapinge out of them without paying their fare p̃tending ţhat they haue nothinge to pay or that they are on the countryes service It is ordred that from henceforth it shalbe Lawfull for any ferriman to demaund & receiue his due before his Boate puts off from shore nor shall he be bound to passe ouer any that shall not giue satisfaction, & any ferry man may Refuse any wampom not strunged or vnmerchantable & such psons whether horse or foot which are passage free by order of Court must shew somthing sufficient for theire discharg or else must pay as others doe, except magistrates & deputies who are generally knowne to be ffree." In the same body it was, May 4th, 1649,³ "Voted: that peage shall still Remayne passable from man to man acording to the lawe in force ;" but under date of May 16, 1649,⁴ the Deputies passed an order, which had been on the 2d of that month passed by the Magistrates,⁵ to this effect: "Itt is Ordered that it shall not be in the liberty of any Toune or pson to pay peage to the Country rate, nor shall the Treasurer accept thereof from time to time."

Under date of October 18, 1650,⁶ (though probably the correct date was October 26th, it being the last record of the session, which was dissolved on that day,) "Itt is Ordered that wampam peage ffiffteene dajes after this present sessions of Courte shall passe Currant in pajment of debts to the vallew of forty shillings the white, at eight a penny ; and the blacke at fower so as they be entire without breaches or deforming spotts except in pajment of Countrje rates to the Treasurer which no Towne nor person may doe nor he accept thereof from time to time :" while in 1661,⁷ May 22d, the law relating to wampum was repealed in these words : "on observation of much Incon-

---

¹Mass. Records, ii. p. 222 ; ²iii. p. 160 ; ³iii. p. 218 ; ⁴iii. p. 233 ; ⁵ii. p. 237 ; ⁶iv. p. 32 ; ⁷iv. p. 369.

venience of the lawe for payment of forty shillings in wampampeage, in sattisfaction of debts & payments except to the Tresurer, page 78, It is ordered by this Court & the Authoritje there of that the sajd lawe be henceforth Repealed." Later than this we learn nothing more from the records relating to wampum as a currency, although it is said to have been in use among the people until the time of the Revolutionary war,[1] and is still, as well as some kinds of shells in their natural state, used among some of the Indian tribes remaining in the land. In fact, samples of wampum can to this day be obtained from the Penobscot and other friendly Indians.

Strings of wampum were also used by the Indians as necklaces and bracelets. And another kind, made in wide bands, and composed of various materials, were generally worn by the belles of the tribes. Sometimes a young brave would receive one of these ornaments as a gift from his betrothed, and wear it as an amulet, in the firm belief of its power to protect the wearer from all danger. A modern poet has made this tradition the subject of his verses, and thus a dusky maiden sings to her warrior lover:

"Brave son of a chieftain! beloved Cherokee!
This token of wampum is woven for thee!
A token to flutter and shine on thy breast,—
My bravest and brightest, my wisest and best!

'Tis woven with coral, with beads, and with shells;
It shall lie on thy breast the most potent of spells,
To save thee from ambush, to shield thee from harm,
To quicken thy sight, and give strength to thine arm."[2]

Wampum also served another purpose, as important as its other uses. This was when, usually in the form of belts, it was given as a pledge of friendship, in ratification of treaties, or to establish friendly relations in their preliminary stages.

We find it frequently mentioned in the Documents relating to the Colonial History of New York, as "strings of wampum," "belts of wampum," "a large black belt," "a large covenant belt," "a belt black wampum," "a belt of invitation;" and an Indian says, in presenting, "a prodigious large belt."

"Be attentive to what we now propose. * * Look upon this Belt as

---

[1] Drake's Hist. Boston, p. 326.     [2] E. Sargent, Jr.

a pledge of our inviolable attachment to you, and of our unshaken resolution of joining you in all your measures."

This belt had wrought into it a figure of the sun, as an emblem of light, to signify that their eyes were opened to the true light, and that they were convinced of the truths of all things then proposed.

In addition to the articles already enumerated, boards and cattle, which latter included horses, sheep, swine, goats, and "ases," formed no *small* part of the circulating medium, a mixture which should have furnished a variety sufficient to satisfy the demands of the most exacting.

To show the source whence much of the silver which afterwards found its way to the mint, flowed hither, as well as the effect of the financial disturbances of the period, we quote some passages from Winthrop's Journal,[1] August 27th, 1639 : "Here came a small bark from the West Indies, one Capt. Jackson in her, with commission from the Westminster company to take prize, etc., from the Spaniard. He brought much wealth in money, plate, indico and sugar."

[2]October, 1640, " The scarcity of money made a great change in all commerce. Merchants would sell no wares but for ready money, men could not pay their debts though they had enough, prices of lands and cattle fell soon to the one half and less, yea to a third, and after one fourth part." Winthrop relates that[3] " The wars in England kept servants from coming to us, so as those we had could not be hired, when their times were out, but upon unreasonable terms, and we found it very difficult to pay their wages to their content (for money was very scarce). I may upon this occasion report a passage between one of Rowley and his servant. The master, being forced to sell a pair of his oxen to pay his servant his wages, told his servant he could keep him no longer, not knowing how to pay him next year. The servant answered, he would serve him for more of his cattle. But how shall I do (saith the master) when all my cattle are gone ? The servant replied, you shall then serve me, and so you may have your cattle again."

The first action taken by the General Court for fixing the value of foreign coin, appears in the following extract from the Records,[4] under date of September 27th, 1642 : "This Co$^{rt}$ considring the oft occasions wee have of trading w$^{th}$ the hollanders at the Dutch plantation & otherwise ; do therefore order that the holland ducatour being worth 3 gilders shalbee

---

[1]Winthrop's Journal, vol. i. p. 369 ; [2]vol. ii. p. 21 ; [3]vol. ii. p. 269.   [4]Records, vol. ii. pp. 23-24.

currant at 6ˢ in all paymtˢ wᵗʰin oʳ iurisdiction, & the rix doller being 2½ gildrs shalbee likewise currant at 5ˢ & the ryall of 8: shalbee also currant at 5ˢ."

The old English coins known as Nobles[1] and Marks[2] were also sometimes made use of, at least by name, as we find in the records, October 18th, 1645,[3] that "The Couʳte being often troubled wᵗʰ yᵉ suits of p̃ticuleʳ psons, doe oʳdeʳ yᵗ mʳ Smith shall pay twenty nobles for ye defraying ye chardge of ye Courte in yᵉ hearing of his Cawse ; " and entered as the same date,[4] "Itt is oʳdered yᵗ mʳ Rawson shallbe allowed out of the treasury the som̄e of twenty markes for the seʳvice he hath donne in keeping & transcribing the records of the Howse of Deputs for the time past."   Also, in 1690, " The Magistrates Ordered that the Said Thoˢ Hawkins pay Twenty marks in Money for the Charges of His Prosecution and Imprisonment."[5]

Still the scarcity of money proved detrimental to business in every department ; and though this mixed currency passed very well for a time, and served the purposes of trade between the colonists and the Indian tribes, yet, for the reasons that much of it had no real intrinsic value, and that no method was provided for the redemption of that which was otherwise valueless, as well as the perishable nature of many, and the difficulty of transporting most of the articles which it comprised, it rapidly disappeared before the influx of Spanish, English, and Dutch money, obtained by trade with the West Indies and with the mother country.

This influx of the various foreign moneys, after a time, becoming burdensome on account of the large amount of base and counterfeit coin found amongst it, as well as by reason of the confusion incident upon the use of coins of so many differing standards of value, occasioned the issue of a printed order, by the General Court, for its alleviation.  Although no copy of this order is known to be now in existence, it was, beyond a doubt, as will be seen by the reference to it in the preface to the act of May $\frac{26}{27}$, 1652, for the purpose of authorizing the appointment of some person or persons, whose duty it should be to examine and test the quality and worth of the foreign moneys in circulation, and to stamp upon each piece its proper value, according to some uniform standard, probably sterling.  This preface was not consented to by the deputies, but its omission was made one of the conditions of their consent to the remainder of the bill.  The preface referred to was as

---

[1]A gold coin of about $1.61.   [2]A gold coin of about 3.22.   [3] Records, vol. iii. p. 50 ; [4] vol. iii. p. 61 ;   [5] Provincial Records, Council & Court, vol. 6. p. 118.

follows : "fforasmuch as the new order about mony is not well Resented[1] by the people and full of difficultjes, and vnlikely to take effect in regard no psons are found willing to try and stampe the same."

The printed order mentioned in the act last referred to, is the first legislation of the New England colonies, regarding coinage, of which we have been able to find any trace ; and it is the earliest known authority for the affixing of a stamp upon foreign coin as a token of its acceptance or endorsement by the colonies, in lieu of a coinage of their own ; but on account of its failure to effect the objects aimed at, they were soon compelled to resort to the establishment of a mint.

How much earlier than the passage of the act of May $\frac{26}{27}$, 1652, the printed order was passed, it is impossible to say, as that act contains the only reference we find thereto. It is probable, however, that not many months were suffered to pass in unsuccessful efforts to find "psons willing to try & stampe the same," the necessities of the colonists rendering it imperative that some plan be resorted to which should induce a supply of coin, and that with the least possible delay.

In relation to the causes which led to the establishment of the mint, and the appointment of its officers, we have John Hull's own statement, as written in his Diary.[2] He says "Also upon occasion of much counterfeit coin brought in the country, and much loss accruing in that respect (and that did occasion a stoppage of trade), the General Court ordered a mint to be set up, and to

---

[1] The use of the word *resented*, then used in the sense of favorably received, is appropriately illustrated in the life of Mr. John Wilson, contained in Mather's Magnalia, as follows : "Mrs. Wilson being thus perswaded over into the difficulties of an American desart, I have heard that her kinsman, old Mr. Dod, for her consolation under those difficulties, did send her a present, with an advice, which had in it something of *curiosity*.

"He sent her, at the same time, a brass *counter*, a silver *crown*, and a gold *Jacobus ;* all of them severally wrapped up ; with this instruction unto the gentleman who carried it : that he should first of all deliver only the counter, and if she received it with any show of discontent he should then take no further notice of her ; but if she gratefully resented that small thing for the sake of the hand it came from, he should then go on to deliver the *silver*, and so to the *gold :* but withall assure her, 'That such would be the dispensation of God unto her, and the other good people of New-England : if they would be content and thankful with such little things as God bestowed upon them, they should, in time have silver and gold enough.' Mrs. Wilson accordingly, by her cheerful entertainment of the least remembrance from good old Mr. Dod, gave the gentleman occasion to go through with his whole present, and the annexed advice ; which hath in a good measure been accomplished."

[2] Coll. Amer. Antiq. Soc. vol. iii. p. 145.

coin it, bringing it to the sterling standard for fineness, and for weight every shilling to be three pennyweight ; i. e., 9d. at 5s per oz. And they made choice of me for that employment ; and I chose my friend, Robert Sanderson, to be my partner, to which the Court consented."

Hutchinson[1] gives a short account of this mint, which agrees substantially with the above. He says : "The trade of the province increasing, especially with the West-Indies, where the bucaneers or pirates at this time were numerous, and part of the wealth which they took from the Spaniards as well as what was produced by the trade being brought to New-England in bullion, it was thought necessary, for preventing fraud in money, to erect a mint for coining shillings, six-pences and three-pences, with no other impression at first than N E on the one side, and XII. VI. or III. on the other ; but in October 1651[2] the court ordered that all pieces of money should have a double ring with this inscription, MASSACHUSETTS and a tree in the centre on one side, and NEW–ENGLAND and the year of our Lord on the other side."

"The first money being struck in 1652, the same date was continued upon all that was struck for thirty years after ; and although there are a great variety of dies, it cannot now be determined in what years the pieces were coined. No other colony ever presumed to coin any metal into money. It must be considered that at this time there was no King in Israel. No notice was taken of it by the parliament or by Cromwell ; and having been thus indulged, there was a tacit allowance of it afterwards even by King Charles II. for more than twenty years ; and although it was made one of the charges against the colony when the charter was called in question, yet no great stress was laid upon it. It appeared to have been so beneficial, that during Sir Edmund Andros's administration endeavours were used to obtain leave for continuing it, and the objections against it seem not to have proceeded from its being an encroachment upon the prerogative, for the motion was referred to the master of the mint, and the report against it was upon mere prudential considerations. It is certain that great care was taken to preserve the purity of the coin. I do not find, notwithstanding, that it obtained a currency anywhere, otherwise than as bullion, except in the New-England colonies. A very large sum was coined. The mint master, John Hull, raised a large fortune from it. He was to coin the money of the just alloy of the then new sterling English money ; and for all charges

---

[1] Hist. Mass. 3d ed. vol. i. p. 164.　[2] Evidently an error in the date. See Hist. Mag. vol. iii. p. 197.

which should attend melting, refining, and coining, he was to be allowed to take fifteen pence out of every twenty shillings. The Court were afterwards sensible that this was too advantageous a contract, and Mr. Hull was offered a sum of money by the court to release them from it,[1] but he refused to do it. He left a large personal estate, and one of the best real estates in the country. Samuel Sewall, who married his only daughter, received with her, as was commonly reported, thirty thousand pounds in New-England shillings. 'He was the son of a poor woman, but dutiful to and tender of his mother, which Mr. Wilson his minister observing, pronounced that God would bless him, and although he was then poor yet he should raise a great estate.'"

The earliest document known to us, relating to this mint, is the original draught of the act already referred to, comprising the minutes of the secretary, and showing the erasures and alterations made therein during its discussion by the two houses.

This is the only record known (if we except the copies of it upon the records of the General Court,) making the slightest reference to any action whatever relating to coinage, as having been previously taken or proposed.

It will be seen that the last clause of this act is for repealing of the "all other orders concerning the valuation or coyning of money." This was probably merely for the sake of form, or referring to the printed order, which may have been considered as coining ; but that clause, whatever its intention, was considered of so little importance as to have been omitted from the records of the House of Magistrates, which constituted the law of the colony, nor is it to be found in the printed book of laws, issued in 1660.

In order to show more distinctly the changes made in this act, as well as the peculiar style of chirography of that day, we present a *fac simile* of the draught, copied from the original document by the heliotype process. That the reader may be assisted in deciphering the antique style of writing in which it appears, we present a transcript of this document on the next two pages, and immediately opposite each page will be found the corresponding parts of the original.

---

[1] We find nothing to prove this. On the contrary, the contract was repeatedly renewed upon nearly the same terms. The Records show, however, that in 1660, a committee was appointed to treat with the mint masters and induce them to pay a *bonus* out of their profits. They offered ten pounds as a *gift*, but would then agree to nothing further; but in 1667 they agreed to pay into the public treasury the sum of forty pounds, and yearly thereafter, for seven years, ten pounds. These transactions will be found, at length, at their proper dates.

The erasures in the original are designated in this transcript by italics. Some doubtful punctuation marks are omitted.]

"*fforasmuch as the new order about mony is not well Resented by the people and full of difficultjes, and vnlikely to take effect in regard no psons are found willing to try & stampe the same, the sajd Order is Repealed.*

The Courte therefore Ordereth & enacteth that the p<sup>r</sup>inted orde<sup>r</sup> about

1     mony shall be in force vntill the first of <sub>ᴧ</sub> <sup>Seauenth month</sup> *July* next and no longer

2     <sup>ly</sup>That from and After the first of Septembe<sup>r</sup> next the mony heere

after Apointed & expressed shall be the Currant mony of this Comon

wealth and no other, <sub>ᴧ</sub> <sup>vnless English &</sup> (except *it be at* the Receivers <sub>ᴧ</sub> <sup>consent therevnto</sup> *chojse*). In pu<sup>r</sup>suance

of the Intent of this Courte heerein Bee it further *Acted* Ordered

& enacted by the Authority of this Court ; That all persons what

soeuer have liberty to bring in vnto the mint howse at Boston all

bulljon plate or Spannish Cojne there to be melted & brought to the

allay of sterling Silver by John Hull master of the sajd mint and his

sworne officers, & by him to be Cojned into 12<sup>d</sup>: 6<sup>d</sup>: & 3<sup>d</sup> peeces which

shall be for forme & flatt & square on the sides & stamped on the one

side with N E & on the other side w<sup>th</sup> the figure xɪɪ<sup>d</sup> vɪ<sup>d</sup> & ɪɪɪ<sup>d</sup> =

<sup>according to the valew of</sup>

*peeces which shall bee* each peece, together with a privy marke =

which shall be Appointed euery three months by the Gouerno<sup>r</sup> & known

only to him & the sworne officers of the mint.

3     And further the sajd master of the mint aforesajd is heereby Required

to cojne all the sajd mony of good Silver of the Just allay of <sub>ᴧ</sub> <sup>new</sup> sterling English

mony, & for valew to stampe <sup>two</sup> *three* pence in a shilling of lesser vallew

4:     then the p<sup>r</sup>sent English Cojne & the lesser peeces p<sup>r</sup>oportionably : And

all Such Cojne as aforesajd shall be acknowledged to be the Currant Cojne

of this Comonwealth & passe from man to man in all pajments accordingly

<sup>within this Jurisdiction only.</sup>

5     And the mint master for himselfe & officers for their pajnes & labour in

melting Refining & Coyning is Allowed by this Courte to take one shilling

*six pence* out of euery twenty shillings which he shall stampe as aforesajd

6     And It shall be in the liberty of any pson who brings into the mint howse

any bullion plate or Spannish Cojne as aforesajd to <sub>ᴧ</sub> <sup>be prsent &</sup> see the same melted Refined

& Allajed, & then to take a receipt of the master of the mint for the =

weight of that which is good Silver allajed as afforesajd, for which the

mint master shall deliuer him the like weight <sub>ᴧ</sub> <sup>in currant money.</sup> viz. euery shilling

weigh<sup>to</sup>*ing the* three penny <sub>ᴧ</sub> <sup>troj:</sup> weight & lesser peeces proportionably. deducting

Allowance for Cojnage as before exp<sup>r</sup>ssed : And that this Order being

of So great Concernment may not in any pticular thereof fall to the

ground Itt is further Ordered that m<sup>r</sup> Richard Bellingham m<sup>r</sup>

willjam Hibbens, the p<sup>r</sup>sent Secretary, Capt. John Leueret & m<sup>r</sup> Thomas

Clarke be a Comittee appointed by this Court to Appointe the mint howse

in some Convenjent place in Boston. to Give John Hull master of the

mint the oath suiteable to his place. And to Approove of all other

Moreover as the new order about mony is not well resented by the people and full of difficulties, and unlikely to take effect in regard no persons are found willing to buy the stamped the same, the said order altogether.

1. The Courte therefore Ordereth & enacteth that the printed order about mony shall be in force untill the first of February next and no longer

2. And that from and after the first of September next the mony here after coyned & expressed shall be the Currant mony of this Common wealth, and no other (except it be at the receivers choyce) in persuance of the Intent of this Courte herein. Bee it further Ordered & enacted by the Authority of this Court, that all persons whatsoever have liberty to bring in unto the mint howse at Boston all bullion plate or Spaanish coyne there to be melted & brought to the allay of sterling silver by John Hull master of the said mint and his sworne officers, & by him to bee coyned into 12d : 6d & 3d peeces which shall bee for forme flatt & square on the sides & stamped on the one side with NE & on the other side with these figures XII VI & III = according to the value of each peece, together with a privy marke. = which shall bee appointed every three moneths by the Counsell & knowne only to him & the sworne officers of the mint.

3. And further the said master of the mint aforesaid is hereby required to coyne all the said mony of good silver of the just allay of sterling english mony, & for value to stampe the same in a shilling of lesse value then the present english Coyne & the lesser peeces proportionably. And all such coynes as aforesaid shall bee acknowledged to bee the Currant coyne of this Common wealth & to passe from man to man in all payments accordingly

5. And the mint master for himselfe & officers for theire payne & labour in melting, refining & coyning is Allowed by this Courte to take one shilling out of every twenty shillings which he shall stampe as aforesaid

6. And it shall bee in the liberty of any person who bringes into the mint howse any bullion plate or Spaanish coyne as aforesaid to see the same melted refined & allayed, & then to take a receipt of the master of the mint for the weight of that which is good silver allayed as aforesaid, for which the mint master shall deliver him the like weight viz every shilling weighing three penny weight & lesser peeces proportionably deducting Allowance for coynage as before expressed. And that this order being of so great concernment may not in any particular thereof fall to the ground. It is further Ordered that mr Richard Bellingham, mr william Hibbens, the present Secretary, capt John Leuret & mr Thomas Clarke, by a Committee appointed by this court to appointe the mint howse in some convenient place in Boston, to give John Hull master of the mint the oath suitable to his place And to Approove of all the

offindes and deteremine what els shall Appeare vppon as
necessarely to be donne for the Carrying an end off the
whole order.

And that all oter orders past this Court shalbe repeale [crossed out: concerning vppon the valuation or coyning of mony]

The magists have past this with Reference to the Consent
of their brethren the deputs hereto

Edward Rawson Secrt

The Deputyes Consent hereto provded that
[crossed out] be left out e yt instood of
[crossed out] for Coynare be inserted & only
wth reference to the consent of or honod
magists hereto

william Torrey Cleric.

The magists. Consent hereto

Edward Rawson Secrety

officers and determine what els shall Appeare to them as
necessaryly to be donne for the Carrying an end of the
whole order.

              concerning *money* the valuation or coyning of money
& That all other orders ‸ past this Court shalbe repealed:
The magists have past this with Reference to the Consent
of their bretheren the Depu<sup>ts</sup> heereto

                                    Edward Rawson Secrety

The Deputyes Consent hereto pvided that
the p̄face be left out & yt in steade of
*    *    for Coynage be inserted 1ˢ only
w<sup>th</sup> reference to the consent of o<sup>r</sup> hon<sup>rd</sup>
magists hereto

                           William Torrey  Cleric.

The magists. Consent heereto.

                          Edward Rawson Secrety

It appears that in the original draught[1] of the foregoing act, a larger allowance for the mint master was proposed by the Magistrates, than the Deputies thought proper ; the amount stated in the first instance being one shilling six pence, the words "six pence" having been erased at the suggestion of the Deputies, who returned the paper to the Magistrates with this addition : "The Deputyes Consent hereto pvided that the p̄face be left out & yt in steade of *  *[2] for Coynage be inserted 1ˢ only w<sup>th</sup> reference to the consent of o<sup>r</sup> hon<sup>rd</sup> magists hereto." These conditions were acceded to by the Magistrates, and the bill, thus amended, was passed, and became a law.

The preceding document bearing no date, it is left for us to ascertain that point by the date of its entry upon the Court records.

Two dates are there given, in consequence of which we have referred to this act by the double date, May $\frac{26}{27}$, 1652 ; the first being the date given upon the records of the House of Magistrates, the last, that of the House of Deputies.

For the purpose of completeness we copy both of these records, although one is nearly a repetition of the other.

In the preceding copies we have, in order to exhibit the fashion of that

---

[1] Archives, vol. c. p. 42.

[2] The amount originally written here has been entirely obliterated, for what reason it is impossible to determine ; but it is probable that it was 1s. 6d., there evidently having been figures here, while in the body of the draught the words were written in full.

period, given the extracts from the Records punctuated as in the originals. In those which ensue we shall not follow them, with *exactness*, in that respect, as many of the marks are apparently unintentional, and tend to pervert the meaning, and in some cases there is almost an entire absence of punctuation.

The following is copied from the Records of the House of Magistrates : [1]

"Itt is Ordered and by the Authoritje of this Courte Enacted that the printed Order about mony shall be in force vntill the first of september next and no longer. And that from and after the first of september next the mony heereafter Appointed and expressed shallbe the Currant mony of this Comonwealth and no other vnlesse English (except the Receivers Consent therevnto:) In pursuance of the Intent of this Courte heerein bee it further Ordered and enacted by the Authoritje of this Courte That all persons whatsoeuer have libertje to bring in vnto the mint howse at Boston, all bulljon plate or Spannish Cojne there to be melted and brought to the allay of starling silver by John Hull master of the Sajd mint and his sworne officers, and by him to be Cojned into twelve penny Six penny, and three penny peeces which shallbe for forme flatt and square on the sides and stamped on the one side with N E and on the other side with the figure xii$^d$ vi$^d$ & iii according to the valew of each peece, together with a privy marke which shall be Appointed euery three months, by the Goūno$^r$. and knowne only to him and the sworne officers of the mint. And further the sajd master of the mint aforesaid is heereby Required to Cojne all the sajd mony of good silver of the Just allay of new starling English mony and for valew to stampe two pence in a shilling of lesser value then the present English Cojne and the lesser peeces proportionably. And all such Cojne as aforesajd shallbe acknowledged to be the Currant Cojne of this Comonwealth and passe from man to man in all pajments accordingly within this Jurisdicc̄on only. And the mint master for himselfe and officers for their pajnes and labour in melting Refyning and Coynning is Allowed by this Courte to take one shilling out of euery twenty shillings which he shall stampe as aforesajd and it shall be in the liberty of any person who brings into the minthowse any bulljon Plate or spannish Cojne as Aforesajd to be present and see the same melted Refined and Allajed, and then to take a receipt of the master of the mint for the weight of that which is good silver allajed as aforesajd for which the mintmaster shall deliuer him the like weight in Currant money, viz: euery shilling

---

[1] Records, vol. iv. p. 81.

to weigh threepenny troj weight and lesser peeces proportionably, deducting Allowance for Cojnage as before expressed. And that this Order being of so great Concernment may not in any p̃ticcular thereof, fall to the ground, Itt is further Ordered that m^r Richard Bellingham m^r Willjam Hibbens m^r Edward Rawson Capt̃ Jn° Leueret, and m^r Thomas Clarke be a Com̄ittee appointed by this Court, to Appoint the mint howse in some Convenjent place in Boston to Give John Hull master of the mint the oath suiteable to his place, and to Approove of all other officers and determine what else shall appeare to them as necessarily to be donne for the Carrying an end of the whole order."

The record upon the book of the House of Deputies[1] is as follows :

"It is Ordred by this Court & the Authoritie thereof that the printed Order about money shalbe in force vntill the first of the seuenth mo^th next & no longer. And that from & after the first of September next the money hereafter appoynted & expressed shalbe the Current money of this Common wealth & no other, vnles English, except the receiuers consent therevnto. in psuance of the Intent of this court herein Be it further Ordred & enacted by the Authoritie of this court That all psons whatsoeuer haue libertie to bring in vnto the mint howse at Boston all Bullion plate or Spanish Coyne there to be melted & brought to the Allay of Sterling siluer by John Hull master of the s̃d mint, & his sworne officers & by him to be Coyned into twelue pence Six pence & three pence peeces which shalbe for forme flatt & square on the sides & Stamped on the one side with N E & on the other side with xii^d. vi^d & iii^d according to the value of each peece together with a priuie marke which Shalbe appoynted euery three monethes by the gouerno^r & knowne only to him & the sworne officers of the mint, & further the s̃d master of the mint Affores̃d is hereby required to Coyne all the s̃d money of good siluer of the Just allay of new Sterling English money & for value to Stampe two pence in a shilling of lesser valew then the p̃sent English Coyne & the lesser peeces p̃portionable. And all such Coyne as afores̃d shall be acknowledged to be the Current coyne of this com̄on wealth & pass from man to man in all payments accordingly within this Jurisdiction only. And the mint master for himselfe & Officers for theire paynes & labour in meltinge refineinge & Coyninge is allowed by this court to take one shillinge out of Euery twenty shillings w^ch he shall stampe as affores̃d, & It shalbe in the liberty of

---

[1] Records, vol. iii. pp. 332-333.

any pson who brings into the mint howse any bullian plate or spanish Coyne
as afforeśd to be p̄sent and se the same melted & refined & Allayed & then
to take a receit of the master of the mint for the weyght of that which is
good siluer allayd as aforeśd, for which the mint master shall deliuer him
the the like weight in Current money viz[t]. euery shilling to weigh three
penny Troy weight & lesser peeces proportionably deducting allowance for
coynage as before exprest. And that this Order beinge being of so great
Concernment may not in any perticuler thereof fall to the ground It is
further Ordred that m[r] Richard Bellingham m[r] W[m] Hibbens the p̄sent secrity
Cap̄t. John Leueritt & m[r] Thomas Clarke be a Com̄ittee appoynted by this
court to appoynt the mint howse in some Convenient place in Boston to
giue John Hull master of the mint the oath suteable to his place & to
approue of all other Officers & determine what else shall appeare to them as
Necessary to be done for the Carying an End of the whole order, & that all
other Orders concerning the Valuation or coyning of money past this court
shalbe repealed."

The committee, however, which was appointed "for the carrying an end"
of this work, either meeting with opposition from Messrs. Hull and Saunderson, or being otherwise persuaded that the compensation was insufficient, in
the order soon to follow increased it to the same amount with that originally
awarded : the one penny an ounce for waste, amounting to three pence in
twenty shillings, which, added to the fifteen pence per twenty shillings for
coinage, etc., amounts to just one shilling and sixpence.

A different view of this is taken by the writer of the remarks upon the
coinage of Massachusetts appended to Hull's Diary,[1] owing to the extreme
difficulty of deciphering certain words which, in the *fac simile*, are indeed
illegible, but which a close scrutiny of the original manuscript, and comparison
with like words in other writings by the same hand, show to be six pence
instead of eight pence, as supposed by him.

The theory there advanced is that Hull, refusing to accept the award of
one shilling in twenty, the committee "were compelled, therefore, to increase
his compensation, on their own responsibility, to an allowance of fifteen-pence
in every twenty shillings, besides one penny for waste in every ounce. This
brought the allowance to one shilling sevenpence in every twenty, — nearly
the same as it was in the original draught."

---

[1] Coll. Amer. Antiq. Soc. vol. iii. p. 285.

The ensuing papers show the action taken by the committee having the mint business in charge, the first being a rough, unfinished draught, of which the second is a repetition, in a slightly different form.

[1] "wee whose names are herevnder exp'ssed · R B. m' Whereas, the Gennerall Court have Appointed m' W. H. m' E· R· C: ĩ: L. & m' Th: C: as a Comittee to Conside' and determine of whatsoeuer may best tend for the Carying an end of the order ffor melting Refining & Coyning of Silver haveing spent sometime in Considering of what may, w^{th} most speede & least charge, Carry that buisnes an end Respecting the Countrjes Advantage . . doe hereby declare that thire shall be an howse built at the Countryes Charge of sixteene foote square tenn foote high, substantially wrought and further also, pvide all necessery tooles & Implements for the same at the Countrjes charge: And that the mint m' may not have Just Cawse to Complaine wee Cannot but Judge it meete to Allow the sajd mint master for melting Refyning & Coyning such Bulljon Plate & mony y^t shall be brought vnto them: what in their Judgements & consciences on their experience he shall Judge Aquall So as they exceede not 15^d in a^{lb} ou' & besides a 1^d in eu'y ounce allowed for wast till the next sessions agn^t wch tjme It is to be hoped, such experience will be had of w^t is necessary to be Allowed as there will be no Just occasion of Complaint only wee doe desire & Advise the sajd [                    ]: that there being a likly hood of seu'all sorts of worke in which they are to be Imploied where there is no Refining & so less labor they would take lesse & where both Refining and Cojning is necessary, there if they find" * * * * This draught is left unfinished, but that next given completes the record of this session of the committee.

On the margin of this paper are the names of Symon Bradstreet and Jn° Woodbridge, apparently autographs; "Robert Saunderson, his coptner," probably written by Secretary Rawson, and underneath is the autograph of the mint master, John Hull, a *fac simile* of which is presented underneath the two papers facing page 41, together with representations of some rough sketches of designs for the proposed coinage, which are drawn upon the margin of the back of *this* paper, — not that with which they are there illustrated.

The smallest of these designs is quite interesting, as it shows one plan to have been to place only the numerals xii in the centre, having the date,

---

[1] Archives, vol. c. p. 37.

of which the first three figures only are legible, in the same circle with the legend, NEW ENGLAND.

The completed draught of this action of the committee reads thus : [1]

"20 June 1652

Whereas the Gennerall Courte hath Appointed vs whose names are heerevnder exp'ssed A Comitee to Consider and determine of whatsoeuer may best tend for the Carying an end of the order, for melting Refyning and Coyning of silver having spent some tjme in Considering of what may, with most speede and least charge Carry that buisenes an end, Respecting the Countrjes Advantage ; doe heereby declare, that there shall be an howse built at the Countrjes charge, of sixteene ffoote square. tenn foote high ; substantially wrought ; and further also, Provide all necessary tooles and Implements for the same, at the Countrjes charge all wch is in Acting And that the mint master may not have Just Cawse to Complajne, wee cannot but Judge it meete to Allow the said mint master, for melting Refyning and Coyning such bulljon, plate & mony, that shall be brought vnto them, what in his Judgment and Conscience, on his experience he shall Judge æquall, so as he exceede not 15[d] in twenty shillings ouer and besides a penny in euery ounce allowed for wast till the next sessions Against which tjme, Itt is to be hoped such experjence will be had of what is necessary to be Allowed, as there will be no Just occasion of Complainte only wee doe desire and Advise the sajd John Hull, (there being a likely hood of seuerall sorts of worke: in which he is to be Imployed where there is no Refjning and so lesse labor, he would take lesse : and where both Refining and Coyning is necessary there ; if he finde he Cannot subsist with lesse he may take fiveteene pence, for euery twenty shillings.

Ri. Bellingham  
William Hibbins  
Edward Rawson Sec  
Tho: Clarke

Voted by the whole Court. that they Allowe  
ye Act of the Comittee for minting of mony,  
Respecting the howse & Allowance of 15[d] p 20[s].

28 [8/mo], 1652:      Edw Rawson Secrety.

Comitee about ye mint to stand to ye next sessions                E R S "

---

[1] Archives, vol. c. p. 40.

It is Ordered that this Oath hereunder written shall be
the oath that John Hull and Robert Saunderson shall take
equall officers in the minting of mony &c.

Whereas yow John Hull and Robert Saunderson are Appointed by
the order of the Generall Courte bearing date the 10th of June 1652
to be officers for the Massachusetts Jurisdicion in New England for the
melting Refyning and Coyning of silver yow doe heere sweare by
the great name of the everliving God that yow will faithfully and
diligently performe the duty of yow places that all mony coyned by yow
shall be of the just Allay of English Coyne & that every shilling shalbe
of due weight viz three penny troy weight and all other peeces pro=
portionably according to the order of Courte so neere as yow can
so helpe yow God.

Whereas by order of the Generall Courte Assis Assembled that
all monies coyned heere for this shall be flatt and square, and
whose names are heereunder written appointed by the Generall
Courte as Committee to Consider and determine whatsoever we shall
Judge necessary for the carrying an end of the order wee hereby
determine & declare that the officers for the minting of
mony shall Coyne all the mony that they mint in a Round forme
till the Generall Courte shall otherwise declare their minds

John Hull, minter

It is ordered by this court, and the mint master is hereby injoyned,
of the first Bullion that comes to his hand, to coyne two pence
of silver, in proportion according to the just valleu & allay of
monys allowed heere, to answer the ocasions of the country, for viz
that is the first yeare fifty pounds in sure small mony, for every
pounds by him to be coyned. & for after time twenty pounds in like
mony, annualy for every hundred pounds, that shalbe coyned
order is to continued in force for Heaven yeares any thing
to the contrary notwithstanding. The magistrates haue passed this &c
desire the Consent of their brethren the deputys heereto
Edw. Rawson secrety

Boston 16 May 1662
Consented to by the deputs
William Torrey Cleric

Although this committee exceeded its instructions, their proceedings were approved by the Court in the note appended to the document, and there dated October 28th, while upon the records it appears under date of October 26th.

This discrepancy was occasioned by the custom of the secretary of dating but few of the days of a session, [sometimes he recorded a whole session under one date,] thus rendering it impossible to determine from the records the precise dates of the passage of most of the acts there recorded. Greater apparent errors than this appear in some other entries, which must be attributed to the same cause.

The secretary's record of this vote stands thus :[1] "The whole Courte by their Gennerall vote did Allow and Approove of the acte of the Comittee about minting of money & Respecting their building of the mint howse at the Comon charge, and allowance of the officers 15$^d$ in euery twenty shillings for their paines and Ordered the Comittee to Continew in theire power till the next Eleccon."

Upon the back of the paper which contains the record of the action of the committee mentioned above is found the form of oath to be administered to Messrs. Hull and Saunderson, as "æquall office$^{rs}$ in the minting of mony," in these words :[2]

"Boston : 11 : June. 1652.

Itt is Ordered that the Oath here vnde$^r$ written shall be the oath that John Hull and Robt Saunderson shall take as æquall office$^{rs}$ In the minting of mony &c.

Whereas yo$^w$. John Hull and Robert Saunderson are Appointed by the order of the Gennerall Courte bearing date the 10$^{th}$ of June 1652. to be officers for the massachusetts Jurisdiccon in New England, for the melting, Refyning, and Cojning of silver yow doe heere sweare by the great name of the euer living God that yo$^w$ will faithfully and dilligently pforme the duty of you$^r$ places that all mony Cojned by yow = shall be of the Just Allay of ye English Cojne that euery shilling shallbe of due weight, viz. three penny troj weight, and all other peeces proportionably, according to the order of Courte so neere as yo$^w$ Cann = So helpe yo$^w$ God : "

Jo: Hull depos$^d$ accordingly y$^e$ Same day before ye Comittee.

E. R S :
Rob$^t$ Saunderson deposed 19 $\frac{6}{mo}$ 52 :

---

[1] Records, vol. iv, p. 111.    [2] Archives, Pec. vol. c. p. 40.

We find no reference to this action of the Court upon their records, nor does it appear from them that the Court was in session at the time here mentioned, although, owing to the absence of daily dates, it is impossible to determine precisely upon what day the adjournment took place, June 1st being the last date recorded prior to the adjournment, which was to the 19th of October.

In order further to carry out the provisions of the law, the committee issued the following :[1]

pᵣsent
Rich Bellingham
mʳ Hibbins
Capt Leutt.
Mʳ Clarke
Edw. Rawson.

"Att A meeting of the Comittee for Carrying an end of the ordeʳ conc. mony, on 22 day of June, 1652,
At wch meeting it was determined :

1   that there should be a mint howse & all tooles and Implements necessary thereto, built & pcured At the Countrjes charge wch is in acting & a declaration accordingly made.

2.   That warrants should Issue out to the Constables of Boston, for the pʳessing Isacke Cullimore for that Service wch was donne.

3.   That A warrant should Issue out to the sajd Isacke Culljmore, for ye Impowering him to pʳesse other workemen Carpenteʳˢ &c. as may Joyne wᵗʰ him in the Countrjes Service wᶜʰ was donne.

4.   That the sajd mint howse shall be sett vppon the land of the sajd John Hull : and if It is Agreed betweene the sajd committee and ye sajd John Hull that when euer either by his death or otherwise the said John Hull shall cease to be the mint master, that then the Countrje shall have the ground ye howse stands vppon at such prize as two Indifferent men, equally chosen by the Countrye & ye said John Hull or his Assignes shall determine, or else the sajd John Hull on the like termes shall have the sajd Howse as two Indifferent men shall Judge it to be worth at the choice of the Countrje :

William Hibbins
Edward Rawson Sec:·
Tho : Clarke "

[1] Archives, Pec. vol. c. p. 38.

The extreme scarcity of the coins struck in accordance with this act, and the simple form of the dies with which they were struck, renders it next to impossible to give an intelligible list of their varieties, which were not numerous, not more than some half dozen varieties being known to us. They were made from thin planchets of silver, apparently clipped to the desired size, weight, and form ; and although the latter was ordered by the Court to be "flatt and square," a subsequent decision of the committee determined that they should be coined "in A Round forme," as witness their order here copied, the draught of which is found underneath the form of oath, and on the same paper : [1]

"Whereas: by order of the Gennerall Courte It is Appointed that all monies Coyned heere, for forme should be flatt and square, wee, whose names are heere vnder written, Appointed by the Gennerall Court, as A Comittee to Consider and determine $^{of}_{\wedge}$ whatsoeuer wee should Judge necessary for the Carrying an end of the order $^{\text{Respecting minting of monyes}}_{\wedge}$ doe hereby determine & declare that the office$^{rs}$ for the minting of mony shall Coyne all the mony that they mints in A Round forme till the Gennerall Courte shall otherwise declare their minds = *therein any thing in the former order notwithstanding.*"

A *fac simile* of the record of this action of the committee will be found, together with those of the form of oath to be administered to the mint officers, the draughts of designs for the proposed coinage, the autograph of John Hull, and the order for Twopenny pieces, facing page 41. By reference to that *fac simile* it will be seen that the names of the committee were not affixed to the order as therein stated.

These coins were very irregular in their outlines, which was of little importance so far as the coining was concerned, for the dies, (if they should be dignified with the name of dies,) were simply punches, upon one end of which were sunken the letters for the obverse, or the numerals for the reverse, (which occupied the greater part of their surfaces,) and which were struck upon the planchets at opposite edges, that one stamp might not obliterate or deface the other.

The original clipped and irregular form of this issue rendering it particularly liable to a repetition of the process of clipping by dishonest traders, who did not hesitate, even in those days of honest dealing, (as they are reputed,) to avail themselves of every opportunity for the increase of their worldly

---

[1]Archives, Pec. vol. c. p. 40.

gains at the expense of the public good, it was found necessary to change the design of the impress, in consequence of which this order was issued, under date of October 19, 1652 :[1]

Fig. 1.

"ffor the prevention of washing or Clipping of all such peices of mony as shall be Cojned w[th]in this Jurisdiction. It is Ordered by this Courte and the Authoritje thereof, that henceforth all peices of mony Cojned as afore sajd shall have a double Ring on either side, with this Inscription — Massachusetts, and a tree in the Center on the one side, and New England and the yeere of our lord on the other side, according to this draught heere in the margent."

The entry of this order, as it appears on the records of the House of Deputies,[2] differs from that of the Magistrates but little, even in form, yet we here give a copy of it : "ffor the p̃vention of washing or Cliping all such peeces of money as shalbe Coyned within this Jurisdiction It is ordred by this court & Authoritie Thereof that Henceforth all peeces of money Coyned as afforeẽd both shillings & smaller peeces shall haue a double Ringe⁎ on either side with this Inscription (massachusetts) & a tree in the center on the one side, And (New england) & the date of the yeare on the other side according to a draught herew[th]all p̃sented."

It is a fact to be noticed that no coin is to be found agreeing in orthography with the specifications of this order ; and had the shillings dated 1650 been coined at that date, it is extremely probable that one of these, or at least a draught more nearly resembling them, would have been presented ; whereas no mention of them seems to have then been made.

Our studies of this coinage have led us to a conclusion directly opposed to that generally accepted regarding the coinage of the different varieties of the silver money of Massachusetts.

The only satisfactory theory which presents itself in relation to this point, is the ensuing :·

The earliest issue of this mint was, of course, the N E series, this being in exact accordance with the description given in the act for the establishment of the mint, that bearing a tree following it, in accordance with the order of October 19, 1652, which furnishes the draught of that device.

The cuts on the next page (Figs. 2, 3, 4, and 5,) furnish good represen-

---

[1] Mass. Records, vol. iv. p. 98.    [2] Records, vol. iii. p. 358.

tations of the coins of the series first mentioned. [See also Plate I, Nos. 3, 4, and 5.]

The N E Shilling may be described as a plain, hammered or rolled planchet of silver, in size varying from sixteen to nineteen, clipped to an irregularly circular form; upon the obverse, N E in relief upon a depressed field, which is straight upon three sides but arched at the top. The length of this field is usually somewhat less than one-half the diameter of the planchet, and near its upper edge; the central line of the N is prolonged into a curve under the E, and the top of its right limb is also curved or bent forward, crossing the upright of, and forming the top to, the E.

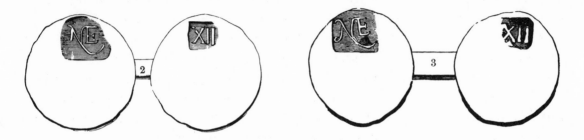

Reverse: upon a field similar to that of the obverse, but smaller, and more nearly square, not being rounded or arched at the top, the Roman numerals XII This stamp also is placed near the edge and at the top of the planchet; not behind that upon the obverse, but so that when held with the numerals upright, that upon the opposite side will usually be at the bottom, though it is occasionally found at one side.

The Sixpences and Threepences differ from the Shilling in the form of the depressed field: that upon the obverse of these, instead of being nearly square, is indented on its four sides, and irregularly quadrilobed, to conform to the outlines of the letters. The reverses differ but little from the Shilling, except in the numerals, which here are VI and III In size the Sixpence varies from twelve to fourteen, and the only Threepence we have measured is size twelve-and-a-half.

But two undoubtedly genuine specimens of the Threepence are known, those in the collections of William S. Appleton, A. M., and Yale College ; those recently sold in New York, as well as the Sixpences and Pennies, having been pronounced forgeries.

Next to the N E series we place the Willow Tree coins, these bearing the rudest resemblance to the draught accompanying the order for a change in the design.

[See Plate I, Nos. 6 and 7.]

The coins bearing this tree are so rude in conception and bungling in execution, (though not partaking of the errors of reversed letters which appear in some varieties of both Oak and Pine,) as to deserve none other than a position among the experimental attempts of novices in the art of coining ; unless, as has been suggested, they are to be considered as counterfeits, which to us does not appear probable. So rude, indeed, are they, that it is difficult to believe them to have been accepted by any people except under urgent necessity for coin of some kind, however imperfect.

Of these we have never met with a perfect specimen, all being doubly struck, and most, very faint impressions and much worn. We find of them three obverse and seven reverse dies for the Shilling, and of the Sixpence only one die of each, obverse and reverse.

## TABLES OF VARIETIES OF WILLOW TREE SHILLINGS.

### OBVERSES.

| Die. | Legends. | Tree. | Roots. | Grains of Ring. | Letters. | Obv. | With Rev. |
|---|---|---|---|---|---|---|---|
| No. 1. | MMAS THVSE IN. / IASA HVETS N | A confused mass of curves and lines. Trunk double and wide. | Long, pointing downward. | Round. Separate. | Large. Heavy. | 1a 1b | A¹ A² |
| No. 2. | MAS THVSE S: IN / SATH ETS: IIN | Angular. Trunk double, with cross lines. | Curved to left and right. | Small. Connected. | Rather light. | 2a 2b | B C |
| No. 3. | MAASATTH SE SS II / MASSATVSETSS IN / MAASSAT ETS TS: N. / MASAATVSETS: IN / MA ATHVS ETS IN | A net-work of curves and lines, more compact than the last. Large dot in centre. Trunk narrow. | Long, open. Pointing right. | Large. Some connected. | Medium. | 3a 3b 3c 3d 3e | D E F G1 G2 |

REVERSES.

| Die. | Legends. | Figures of Date. | Numerals. | Grains. | Letters. | Rev. | With Obv. |
|---|---|---|---|---|---|---|---|
| A | NE NLAN M˙<br>: NE L ND NDOM | Rather large.   2 high. | Large. | Round.<br>Separate. | Rather large. | A1<br>A2 | 1a<br>1b |
| B | ɪEWE NGLAND N DO | Worn. | Medium. | Connected. | Medium. | B | 2a |
| C | NE NGLAN N DOM. | Large. | Medium. | Connected. | Rather light. | C | 2b |
| D | : NEW AND˙AN OM: | Large, heavy. | Large, heavy. | On thread. | Large, heavy. | D | 3a |
| E | NEɪ EWENGLD.ANDOM | Large, heavy. | Large, heavy. | Connected. | Large, heavy. | E | 3b |
| F | NEWEWEND :AAɪNDOM | Rather heavy. | Rather heavy. | Connected. | Small, light. | F | 3c |
| G | NEWNGLAA D AN DOM<br>NEW ENGGLA D ANDOM | Rather heavy. | Rather heavy. | Connected. | Medium. | G1<br>G2 | 3d<br>3e |

The confusion in the legends of these pieces has been thought by some to constitute different varieties. It is occasioned by the intermingling of the letters, by double or triple impressions, of which doubtless many more specimens might be given, were it worth our while to follow so unsatisfactory a pursuit. These few are mentioned as an illustration of the unskillful execution of the coins of this class.

In explanation of this table we would say that the letters in the column following the numbers of the obverse dies, refer to the reverse with which that die is coupled ; and the figures following the letters designating the reverse dies, are those of the obverses with which *they* are coupled. The small letters or figures simply refer to the particular combinations of the letters of the legends caused by double impressions. Thus, 3d G1, indicates that the legends of that particular specimen are as there represented : as it is hardly possible that two pieces can be found showing the same combinations of letters, when doubly struck, this is really of little importance.

Next, the Oak Tree coins. See Plate I, Nos. 8 to 17, and Figs. 6 to 12.

 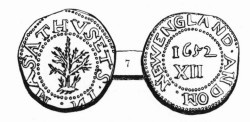

Notwithstanding the fact that the Twopenny pieces, — all of which have for their device an oak shrub, — bear the date of 1662, (which fact we consider does not in the least degree conflict with this theory,) we think these also must have preceded the device of the Pine tree, and for several reasons.

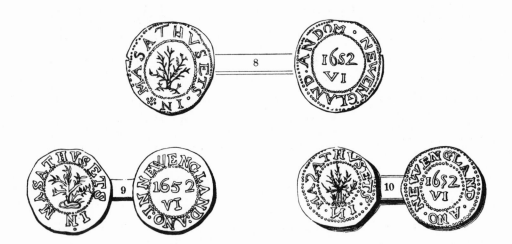

1st.   The resemblance of the device, upon both Oaks and Willows, to the draught presented by the General Court, October 19, 1652, the Willows being the rudest representations of the draught previously illustrated.

2d.   Their general inferiority, in point of execution, to the Pine Tree coins.

3d.   Their size, which varies but slightly from that of the N E series, which preceded ; or the larger, which are believed to be the older of those of the Pine Tree series.

4th.   The stamp of this mint was spoken of by a writer in 1680, as "a New England pine."   Had the Oak Tree device been still in use, this term would not have been then used.

5th.   The scarcity of specimens of these, and the small number of varieties which they furnish, — the Shillings of the Willows numbering but three obverse dies, and of the Oaks nine.

Allowing the coinage of the Oak Tree variety to have commenced very soon after the design was adopted, and to have been continued for ten years or a little longer, about one third of the whole coinage, (exclusive of the

Twopenny pieces,) would be likely to have been issued ; and the Twopenny pieces, with their date of 1662, would be included among these in style.

6th. The punctuation, which we take to be the privy mark ordered to be put upon them, is, upon these of the more simple character ; some having none, and none of the Willow and but few of the Oaks having more than colons for such marks.

7th. Sir Thomas Temple, in 1662, showed at the council table in England, some of this money, which Dr. Eliot, in a letter to Mr. Hollis,[1] written in May, 1768, says had upon it "a pine tree[2] of that sort which is thick and bushy towards the top," [how did he ascertain the particular style of tree upon the coin which was shown in England more than one hundred years before?] informing the king, in answer to his direct inquiry, that it was the "royal oak which preserved his majesty's life." Had this been really a pine tree, Sir Thomas would hardly have been so bold as to have stated it to the king, who was then in no mood to be trifled with, to be an oak. Conceding it to have been an oak, he could hardly have had it in his possession to have shown at that time and place, had not these been coined previous to 1662. It is more probable that those previously coined had been of the Oak Tree variety, and that soon after 1662 a change was made to the Pine.

The whole story here referred to has been considered merely as a pleasant myth, and is called by Ruding[3] a "ridiculous story;" but the fact of the money being so shown by Sir Thomas is sufficiently proved by records still preserved in the State archives, a copy of which will be given on a subsequent page.

Although it may be objected that this story implies that Sir Thomas did falsify in his answer, for the purpose of making his point, we think it more probable, and as much implied, that, instead of making a false statement, he merely turned the truth to his advantage, making it subserve his purpose by his ready wit. He could not have given the king credit for much intelligence to have attempted to foist upon him a pine tree for an oak, when, from the experience of Charles with the latter tree, he should have been supposed to know the difference between it and a pine.

Upon the next two pages are tables of varieties of the Oak Tree coins.

---

[1] Hollis Memoirs, vol. i. p. 397-8.

[2] Probably calling it so in accordance with a custom which continues to this day, of calling all these, of whatever variety, "Pine Tree coins." [3] Vol. i. p. 416.

# TABLES OF VARIETIES OF OAK TREE COINS.

## SHILLINGS. — OBVERSES.

| Legend and Punctuation. | Tree. High. | Tree. Wide. | Rings. Grains, Number, Size, &c. | Rings. Inner. Diam. | Rings. Outer. Diam. | Top limb of tree points | Below the roots. | Shrub. | Roots point, &c. | Letters. | Obv. | With Rev. |
|---|---|---|---|---|---|---|---|---|---|---|---|---|
| MASATHVSETS IN | 8¼ | 8¼ | 51. Medium. | 10 | 17 | Between H and V. | N | None. | Many fine, to left. | Large, heavy. | 1a | D |
| MASATHVSETS IN | 8¼ | 8¾ | 51. Medium. | 10 | 17 | One point each side right foot of H. | N | None. | 5. Fine, to right. | Large, heavy. | 1b | D |
| MASATHVSETS ·IN· | 8 | 8 | 64. Small. | 9 | 16¼ | At right foot of H. | N· | Two. | 3. Forked, to left. | Large, light. | 2 | D |
| MASATHVSETS ·IN· | 7 | 8 | 67. Connected. | 9½ | 16 | At right foot of H. | N· | Two. | Crossing. | Large, medium | 3 | D |
| MASATHVSETS ·IN· | 8 | 8 | 73? Connected. | 9½ | 16 | Just left of H. | N· | None. | Crossing. | Small, heavy. | 4 | C |
| MASATHVSETS ·IN· | 8 | 7¾ | 64? Large. | 9½ | 16 | At H? | N· | None. | Heavy crossing. | Small, heavy. | 5 | A |
| MASATHVSETS ·IИ· | 8 | 7¾ | 48. Large. | 10 | 16¼ | At right foot of H. | И· | 1. To left | Very light crossing. | Small, heavy. | 1a | E1 |
| MASATHVSETS ·IИ· | 7¾ | 7¾ | 48. Large. | 10 | 16¼ | At right foot of H. | И· | Two. | None. | Small, heavy. | 1b | E2 |
| MASATHVSETS ·IИ· | 8¼ | 7¼ | 48. Large. | 10 | 16 | Just right of H. | ɿ· | Two. | 4. To left. | Heavy, forked. | 7 | B |
| MASATHVSETS ? ? | 8½ | 8 | 48. Large. | 10 | ? | Between H and V. | ? | Two. | 4. To left, heavy. | Medium, heavy | 8 | F |
| MASATHVSETS :IN: | 8¾ | 8½ | 66. Med. on thread. | 9½ | 16 | Forked. At M and second A. | ET | Two. | Right. | Medium. | 9 | G, H, I |

## SIXPENCES. — OBVERSES.

| Legend and Punctuation. | Tree. High. | Tree. Wide. | Rings. Grains. | Rings. Inner. Diam. | Rings. Outer. Diam. | Top limb of tree points | Below the roots. | Shrubs. | Roots point, &c. | Letters. | Obv. | With Rev. |
|---|---|---|---|---|---|---|---|---|---|---|---|---|
| MASATHVSETS ·IИ· | 6½ | 6½ | 43. Irregular. Medium. | 7 | 12¼ | At left foot of H, curving to left. | И | Two. | Light; point left and right. | Small. | 1a | D |
| MASATHVSETS ·IИ· | 6½ | 6½ | | 7 | 12¼ | | | Two. | | | 1b | D |
| MAƧATHVSETS ·IИ· | 6½ | 6½ | | 7 | 12¼ | | | Two. | | | 1c | D |
| MASATHVSETS ? IN· | 6 | 7½ | Large, connected. | 7½ | 13 | Between T and H. | I | None. | Faint. | Medium. | 2 | B |
| MASATHVSETS IN | 6 | 8 | 57. Medium, close. | 8¼ | 13¼ | At H. | N | None. | Circular. | Med., heavy. | 3 | E |
| MASATHVSETS ⁏ IN: | 5¾ | 6¼ | Small, connected. | 7½ | 12½ | Left of H. Tree tall. | ; I | None. | None. | Med., light. | 4 | C |
| MASATHVSETS ·IN⁙ | 7 | 7¼ | Medium, connected. | 8¾ | 14 | Between T and H. | N | Two. | 2. Right. 2. Left. | Medium. | 5 | A |
| MASATHVSETS ⁙ | 6¼ | 7 | 50. Medium. | 7½ | 12¼ | At right foot 2d A. | 3d s. | Two. | Right and left. | Large. | 6 | F |

## THREEPENCES. — OBVERSES.

| Legend and Punctuation. | Tree. High. | Tree. Wide. | Rings. Grains. | Rings. Inner. Diam. | Rings. Outer. Diam. | Tree points | Below the roots. | Shrub. | Roots point, &c. | Letters. | Obv. | With Rev. |
|---|---|---|---|---|---|---|---|---|---|---|---|---|
| MAƧATHVƧETƧ ·IN ⁘ | 4 | 4½ | 45. Small, connected. | 5 | 9½ | At group. | HV | None. | None. | All Ss reversed | 1 | A1 |
| ·MAƧATHVSETS ⁘ | 4 | 4½ | 36? Large, connected. | 4¾ | 9 | At M. | HV | None. | 3. Left. | 1st S reversed. | 2 | A1 |
| MASATHVSETS ⁙ | 3½ | 3¾ | 36. Large and small. | 5 | 9 | Bet. group and M. | HV | None. | 2. Right. | Heavy. | 3 | A2 |
| MASATHVSETS ⁙ | 4 | 4 | 36? Medium. | 5 | 10 | At M. | HV | Two. | None. | Light. | 4 | A2 |
| MASATHVSETS ⁙ | 4¼ | 4 | 30. Large. | 5 | 10 | At M. | HV | Two. | Left. | Heavy. | 5 | B |
| ATHVS ? ? | ? | ? | Medium. | 5 | ? | At T H. | Group? | ? | ? | Small. | 6 | C |

## TWOPENCE. — OBVERSE.

| Legend and Punctuation. | Tree. High. | Tree. Wide. | Rings. Grains. | Rings. Inner. Diam. | Rings. Outer. Diam. | Tree Points | Below the roots. | Shrub. | Roots point | Obverse. | With Reverses. |
|---|---|---|---|---|---|---|---|---|---|---|---|
| MASATHVSETS · IN: | 3¾ | 4¼ | 26. Large, round. | 4½ | 8½ | At H. | N: | Two. | Left | 1 | A1 A2 A3 |

# TABLES OF VARIETIES OF OAK TREE COINS.

## SHILLINGS. — REVERSES.

| Legend and Punctuation. | Centre Marks. | Diam. Rings. Inner. | Diam. Rings. Outer. | Grains of Inner Ring. No. | Grains of Inner Ring. Size, &c. | Below XII. | Letters. | Date. | Numerals. | Reverse. | With Obverse. |
|---|---|---|---|---|---|---|---|---|---|---|---|
| NEWENGLAND AN DOM | Small. | 9½ | 15¾ | 61 ? | Medium, irregular. | DO | Low, irregular. | Light. | Small. | A | 5 |
| NEWENGLAND · AN DOM . | None. | 10 | 16 | 52 | Large. | OM . | Heavy, irregular. | Medium. | Heavy. | B | 7 |
| NEWENGLAND · AN · DOM· | Two. | 9½ | 15½ | 79 ? | Large, connected. | DO | Small, heavy. | Medium. | Heavy. | C | 4 |
| NEWENGLAND · AN · DOM· | Small. | 9½ | 16½ | 68 | Medium, close at top. | OM | Large, medium. | 6 large. | Large. | D | 1a, 1b, 2, 3 |
| NEWENGLAND · AN · DOM . | Large. | 10 | 16 | 52 | Large, regular. | OM . | Small, medium. | 1 heavy. | Heavy. | E1 | 6a |
| NEWENGLAND · AN · DOM . | None. | 10 | 16 | 52 | Medium. | OM . | Small, medium. | Light. | Light. | E2 | 6b |
| NEWENGLAND ? AN ? DOM ? | None ? | 10 | ? | 52 | Medium, irregular. | OM | ? | Medium. | Large. | F | 8 |
| NEWENGLAND · AN · ? | Very small. | 9½ | 16 | 67 ? | Small, connected. | GLA | Medium. | Large. | Large. | G | 9 |
| NEWENGLAND : AN · DOM· | Joins 5. | 9½ | 16 | 69 ? | Medium, connected. | ND: | Large, medium. | Medium. | Large. | H | 9 |
| NEWENGLAND ? AN ? DO ⁘ | Large. | 10 | 15½ | 70 ? | Med., many connected. | 1st AN | Large, medium. | Large. | Medium. | I | 9 |

## SIXPENCES. — REVERSES.

| Legend and Punctuation. | Centre Marks. | Diam. Rings. Inner. | Diam. Rings. Outer. | Grains of Inner Ring. No. | Grains of Inner Ring. Size, &c. | Below VI. | Letters. | Date. | Numerals. | Reverse. | With Obverse. |
|---|---|---|---|---|---|---|---|---|---|---|---|
| NEWENGLAND · AN DOM · | None. | 9 | 14 | | Medium, connected. | LA | Medium. | Central. | Low. | A | 5 |
| NEWENGLAND ? AN ? DOM | ? | 7¼ | 13 | | Large, connected. | EN | Medium. | Very high, | Large. | B | 2 |
| NEW : ENGLAND : AN : DOM : | Small. | 7¼ | 13 | | Small, connected. | 2d N | Light. | High, light. | Light. | C | 4 |
| NEWENGLAND · A NO · | Joins 5. | 7 | 12 | | 42. Large. | NO | Heavy. | 52 larger. | Small. | D | 1a, 1b, 1c |
| IN NEWENGLAND : ANO : | ? | 8½ | None | | 57. Medium. | 2d N | Large. | Large, cent'l | Low. | E | 3 |
| IN NEWENGLAND · ANO ⁘ | Bet. 5 & 6. | 7½ | 12½ | | 52. Medium. | NO | Medium. | 16 larger. | Low. | F | 6 |

## THREEPENCES. — REVERSES.

| Legend and Punctuation. | Centre Marks. | Diam. Rings. Inner. | Diam. Rings. Outer. | Grains of Inner Ring. No. | Grains of Inner Ring. Size, &c. | Below III. | Letters. | Date. | Numerals. | Reverse. | With Obverse. |
|---|---|---|---|---|---|---|---|---|---|---|---|
| NEWENGLAND ⁖ | Small. | 5 | 9½ | | 43. Small. | GL | Medium. | Large. | Heavy. | A1 | 1, 2 |
| NEWENGLAND ⁖ | Small. | 5½ | 9¼ | | 38. Medium. | GL | NG double lined. | 2 heavy. | Irregular. | A2 | 3, 4 |
| NEWENGLAND ⁘ | ? | 5¼ | 9¾ | | 36 ? Some double. | GL | Medium, irregular. | Medium. | Light. | B | 5 |
| NEWENGLAND ⁙ | Large. | 5 | 9¾ | | 30. Large. | D ⁘ | Small, heavy. | Small. | Heavy. | C | 6 |

## TWOPENCE. — REVERSE.

| Legend and Punctuation. | Centre Marks. | Diam. Rings. Inner. | Diam. Rings. Outer. | Grains of Inner Ring. No. | Grains of Inner Ring. Size, &c. | Below II. | Letters. | Date. | Reverse. | With Obverse. |
|---|---|---|---|---|---|---|---|---|---|---|
| NEWENGLAND ⁘ | None. | 4¾ | 8½ | | 26. Large below, close above. | Group. | Small, heavy. | 1 large, 2 full size. | A1 | 1 |
| | | | | | | | Crack over A. | 1 light, 2 very small. | A2 | 1 |
| | | | | | | | Crack from A to 2. | Small, heavy. | A3 | 1 |

Some notes may be necessary for the greater ease in distinguishing the varieties of these coins, which we will here endeavor to supply.

The consecutive numbers and letters on the tables indicate the different dies used upon these coins, — figures being used to represent the obverses and letters for the reverses.

The superior letters, or figures, affixed to some of the figures, or letters, indicate that those dies have undergone alterations, — the superior characters indicating the number of different forms in which they appear.

An interrogation mark is used where a point is doubtful, or where no specimen is found sufficiently clear to give the particulars of the portions indicated thereby. The measurements of the tree, and the inside diameters of the rings, are made in sixteenths of an inch.

## SHILLINGS.

The first die showing alterations is No. 1. In $1^a$ the tree is covered with coarse spines, lying pretty closely upon the branches; the lower limb at the left curves upward, pointing at H. The roots are many, and very fine. $R^6$.

In $1^b$ the spines are lighter and more open, and the lower branch points at the second A. The roots are less numerous and heavier. It is this variety that Wyatt's counterfeit most closely resembles. See Plate I, No. 10, and Fig. 6. $R^3$. For Wyatt's counterfeit see Plate I, No. 21.

No. 2 has the inner ring nearly round, the grains separate, and the lower branches of the tree curving equally. Plate I, No. 9. R.

In No. 3 the ring is longer horizontally, many grains joined, and the lower limb at the right is low, pointing at the third S. Plate I, No. 8. $R^4$.

No. 4. In this the ring is nearly round, with the grains joined above and below; the trunk is very broad, and of several lines. $R^3$.

No. 5 is much like No. 4, but the grains are round and separate, the trunk narrower, and of but two upright lines. $R^6$.

$6^a$ and $6^b$ closely resemble each other, but may be distinguished by the lower limb at left, which in $6^a$ curves upward, pointing at the second A, and the shrub under it is midway between the trunk and the ring; while in $6^b$ the limb points near the right foot of the first A, and the shrub is as near to the tree, as is the one at the right. The N is reversed. $R^4$.

No. 7 has a tree covered with spines, and the letters are mostly forked at the ends. It is represented at Fig. 7. The N is reversed. R.

Of No. 8 we have found but a single specimen, and that, unfortunately, is so much clipped that a full description of the die is impossible. It may be seen on Plate I, No. 12. R⁶.

No. 9 has a ring more high than wide, the grains joined under SETS, and upon a thread in the rest of the ring. It is represented with reverse H, on Plate I, No. 11. 9-G R⁶.; 9-H R².; 9-I R⁶.

## SIXPENCES.

No. 1 is most frequently met with. 1ᵃ has the letters MASATHVSETS correct, and in their proper positions. R.

In 1ᵇ, M and A are joined below, and the first S rests upon the inner ring.

In 1ᶜ, M and A are separate, as in 1ᵃ, but the S is reversed, and here also rests upon the inner ring. The N is reversed in all. Fig. 10. R³.

No. 2 is a variety rarely found, and all very poor specimens. The tree seems to stand upon a hillock, which, as well as the trunk, is cleft; the grains of the ring are so closely connected as to render a count impossible. Its reverse is peculiar, the date being often mistaken for 1650, on account of the 2, which seems to have been first cut reversed, then altered, thus resembling a cipher resting upon a line. The date is very high in the field. R⁵.

No. 3 is a curious variety, and can be better understood by reference to Fig. 9 than by any written description. This variety has IN on both sides, but has no beaded ring outside of the legend. R⁶.

No. 4 has a tall tree of fine branches, many fine cross lines in the trunk, standing upon a hillock, cleft. The points of the first colon are diamond shaped. Plate I, No. 13. R⁴.

No. 5, the largest Sixpence we have found, is represented by Fig. 8. R⁶.

No. 6 is peculiar in that the word IN is omitted from the obverse; it is, however, found upon the reverse die. R³.

## THREEPENCES.

No. 1 has every S reversed, and the dots of the group very small and close together. The grains of the inner ring are very small, some being connected by a fine line or thread. The trunk is double, curving left. Plate I, No. 15. R⁵.

No. 2. The tree is heavier on the right, with trunk double and cross-lined. The first S only is reversed, the dots of the group large, the grains of the ring large and so joined as to render an accurate count impossible. Plate I, No. 14. R⁵.

No. 3 has a more evenly-balanced tree, with trunk double, but no cross-lines. The grains are mostly separate, but slightly joined at the top of the ring. Fig. 11. R⁶.

No. 4. The tree leans to the right, trunk double, ground joins ring at both sides, and no roots visible. R³.

No. 5 resembles No. 4. The tree leans to the right, the trunk is single, and the ground does not reach the ring. Several fine roots point left. R².

No. 6. The only specimen of this variety known to us is so much worn upon its obverse as to render a description impossible. We can only say that it strongly resembles the Twopenny piece, but *appears* to have been punctuated with a group of dots. R⁶.

## TWOPENCE.

The varieties of this are found simply in alterations of the reverse die, A¹, having the figure 2 uniform in size with the other figures of the date, (Plate I, No. 17,) A² having the 2 very small, (Plate I, No. 16,) and on A³ it is broken, resembling ℃.

The letters R to R⁶, in the notes, indicate the comparative rarity.

The latest issue we take to be those bearing the device of a Pine Tree.

The following cuts (Figs. 13 and 14,) represent varieties of the Pine Tree Shillings not given upon Plate II.

These coins (the larger of which we consider to have been the first coined,) as they diminish in size increase in the complexity of their punctuation, — some of the largest having none, others single points, (one variety only of the larger ones having a group,) while the medium and smaller sizes have groups of dots or pellets, consisting of from four to eight each, and in some instances combinations of groups with single points. This type furnishes at least twenty-four obverse dies of the Shilling, or about double the number of both Willows and Oaks, and are met with in about the proportion of four of these to one of those. This is the result naturally to be anticipated had the Pine Tree replaced the Oak at about 1662, and continued until the suspension of the operations of the mint, whose legal existence is supposed to have terminated about June 3d, 1682, they having been coined for about twice the number of years covered by the preceding issues ; and having made their appearance at from twenty to thirty years later, might reasonably be expected to be more frequently found, and in a better state of preservation, than would their predecessors, which is the case.

This theory of their order of coinage seems to reconcile all the difficulties besetting that which regards the Pine Tree coins as taking precedence, and the Oak as following them at about 1662, while it does not conflict with the basis of that theory, — that basis being, if we mistake not, simply that the date of the Twopenny pieces, all of which bear the Oak Tree, is 1662, which, it should be remembered, is the date of the order by authority of which they were coined. [See *fac simile* facing p. 41.]

Neither Folkes nor Ruding seem ever to have known of the act authorizing a coinage of this denomination, which accounts for their doubts respecting this date.

An arrangement, according to the punctuation, gives a gradual reduction in size, (though not with perfect regularity, as different coins from the same dies often differ in thickness, and consequently in size,) from the N E coins to the smaller Pine Tree Shillings, the economy of which change may have been suggested by the superior durability of the smaller dies, as proved by the greater relative proportion of the smaller Shillings, as well as the greater number of Oak Tree coins found among the smaller denominations than among the larger, the dies probably being made use of until they were so much worn or broken as to render them worthless ; and even when much worn they seem to have been recut, and slightly altered, to fit them for still further service.

If we place the Pine Trees first, and suppose either a gradual decrease, or increase in size, one of which seems very probable, we are compelled to make a sudden change, either from the small Pine Tree Shilling to the larger Oak, in the first case, or, in the last, from the large N E to the small Pine Tree Shillings. This sudden change, in either case, is by the foregoing theory avoided, which to us appears to strengthen the probability of its correctness.

# TABLES OF VARIETIES OF PINE TREE COINS.

## SHILLINGS. — OBVERSES.

| Legend and Punctuation. | Tree. High. | Tree. Wide. | Tree. Points at | Direction of Roots, &c. | Diam. Rings. Inner. | Diam. Rings. Outer. | Grains. No. | Grains. Size, Form, &c. | Letters. | Obv. | With Rev. |
|---|---|---|---|---|---|---|---|---|---|---|---|
| MASATHVSETS IN | 9 | 7½ | Right foot of H. | Irregular, horizontal. | 10 | 17 | 53 | Irregular, round. | Large, heavy. | 1a | C |
| MASATHVSETS ·IN· | 9 | 7½ | Right foot of H. | Crossing, heavy. | 10 | 17 | 53 | Medium, oval. | Large, heavy. | 1b | C, D |
| MASATVSETS ·IN· | 8 | 8½ | Left part of 2d S. | Indefinite, heavy. | 10 | 17 | 46 | Large, oval. | Medium, heavy. | 2a | A1 |
| MASATVSETS ·IN· | 8 | 8½ | Left part of 2d S. | Curve left and right. | 10 | 17 | 46 | Large, oval. | Medium, heavy. | 2b | A2 |
| MASATHVSETS ·IN· | 9 | 9½ | Left part of V. | Heavy, very short. | 11 | 18 | 56 | Small, mostly oval. | Large, medium. | 3 | F |
| MASATHVSETS ·IN· | 10 | 7 | Just left of foot V. | Fibrous, left and right. | 11 | 18 | 57 | Medium, oval. | Large, heavy. | 4 | F |
| MASATHVSETS ·IN· | 9 | 8 | Right foot of H. | Three left, four right. | 10 | 17 | 54 | Small, oval. | Large, medium. | 5 | B1, B2 |
| MASASTHVSETS⁘IN⁘ | 7½ | 6 | Just left of H. | Four to left. | 10 | 16 | 48 | Large, oblong square. | Small, open. | 6 | K |
| MASATHVSETS ·IN· | 10 | 7 | Between V and S. | Long, crossing. | 11 | 17 | 60 | Small, oval. | Large, thin. | 7 | B3 |
| MASATHVSETS? IN? | 8 | 8½ | At V? | Short, right. | 10½ | ? | 42? | Large, oval. | Large. | 8 | E |
| MASATHVSETS? IN? | 8 | 9 | At S. | Left and right. | 10 | 17? | 53? | Medium, oval. | Large, thin. | 9 | G |
| MASATHVSETS •IN• | 8½ | 8½ | At left part of V. | Left, down, and right. | 9½ | 16½ | 30 | Very large, ob. square. | Large, wide. | 10 | P |
| MASATHVSETS ·IN⁙ | 9 | 7½ | At S. | Left and right. | 12 | 18 | 51 | Large, round. | Large. | 11 | H |
| MASATHVSETS ·IN⁙ | 8 | 7 | At S. | Four long, right. | 11 | 17½ | 51 | Small, oval and ob. sq. | Medium. | 12 | I |
| MASATHVSETS⁘IN⁘ | 7 | 7 | To left of V. | Short, down. | 8 | 14½ | 47 | Large, oblong square. | Small. | 13 | S |
| MASATHVSETS⁘IN⁘ | 7½ | 7 | Between H and V. | Undefined. | 8½ | 14½ | 48 | Large, oblong square. | Small. | 14 | R |
| MASATHVSETS⁘IN⁙ | 6½ | 7 | Just right of V. | To left. | 8 | 14½ | 39 | Round and oval. | Medium. | 15 | O |
| MASATHVSETS⁙IN⁙ | 7 | 7 | At right part of V. | Seven to left. | 7½ | 14½ | 42 | Medium, oval. | Small. | 16 | L, M, O |
| MASATHVSETS ⁙?IN⁙ | 6¼ | 6½ | At right part of V. | Four to left. | 7 | 14 | 37 | Oval and ob. square. | Small. | 17 | L |
| MASATHVSETS ⁘IN⁘ | 7 | 7 | Between H and V. | Short, to left. | 8 | 15 | 39 | Medium ob. square. | Small. | 18 | L, Q |
| MASATHVSETS⁙IN⁙ | 7 | 7½ | Between V and S. | Short, to right. | 8½ | 15 | 32 | Large, oval and ob. sq. | Medium and small. | 19 | Q |
| MASATHVSETS⁙IN⁙ | 6 | 6¾ | Right of V. | Very light, left. | 7 | 14 | 36 | Medium ob. square. | Small. | 20 | L |
| MASATHVSETS⁙IN⁙ | 6½ | 6 | Left part of S. | Short, down. | 7 | 14 | 41 | Medium ob. square. | Medium. | 21 | L |
| MASATHVSETS⁙IN⁙ | 6 | 6½ | Between V and S. | Short, right. | 7 | 14 | 41 | Medium, irregular. | Medium. | 22 | L |
| MASATHVSETS ⁙ IN ⁙ | 7 8 | 7½ | Just left of V. | Left and right. | 8½ | 14½ | 46 | Medium, oval. | Medium. | 23 | L, M |
| MASATHVSETS.⁙IN·⁙ | 6¾ | 8 | At S. | Many short, to right. | 8½ | 14 | 37 | Large oblong square. | Small. | 24 | N |
| MASSAT ? ETS ·IN· | | 7 | Between T and V? | Indistinct. | 8 | 13½ | 37 | Large, round. | Medium. | 25 | T |

## SIXPENCES. — OBVERSES.

| Legend and Punctuation. | Tree. High. | Tree. Wide. | Tree. Points at | Direction of Roots, &c. | Diam. Rings. Inner. | Diam. Rings. Outer. | Grains. No. | Grains. Size, Form, &c. | Letters. | Obv. | With Rev. |
|---|---|---|---|---|---|---|---|---|---|---|---|
| MASATHVSETS ·IN· | 6 | 5¾ | H. | Down, short. | 7 | 11½ | 35 | Medium, round. | Heavy. | 1 | A |
| MASATHVSETS? IN:⁙: | 6 | 7 | Between V and S. | ? | 7 | 12 | 37 | Medium, round. | Irregular. | 2 | Oak D |

## THREEPENCES. — OBVERSES.

| Legend and Punctuation. | Tree. High. | Tree. Wide. | Tree. Points at | Direction of Roots, &c. | Diam. Rings. Inner. | Diam. Rings. Outer. | Grains. No. | Grains. Size, Form, &c. | Letters. | Obv. | With Rev. |
|---|---|---|---|---|---|---|---|---|---|---|---|
| MASATHVSETS · · | 4 | 5 | M | Right, short. | 5½ | 10 | 30 | Large, round. | Heavy. | 1 | A1, A2 |
| MASATHVSETS ⁙ | 4 | 4 | Left foot of M. | Left, long. | 5 | 9½ | 33 | Small, round. | Light. | 2a | B |
| 1st A narrow; 2d, high. | 4 | 4 | ? | ? | 5 | ? | ? | Small, round. | Irregular. | 2b | B |

# TABLES OF VARIETIES OF PINE TREE COINS.

## SHILLINGS. — REVERSES.

| Legend and Punctuation. | Diam. Rings. Inner. | Outer. | Grains of Inner Ring. No. | Size, &c. | Below XII. | Letters. | Numerals. | Figures. | Reverse. | With Obverse. |
|---|---|---|---|---|---|---|---|---|---|---|
| ИEW EИGLAИD AИ DOM | 10½ | 17 | 61 | Medium, oval. | M | Small, Ns reversed. | Medium. | Small. | A1 | 2a |
| ИEW EИGLAИD : AИ : DOM : | 10½ | 17 | 61 | Medium, oval. | M : | Heavier. | Heavier. | Heavier. | A2 | 2b |
| NEW · EИGLAND · AN · DOM · | 10½ | 17 | 57 | Small, oval. | M · | Medium, light. | Large. | Light. | B1 | 5 |
| NEW EИGLAND · AN · DOM · | 10½ | 17 | 55 | Larger. | M · | Recut. | Recut. | Recut. | B2 | 5 |
| NEW EИGLAND · AN · DOM · | 10½ | 17 | 55 | Still larger. | M · | Again recut. | Recut. | 6 large. | B3 | 7 |
| NEW EИGLAND · AN · DOM · | 10½ | 17 | 58 | Medium, oval. | M · | Medium, heavy. | Large. | Large. | C | { 1a, 1b |
| NEW ENGLAND · AN DOM · | 10 | 16½ | 45 | Large, oval. | OM · | Medium, heavy. | Medium. | Medium. | D | 1b |
| ? | 11 | ? | 46 ? | Large, oval. | ? | Large, illegible. | Large. | Light. | E | 8 |
| NEW ENGLAND · AN · DOM · | 11 | 18 | 56 | Medium, oval. | OM · | Large, heavy. | Large. | Heavy. | F | { 3, 4 |
| ? ENGLAND · AN ? DOM ? | 10 | 17 ? | 50 ? | Medium, oval. | NE ? | Large, light. | Large. | Heavy. | G | 9 |
| NEW ENGLAND : AN : DOM ⁘ | 12 | 18 | 53 | Large, round. | M ⁘ | Medium, heavy. | Large. | Medium. | H | 11 |
| NEW ENGLAND : AN : DOM ⁘ | 10¾ | 17 | 74 | Medium, oblong square. | ⁘ | Medium, heavy. | Small. | Medium. | I | 12 |
| ИEW ⁖ EИGLAИD ⁖ AИ : DO : | 8 | 14 | 39 | Medium, nearly square. | DO : | Small, irregular. | Heavy. | Medium. | K | 6 |
| NEW ENGLAND · AN · DO · | 7½ | 13¾ | 41 | Medium, oval. | AN · D | Medium, heavy. | Large. | Heavy. | L | { 16—21, 17—22, 18—23, 20 |
| NEW ENGLAND · AN · DO · | 8 | 14½ | 46 | Medium, semi-oval. | O · | Medium, irregular. | Heavy. | Heavy. | M | { 16, 23 |
| NEW ENGLAND · AN · DO · | 8 | 15 | 32 | Large, oblong square. | ƆO · | Small, irregular. | Wide. | Heavy. | N | 24 |
| NEVV ENGLAND · AN · DO · | 8 | 14 | 43 | Medium, irregular oval. | · DO | Medium, irregular. | Heavy. | Heavy. | O | { 15, 16 |
| NEW ENGLAND • AN • DO • | 10½ | 18 | 31 | Very large, oblong square. | DO • | Medium. | Large. | Large. | P | 10 |
| NEW ENGLAND · AN · DO · | 8½ | 15 | 33 | Large, oval and ob. square. | DO · | Large, ill formed. | Wide. | Wide. | Q | { 18, 19 |
| NEW ⁞ ENGLAND ▮ AN ⁞ DO ⁞ | 8 | 14¼ | 47 | Large, oblong square. | DO | Small. | Heavy. | Heavy. | R | 14 |
| NEW · ENGLAND ∴ AN ∵ DO ∴ | 8 | 14½ | 45 | Large, oblong square. | DO · | Small. | Heavy. | Heavy. | S | 13 |
| NEW ENGLAND · | 7½ | 13½ | 35 | Large, round. | D · | Medium, heavy. | Large. | Large. | T | 25 |

## SIXPENCES. — REVERSES.

| Legend and Punctuation. | Diam. Rings. Inner. | Outer. | Grains of Inner Ring. No. | Size, &c. | Below VI. | Letters. | Numerals. | Figures. | Reverse. | With Obverse. |
|---|---|---|---|---|---|---|---|---|---|---|
| NEW ENGLAND · ANO · | 7 | 11½ | 35 | Medium, round. | AN | Large, heavy. | Wide. | Heavy. | A | 1 |

## THREEPENCES. — REVERSES.

| Legend and Punctuation. | Diam. Rings. Inner. | Outer. | Grains of Inner Ring. No. | Size, &c. | Below III. | Letters. | Numerals. | Figures. | Reverse. | With Obverse. |
|---|---|---|---|---|---|---|---|---|---|---|
| NEW ENGLAND · : · | 5½ | 10 | 29 | Large, round. | A | Large, heavy. | Heavy. | 6 high. | A1 | 1 |
| NEW ENGLANᗡ · ANO | 5½ | 10 | 29 | Medium, round. | A | Irregular, lighter. | Light. | 2 large. | A2 | 1 |
| NEW ENGLAND ⁘ | 5¼ | 9½ | 39 | Small, round. | A | Small. | Small. | Light. | B | { 2a, 2b |

In the following notes the figures representing the trees, as 8 3 7, indicate that the tree has eight branches on the left, three small points at the top, and seven branches on the right of the trunk.

Branches are said to be in pairs when springing from the trunk opposite each other; alternate, when between two branches of the opposite side.

No. 1ᵃ. Tree of 7 3 7, all in pairs. The second limb on left, and second and third on right, forked; a break near the trunk, between the third and fourth limbs on the right; trunk cleft to fifth pair of limbs. R⁴. ·

No. 1ᵇ. Tree similar, but third limb on right not forked, but long, extending nearly to s; no break in the tree. Fig. 13. R.

No. 2ᵃ. Tree of 8 3 7, the ten lower in pairs. Seventh limb on left, and third and fourth on right, do not join the trunk, which is heavy below the second pair of branches, then suddenly contracts. R⁴.

No. 2ᵇ. Tree similar, but all limbs join the trunk, which tapers gradually, and is cleft to the sixth limb on the left. Fig. 14. R⁵.

No. 3. Tree of 8 2 7, ten lower in pairs. The lowest pair short, all joining the trunk, which is solid, but heavier below the second pair of branches. Plate II, No. 2. R⁵.

No. 4. Tree of 7 3 6, alternate. The limbs rise sharply, and are rigidly straight; the two lower are very short. The trunk tapers from the ground to the fourth limb. Fig. 15. R³.

No. 5. Tree of 8 2 7, mostly alternate. The second and third on the right are forked; the trunk tapers from the ground to the top. Plate II, No. 1. R³.

No. 6. Tree of 6 2 7, six upper in pairs. Trunk very tall below the branches. Plate II, No. 6. R⁶.

No. 7. Tree of 8 1 8, mostly alternate. Two lower limbs very light, that at the right forked; trunk heavy to seventh limb. Plate II, No. 3. R⁴.

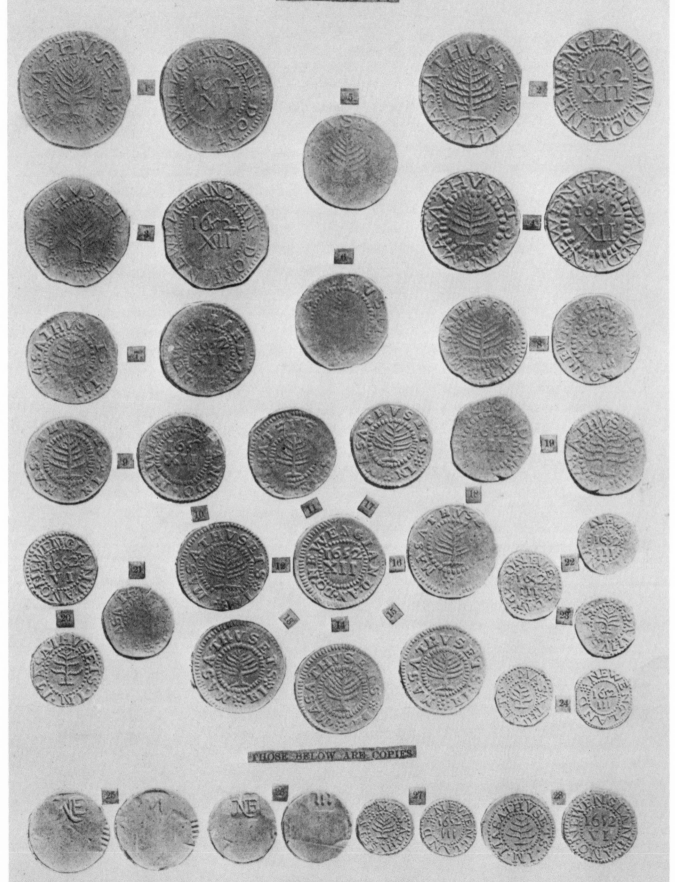

PLATE II

THOSE BELOW ARE COPIES

No. 8. Tree of 4 ? 4, all in pairs. The limbs are very heavy, and curve uniformly; trunk heavy, tapering slightly. The only specimen we find of this variety is so much clipped and worn that a full description cannot be given. R⁶.

No. 9. Tree of 6⁴6, alternate. Trunk heavy, tapering to the top, and bending to the left. This variety is as rare as the last, and in but little better condition. Plate II, No. 5. R⁶.

No. 10. Tree of 6³6, mostly in pairs. The branches on the right are nearly horizontal, and but slightly rising on the left. The trunk tapers but little; the points and the grains of the rings are very large and heavy. Plate II, No. 4. R⁵.

No. 11. Tree of 7²7, alternate and irregular. The lower branch at the left is very near the ground; the trunk is crooked. Four heavy roots left of the trunk below, and two above the ground at right, point to the right. The legend on this variety is enclosed in a plain ring, not beaded. Punctuated with a point and a group of seven. This may be an early counterfeit. R⁶.

No. 12. 6³7, alternate. The trunk tapers very slightly; four long light roots below the ground, and three above, point to the right; a pellet at each side of the trunk. Point, and group of seven. Fig. 16. R.

No. 13. Tree of 4⁴4, all in pairs. The limbs are rather heavy, curving slightly; the trunk heavy, tapering slightly at top. Two groups of four each. R².

No. 14. Tree of 5³5, eight in pairs. The lower limbs are straight near the trunk, but curve upward at the ends. The third and fifth limbs on the left are short. Two groups of four each; second group joined. Fig. 17. R².

No. 15. Tree of 5¹5, eight in pairs. The branches are rather light, curving uniformly; the trunk heavy to above the third pair. The first T is defective at the right of cross, and the group of five, usually faint in the first and outer points. Groups of five and seven. Plate II, No. 7. R⁴.

No. 16. Tree of 5²5, all in pairs. Trunk bulges at the left near the ground, and tapers very little till near the top; T and V double cut. Groups of six and seven. Plate II, No. 9. R⁴.

No. 17. Tree of 5¹5, four lower in pairs. The trunk is nearly straight from ground to tip; second A, V, and S double cut. Groups of seven(?) and six. The position of the points in the first group is such that there may have been two more in the die, which, for some unknown reason, fail to appear on this coin, of which we find no duplicate. Plate II, No. 11. R⁶.

No. 18. Tree of 6¹7, alternate. The lower branches curve more at their points; a heavy line is between H and V, and a break joins the fifth and sixth branches, near the trunk; another break extends from the ground to the first s. Groups of seven and six. Plate II, Nos. 16 and 18. R⁴.

No. 19. Tree of 5¹5, all in pairs. The branches are nearly horizontal, but double curved; HVS small. Two groups of seven. Plate II, No. 19. R⁵.

No. 20. Tree of 5³5, four lower in pairs. The trunk is irregular; second T and I double cut; a break extends from first A to edge. Groups of seven and eight. Plate II, No. 17. R³.

No. 21. Tree of 6³5, six in pairs, others alternate. The trunk tapers but very slightly; the second and third limbs on left join at points; first A and second s, double cut. Groups of seven and eight. Plate II, No. 14. R.

No. 22. Tree of 7²5, mostly alternate. The trunk curves slightly to the right; ring double over AS, H double cut. Groups of seven and eight. Plate II, Nos. 13 and 15. R. This variety was duplicated on the plate by mistake. One of these obverses should be the same with that of No. 9, which has the reverse of this as well as the one there given.

No. 23. Tree of 7³7, mostly alternate. The trunk is nearly the same size from the ground to its tip, and curves slightly to the left; two roots under the trunk are separate and low. Groups of eight and seven. Plate II, Nos. 10 and 12. R⁴.

No. 24. Tree of 7³6, two lower and four upper in pairs. The trunk tapers gently to the upper pair of limbs, then turns slightly to the left; second A double cut, HVS small. Groups of eight and seven, each preceded by a single point. Plate II, No. 8. R³.

No. 25. Tree of 5²5. Branches all in pairs, curving parallel, full of fine leaves; the trunk tapers from the ground to the top; the legend is not distinct, but probably is MASSATVSETS · IN · This piece has a modern appearance, and its genuineness is doubted. R⁶.

## SIXPENCES.

Of these, the only variety often met with is No. 1. It is a tree of 4²4, the limbs all in pairs, the lower pair being doubly curved; the others are more nearly straight. It has a pellet at each side of the trunk, like No. 12 of the Shillings. Plate II, No. 20, and Fig. 18. R.

No. 2. Tree of 4²4? The branches are covered with spines. The only specimen of this variety we have found is so much worn and mis-struck that it cannot be fully described. It may be identified by its punctuation, which is a colon, a group of eight, and a colon. Its reverse is from the same die with that of No. 1 of the oak tree sixpences, D. Plate II, No. 21. R⁶.

## THREEPENCES.

No. 1 has a tree of 4²4, and is of a design much like No. 1 of the Sixpences, having, like that, a pellet at each side of the trunk. It is shown on Plate II, No. 23. No. 22 should represent the same obverse, with the reverse above it. This mistake was caused by the misplacing of the obverse and reverse of No. 23, which should have been transposed.

No. 2ª. Tree of 3³4. The second branch on the right is partly double; sa very close upon the inner ring. Group of nine. Plate II, No. 24. R³.

In No. 2ᵇ the only difference to be noted in the worn specimen which alone is found, is in the letters, the first a being narrow, the second heavy, sa higher than the others, and h double cut. R⁶.

A few words here in regard to the "mint mark," as the group of dots or points has been called.

It will be seen, by reference to the order for the establishment of the mint, May $\frac{26}{27}$, 1652, that one of its requirements is that there shall be stamped upon the coins "a privy marke which shall be Appointed euery three months by the Gouno.ʳ and knowne only to him and the sworne officers of the mint." The probability is that these groups, differing in number, and in the number of points of which they are composed, as well as other variations in the punctuation, are the "privy markes," changed in accordance with this provision ; nor is it unlikely that the forms of the trees, and the peculiarities of reversed letters, which is usually confined to the N of IN on the obverse, and the first N of ENGLAND, on the reverse, may also have been intentional, and with the same design.

Had this regulation been strictly complied with it would have necessitated at least one hundred and twenty varieties of each denomination, (excepting the Twopennies,) that is, supposing the coinage of all denominations to have been continuous, and for the period of thirty years. The number of varieties known to us falls so far short of this that it is reasonable to suppose it to have been but partially regarded.

Attempts have been made to cast ridicule upon the coinage of this mint, because, forsooth, the devices adopted upon it do not conform to the precise pattern which some minds have imagined as proper to be followed.

It may be remarked that the records make no mention of the pine tree ; neither do they specify any particular species of tree which should be represented, but leave it entirely optional with the mint master as to what tree he would adopt, or to change it as reason, fancy, or that clause of the act relating to a privy mark might dictate ; and we think none will hesitate to concede that the pine tree device is a vast improvement upon most of those which preceded it.

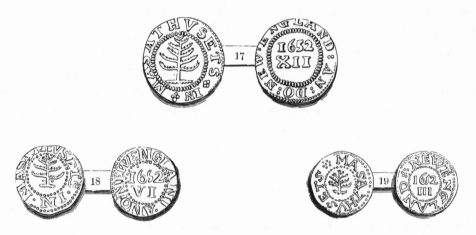

These coins were known in their early days as Boston or Bay Shillings.[1] The first application we find of the name of "pine" to them was in May, 1680, in a proposition to make the mint free, (which will be found upon another page;) and it seems not improbable that this name was given them soon after the change from the oak to the pine as a device ; as were there any interest whatever taken in the subject by the people in general, (and it would seem there must have been,) so decided a change must have occasioned remark, and would naturally lead to the application of some popular name to so popular a commodity, and one from which so much benefit was expected.

We find no reason to believe that any action was taken toward establishing a coinage, earlier than the year 1652, notwithstanding the existence of certain Pine Tree Shillings bearing the date of 1650, these being evidently

---

[1] New York Records, 1672, and Lambert's Colony of New Haven, p. 193.

nothing more than modern results of the reprehensible passion for possessing coins merely on account of their rarity, without regard to their historical value.

Although it has been declared probable that these pieces "were all returned to the crucible in 1652," that assertion is the only reference we have found relating to the issue of coin in the colonies previous to the year 1652.

It is thought that the following letter, from Dr. Ammi Brown, of Boston, who first brought these pieces into notice, will be considered as sufficient confirmation of the opinion we have expressed regarding them:

BOSTON, SEPTEMBER 21st, 1868.

DEAR SIR, — I will give you the history of the 1650 Massachusetts Shillings as correctly as my memory will serve me. I have mislaid the letters relating to them, but as they would only fix the date of receiving the pieces they are of no especial value at this time.

In the Fall of 1854, while residing in Salem, Mass., a young man named ——, from Boscawen, N. H., called on me and wanted to buy coins. I told him I did not sell, but kept duplicates for exchange; that I was much interested in the colonial series, and desired to secure as many varieties of Massachusetts pieces as possible; and if he would find some that I did not possess I would give him Roman coins, which he much desired, in exchange for them.

He appeared to have no knowledge whatever of numismatics, but was merely a collector of curious pieces. He said he had some of the Massachusetts shillings at home, that he had bought from an old person in New Hampshire, in a lot of silver, some of which was Spanish, and that the dates were 1650 and 1652.

I told him that he was probably mistaken about the dates, — that they were all of 1652; but if any were of 1650 I should like to have them. He offered to exchange a 1650 shilling for one of my 1652 duplicates and a Roman coin worth about fifty cents. In about a week he sent by letter the large shilling of 1650, with fruit or cones upon the branches. I returned by mail what was agreed upon, and he expressed himself perfectly satisfied with the exchange, and said that he would bring the others and exchange them also. A short time after this he called with the other pieces, consisting of three shillings of 1650, small size, all fine, same die, but one imperfectly struck, and several of 1652. Those of 1652 were of ordinary types and undoubtedly genuine, being from the same dies as some in my collection. He wanted a Massachusetts Twopence, very much, and I gave it to him for one of the shillings of 1650. The market value of a twopence, (if it could be said to have any,) at that time was perhaps $2.50. For the other two shillings of 1650 I gave him some Roman coins, the cost to me certainly not exceeding two dollars each. I also obtained, by exchange, two of 1652, which were very fine, on very favorable terms. During the winter of 1856 or 1857, after I had moved to Boston, he sold me a shilling, and I bought it with the understanding that it had been altered from 1652 to 1650. It was cleverly done, although I easily detected the tooling. I gave him five dollars for it, as he said he had obtained it for me of another person, after some trouble. It was in fine condition, and different from any in my possession.

I saw him once or twice after that, but had no dealings with him. He had been among coin collectors and brokers, and I found had got his ideas somewhat raised in regard to the prices of coins. The possession of these pieces by me created considerable interest among collectors, some of whom he knew and had dealings with ; and reports of their extreme rarity and value must have reached his ears, although I heard nothing from him on the subject.

In the year 1858 I sold my collection, — the large shilling, one of the small ones, and the altered piece, passing into the hands of Mr. Mickley. One of the small pieces went with the rest of the collection to Mr. Brooks, of Salem, who afterwards sold it to Mr. Finotti. The third is still in my possession.

A short time after I had sold the pieces above-named, I received a letter from Mr. ———, saying that he had experienced religion, and was very sorry for many things he had done ; that in our exchange of coins he had taken advantage of me ; that *all* the pieces he let me have were false ; and he desired very much to get them again into his possession, and make restitution of the amount he had defrauded me. He enclosed the Massachusetts two-pence, and desired me to return one of the 1650 shillings, and let him know how much money he should send me for the remaining pieces, as he had parted with the pieces I had given him.

There was something about this letter that did not appear exactly right; and it occurred to me that, finding out the value of the pieces, he was willing to acknowledge himself a trickster for the purpose of obtaining them again, and to test the matter I cut one of the 1652 shillings into ten or fifteen pieces, and enclosed them in a letter to him, saying that it would take some time for me to obtain the others, as they had passed out of my hands; but as soon as I got them back I proposed to mutilate them as I had done with that enclosed, and would send the pieces to him, that I might be sure no other person was deceived as I had been, at the same time asking him to give me some information as to how, when, where, and by whom they were fabricated. To this letter, and to another that I sent soon after, asking the same questions, I received no answer; nor did he ever send any more coins or any money to me.

If these pieces are fabrications they must have cost a considerable sum, and could only have been made for the purpose of gain. At that time a shilling of 1652, in fair condition, could be obtained for $1.00. I imported several fine ones from England for $1.50 each; and a twopence, the finest specimen I ever saw, for sixty-two cents. There was no enthusiasm whatever in regard to the Massachusetts money. These 1650 shillings did not cost me more than $2.00 each, and at that time it would have required large sales to make it pay as a swindle.

If the pieces are false, and his repentance sincere, I shall deeply regret having doubted him when he offered to repair the wrong he had done; but his subsequent course strengthened the suspicion I at first entertained.

I have been offered $50.00 for the one I possess, by a person who knows all the facts connected with it, but I decided not to sell it while any doubt of its genuineness remains. If it is a fabrication, it is worthless; if genuine, it is worth a great deal more.

Make any use you please of the information herein conveyed, if it will help to settle the question, but do not make any mention of Mr. ———'s name publicly. Whatever he may have been, I have no wish to publish him.

Yours, truly,                                             AMMI BROWN.

Our belief in regard to the transactions related in the foregoing letter is that the person from whom these coins were obtained was honest in his statement that he had procured them with a lot of other silver, and that neither he, nor the one from whom he obtained them, knew of the non-existence of genuine pine tree money dated 1650; but, that this lot of silver had previously belonged to some person possessed of shrewdness enough to know that no such coin, of that date, existing, if he could produce one which should be believed to be genuine, it would afford him a handsome profit, even at that time, when the "coin fever" had not reached its height; that he so far carried out his design as to make, or procure, dies for their production, and had pieces struck; but that he was prevented, by some cause, possibly death, (perhaps he experienced religion with a more beneficial effect upon his life than he who in his letter claimed to have done so,) from consummating his plan, and the coins were left to be disposed of by his executor, who perhaps was the party from whom Mr. ———— received them. That Mr. ————, after disposing of them, found that they were creating an excitement among collectors, and devised the plan of procuring them again by confession of a pretended fraud, designing to dispose of them in a more judicious manner, at some future time, which plan was frustrated by the quick perception of his purpose, and the attempt to draw from him the full particulars of their origin.

We can readily excuse the former owner of these pieces for hesitating summarily to condemn them as forgeries without *positive* evidence; yet the writer of the letter therein acknowledges that some person had taken the trouble to alter one of the coins he bought, and has said to us that the three small shillings, all of which were from the same dies, were the only ones to which the slightest credit could be given. If *these* are genuine it would certainly appear very strange that three specimens, the only ones known, should have been preserved unseparated for upwards of two hundred years, or should have again come together, after a separation of many years, with no tradition proving any unusual interest attaching to them.

The fact, that from the same source was obtained one an acknowledged alteration, and another evidently a counterfeit, and so pronounced by all experts whose opinions upon this subject we have heard stated, as well as by Dr. Brown himself, thus proving that pine tree coins had, at that time, been considered by counterfeiters as worthy of their attention, together with that of no other impression from the dies of the smaller pieces being elsewhere found, while *three* of these spring from this deposit, is sufficient to condemn the whole of them.

It remains for us to mention one other piece belonging to this series, the genuineness of which has been doubted. We refer to the Good Samaritan Shilling, whose claim to a place among the issues of this mint we consider as being fully established by the specimen in the collection of Charles I. Bushnell, Esq., of New York. See Fig. 22.

For the argument in favor of this piece, which, had it not been so generally thought to owe its origin to a more recent period, we should consider as needing no argument to establish its claim, we are indebted to the kindness of the owner, and we here give it place in his own words:

"The Good Samaritan Shilling in my possession differs materially from the one formerly in the Pembroke Collection, and from the variety engraved in Ruding, Plate XXX, No. 10, reverse not given, the existence of which is very doubtful. Ruding incorporated the plates which had been engraved for the work of Folkes, so far as they would serve his purpose, the Plate XXX being one of them; and he expressly says he knows not on what authority this shilling is there given. Snelling, in describing the piece, remarks, 'It is said to be in the Pembroke Collection,' proving that he himself had never seen it, (though his statement turned out to be true when the collection was dispersed;) but, curiously enough, in his representation of it, [Fig. 23,] copied the obverse of Ruding's, or rather, Folkes's plate, and the reverse from the Pembroke plate, and thus, by not copying both sides from the latter, he has given a representation for which there was no existing authority whatever, his obverse differing from the only known specimen in the Pembroke Collection by having MASATHVSETS ○ IN · ○ in full, instead of only IN MAS with dots in place of the remaining letters.

My specimen is not only unique, but is the most perfect. It has a well-executed representation of the incident of the Good Samaritan, and the words MASATHVSETS ○○○○ IN: in full. The subject is allowed to speak for itself, as the words 'Fac simile,' on the specimen engraved are omitted on mine. The reverse has also an important difference, the circumscription reading IN NEW ENGLAND · ANO: and in the centre $\frac{1652}{XII}$ without the ○ beneath. It is, moreover, five grains heavier than the Pembroke one, and is a perfectly genuine struck coin. The reverse die was evidently in the act of breaking, from a flaw, the effect of which, while it fortunately destroyed no part of the impression, in this instance has an appearance rendering it probable that no other could be struck from it. The style of work and letters correspond, moreover, with that on the Pine Tree Shilling of the same date.

I think there is little doubt of these having been pattern pieces, and, for some reason, not adopted by the authorities. The fact of no mention being made of it in the records is no argument against its genuineness, for no such mention would in any case be made of pattern or trial pieces, but would be confined entirely to those coins which were intended for circulation as authorized coinage, if indeed any such records were so accurately made in a new and thinly-populated state.

The catalogue describes the Pembroke specimen to have been much rubbed; mine is not so, but only unevenly struck, — the last five letters in MASATHVSETS have not come up as prominently as the others.

I do not at all consider the specimen in the Pembroke Collection in any way spurious, nor can I attach the least importance to the note to the lot describing it, in the sale catalogue of that collection, of 1848. That catalogue was drawn up by the late Mr. Burgon, who was chosen for this duty on account of his being justly considered the most competent authority on Greek and Roman coins, to which he had directed his studies exclusively, thinking them alone worthy of his attention or appreciation.

It is also necessary to bear in mind some particulars relating to the Pembroke Collection. The Earl Thomas, by whom that celebrated collection was formed, succeeded to the title as early as 1683, and died in 1733. The fourth volume of plates issued in his name was not completed and published till 1746, by his son and successor. The collection, however, remained intact until its dispersion by the present earl, in 1848, under the superintendence of his half brother, Mr. Sidney Herbert, — the earl being a constant resident abroad, which may probably account for the collection being wholly unknown, except through the volume of 1746; indeed, it seems seldom, if ever, to have been exhibited since the decease of the original collector, for Snelling, when publishing his work, had no access to it, and obtained all his information from the plates; and, in fact, when he speaks of coins said to be existing in the Pembroke Collection, acknowledges that he had no opportunity of judging for himself in the matter. I cannot give the date of the birth of the Earl Thomas, but as he succeeded his brother in 1683, [his father having died as early as 1669,] the latter, at least, must have been living at the date of this coin or pattern.

I am to a considerable extent justified in regarding it as genuine, in the absence of anything like proof to the contrary, as there could be no motive or interest to be gratified by fabricating a spurious piece relating to a distant possession of so very recent date as was 1652, at the time when the collection was formed.

Ruding's Plate XXX, first published by Folkes in 1763, is not copied from the Pembroke plate, as it is altogether different; and although the specimen it purports to represent may not be now known, I cannot think that any one will venture the supposition that so eminent a gentleman and antiquary as was Sir Martin Folkes, could have published such a piece without having sufficient authority for so doing.

Snelling's engraving goes for nothing, as he had seen no specimen; but finding such good authority for the existence of the piece, he could not but notice it without damage to the completeness of his work, and therefore copied the obverse from Folkes and the reverse from Pembroke.

Now comes the specimen I have, differing from the Pembroke, and five grains heavier; from Folkes, and also from Wyatt's even. I am quite at a loss to conceive what the inducement could be for fabricating a piece of so little interest and value, for certainly until very recently it could possess neither; yet, before the least attention could be attracted to its existence, here are evidently two pieces struck from dies altogether different, — the Pembroke and mine, to say nothing of Folkes.

It could never answer to coin spurious specimens in such small numbers, as that, after the lapse of two centuries, only two specimens alone should be known, and both of these unique varieties.

I am in the belief that they were pattern pieces, struck and submitted when the issue of a coinage was first contemplated in the colony; and this supposition will alone account for the unfinished character and rarity of these pieces, and, since they were not adopted, for the absence of any mention of them upon the records.

It will be seen that the date side of the Pine Tree Shillings is different and more complete than is the corresponding side of either of the pieces in question.

The die from which mine is struck was evidently soon broken; probably no other could have been struck from it, hence the necessity for a new one being made, even for the limited service of a pattern.

It must be remembered that it was particularly the custom to strike pattern pieces, — witness those for the entire sets of silver for the Commonwealth coinage, by Ramage and by Blondeau, the former the most beautiful, while the design of the latter was adopted. Now all these patterns were struck in 1651, and are now much in request, and always produce high prices."

We can only add to the foregoing statement that, having examined the Good Samaritan Shilling, we can with confidence say that the piece is of a character agreeing with other coins of that period, and bears no evidence of having been tampered with, but, on the contrary, was evidently struck from dies. A certain proof that it could have been no alteration from the common issues of that date is found in the legend upon the reverse, it being IN NEW ENGLAND · ANO:, which is found upon none of the Oak or Pine Tree Shillings.

Much trouble being occasioned by the exportation of the issues of this mint in such quantities as to increase the scarcity of silver coin in the colonies, as a means of preventing its loss to the country, the Court, on the 22d of August, 1654,[1] passed an order for preventing the exportation of this specie in any amount exceeding twenty shillings, which we here copy:

1654 22 August. "Itt is Ordered by this Court and the Authoritje thereof, that no Inhabitant of this Jurisdiccon, or strannger, shall from henceforth send, Carry, or transport out of this Jurisdiccon, directly or Indirectly, by sea or land, any of the mony that hath binn or shall be Cojned w^{th}in this Jurisdiccon, except twenty shillings for necessary expences, on the pœnalty of Confiscation, not only of such money so cojned, but also all the vissible estate of him that shall any way be found sending or exporting any of the Cojne aforesajd, one third whereof shall be to the vse of the Informer, or officer, the other two thirds to the Countrje ; and that this lawe

---

[1] Massachusetts Records, vol. iv, p. 174, and vol. iii, p. 430.

may be duely observed and executed, Peter Oliuer and Jn° Barrell for Boston, Jacob Greene for Charles Toune, George Willjams and Samuel Archer for Salem, Robert Lord for Ipswich, Henry Rice for Sudbury, Henry Sherborne for Piscataque, and Hercules Hawkins for the Ile of Shoales, are heereby Appointed and Authorized as serchers to examine and search all psons, vessells, Packs, truncks, chests, boxes, or the like, that shallbe transporting out of this Jurisdiccōn, and finding any mony shall seaze the same, and forthwith Informe the next magistrate thereof, who shall Issue out his warrant for the present seazure of the whole vissible estate of the partje so transporting contrary to this lawe, for the vse of the Comōn-wealth and partje seazing or Informing, as is above exprest. And Itt is heereby further declared, that all such masters, marriners, or other persons that shallbe found to be privy or Consenting to the exporting of any of the Cojne aforesajd out of this Jurisdiccōn, he or they shall for euery such offence forfeite the somē of twenty-pounds a peece, to be to the vses aforesajd : and the sajd Serchers are to take the oath for searchers, only insteede of halfe, a third p̄'te to be Inserted, and to certify the next magistrate instead of the Auditor. And in all other Tounes the Constables are by theire oathes bound to see to the executjon of this order."

It does not appear that this action of the Court had the desired effect, as we find the same trouble repeatedly referred to on later pages of the Records.

Under the impression that the agreement with the mint masters was too favorable to them, action was taken by the Court, under date of October 16, 1660,[1] with the intention of obtaining terms more advantageous to the country, namely: "Itt is Ordered : that Capt̄ Gookin & yᵉ Tresurer, mʳ Anthony Stoddard, & mʳ wᵐ Parks, shall be a Comīttee & are hereby Impowred to treate wᵗʰ the mintmaster for Allowing such an Annuall somē as may be Agreed vpon, as a meete honorarium to the Country for the yearely bennefitt they receive by minting, that so the Country may Reape some bennefitt after so long a forbearance, hauing Given them the bennefit thereof for the tjme past, or otherwise to declare that this Court Intends to agree wᵗʰ some other meete person to minte the money of this Country; making theire report to the next Court what they shall doe heerein."

In observance of this order the committee reported in these words :[2]

---

[1] Massachusetts Records, vol. iv, p. 351.   [2] Archives, vol. c, p. 79.

"Returne of the Comittee impoured to treat w$^{th}$ the mint master.
wee haue, acording to order, treated w$^{th}$ the mint masters, m$^r$ Hull & m$^r$ Sanderson, and find y$^m$ vtterly vnwilling to pay any certaine ꝑportion to ye
country of the allowance paid them for coyning mony; only they offered
tenn pounds as a free gift to the country in Case they will please to accept
it; but the comitte refused that ꝑffer, aledging that the vse of the mint &
house required in justice some certaine ꝑt of the income recvd by y$^m$, w$^{ch}$
vpon examination wilbe found to bee (62$^1$) vpon euery thousand pound; out
of w$^{ch}$ the comity ꝑpounded they should allow one twentieth part for the
country: but they consented not this is the ꝑsent state of that affaire, leauing
it to the court to take such further order therein as vnto y$^m$ seemes meet.
datted the 6th of June 1661.

The deputyes thinke meete that this Comittee
be reimpowred to treat w$^{th}$ the mintmaster, & to
receive the ten pound aboue mentioned & what               Daniel Gookin
else they can gett by way of recompenc for the             Richard Russell.
mint howse for the time past, & y$^t$ it be deliuered        Anthony Stoddard
to the Treasurer to be bestowed in powder & oill,          William Park
with reference to the Consent of o$^r$ Hon$^{rd}$ magists
hereto.                                        William Torrey Cleric.


7 June 1661 : Consented to by the magists.

                              Edward Rawson Secret.


The foregoing is copied from the original return made by the committee,
and it will be noticed that it bears date the 6th and 7th of June, while the
entry upon the book of the secretary is under the date of May 22d.[1]  The
decision of the Court thereon is recorded as follows : "The Court Judged
it meet to order that this Comittee should be reimpowred to treate w$^{th}$ the
mint maste$^r$s, & to Receiue the ten pounds aboue mentioned, & what else
they Cann Gett by way of Recompence for the mint house for the tjme past,
& that it be deliuered to the Tresurer to be bestowed in pouder."

The Shillings, Sixpences, and Threepences which were issued from this
mint, with the exception of those of the N E type, (which bore no date,) all
bear the date of the establishment of the mint, 1652, (which circumstance

---

[1] Massachusetts Records, vol. iv, p. 375.

was one of the objections urged against the mint, by its enemies,) although it is altogether likely that their coinage continued from that year to the year 1682 ; but when the Twopenny pieces were coined, the date of 1662 was placed upon them, that being the date of the year in which the order by authority of which they were struck was issued ; and these bear no other date.

The coinage of these pieces was ordered to continue for seven years, but it seems certain, from the mention made of them by John Hull, in his paper of June 6th, 1680, (to be given on a later page,) that they continued to be coined for a much longer time. The small size of the dies, and their consequent durability, may account for the absence of varieties other than those caused by repairs of the reverse die, from among them. The draught of the order for their coinage is still preserved in the Massachusetts Archives,[1] though in a somewhat mutilated condition, [see *fac simile,* facing page 41,] a copy of which we next present :

> It is ordered by this court, and the mint master is hereby inioynt
> of the first Bullion that comes to his hand, to coyne two pen
> of Siluer, in proportion according to the iust vallew & alloy of
> monys, alowed here, to answer the occasions of the contrey for exch
> that is the first yeare fifty pounds in such small mony for eue
> pounds by him to be coyned ; & for after time twenty pounds in lik
> mony anualy for euery hundred pounds, that shalbe coyned
> order is to continue in force for seauen yeares. any law
> to the contrary notwithstanding . The magists haue past this w^th Ref
> erence to the Consent of their brethren the Deputys hereto.

Boston . 16 · May 1662.                    EDW · RAWSON Secrety.

Consented to by the depu^ts          WILLIAM TORREY Cleric."

The following is a copy of the same, as entered upon the Court records :[2]
" It is Ordered by this Court, & the mint master is hereby enjoyned out of the first bullion that Comes to his hand to Coyne two penny peeces of Siluer, in proportion to the just value & allay of other monys allowed heere, to Answer the occasions of the Country for exchange ; that is the first yeare

---

[1] Vol. c, p. 86.    [2] Massachusetts Records, vol. iv, p. 401.

fifty pounds in such smale money for euery hundred pounds by him to be Coyned, & for after time twenty pounds in lik smale money Annually for euery hundred pounds that shall be Coyned. & this order is to Continew in force for Seuen yeares, any lawe to the Contrary notw^{th}standing."

The first of the preceding copies must be considered as bearing the correct date of the passage of this act, although it is entered upon the records under date of May 7th, which was that of the commencement of that session of the Court, and the only one recorded during the session, which date has accordingly been quoted as that of its passage.

No authority is to be found for the coinage of a piece of the value of a penny, although Sir Martin Folkes, whose work was published in 1763, gives an illustration of a piece purporting to be such ; yet if any pieces of this denomination were ever coined, none are known to have descended to our time.

The illustration given by Folkes [Plate XXX, No. 14 — see Fig. 24,] somewhat resembles a pine tree, and bears date 1652 ; while two specimens now known, and claimed to be genuine and original pennies, are of the oak tree variety, as are all the twopenny pieces, certainly from the same obverse die with them, and, like them, are dated 1662.

Both these pieces, though differing slightly from each other in the date and numerals, while one of them has a pellet at each side of its numeral, bear so strong a resemblance on the reverse, to the twopenny pieces, (the obverse die being identical with them,) as to render it almost certain that they have been altered from coins of that value.

The fact that one of these, the only one the weight of which we have been able to ascertain, (although from a rubbing of the other, in our possession, we should judge its size, and, from our recollection of it, its weight, to be about the same,) is eleven grains, being but one grain less than the legal weight of the twopenny piece, renders it still more certain that they were coined for pieces of the same value. It would certainly be an anomaly in the history of coinage to issue two silver coins from the same mint, the smaller of which was but half the nominal value of the larger, while containing an amount of silver but one-twelfth less than it.

In this year, 1662, occurred the incident which gave rise to the anecdote about Sir Thomas Temple,[1] which has been so often related, the truth of which is by some doubted, and is called by Ruding[2] a "ridiculous story." The fact of the exhibition of the money at the council table is proved by the extract from a draught of an address to the king, which follows the story now to be related. What remarks this occurrence provoked must remain unknown, unless their gist was correctly reported in this anecdote.

"Sir Thomas Temple, brother to Sir William, resided several years in New England during the interregnum. After the Restoration he returned to England. The king sent for him, and conversed with him on the state of affairs in the Massachusetts, and discovered great warmth against that colony; among other things, he said they had invaded his prerogative by coining money. Sir Thomas, who was a real friend to the colony, told his majesty the colonists had but little acquaintance with law; that they had no ill design, and thought it no crime to make money for their own use. In the course of the conversation Sir Thomas took some of the money out of his pocket, and presented it to the king. On one side of the coin was a pine tree, of that sort which is thick and bushy towards the top. Charles inquired what tree that was? Sir Thomas informed him it was the royal oak; adding, that the Massachusetts people, not daring to put his majesty's name on their coin, during the late troubles, had impressed upon it the emblem of the oak which preserved his majesty's life. This account of the matter put the king into good humor, and disposed him to hear what Sir Thomas had to say in their favor, calling them a parcel of honest dogs.

"In 'A collection of original papers relative to the history of the colony of Massachusetts Bay,' published at Boston, 1769, the following description of this money, by Edward Randolph, is inserted :

"'As a marke of soveraignty they coin mony, stamped with inscription, 'Mattachusets,' with a tree in the centre, on the one side, and 'New England,' with the year 1652, and the value of the piece, on the reverse. All the money is stamped with these figures, 1652, that year being the era of the common-wealth, wherein they erected themselves into a free state, enlarged their dominions, subjected the adjacent colonies under their obedience, and summoned deputies to sit in the general court ; which year is still commemorated on their coin.'

---

[1] Hollis's Memoirs, vol. i, pp. 397, 398.     [2] Vol. i, p. 416.

"This is extracted from a long invidious narrative, sent by this Randolph, (who appears to have been a court spy upon the people of Massachusetts,) in the year 1676, to 'the right honorable Lords of his Majesty's most honorable privy council, appointed a committee for trade and plantations.'

"The editor of this 'collection,' in a marginal note upon the latter of these paragraphs, says, 'This is a misrepresentation. The first money of this impress being stamped in 1652, they never altered the date, although they stamped more annually for thirty years together.'

"Some of this money must be yet in being. It is not improbable but Mr. Hollis must have had some of it. A professed antiquary will, in some remote period, seek for it with avidity."

In the Massachusetts Archives[1] we find this passage, written October 30, 1684, which proves the foregoing anecdote to have some foundation in fact, even if not wholly correct: "And as for the minting or stamping pieces of Silver to pass amongst our selves for xii$^d$, vi$^d$, iii$^d$, we were necessitated thereunto, having no staple Comodity in our Country to pay debts or buy necessaries, but Fish & Corn; which was so cumbersom & troublesom as could not be born. And therefore for some years Paper-Bills passed for payment of Debts; w$^{ch}$ were very subject to be lost, rent, or counterfeited, & other inconveniences. Then comes in a considerable quantity of light base Spanish Money, whereby many people were cousened, and the Colony in danger of being undon thereby; Which put vs upon the project of melting it down, & stamping such pieces as aforesaid to pass in paym$^t$ of Debts amongst our selves. Nor did we know it to be against any Law of England, or against His Majesties Will or pleasure, till of late; but rather that there was a tacit allowance & approbation of it. For in 1662, when our first Agents were in England, some of our Money was showed by Sir Thomas Temple at the Council-Table, and no dislike thereof manifested by any of those right honourable Persons: much less a forbidding of it."

There seem to have been no proceedings against the mint, taken by the king or his emissaries, sufficient in importance to cause much apprehension in the minds of the colonists, until 1665, when, in May, recorded at the 8th,[2] the king's commissioners sent the following letter to the General Court:

"Gentlemen: Wee in his Majestjes name desire a booke of your lawes may be sent vs, that wee may haue the pervsall of yo$^r$ lawes, that such as are

---

[1] Vol. cvi, p. 336.    [2] Massachusetts Records, vol. iv, p. 500.

against this act, & such as are Contrary & derogatory to the king's authority & Gouernment, mentioned in his gracious letter of June 28th, 1662, may be anulled & repealed."

The commissioners, having received and examined the book of laws, on the 24th of May, 1665, addressed another letter to the Court, from which we give extracts:[1] "Vpon pervsall of the booke entituled the booke of the Generall Lawes & libertjes Concerning the Inhabitants of the Massachusets, wee finde Just reason to propose in his Majestjes name, that these ensuing alterations & necessary additions be made." Here follows a list of twenty-six articles which they require to be repealed or amended, of which the twenty-second is, "That page 61, title money, the law y[t] a mint house, &c., be repealed, for Coynig is a Royall prerogatiue, for the vsurping of which y[e] act of indemnity is only a Salvo."

The copy of the law referred to in this letter is so nearly a repetition of the acts already printed, on pages 36, 37, 70, and 71, that it will be unnecessary to copy it here.

The colonists, hoping to avert the wrath of the king, who had now begun to make his displeasure, on account of the mint, felt by them, though not on that account only, decided, as a means of propitiation, to send him a present. Accordingly an order was passed, May 18th, 1665,[2] for something "in the best Comodity that may be procured in this his Colony, meete for transportation & accomodation of his Majestje's Navy to the value of five hundred pounds." This order was not effectual at this time, probably owing to "The occasions of the Country calling for more than ordinary disburse this yeere."

The subject recurs, on September 11th, 1666,[3] when "two very large masts" were ordered; and on October 10th, 1666,[4] "a shipps loading more to be bought & Contracted for," as a present for the next year.

These were obtained and sent in the ship "Royall Exchange," under the charge of Capt. John Pierce, to be presented to the king, by agents in England, together with suitable letters declaring their continued loyalty and respect to his majesty.

Hull refers to these gifts, in his Diary,[5] under date of September 12th, 1666: "They concluded to write, and send a present, two brave masts, but sent no person to answer in our behalf;" and, May, 1668,[6] "The Generall Court sent a shipload of masts as a present to the king's majesty."

---

[1] Massachusetts Records, vol. iv, p. 512; [2] vol. iv, p. 468; [3] vol. iv, p. 575; [4] vol. iv, p. 580. [5] Coll. Amer. Antiq. Soc., vol. iii, p. 223; [6] p. 227.

Notwithstanding the protest of the commissioners, the law relating to the mint was not repealed, but on the 15th of May, 1667,[1] another committee was appointed to treat with the mint master, as appears in the order next quoted :

"m^r Thomas Danforth, Majo^r Generall Jn° Leueret, Cap͡t Georg Coruin, m^r Anthony Stoddard, & m^r w^m Parks, are Appointed a Com͡ittee to treat & Agree w^th the master or masters of the mint in refference to some allowance anually, or otherwise, for & in Consideration of the charge the Country hath binn at in erecting a mint house, & for the vse of it for so many yeares w^thout any Considerable sattisfaction, & to make returne thereof to the next session of this Court ; and in Case they Cannot Agree w^th the present mint masters, they are Impowred to make such agreement as they Cann w^th any other."

The report of the above-mentioned committee is recorded under date of October 9th, 1667 :[2]

"Boston, in New England, october 4^th, 1667.

In Observance of an order of the Generall Court held the 15^th of May, 1667, nominating & Impowring vs, whose names are subscribed, to treat & agree w^th the master^s of the mint, wee hauing duely weighed the Country^s Interest in the ædiffices apperteyning to the sajd office, and Agitated the matter w^th m^r Jn° Hull & m^r Robert Saunderson, the present mint masters, haue agreed w^th them as followeth, namely : In Consideration of the Country^s disbursments on the sajd ædiffices, & for the Interest the Generall Court hath therein, to pay vnto the publick Tresury, w^thin six months next Coming, forty pounds in money, & for seven yeares next Coming [the sajd Hull & Saunderson, or either of them, personally abiding in the sajd Imploy,] to allow the publick Tresury annually, in money, tenn pounds ; the sajd terme to beginne from the date aboue named. In witnes hereof the sajd Hull and Saunderson haue herevnto put their hands, the day & yeare aboue written.

|                    | Jn° Leueret        |
|--------------------|--------------------|
| John Hull,         | Tho: Danforth,     |
| Robert Sanderson.  | Anthony Stoddard,  |
|                    | W^m: Parke.        |

The Court thankfully acknowledgeth the good service of the Gent^n subscribers in the premisses, and order It to be recorded.

---

[1] Massachusetts Records, vol. iv, p. 584 ; [2] vol. iv, p. 591.

Another order was passed, May 19th, 1669,[1] with intention similar to that of August 22d, 1654, and probably with no more effect in remedying the evil. It here follows:

"Order to preuent exportation of money out of this Jurisdiction: ffor the better Execution of the Law, page 62: sect: 2: for the restraiñg the Exportation of money, it is ordered by this Court & the Authority hereof, that the persons hereafter named, viz[t]:

"For Boston, Capt: James Olliuer & m[r] Thomas Brattle, or either of them; For charls towne, Captaine John Allen; For Salem, m[r] Edmond Batter; For Piscattaqua, m[r] Elias Stileman; For marble head, m[r] Samuell Ward; For Dedham, Ensigne ffisher; For Braintry, moses Paine; For Mãlboro, William Kerley; For Springfeild, Lawrence Bliss.

"Bee all & euery of them appointed, impowred & required to search for & seize all moneyes of the Coyne of this Jurisdiction that shall bee found or discouered in any ship, or any other uessell, that hath weighed Anchor to depart from that Port where shee ladeth, or all such money that shall bee found in any person's pocket, cloake, bag, Portmantle, or any other thing belonging to them after such Person hath taken horse back, to proceed & trauell in his or their jorney, out of this Jurisdiction, from the first Towne or station whence such Persons begin their trauell; & all money that such searcher shall find (except soe much as is allowed by Law,) hee shall safely keepe it vntill the next Court of the shire, & then p̃sent the same vnto the sajd Court; and if it bee judged by the Court to bee forfeited according to Law, then the sajd Court are required to Order the deliuery of one third part to the officer that seized ye same, and the other two parts to returne to the publike Treasury of the Country. & it is further Ordered that the *the* searchers before named are hereby impowred to breake open any chest, Trunck, Box, Cabbin, Cask, Truss, or any other suspected place or thing where they or any of them conceiue money may be Concealld, & seize the same; and also they or either of them are impowred to require such assistants from any Constables or others as to them may seeme Expedient, who are to ajd them, vpon the penalty of fforty shillings fine for euery neglect."

At the session held May 15, 1672, it is recorded,[2] "In Ans[r] to the Humble proposall of Joseph Jencks, Sen., for y[e] making of mony, &c., the Court Judgeth it meet not to Grant his request." This Joseph Jencks, Sen., had

---

[1] Massachusetts Records, vol. iv, pp. 632, 633; [2] vol. iv, p. 701.

previously been said to be "of Linn," and it is supposed it was he who cut many of the dies for the coinage of this mint.

It does not appear that the amount of silver here coined was sufficient, even protected, as it was, by stringent legislation, entirely to relieve the distress occasioned by the dearth of authorized coin ; and as there still continued to be a lack of silver presented at the mint for coinage, on account of the greater profits accruing from the exportation of foreign money, by reason of the expense incident to its conversion into current coin, an act was passed, October 8th, 1672, designed to obviate this difficulty.[1]

"Whereas peeces of eight are of more value to Carry out of the Country then they will yield to mint into our Coyne, by reason whereof peeces of eight, which might else Come to Coyning, are carrjed out of the Country, It is therefore Ordered by this Court & the authority thereof, that all peeces of eight that are full weight & good siluer, that is sixe shillings of new England money, of mexico, sivil & pillar, & so all lesser peeces of each Sort shall passe in this Jurisdiction as Current as our oune money ; peeces of eight at sixe shillings a peece, and all lesser peeces proportionably therevnto: Provided that all such peeces that shall passe in this Jurisdiction haue a stampe affixt vpon them, wch shall be NE: to euidence that are of right allay, and due weight ; and that m$^r$ John Hull & m$^r$ Robert Saunde$^r$son, or either of them, be the persons for the tryall & stamping of such money, & that therby fower pence vpon the pound pajd for the rest, one fowerth thereof to the officer & the rest to the Country Tresurer.

"whereas peeces of eight, weighing sixe shillings, are ordered to passe for sixe shillings, & ordered to be stamped, &c., according to the sajd law, refference thereto being had ; and for asmuch as few or no peeces of eight are of that weight, and so the intent of Good to the Country therein will be disappointed, as an addition to the sajd lawe, Be it ordered & enacted by this Court & the authority thereof, that peeces of eight vnder the weight of sixe shillings shall likewise be passable for so much of new England money as they shall weigh, and that it be impressed vpon the stampe how much each peece doth weigh, in legible figures, w$^{th}$ the other letters on y$^e$ same, & of the same Alloy."

We have been unable to find any coins proving this act ever to have been put in execution, although we have long sought for them.  The writer

---

[1] Massachusetts Records, vol. iv, p. 706.

of the remarks on "the coinage of Massachusetts," appended to the Diary of John Hull, before referred to, says,[1] "Some of these worn Spanish pieces, which had wholly lost their original impression, stamped with N E on the one side, and the figures 12, 6, or 3 on the other, exist in some of the English collections. Both Folkes and Ruding are puzzled by them, and the earliest authorities supposed they were stamped at Newcastle. Folkes's copies of them are copied in Mr. Felt's 'Currency of Massachusetts.'"

The writer of the foregoing strangely overlooked the possible existence of some specimens of the coinage first ordered, May $\frac{26}{27}$, 1652, which exactly answered to this description, making due allowance for the evident mistake of writing "12, 6, or 3," instead of xii, vi, and iii, — (the iii is not illustrated,) as may be seen by reference to the illustrations referred to. For these coins we need not search England, as they are to be found in American collections, although they may be reckoned among the rarest of our coins.

It will also be noticed that this order provides for no stamp upon both sides, but says, in the addition to the said law, "that it be impressed vpon the stampe how much each peece doth weigh, in legible figures, w[th] the other letters on y[e] same, & of the same Alloy." May not this provision have caused a complication sufficient to have thwarted the whole intent of the order?

At the session of the Court convened upon the 12th of May, 1675,[2] a third committee was appointed to confer with the mint masters, which authority is given in the ensuing form:

"Whereas the time formerly agreed vpon w[th] the mint masters is now expired, for the future well setling of that matter This Court doth desire & Impower the Honoured Gou͂ne[r] and magistrates residing in Boston, or any three of them, to be a Com͂ittee to treate w[th] such persons as they shall thinke meet, and to make such an Agreement w[th] them for the Coyning of the mony of this Jurisdiction as may be most Incouraging to all persons that haue bulljon, to bring the same to the mint."

The report which follows gives the action of this committee in their own words, and is found in the Records[3] under date of July 9, 1675.

"In pursance of an order of the Generall Court, held May the 12th, 1675, relating to the future Setling of the mint, It is Agreed by vs, the Subscribers, as a Com͂ittee appointed therevnto, as followeth, i. e.

"That the former masters of the mint, viz[t], Robert Saunderson & John

---

[1] Hull's Diary, Am. Antiq. Soc. Coll., vol. iii, p. 297. [2] Mass. Rec., vol. v, p. 28; [3]vol. v, p. 41.

Hull, doe Continue to mint what Siluer bulljon shall Come in for this Seven yeares next to Come, if either of them liue so long, and doe receive of those that bring bulljon to the mint, as a full reward for their paynes, twelve pence for euery twenty shillings, & three pence for the wast of euery three ounces of sterling Siluer that they shall so mint, vizt: fiueteen pence in the whole for euery twenty shillings. and the sajd minters are to pay in to the Treasurer of the Country, in mony, twenty pounds ⅌ Anno during abouesajd terme. that this is our Agreement wittnes our hands heerevnto put the 3ᵈ of June, 1675.

John Leueret
Symon Bradstreete

The Court Approoves of this Returne and the        Edward Tyng
Setlement of the mint accordingly.        Robeʳt Sanderson
        as Attests,        Edward Rawson, Secrety.        John Hull."

Still hoping to escape the consequences of the king's displeasure, which was yet directed against the colonists, and partly on account of their mint, another present was sent to him, in pursuance of an order recorded October 10th, 1677 : [1] "It is ordered that the Tresurer doe forthwith prouide tenn barrells of Cranburyes, two hogsheads of speciall Good Sampe, and three thousand of Cod ffish, to be sent to ouʳ messengeʳs, by them to be presented to his Majesty as A present from this Court."

In a letter to the agents of the colony, Messrs. William Stoughton and Peter Bulkley, the Court writes, October 22d, 1677,[2] "As for the Coynage, or any other Additionall priuiledge offered, (not prejudiciall to our charter,) wee would not slight but humbly accept   *   *   *   * As for a present to his majeᵗʲᵉ wee are Considering of some thing to send, wᵗʰ hope Piscataqua men & others will prouide a ships loading of masts, if his majᵗʲᵉ please send a ship, & ourselues some Cor fish, sampe, & Cranburyes."

In the letter book of the treasurer and mint master, John Hull,[3] we find this letter to the agents, dated at Boston, December 22d, 1677, giving some further information upon the same affair :

"Gent., I have sent you in this ship, — the 'Blessing,' John Phillips, master, — eighteen hundred and sixty codfish. There is about seven hundred of them very large fish, between two and three feet long, the other under two feet ; they are well salted down in the ship's bread room.

---

[1] Mass. Records, vol. v, p. 148; [2]vol. v, p. 156.    [3] Coll. Amer. Antiq. Soc., vol. iii, p. 131.

"Also ten barrels of cranberries and three barrels of samp, as by the invoice and bills of lading enclosed, you will see more particularly.' The 'invoice of fish, cranberries, and samp, shipped on board the 'Blessing,' John Phillips master, on account of the Massachusetts Colony, and consigned to William Stoughton, Esq., and Mr. Peter Bulkley,' is as follows : —

'Eighteen hundred and sixty codfish, whereof the very large fish cost,

| | |
|---|---|
| with all charges on board - - - - - | £35 10s 0d |
| Ten barrels of cranberries - - - - - | 6 0 0 |
| Three barrels of samp - - - - - | 7 0 0 |

JOHN HULL, Treasurer.' "

In another letter to the same agents, dated "Boston, 10.8.78," but found in the Records[1] under date of October 2d and 7th, 1678, the Court writes, "As for that particcular of our Coyning money wth our oune Impress, His Majty of his Gratious Clemency towards us hath not binn pleased as yet to declare his pleasure therein ; and wee haue Confidence that when he shall truely be informed of the symplicity of our Actings, the publicke Joy thereof to his subjects here, and the great damage that the stoppage thereof will Inevitably be to our necessary Comerce and abatement of his Majties Customes yearely Acruing by our merchants & Nauigation, & is pajd at London, his majtye will not Account those to be freinds to his Croune that shall seeke to Interrupt us therein ; and for the Impress put vpon it wee shall take it as his majties signall ouning vs if he will please to order such an Impresse as shall be to him most Acceptable."

Joseph Dudley and John Richards, Esqs., having been chosen, the former on the 20th, the latter on the 23d of March, 16$\frac{81}{82}$, to be "Agents to goe & wayte on his majty, &c.,"[2] their instructions, which were dated 15th February, 1681 (-2,) commence as follows: "1. Yow shall most humbly present the Humble Address of this Court to His Royall majesty, with our humble thanks for his Gracious respect to the peace & weale of his subjects scittuate so remote from his Royall Court, And with refference to Complaints exhibbited against us ; 2. You shall Informe his majtie That we tooke vp stamping of silver meerely vpon necessitje, to prevent cheats by false peeces of eight, which were brought hither in the tjme of the late Confusions ; and wee haue been well Informed that his majtie had knowledge thereof, yet did not manifest

---

[1] Vol. v, p. 194 ; [2] vol. v, p. 343.

any dissatisfaction thereat vntil of very late ; And if that be a Trespasse vpon His maj^stjes Royal Prerogative, of which wee are Ignorant, wee Hunbly beg His Maj^tjes pardon and Gratious Allowance therein, It being so exceeding necessary for our Civil Commerce, & no way, as wee humbly Conceive, detrimentall to His Royal Majtje."

That the Court considered these instructions of great importance may be inferred from the fact that they were a long time in agreeing upon the letter, of which this forms a part, which is shown by the several draughts of that letter now preserved in the Archives,[1] each of which indicates a different form of instructions for "A. B. Agents," not then appointed.

The section relating to the mint, however, appears in all, and in substantially the same form.   Their dates are "25ᵗʰ of ffebruary, 1680," this having the date repeated thus : "25: 12 · $\frac{80}{81}$ =" One has no date, one "21ᵗʰ ffebruary, 1681," and the other, "29 of March, 1681," more than a year having passed between the date of the first, and that of the letter as recorded.

Two other draughts appear in the Archives,[2] one of which is dated "March 16, 1681," in which are these words : "Hoping also and humbly praying your Maj^tys favour for the continuance of our liberty of Coyning." Neither of these was adopted.

Not being able to effect either the recoinage, or the stamping of the weight, etc., upon the foreign coins in circulation, and despairing of being able to keep their coin at home by actual prohibition of its exportation, but still hoping to retain it in the country by further legislation, the Court regulates its value, in the act of May 24th, 1682 :[3] "This Court, taking into Consideration that by the frequent exportation of our New England Coyne out of the Country, whereby Com̄erce and trade is very much obstructed, As an expedient to keepe money in the Country, It is Ordered that all peices of $\frac{8}{8}$ as pillar, Civil, & mexico Coyne, that are good siluer, shall passe amongst us as Currant mony of New England, according to their weight in the present New England Coyne ;" and, bearing date the 11th of October, 1682,[4] we find this action, explanatory of the last : "The Court, on the 24ᵗʰ day of may last, taking into Consideration the Frequent exportation of ouʳ new England Cojne out of the Countrey, whereby Com̄erce and trade is very much obstructed, as an epedient to keepe money in the Countrey, did order that all peices of

---

[1] Vol. cvi, pp. 222, 227, 230, 248 ; [2] vol. cvi, pp. 238, 252.   [3] Mass. Rec., vol. v, p. 349.   [4] Mass. Rec., vol. v, p. 372.

eight, as pillar, sevil, and mexico Coyn, that are good siluer, should passe amongst us as Currant money of new England, according to their weight in the present new England Coyn. As an explanation of that law, It is to be vnde<sup>r</sup>stood, and It is heereby declared that those peices of eight in the law mentioned shallbe pajd and received at sixe shillings eight pence p ounce Troy weight, and all smaller peeces of the like Coyn, that are good siluer, shall passe at the same price & weight."

The original draught of the act last copied,[1] will be found to differ little, except in form and date, from that of the Records.

### "24 May 82

"This Court taking into Consideration y<sup>t</sup> by y<sup>e</sup> frequent Exportation of o<sup>r</sup> New England Coyne out of the Country, whereby Com̄erce & trade is very much Obstructed, As an Expedient to keep money in the Country it is ordered that all peeces of $\frac{8}{8}$, as Piller, Civil, and Mexico Coyne, y<sup>t</sup> are good Silver, shall pass amongst us as Currant money of New England, according to there weight in the present New England Coyne.

"As an Explanation of y<sup>e</sup> law, title peeces of $\frac{8}{8}$, it is to be vnderstood & declared that those peeces of $\frac{8}{8}$ In that law mentioned, shalbe payd & Receaued at Six Shillings Eight pence the ounce, troy weight. the Magis<sup>ts</sup> haue past this, their brethren the deputyes heereto Consenting.

12 Octo 1682.             Edw<sup>d</sup> Rawson Secret.

"Consented to by y<sup>e</sup> Deputys, & ordor also that all Smaller peces of the like Coyne y<sup>t</sup> are good Siluer Shall pass as Curant mony at Six Shillings Eaight pence the ounce, troy waight, o<sup>r</sup> hon<sup>rd</sup> Maj<sup>strats</sup> Consenting.

Oct. 16: 1682:             Elisha Hutchinson p<sup>r</sup> ord<sup>r</sup>.

"Consented to by the majjis<sup>ts</sup>.             Edw<sup>d</sup> Rawson Secret."

This is the latest action upon the subject we find to have been taken previous to the cessation of coining in New England.

In 1680 Randolph still complained of the "Bostoneers," that "They coyne money of their owne impress."[1] And in his "Articles of high Misdemeanor,

---

[1] Archives, vol. c, p. 285.      [2] Hutchinson Papers, vol. ii, p. 265.

exhibited against the General Court sitting 15th February, 1681," "The said faction have neglected to repeale all laws of their colony contrary to the laws of England, though required thereunto by his Majesty's letters of 28th of Feb. 1662, and the observance thereof promised by their agents at that time ; and also by particular direction from the right honourable the Lords of the committee of trade and plantation to their late agents, in 1678, by which meanes coining of money (acknowledged in their agents' petition to his Majesty, a great crime and misdemeanor, who then craved his Majesty's pardon to the government for the same,) is continued to this day, &c."

Lord Culpepper states, August, 1681, Randolph's papers having been sent to him, "'I have perused Mr. Randolph's writings sent me, and, during my stay in Boston, did hear most of the matters of fact specified therein.' He added, 'that the coinage of New-England was greatly prejudicial to the king's subjects.'"[1]

The committee on plantation, in April, 1678, expressed the opinion "That though his majesty may, upon due application, grant the colony a charter, with power of coining, yet they must solicit his majesty's pardon."[2]

In a letter from the king to the Court, October, 1681, the accusation is made "That you presume to continue your mint, without regard to the penalties thereby incurred ;"[3] and in June, 1683, Randolph says, "They persist in coining money, though they had asked forgiveness for that offence."[4]

Thus the mint appears to have been a fruitful source of dissatisfaction, furnishing a ready and acceptable weapon for the enemies of the colony, and finally called forth the proceedings recorded in the ensuing documents.

The following letter, found at the State Paper Office, in London,[5] is the first of a series of documents bearing upon the reëstablishment of the mint in New England :

"Letter to Mr. Guy, about Instructions to be prepared by y[r] Comm[rs] of y[e] Customs for New England — Monopoly — The Mint :

"S[r]                                    Council Chamber, 22 November, 1684.

"His Ma[ty] having thought fit to appoint Col. Kirk[6] to be Governor of the Colony of Massachusets Bay and other adjacent Provinces in New England,

---

[1] Chalmer's Annals, Book i, p. 438;  [2] ibid, p. 440;  [3] ibid, p. 448;  [4] ibid, p. 462.   [5] Colonial Entry Book, vol. lxi, p. 218.   [6] Col. Percy Kirke, — he never entered upon the duties of Governorship, to which he was appointed.  See Drake's Hist. Boston, p. 458.

and the R^t hono^bl the Lords of the Committee for Trade & forrein Plantations, having under consideration the preparing such Instructions for Col.
Kirk as may be most proper for the Goverment of those Colonyes, have
ordered me to acquaint the Lords Comm^rs of the Treasury, with the desire
that the Comm^rs of the Customs may be directed to consider of and prepare
a draught of such Instructions (from his Ma^ty to the Governor,) relating to
Trade and Navigation, as may best Conduce to the Execution of the Acts of
Parliam^t in that behalf. And that the Comm^rs of the customs may likewise
consider of the clause herevnto annexed concerning trade and Engrossing of
Comodities, and return their opinion thereupon. Their Lo^ps having likewise
taken notice that a mint has hitherto been kept up and imployed at Boston
in New England, for the Coyning of money different in value and alloy from
that of England, and it being now in his ma^tys power to continue or set
aside the further exercise of such a mint, as shall be found most requisit for
his Service, Do further desire the Lords Comm^rs of the Treasury to receive
the opinion of the Comm^rs of the Mint in this matter, that his ma^tys pleasure
may be knowne thereupon, and Instructions given to Colonel Kirk accordingly.

"22 November 1684."

Neither of the letters from Mr. Guy, referred to in the following reports,
can be found :

"To the R^t Hon^ble y^e L^ds Comm^rs of his Majesty^s Treasry.

"May it please yo^r Lordp^s,

"In Obedience to yo^r Lordp^s Comands signified by m^r Secretary
Guy, ye 24 of Novb^r last, in Reference to a Mint w^ch hath been hitherto kept
up & imployed at Boston in New England,

"Wee haue mett with a Copy of what was ordered by the then Court
as they termed themselves, being of the Collony of Massachusets, & sitting
at Boston, in N E aforesaid, did in y^e year 1652, Settle y^e s^d Mint, w^ch manor
of settlem^tt Wee put down in their owne words (Viz.)

"Itt is ordred by this Court & y^e Authority thereof, that a Mint house
be erected in Boston, Año Dom, 1652, and that y^e mastor of y^e s^d Mint & all
y^e officers thereof, shall be sworne & allowed by this Court or by such as
shal be Authorized by this Court for that purpose. And all persons whatsoeuer
haue Liberty to bring into y^e s^d Mint all Bullian, Plate, or Spanish Coyne,
there to be Melted & brought to Allay of starling mony by the mastor of y^e
s^d Mint & his sworne officers, from time to time, by him or them to be

Coyned in to 12 peny, 6 peny, or 3 peny Pieces, w^ch shal be Stamped with a double Ring on either side, with this Inscription: Massachusets and a tree in y^e Center, and on y^e one side, New England, with the year of o^r Lord & the figuers xii. vi. iii. according to the uallue of each piece, on the other side, to gether with a privy Marke, w^ch shalbe appoynted euery three Months by y^e Gouernor, & only knowne to him & the sworn Officers of the Mint; and y^e mastor of ye Mint afore said is Requiered to Coyne all the said Mony of good silver, of y^e Just allay of new starling English Mony, and for Value Two pence in y^e shilling of Less Vallue then y^e present English Coyne & the Lesser pieces proportianably; and all such Coyn as aforesaid (& no other, Except English,) shal be acknowledged to be the Currant Mony of this Comonwealth, and to pass from man to man in all payments accordingly w^th in this Jurisdiction.

"And the Mint Mastor, for himselfe & officers, for their pains & Labour in Melting, Refining, & Coyning, is allowed by this Court to take One shilling out of euery twenty shillings w^ch he shal stamp as aforesaid. And it shal be in the Liberty of any person who brings into the Mint house any Bullion, Plate, or Spanish Coyn, to be present & to se the same Melted, refined, & allayed, & then to take a Receipt of the Mastor of the Mint for y^e weight of that w^ch is good siluer, allayed as aforesaid, for w^ch y^e Mint mastor shall deliver him the Like weight in Currant Mony, (Viz) euery shilling to weigh 3 pene Troy weight, & lessor pieces proportianably, deducting allways for Coynage as before is exsprest. And it is further ordered that a Comittee be Chosen to appoynt a Mint house in sum Conveniant place in Boston, & to approue & Swear y^e Mastor, & to ordor & determine what shal further appere Necessary to cary on this Order to effect.

"Wee haue examined y^e 12 pene, 6^d, & 3^d pieces coyned at y^e Mint in Boston in N E aforesaid, for weight & allay, & do finde as to y^e allay it is equal to his Maj^ts silver Coyns of England, but different in weight, being Less by about 21 grains upon the shilling, & so proportianobly in the other Coyns from his Majesty^s shilling Coyne, w^ch is near two pence three farthings upon the shilling, & is about $22\frac{1}{2}$ p Cent; besides a third more is allowed for the Coynage then what hath been allowed for the Coynage of his Maj^ts Silver Mints in England.

"The preserving of one certain Standard for weight & fineness of his Maj^ts silver Coyns, in all his Maj^sts Kingdoms & Dominians, is Very much for the Security & advantage of his Maj^sty and the altering thereof, w^ch are y$^e$ Comon measures given by his Maj$^{sty}$ unto his people, cannot well be done in any one of his Maj$^{sts}$ s̃$^d$ Dominians without eminent prejudice to the Rest.

"Besides, according to y$^e$ advantage before set downe, it will be a great Encoragem̃$^{tt}$ for y$^e$ drawing away y$^e$ Current Cojns of this Kingdom, so farr as that trade may promote it. It will also be y$^e$ occasian of makeing all Marchandize & other goods rise in proportion to that Mony.

"Wee are humbly of opinian, if his Maj$^{sty}$ shal think fitt to settle a Mint in N E, for making of Coyns of silver, of 12 pences, 6$^d$, & 3$^d$, that they be made in weight & fineness answerable to his Majestys Silver Coyns of England, & not otherwise.

"And for smaller pieces, (Viz) farthings, half penc, and peny pieces, if his maj$^{sty}$ shal so think fitt, that they be made of Tinn, & so supplyed from hence, which will be to his Maj$^{sts}$ advantage.

"It also may be observed, that tho' they haue Continued this unwarrantable way of Coyning of Monys euer since y$^e$ year 1652, yet there is no alteration of date appears upon their Coyne of 12$^d$, 6$^d$, & 3$^d$ pieces, but the same date (Viz) 1652, as was at first coyning of them.

"Itt is also further to be obserued that for y$^e$ Incoragem̃$^{tt}$ of bringing Silver to their Mint to be Coyned, they do promis that there shall be but two pence in y$^e$ shilling Less in Vallue then the English shilling. but aftor the Mint master hath the same in Custody & Coyned the same, they order him to pay y$^e$ Mony out by weight at 3$^d$ Troy weight for their shillings & lessor pieces proportianably, w$^{ch}$ 3 pene Troy is about 9$^d$ $\frac{1}{9}$ Starling, and makes out the amõ$^{tt}$ as before about 22$\frac{1}{2}$ p Cent besides the Charge of Coynage. all w$^{ch}$ we humbly Leaue to yo$^r$ Lordps further Considoration.

"Dated at y$^e$ Mint y$^e$ 15 day of Jan$^{ry}$, 1684.   Tho Neale
              Cha. Duncombe
              Ja. Hoare."[1]

"To the R$^t$ Hon$^{ble}$ Lawrence, Earle of Rochester,[2]
        Lord high Tresurer of England,
"May it please yo$^r$ Lo$^p$

"In obediance to yo$^r$ Lord$^{ps}$ Comands, Signified to us y$^e$ 10$^{th}$ of this month, by Letter from Henry Guy, Esq$^r$., Wee haue Considored of the papers enclosed to us in y$^e$ s$^d$ Letter concerning a Mint to be reëstablisht in New England, & doe find that vpon alike reference from y$^e$ L$^{ds}$

---

[1] Archives, vol. c, p. 350 ; [2] vol. c, p. 388.

Com<sup>rs</sup> of the Treasury, of y<sup>e</sup> 24 Noub<sup>r</sup>, 1684, of this Matter the officers of the Mint did by their Report of the 15 of Jan<sup>ry</sup> following deliver their opinion concerning y<sup>e</sup> same, a Copy of w<sup>ch</sup> Report is hereunto annext, no cause appering to us to ater our Judgm<sup>tts</sup> therein, presuming only to add this further, that when a grant was obtained by S<sup>r</sup> Thomas Vyner & others, in y<sup>e</sup> year 1662, for Coyning Small Silver monys in Ireland, aftor it wass by his Maj<sup>sty</sup> in Council refered to the Lord Tresurer & Chancellour of the Exchecq<sup>r</sup>, who heard the pattentees & the officers of the Mint upon Report of their Lord<sup>ps</sup>, His Late Maj<sup>sty</sup>, by his ordor in Council of the 14th of November, 1662, was pleased to Comand the s̅<sup>d</sup> Lettors Pattents to be delivered up at the borde to be canceled for waighty Reasons exprest in the s̅<sup>d</sup> Report.  Wee may likewise obserue to yo<sup>r</sup> Lord<sup>ps</sup> that when in y<sup>e</sup> year 1678 the Earle of Carlisle did make application for power to Erect a Mint in Jamaca, of w<sup>ch</sup> Island he was Gou<sup>r</sup>, it was then found Impracticable, under the termes of keeping the weight & fineness of the Moneyes to English Standard, (w<sup>ch</sup> can not be altered, as we humebly Conceive,) with out dishon<sup>r</sup> to his Maj<sup>sts</sup> Coyns, & prejudice to his subjects of his other Dominians, in w<sup>ch</sup> opinion we are Confirmed by y<sup>e</sup> Report made upon this occasion by y<sup>e</sup> Lords of y<sup>e</sup> Comitte for trade & forraigne Plantations, y<sup>e</sup> 8<sup>th</sup> of ffeb<sup>r.</sup> 1678. As for the second part of m<sup>r</sup> Guys Letter, w<sup>ch</sup> directs us to think upon some other Inscriptions more agreable to the Kings prerogative, to be stampt upon y<sup>e</sup> Coyne of New England, if a Mint be settled there, Wee craue some time to Considor of, after yo<sup>r</sup> Lord<sup>ps</sup> shal have perused these papers, & will be redy to obay yo<sup>r</sup> Lord<sup>ps</sup> therein.

" Dated at the Mint the 15<sup>th</sup> day of July, 1686.

Phil  Loyd

Tho.  Neale

Cha:  Duncombe

Ja:  Hoare."

It has been the opinion of most writers upon the subject that this coinage was continued until suppressed by action of the authority of the crown, during the administration of Sir Edmund Andros.  This could hardly have been the case, as Andros did not reach this country until the latter part of December, 1686, before which time the foregoing papers show the reëstablishment of the mint to have been proposed.

The information already given upon this point favors the belief that it terminated, (the machinations of its enemies probably being not without influence in producing this result,) with the expiration of the agreement with the mint masters, dated June 3d, 1675, although it is impossible now to determine with certainty.

The final closing of the mint would, in this case, probably have been somewhat later than June 3d, 1682, as the committee report, June 3d, 1675, "that the former masters of the mint, vizt. Robert Saunderson & John Hull, doe Continue to mint what siluer bulljon shall come in for this Seven yeares next to Come, if either of them liue so long," — its actual termination would therefore be extended more, or less, from that date, according as there happened to be much, or little, uncoined silver on hand at that time.

It appears certain, however, that coining was discontinued, and the mint abandoned, as early as 1684, as may be seen from the letter of the officers of the king's mint, already given, dated January 15th, 1684 (-5,) referring to a letter dated November 24th, 1684, which spoke of "a Mint w$^{ch}$ hath been hitherto kept up & imployed at Boston in New England," — a vague expression, but explained by a later sentence in the same, where the officers state, "Wee are humbly of opinian, if his Maj$^{sty}$ shal think fitt to Settle a Mint in N E," and also by a reference in the letter of July 15, 1686, from the same, to the lord high treasurer of England, where they say, "Wee haue Considored of the papers enclosed to us in y$^e$ s$^d$ Letter concerning a Mint to be reëstablisht in New England, & doe find that vpon alike reference from y$^e$ L$^{ds}$ Com$^{rs}$ of the Treasury of y$^e$ 24 Nov$^r$, 1684, of this Matter," thus proving that the letter of November 24th, 1684, had reference to the *reë*stablishment of the mint, which, as a matter of course, must previously have been discontinued.

"Letter from M$^r$ Guy to M$^r$ Blathway$^t$, w$^{th}$ papers about a Mint, &c.[1]
"S$^r$

"By my Lord Treasurers Command, I send you the two inclosed Papers about reëstablishing a Mint in New England, w$^{ch}$ his Lo$^p$ desires you to lay before the Lords of the Comittee for Trade and Plantations.

"I am, S$^r$, Yo$^r$ most humble Servant,      Hen. Guy.
"Treasury Chambers, 23 7bris, 1686."

"Reasons for a Mint in New England.[2]
"1$^{st}$. Money is the measure for the valuation of Houses, Lands, or Goods,

---

[1] Colonial Entry Book, vol. lxi, p. 137 ; [2] Ibid.

but because the Stock of Lands & Goods in every Country is one hundred times more then the Stock of Money, there fore the value of Money must of necessity depend upon & be governed by the value of Goods. Witness the rising & falling of Money in Bills of Exchange every weeke.

"2. Although the Standard of the Money of England hath been kept in its purity and fineness, yet the value and weight thereof hath been very often changed, according to the Rate of Silver and Increase of Trade, So that the Old Easterling penny of the Conqueror was raised to three half pence by King Henry the 6th, thence to Two Pence by King Edward the 4th, and thence to three pence by Queen Elizabeth.

"3. The Trade of New England consisting cheifly in Fish, Provisions, and Lumber, exported to His Ma<sup>tys</sup> Southern Plantations in America, and to the Dominions of the King of Spain in Europe, The returns from the former are made in Sugar, Tobacco, and other Commodities of the growth of those Parts, w<sup>ch</sup> are again reshipped for England, and thereby Imploy a double navigation ; but from Spain are brought pieces of Eight, which being of unequal weight and value, did necessitate the then Governm<sup>t</sup> of New England (neer forty yeares since,) to Erect a mint for making of Silver moneys, to be currant in that Country, as the Standard and measure of Trade, all payments being since made in that money, which is in fineness equal to the money of England, but less in weight, the shilling being in value nine pence farthing, and smaller Pieces proportionable, and frequently brought into England for want of other Returnes.

"4. The Rents of Houses and Land have been paid, and all Goods bought & Sold for many years in New England, by this measure, and the altering of it, and bringing it to the standard of Old England, would enrich the Landlord and Creditor, but it would ruyne the Tenant and Debtor, destroy the Trade of that Country, and bring no advantage, but loss to the King, whose Customes and Poundage Circulats in that Coyn, as well as in any other.

"5. In case his Ma<sup>ty</sup> shall not upon these Considerations, think fit to settle or Continue a Mint in New England, It will be absolutely necessary and not to be avoyded without y<sup>e</sup> Ruyne of the Plantation, that Pieces of Eight, which is a Forrein Coin, Bee made Currant there (as they are now in all the other Plantations in America,) at the same Rate as are now proposed for his ma<sup>tys</sup> Coin, which leaves the same inconvenience, if any, as is apprehended by the officers of the Mint, in case the mint be continued in New England.

"Lastly. It is not proposed that Letters Patents be granted to any one for a Mint in New England, as in the case of S$^r$ Thomas Viner, but that every thing be performed by his ma$^{tys}$ officers, and the Profit that shall arise by the Coinage, applyed to his Ma$^{tys}$ use.

" Memorand

"A Copy hereof being sent to the officers of the Mint, They attended their Lo$^{ps}$ and presented the following Answer thereunto.

"Answer to Reasons for a Mint in New England.

"1. Wee agree that money is the measure of Lands, Goods, Houses, &c. and therefore do deny that Lands, Houses, and Goods (tho' never so much,) can be the measure of Money, It being an absolute contradiction. As to the rising and falling of money by Bills of Exchange, it depends intirely upon the Plenty or Scarcity of money, and not upon the number of Houses or Extent of Lands.

"2. As to the standard of the money of England in weight and value, wee do own it hath been often altered, occasioned by the increase of Silver, &c., But that is no reason why the Mint in one part of His Ma$^{tys}$ Dominions should not hold equal Balance with that of the other.

"3. What their Trade of Fish, Provisions, and Lumber, or Returnes in Pieces of Eight from Spain, relates to the Erecting a Mint in New England differing from the Mint here, wee do not understand.

"4. That their Rents, Houses, and Lands, and all Goods, have been negotiated at 9$^d$ for a shilling (w$^{ch}$ is about 25 per cent less then the money of England,) and that if they should be ordered to make their Mint agree with that here, it would ruyne the Tenant and Debitor, and destroy the Trade of the Country, &c. To which wee Answer, that as to their future Trade, it will most certainly conform it self to y$^e$ intrinsick value of the money. And as to former Rents & Debts care may be taken that they may be discharged at 15$^s$ per pound, w$^{ch}$ holds proportion with the current money of England, upon which, if their new Mint be made agreeable to his ma$^{tys}$ here, in our humble opinions there can ensue no dishonnor to his ma$^{ty}$ nor loss to the People.

"5. In case his ma$^{ty}$ shall not think fit to settle a mint in New England, then to make pieces of Eight Current there, &c., To w$^{ch}$ wee answer that pieces of $\frac{8}{8}$ are but a Commodity as other merchandizes are, and they may be left at liberty to Barter the one against the other, as their Interest Guides them.

"6.   When his ma^ty thinks fit to settle a mint in New England wee shall be ready humbly to offer the best Rules and Instructions wee can for its Establishment.

O. Wynne, Tho, Neale, Ja. Hoare.

"Mint, 23^th October, 1686."

"At the same time was presented the two following Reports to my Lord Treãr from the Comm^rs of the Mint, touching a Mint in New England."

Here follow the reports of January 15, 1685, and July 15, 1686, already given on pages 87 to 90.

"Report of the Committee ab^t a Mint in New England, &c.

"May it please yo^r Ma^ty

"Wee have lately had under Our Consideration a Proposall made unto us for reëstablishing a Mint in yo^r ma^tys Territory of New England vnder the Governm^t of S^r Edmund Andros ;  And having consulted the Comm^rs of yo^r mat^ys Mint here in England in that behalf, Wee do not find that the reëstablishing a Mint for the Coining of money in New England may be for yo^r ma^tys service there, But wee humbly offer Our opinions to yo^r Ma^ty that for the benefit of the Trade and Commerce of those parts, S^r Edmund Andros may have power, by Proclamation, to Regulate pieces of Eight and other forreign Coin Imported thither, to such current value as he shall find most requisite for yo^r ma^tys Service and the Trade of yo^r Subjects there.

"Council Chamber, 13 October, 1686."

"Order of Councill ag^st a Mint, but y^t pieces of 8 shall passe in N. England.

"At the Court at White hall, the 27^th of October, 1686.

"By the King's most Excellent ma^ty & the Lords of his ma^tys most hono^ble Privy Councill.

"Whereas the R^t hono^ble the Lords of the Committee for Trade and Plantations, did by their Report this day read at the Board, Represent that they have lately had under consideration a Proposall made unto them for reëstablishing a Mint in his ma^tys Territory of New England, under the Governm^t of S^r Edmund Andros, And having consulted the Officers of his ma^{tys} Mint here, in that behalf, Their Lo^{ps} do not find the same to be for his ma^{tys} Service, But offered it, as their opinions, that for the benefit of Trade & Commerce in those Parts, S^r Edmund Andros may have Power, by Proclamation, To Regulate the Pieces of 8 and other Forrein Coines Imported thither, to such current value as he shall find most requisite for his ma^{tys} Service and the Trade of his subjects there, w^{ch} his ma^{ty} taking into Consideration, was pleased to approve of their Lo^{ps} opinion, and accordingly did order that S^r Edmund Andros be, and he is hereby authorized & Impowered by Proclamation to Regulate Pieces of 8 and other forrein Coine within the said Territory of New England, to such current value as he shall judge most requisite for his ma^{tys} Service, and the Trade of His Subjects there.

John Nicholas."

"His Ma^{tys} Letter for the valuation of Pieces of 8, &c., in New England.

"Trusty and welbeloved, wee greet you well. Whereas it may conduce to the benefit of Trade & the Commerce of Our Subjects within our Territory and Dominion of New England, that the Currant value of Pieces of Eight and other forreign Coyn be forthwith setled according to the usage of Our other Plantations ; Our will and Pleasure there fore is, That by Proclamation under Our Seal for Our said Dominion in New England, you Regulate the Price of pieces of Eight and other forrein Coyn Imported thither, in such manner & to such a Currant value as you, with the advice of Our Councill, shall find most requiset for our Service and the Trade of Our Subjects there.

"And for so doing this shall be yo^r warrant.

"Given at Our Court at Whitehall, the 31^{st} day of October, 1686, in the second year of Our Reign.

"By his ma^{tys} Command.                                        Sunderland."

Chalmers says that "Andros arrived at Boston in December, 1686." "In order to facilitate the colonial commerce, Andros applied for leave to continue the practice, that had commenced in the year 1652, that had been pursued to this time, notwithstanding the prohibitions of Charles, of coining money at Boston. But the project being referred to the officers of the mint, they confuted his arguments, and decided against his application. But he was empowered to regulate the circulation and value of foreign coins." [1]

---

[1] Polit. Annals, p. 421.

It would appear from the preceding documents found at the State Paper Office, in London, that the plan of authorizing Andros to regulate the value of foreign coin, must have originated there, and was probably consummated while he was upon his passage ; but we see no reason to believe that he exercised that privilege, or indeed, troubled himself in any manner as to the financial affairs of the colony.

We find in the records of the Council and Court,[1] January 24th, $16\frac{89}{90}$, which was after the overthrow of Andros, this, among the instructions to Sir Henry Ashurst, Elisha Cooke, M$^r$ Increase Mather, and D$^r$ Thomas Oakes, agents, soon to depart for England, "9$^{thly}$, You are to Solicite, That the Liberty of Coynage may be allowed us."

What action was taken by these gentlemen toward the fulfilment of this part of their duty is unknown, except so far as may be inferred from the ensuing report,[2] which was evidently called forth by their petition, which we have been unable to find.

"To the R$^t$ Hon$^{ble}$ the Lords Com$^{rs}$ of their Ma$^{ties}$ Treasury :

"May it please your Lop$^s$, —

"In Obedience to your Lp$^s$ Reference of the 12 Jan. Instant, Signified to Us by M$^r$ Secretary Guy, touching the Proposalls, and Reasons offered to their Ma$^{ties}$ by Sr William Phipps,[3] etc., for obtaining their Ma$^{ties}$ Royall favour to be granted to the Generall Court in the Province of the Massachusetts Bay in New England to Privelige them with Liberty of Coyning for the Benefitt of their Ma$^{ties}$ Subjects in that Territory,

"Wee haue considered their Reasons, And humbly offer to your Lop$^s$ our Opynions in Answer thereunto.

"As to the first, second, and third Reasons, wee Conceive it very probable, That most of the Monies which have been coined in New England from the year 1652 (when they had the priveledge of Coyning,) may still remain there. The Lightness of those Coines from Jamaica, Barbadoes, and other places, in Returns of Trade, (some of which might prove Counterfeit,) soe that it is scarse credible (as they suggest,) that shoppkeepers and those that are buyers should labour under such difficulties for want of Small Monies for

---

[1] Vol. vi, p. 105 ; also Archives, vol. xxxv, p. 181.    [2] Treasury Papers, London.

[3] Phipps arrived in Boston, as Governor, in May, 1692, and with him returned Dr. Increase Mather.—*Drake's Boston, p.* 498.

Change, Since the coyned monies of New England are the shilling, Sixpence, three Pence, and two Pence, Besides Small Spanish coins, which are current there as well as in the other English Colonies. And in Lieu of Smaller Pieces (if there Ma^ties shall think fitt,) They may be Supplyed with Pence, Halfe Pence, and farthings of Tinn, from England, to their Ma^ties Advantage.

"As to the Priviledges of Coynage which (they say,) has been granted to some other English Plantations, To the East India Company, &c., Wee answer The Priveleges of Coynage has not been granted to any of the English Plantations, (as is represented,) But on the contrary The Greate and Repeated Applications which were made to their late Ma^ties by the Respective Governors of Jamaica and New England, for obteining of such a Privelege, were ineffectuall.

And the Instance of the East Indian Company is very different from the present case. Their Privelege of Coynage being restrained and limitted to their Forts in India, And to the Coines of Monies Current in the Dominions and Territories of those Indian Princes onely.

" But if their Ma^ties shall be graciously pleased to grant the Priveledge of Coyning Monies to the Generall Court in the said Province of the Massachusetts Bay in New England,

" Wee humbly Propose to your Lordshippes that it may be directed and appointed, That the Monies to be made and Coined there may be in weight and fineness according to the standard of their Ma^ties Mint in England.

" Since the Preservening of one Certain Standard in weight and ffineness of there Ma^ties Silver Coines, in all their Kingdomes and Dominions is very much for the Security and Advantage of theire Maj^tys and their Subjects, (Being the Common Measure given by their Ma^ties to their People,) The Altering whereof in any one of their Dominions can not but occasion Eminent Prejudice to the Rest.                    Ben Ouerton,
                                                    Tho Neale,
" Mint, Jan. 19, 1691.                              Ja Hoar."

John Hull was not living at the time of the final action of the officers of the crown, upon the restoration of the mint, he having died October 1st, 1683.

His residence was in what was at that time the south part of the town, but is now north of the centre of the city, — its site being on Pemberton Hill, a little southerly of the entrance to Pemberton Square.

Rev. John Cotton, of Boston, says in his will, proved January 27th, 1652-3, "and because the south part of my house, which Sir Henry Vane built while he sojourned with me, he by a deed gave it at his departure to my son Seaborne, I doe yrefore leave it unto him as his by right," &c. Rev. John Cotton, of Plymouth, (son of the above-named,) in 1664 confirmed this devise to Seaborne, and he sells this part to John Hull. In 1677 Nicholas Paige bought the residue of the estate ; and in 1682 this also was bought by Mr. Hull. It was afterwards occupied by Hull's son-in-law, Judge Samuel Sewall, who is said to have received with the daughter of the mint master her weight in the coinage of his mint. Part of this estate was subsequently owned by Gardiner Greene.[1]

Without a wish to detract in the least from the well-earned laurels of John Hull, we cannot but think that injustice has been done to the memory of Robert Saunderson, by all who have attempted a history of this mint. He was appointed, as Hull states, at his especial request, as his equal in office, (the records frequently mentioning the "mint masters.") In the agreement of June 3d, 1675, he is first named, and his signature precedes that of Hull ; and why all the honors of the office should, in later years, have been accorded to Hull, we are unable to imagine.

Robert Saunderson and Lydia, his wife, were among the earliest settlers in Hampton, in 1638. He soon removed to Watertown, and, about the year 1642, married Mary, widow of John Cross. Here he remained until about 1653, when he moved to Boston, where he filled the office of deacon in one of the churches, and, Savage says, "was partner in gainful business with John Hull, the mint master." His death occurred October 7th, 1693.

In 1696 another effort was made to prevent the exportation of money, and the following order was passed :[2]

"By the Hon[ble] the Lieu[t] Gov[r] and Council.
"Ordered,
          That Sam[l] Sewall, John Foster, and Eliakim Hutchinson, Esq[rs], be a Comittee of this Board to confer with a Comittee to be appointed by the Assembly, upon some Proposals offered as an Expedient to prevent the Exportation of the money currant of this Province out of the same : And to prepare and bring in a Bill for that purpose, If they thinke it advisable.
"May 30th, 1696.                                        "John Addington, Secry."

<hr/>

[1] Drake's Old Landmarks.        [2] Archives, vol. ci, p. 55.

"Capt. Nathan[l] Byfield, M[r] Nehemiah Jewet, M[r] Nathan[l] Oliver, and M[r] John Eyre, are appointed by this House to joyne with the Gent[ln] abovenamed.

"May 30th, 1696. Penn Townsend, Speaker."

Upon the back of the paper containing the last order, is this proposition of the committee :

"In addition to the Act against Counterfeiting, Clipping, Rounding, Filing, or impairing of Coyne, 'Tis humbly proposed, That the Coyne of the late Massachusetts Colony, and Mexico, Sevil, & Pillar pieces of Eight, & half pieces, be made to pass currant at Seven shillings p ounce, Troy weight.

"And that a Suitable Clause be drawn up, to prevent the Exportation of Money. Sam[l] Sewall, in the

"June 2[d], 1696. name & behalf of y[e] Comittee."

Failing in all attempts to secure a coinage of their own, the Assembly, in 1692, passed an act entitled "An Act against the Counterfeiting, Clipping, Rounding, Filing, or Impairing of Coynes,"[1] which, beside providing a penalty for counterfeiting, also regulated the value of coins. This was the act referred to by the committee last appointed :

"Whereas divers false and evil disposed persons have attempted and practised, for wicked lucre and gain's sake, to diminish, impair, and falsifie the money and coynes currant within this province, by counterfeiting or clipping, rounding or filing thereof, not only to the great discredit of the province and the government thereof, but also to the great loss and damage of their majesties' subjects ; and more is like to be if the same be not speedily met withal and prevented ; for remedy whereof,—

"Be it enacted, and declared and established by the Governour, Council, and Representatives, in General Court assembled, and by the authority of the same,

"[Sect. 1.] That the coyn of the late Massachusetts Colony shall pass currant at the rate it was stampt for. And pieces of eight, sevil, pillar, and Mexico, of full seventeen penny-weight, shall pass currant at six shillings per piece, and half pieces of due weight, pro rata, and quarter pieces of the same coin at sixteen pence per piece, and realls of the same coin at eightpence per piece.

---

[1] Province Laws, vol. i, p. 70.

"[Sect. 2.] And whosoever, from and after the publication of this act, shall attempt and practice the counterfeiting, or clipping, rounding, filing, or otherwise diminishing or debasing any of the monies and coins currant within this province, being thereof lawfully convicted before the justices of assize, shall forfeit double the value of the money so counterfeited, clipped, rounded, or filed, one half to their majesties towards the support of the government, and the other half to the informer ; and shall also stand in the pillory, in some open place in the shire town of that county where the offence is committed, and there have one of his ears cut off. [Passed November 24."

A note following the act says, "'The Act, &c., is also repealed, [August 22, 1695,] the punishment thereby inflicted being only forfeiture of double the value of yᵉ Coin impaired, & standing in yᵉ Pillory and loosing an ear, it being thought fit that these Crimes ought to be punisht as in England.'"

An act was passed, October 19, 1697, reviving Section 1 of the act of 1692, but omitting the objectionable features which caused the repeal of that act. It was in these words : [1]

"An Act For ascertaining the value of Coynes Currant within this Province.

"Whereas for many yeares past the money coyned in the late Massachusetts Colony hath passed currant at the rate or value it was stampt for, and good Sevil, pillar, or mexico pieces of Eight of full Seventeen penny weight, have also passed Currant at Six Shillings p piece, and halfe pieces of proportionable weight pro-rato, quarter pieces of the same Coin at sixteen pence p piece, and Reals of the same Coin at eightpence p piece,

"Be it therefore Enacted and Declared by the Lieutenant Governour, Council, & Representatives convened in General Assembly, And by the authority of the Same, That all & every the Coynes before mentioned shall stil be and continue currant money within this Province, and shall be accepted, taken, and received at the respective values aforesᵈ, according as hath heretofore been accustomed.

"Provided, alwayes, That such of the sᵈ Coynes as pass by tale, be not diminished by washing, clipping, rounding, fileing, or scaling.

Read in Council, Votᵈ, and sent down to
"Octobʳ 19ᵗʰ, 1697.      the Representatives for Concurrance.

Isᵃ Addington, Secry.[2]

---

[1] Archives, vol. ci, p. 93, and Province Laws, vol. i, p. 296.      [2] An error on page 98 makes this name "*John* Addington."

"Octob.<sup>r</sup> <sub>19:</sub><sup>th</sup> 1697.        Read in the House of Representatives
                              a first and Second time and debated.
" Read                        Read a third time.
   18<sup>th</sup> octo.                              Voted A Concurrance.
   19<sup>th</sup>
                              Penn Townsend, Speaker."

One other act was passed this year,[1] possibly in accordance with the proposition contained in the committee's report of June 2d, 1696. This is the last act we find passed, during the seventeenth century, having reference to the monetary affairs of the colony :

" Province of the Massachusetts Bay, ss.

" An Act prohibiting the Exportation of money and Bullion.

" Upon Consideration of the scarcity of money within this Province, and the maney difficultys ariseing thereby, not onely w<sup>th</sup> respect to Trade and commerce, But also for carrying on the publick Affajres of the Governm<sup>t</sup> necessary for his Ma<sup>tys</sup> Service, more especially during the Rebellion & troubles with the Indians,

" Be it Enacted by the L<sup>t</sup> Gov<sup>r</sup>, Council, and Representatives in General Court assembled and by the Authority of the same, That no person or persons whatsoever shall or may export, Lade, or put on board any Ship or other Vessell, in order to export out of this Province any Coyne or Silver moneys currant within the same, or Bullion over and above the Sum of Five pounds for such person's necessary Expences, on Pain that all such money or Bullion Ship't or put on board any Ship or other Vessell, for exportation contrary to the true intent and meaning of this Act, shallbe liable to Seizure and become Forfeit, and the Shipper to Forfeit the like Sum or value over and above.

" And if it happen any money as afores<sup>d</sup>, or Bullion, (except to the value aboves<sup>d</sup>, for any particular person's own Expence,) to be exported out of this Province before Seizure thereof be made, or carried into any of the neighbouring Governm<sup>ts</sup> & exported from thence, the person or persons that Ship't or caused such money or Bullion to be carryed out of the province, laden, or put on board any Ship or other Vessell, or the person or persons that knowingly carried out or exported the same, being thereof convicted shall

---

[1] Archives, vol. ci, p. 106, and Province Laws, vol. i, p. 306.

incur the penalty and Forfeiture of double the Sum or value of the money or Bullion so exported, Provided that Information, Suit, or prosecution for the same be had and made within the space of 18 months next after the offence comitted, and not afterward.

"The aforementioned several Forfeitures to be recovered by action, Bill, Plaint, or Information in any of his Maj^tys Courts of Record within this Province, and to be imployed and disposed of two-thirds thereof for and towards the Support of his Ma^ts Governm^t within the same, and the other third to him or them that shall Informe & Sue for the same.

"And it shall and may be lawful to and for every Justice of the Peace, upon Information given of any money or Bullion put on board any Ship or other Vessell, for exportation or carrying out of y^e Province to be export^d by warrant under his hand & Seal, to cause the same to be Seized and secured, in order to Tryal. And all officers imployed and about the customs or Imposts, are hereby Impowred and required, ex officio, to cause Seizure to be made as afores^d.

"And be it further Enacted by the Authority afores^d. That every Master of any Ship or other Vessell, before such Ship or Vessell be cleered at the Impost office, shall make Oath to the following, That is to say,

"I, A. B., do Swear, That neither my selfe, nor any of the Company belonging unto the Ship or Vessell whereof I am now master, nor passengers goeing upon the same, have or shall by my knowledge, privity, or consent, take on board or export in the s^d Ship or Vessell, any Bullion, Coyne, or Silver money currant within the Province of the Massachusetts Bay, over and above y^e sum or value of Five pounds for my own or any of my marriners or Passengers particular expences. So help me God.

"Which Oath the Comission^r for Impost or Receiver are hereby respectively Authorized and Impowred to Administer.

"Provided this Act shall remain in force until the end of the Session of the General Assembly to be held upon y^e last Wednesday in May, which will be in the Year of our Lord 1700, and not afterwards.

"Decemb^r 21^st, 1697. Read in the House of Representatives.

"Read a Second time ; Read a Third time.

"Voted, And sent up for Concurrance.

"21° Dec^r, 1697.                                    Penn Townsend, Speaker.

"Read in Council and vot^d a concurrance
to be Engros't.                                    Is^a Addington, Secry."

The preceding papers comprise all known to us, which formed a part of the laws authorizing or regulating the silver coinage of New England. Those which follow are all, not already printed, that we find preserved in the Archives, relating to the same subject, and serve to show the different plans submitted, at various times, some of which, though not adopted at the time of their first proposal, were, at a later period, while all attempts to render the coinage free, failed entirely.

The first of these papers, the petition of John Mansfeilld and his wife, though of slight importance in its relation to the history of the mint, we present as a quaint specimen of one among many petitions requiring the attention of the Court at that period, this being, however, the only one having any reference to the mint. This is endorsed "Jnº Mansfield, 1654. perused."[1]

"To the Right Worshippfull gouernour, Depputie gouernour, with the rest of the Maiestrats & depputies,

"May it please your worshipps to take into considderation the poore Estate of John Mansfeilld, of charlstoune, that whereas your worshipps was pleassed by an order, one gennerall Court, to turne us ouer for reliefe of this towne, myselfe, wife, & children, & wee can not haue it when wee do need it unlesse wee part with our Children, contrary to that order, the which Children, being young, will pine away, to the greate hassordinge of there liues, if wee should give them away ; besides, they are the greatest comfortt in this world, and doe learne there bookes & thriue better with us, & are soe loueing to us, & wee to them, that wee can not till how to part One from other. And I, for my part, do verryly beleeife my wife would runne quite Madd if anny of them should be taken from hir.

"And therfor your poore humblle petitionour do desire your Worshipps would now be pleassed to lett your poore petitionours know what wee may demaund on yᵗ ordeʳ weekly of our Genˡˡ tounes men ; while our Children are ablle to goe to seruice, and haue had there learninge soe that wee there parents might be better that keeps them. And alsoe your poore humble petitioner morst humbly desires your worshipps would be pleassed to graunt me to be the Country searuantt for helping to quine & melt & fine siluer with mʳ Hull & good man Saunders, in the country howse withe them, for I serued 11 yeares & ½ prentiz to the same arte, & am a free man of London, and am also sworne to be trew to the Country, as I hoope I shall, which, if

_____

[1] Archives, vol. cv, p. 4.

soe greate a fauor be now graunted me, your poore Supplicants, my selfe, my
wife, & Children, shall haue Cause Euer after to pray for your Worshipps'
health, peace, & prosperitie heare in this life & euerlast reward with God
aboue.

"our howse do take fire manny times because it wants mendings, is like
to fall uppon our headds before we be awarr, & wee are not able to mend
it ; but is in great want of foode & other nessessaries both for ourselves &
Children, my selfe broaken bellied, my Wife much troubled in hir Mind
because of som Wrongs & to see how hard it is with us and how wee run
our selues in debt & all for the belly, and No worke stirring ; nor are wee
respected heare because we are soe poore & can not haue imployment in our
callings ; & we haue both ben Wronged both in our Estats & good Name,
& noe healpe as yet, but patiently abide the Lord's pleassure.

"Your poore petitioners,

"John Mansfeilld,
& Mary Mansfeilld his
wife."

The first attempt to prohibit the exportation of coin met with defeat,
as, after being passed by the Magistrates, it was negatived by the Deputies.
The acts of August 22d, 1654, May 19th, 1669, and December 21st, 1697,
prove that this project met with more favor at a later date than when first
proposed.  This proposition was made in 1654 : [1]

"Whereas, the end of Coyning mony w'hin this Comõnwealth is for the
more easy managing the traficque thereof w'hin itself, & not Intended to
make Returnes to other Countrjes, which cannot Advance any proffitt to
such as send it, but Rather a fowe'th part Losse Vnlesse such persons doe
oppresse & extort in the sale of theire goods to make vp the sajd losse,
which practice occasioned heereby (through some men's preferring theire oune
gaine before the publick good,) doth bring an vndervalue vppon all Comõd-
itjes Raised among ou'selves, and vtterly frustrate the end & vse of mony
amongst vs.  This Court doth therefore order & enact that whatever person
or persons, be they stranngers or Inhabitants, that shall directly or Indirectly
export out of this Jurisdicõon any of the Cojne of this Countrje, after the
publication heereof, shall forfeite his or theire whole estate, one halfe to the
Countrje & the other halfe to such psõn or psõns as shall sue for the same,

---

[1] Archives, vol. c, p. 46.

& to the end that the breakers of this Lawe may be discouered, Itt is Ordered that the County Court shall choose & Appointe in euery Port Toune w^hin theire seuerall Countjes a water Bayly or Searcher, that is heereby Impowered to search any suspitious persons or Vessels, chests, truncks, or any other thing or place, & vppon discouery of any som̄es of money about to be transported, shall cease the same, and p^resent the Case to the next County Court, who shall determine whither the said mony was Intended, or about to be transported ; and if they so finde it, then to forfeite the same, on halfe to the officer and the rest to the Countrje ; & if any shall travill by land & be suspected to Cary mony, any pson, w^th a Constable, may search for the same ; if it be discouered it shall be forfeited, one halfe to the Constable & the other p̃t to be œqually to be divided betweene the pson & Constable y^t doe search for it. The majists haue past this w^th Reference to the Consent of theire bretheren the depu^ts heereto.

Edward Rawson, Secrety.

"Boston 12·· may, 1654.

"The deputyes Cannot Consent hereto.

William Torrey, Cleric."

There seems to be a clerical error here, in regard to the division of the forfeited money, as it gives three quarters to the constable. It probably was intended to be, one half to the country, but the manuscript reads, "one halfe to the Constable," etc.

In June, 1669, we find a proposition for the trial and stamping of the foreign coin yet in circulation.[1] This measure was passed by the Deputies, but failed in the House of Magistrates."

"This Court being sensible of the great necessitie of money for the more easie & Equall Carying on of Commerce amongst vs, & finding that Coyninge hath not fully answered the Court's expectations, but there still remaynes great want for a further supply, It is there fore ordered by this Court & Authority thereof, & be It hereby enacted, that peeces of eyght that are full weight, & of the finest of Sterlinge money, shall passe in all payments of money of new england, at the price of 6^s, & halfe peeces, quarter peeces, and halfe quarter peeces in like pportion. & for the better p^rvention of deceite herein, that Counterfeit & light peeces may not be be brought, to

---

[1] Archives, vol. c, p. 136.

the deceiuinge of the people, This Court doth further order that some meete person shalbe appoynted to try & waygh all peices as affores[d], & all such as he finds full weight, & to be of the finest of Sterling money, he shall put a Stamp or marke vpon It, & receiue 4[d] for the Stamping of each peece of eyght, & in proportion for lesser peeces, which shall be for the vse & benefitt of the Country; & without the marke or stamp aboues[d] no man shall be Injoyned to receiue Spanish coyne as lawfull payment in this Jurisdiction. & It is further ordered, that the person appoynted to try and marke Spanish Coyne shall keepe a Just account of the Number he markes, & for whom, & giue an account to the Treasurer of the Country every quarter of a yeare or oftener if required; & the money he receiues for the marking, only deducting what shalbe due vnto him, according to what shall be agreed from time to time. The deputyes haue past this w[th] refference to the Consent of o[r] hon[rd] magists hereto.

William Torrey, Cleric.

"2 of June, 1669.

"The magists Consent not heereto. Edw. Rawson, secrety."

Next in order comes a paper without date, but placed by Mr. Felt in 1671. It is endorsed

"Mr. Wharton's paper about raising of money."[1]

"That all former Accompts, debts, and transactions be Satisfyed, paid, and discharged in specie, according to obligation, Agreement, or former Customes saving in want thereof in pieces of eight, exept peru, at 6[s] 8[d] per ounce.

"That from and after

the money formerly Coyned in New England shall on all future contracts, dealings, Transactions, and paym[ts], pass Curr[t] at the ualew hereafter ascertained, Viz :

|  |  |  |
|---|---|---|
| euery New Engld shilling at | | 14[d] |
| euery: New Engld Six pence at | | 7[d] |
| euery: | three pence at | 4[d] |
| euery: | two pence at | 3[d] |

"Prouided noe pson be compelled in any one payment to accept more then in Such : 4[d]. : and : 3[d]:

"That all mexico, Pillar, Siuill, and other p̄ces of ⅜ Bulloine or Plate, or

---

[1] Archives, vol. c, p. 162.

any manner of Broken Siluer, or other money or Plate being of the fineness of Sterling money or better, shall pass Curr$^t$: in all payments at Seuen shill Six pence p oz : But noe Plate, Bulloine, or unknowne Coyne to be imposed in payment under

"That Spanish Pisstolls of Gold: q$^t$: 4$^d$ 6: gr: shall pass at : 24$^s$ p $\overline{peec}$; Double ones, the ffrench Lewis, and other Gold greater or Less of the Same fineness, shall be ualewd and pass Curr$^t$ Pro rato.

"That all whole Rialls of plate shall be Curr$^t$ at nine pence, double Rialls at : 18$^d$ : half $\overline{pies}$ : $\frac{8}{8}$ : at : 3$^s$ : Prouided none shall be compelled to receiue in any one paym$^t$ : aboue : 10$^s$ : in Rialls and double Rialls, nor aboue : 20$^s$. in halfe $\overline{pies}$ : $\frac{8}{8}$ : exccept by Weight at the Rate aboue said.

"That for Auoiding frauds & contrauercesyes in great payment there be in Boston and Salem, &c., Sworne officers to touch, try, or essay, and to weigh all Gold and Siluer that shall bee brought in to them for that end, who shall haue allowed y$^m$ for Weighing                    for touching
for Essaying

"That if any pson shall counterfeet, corrupt, clip, Wash, or any Way Lessen or debase Coyned money, or Knowingly bring into his Majestyes Dominion, or pass away or offer in paym$^t$, Barter, or exchange, any Counterfeet Gold or Siluer, Coyned or uncoyned, shall forfeit the same or the ualew thereof, one halfe to his Ma$^{tye}$: for Subport of his Gouerment heer, and the other halfe to him or them that shall sue for the same, &c., or be sett in the Pillory or otherwise punised according to the Circumstances of his offence, Prouided neuertheless that any psons may bring in any Course, base, or mixed mettles to haue the same refined, or may expose the Same to Sale to any Gold smith or to any psons, the Sworne officers for trying and Essaying being p$^r$sent and priuy to such sale, or the seller making first Knowne to the buyer the Baseness or mixture of Such Gold or Siluer."

The following minutes, in another hand, are found on a slip of paper following the last :

"All former Accompts & Debts be pay$^d$ according to Contract & former Custom, saving in want thereof in peices of $\frac{8}{8}$, except Peru at 6$^s$ 8$^d$.

"All whole peices of $\frac{8}{8}$, Except peru, weighing 15$^d$ weight and upwards, shall pass Currant at six shilling.

"all other. Bullion & plate of sterling alloy shall pass Currant at six shillings eight pence per ounce.

"All Peru peices at 15$^d$ at 6$^s$."

At about this period, 1677 to 1680, there were several propositions for making the mint free. The first of these[1] seems to have originated in a committee of both houses, but we find no record of any action thereupon.

"In pursuance of an order to obtain the Coynage of Bullion, & stoppage of Transportation of Money, we have descoursed Capt Hull & others, & find no other expedients but the raysing of the vallue of our Coyn, or Making our Money for future lighter by 9 or 12 graynes, or Making the Mint free. for the first, if it be done three half pence in the shilling, & the law for exportation of Money duly attended, we hope it may obtain what is desired ; the Paying Coynage out of the Treasury, we find the Charge uncertain but great, & both expedients attended with Difficulty, & therefore Judge them worthy of further Consideration. In the Mean time, we Judge it meet to Double the Custom of all wines, brandy, & rhum Imported, which being drawn into the treasury, part of it May pay the Charge of a free Mint, if the Court afterwards see meet so to Improve the same.

"June 2, 1677.

Joseph Dudley,
Richard Waldron,
Daniel ffisher."

Another proposition regarding the valuation of coin comes from the Deputies,[2] but is defeated by the Magistrates :

"For the encouragem$^t$ of the importation of bullion & encrease of money in these p̃ts,

"This Court doth Order & Enact, & it is hereby Enacted, That henceforth All peeces of eight, of good Silver, & of the Coine of Mexico or Sevill, & pillar peeces, shall passe currant att Six shillings p peece. And halfe peeces of Same Sorts att three shillings, and all Smaller peeces of Said Sorts after five shillings p peece of Eight.

"The Deputyes haue passed this w$^{th}$ reference to the Consent of our honoured Magistrates.                     William Torrey, Cleric.

"Octo 31, 1679.

"not Consented to by y$^e$ magis$^{ts}$.              Edw$^d$ Rawson, Secrety."

The second plan for a free mint[3] contains the earliest application we have found, of the name Pine, to the money of New England. It is without

---

[1]Archives, vol. c, p. 222 ; [2]ibid, vol. c, p. 241 ; [3]ibid, vol. c, p. 243.

signature, but in the handwriting of Isaac Addington, the secretary of the General Court:

"To the Honoured Generall Court sitting in Boston, 19: May. A⁰. 1680.

"The decay of Trade and decrease of money in the Land, (being a generall complaint throughout the Country,) craves some Speedy and effectuall Remedy: And the most probable expedient that offers is to make the mint free; which, it's hoped, wilbee manifest from these Considerations following.

"1ˢᵗ  All the money that now passeth the mint (besides the waste there,) returns to the Owner at least Six and a quarter in the hundred lighter then it entred, And the impress adds nothing to the intrinsick value, a spanish Cross in all other places being as well esteemᵈ as a New England pine.

"2ᵈ  The least Loss being Six and a quarter p Cent, and comonly more, is so considerable for the meere stamp, that nothing but necessity makes it tolerable: Those who are able chooseing rather to lay up, or send their plate, Bulloin, or peeces of ⅛ abroad, and others to sell to those that export the same, having something more then the mint will yeild; By which discouragement little of late yeares (compared to what is laid up and carried away,) hath been coyned; and of that little, much dispersed into other Colony's, and thence consequently groweth the great difficulty & decay of trade.

"3ᵈ  A free mint will soone open all the Coffers in the Country, Security from loss and charge will effectually perswade to convert dead treasures into currant coyn, and those that have no Bancks through whose hands Materials to make money often pass, will finde the Mint their surest and highest market; Besides, Strangers from forrreign parts, and our own Plantations, being thus secured from loss in the mint, will, to purchase ffish, provisions, and what else they want, rather choose to send peices of ⅛, plate, or Bulloin, then run the hazard of an uncertain market for those goods which they may with less loss send to other parts.

"The benefit of a free mint, both to the publique and every perticular person, will far Surmount the charge. It being very observable that in all Country's where money abounds, the price of all Comodity's and provisions of their place advances, and the goods imported abate proportionably, And less trouble, time, and discharge, dispatches all matters of trade, then where it depends upon truck, barter, &c. And as wisdom, so is money as defence against the designes and power of fforreign or Intestine Enemies. So also it will prevent many Suits, controversy's, and inconveniencies amongst neighbours and ffreinds.

"And upon approbaꝏn of the meanes it's hoped the charge will not discourage, which may either bee levyed by some easy rate, or by Excise upon some of those improfitable coṁodities which are consumed to nourish lust and vice."

The following is in the same handwriting with the last, and appears to be a form of order submitted to the Court by its author. It is without date, but is presumed properly to follow the foregoing statement, and was so placed by Mr. Felt, who arranged these volumes of papers.

"ffor incouragement of the importation of plate, Bulloin, and Spanish coyne into this Colony;  And of all persons who have, or may have, any such in their hands to minte the same, whereby there may bee greater plenty of money in the Country, and Trade and coṁerce thereby revived and facilitated.

"It is Ordered by this Court and the Authority thereof, that henceforth our Mint bee made free, and that the Master of the sᵈ mint do from time to time receive all such plate, bullion, or fforreign Coyne as shalbee brought to him to bee coyned, by any person or persons whatsoever, as well strangers as our own Inhabitants, who shall forthwith refine and mint the same, bringing it to the due Alloy prescribed in the Law title Money, and shall deliver again to the sᵈ person or persons the just weight thereof so refined, in currant money of this Colony, cleer of all costs and charges: The sᵈ Mint Master to bee allowed and paid yearely by the Country Treasuroʳ, the usuall rate for coynage as the former Law provided to bee paid by perticular persons."

Another draught of an order, of much the same tenor as the last, is found[2] in the handwriting of John Saffin, afterwards a member of the House of Deputies, and, in 1686, Speaker of that House :

"Whereas, upon mature Consideration & by Dayly Experience, it doth Evidently Appeare unto this Court That the Money of our Coyne is much diminished & become very scarce throughout the Country, whereby Tradeing is groune very Difficult, Delatory, & much Decayed, so that Persons Generally (haveing otherwise competent Estates,) are by Reason there of, in the carrieing on and management of their Respective Affayres, greatly straightened and Disappoynted, suites of law increased, for Reparration where of it is Thought meete & most Expedient for the facillitateing of Commerce and Quickening of Trade amongst us, both in Towne & Countrey, To take Order that our Mint be made ffree, so as all persons, strangers as well as our Owne

---

[1]Archives, vol. c, p. 244; [2]ibid, p. 260.

Inhabitants, may be Encouraged to bring in Either Plate, Bullion, or fforraigne Coyne, to be minted into New England, for their owne Advantage and the good of the Publick.

"It is Therfore Ordered by this Court, and by the Authority there of Ordained, that a Mint-Master be hence forth Appoynted and Duely Sworn, who shall from time to time Receive, Refine, & mint into New England money of good Alloy, (According to the Order & Prescript in that case provided,) all such Plate, Bullion, or fforraigne Coyne, as any person or persons shall Deliuer to the said Mint master to be coyned as aforesaid, who shall, with all Convenient speed, Refine the same & bring it into true Alloy, and shall deliuer the Just waight thereof so Refined, &c., in New England Money, cleare of all Costs & Charges, the said Mint-master to be Allowed, and payed yearely by the Country Treasurer, according to the Usuall Rate of Coynage formerly payed by perticular persons. And this order to be and Remaine in force the terme of Three years Next Ensueing the date of this sessions."

The next plan for the advancement of the New England coins comes from the mint master himself, though wanting his signature.[1]

"Boston, June 6, 1680.

"If forreigne Coyne be Advanced without great regard both to weight & fineness, and also without there be a great quantity of it in the Countrey before it be advanced, It will be much loss to the Countrey that so Advances it. And the gaine is onely to strangers $y^t$ bring it in.

"If o$^r$ owne Coyne be Caried out of the Countrey it is a signe it is not soe light as it may be, & that it would be for Publique advantage to make it lighter, unless wee had some Publique income by wines, as $y^e$ Spanyard hath.

"If every shilling be made 12 graines lighter, then all those that have good Peices of eight, i. e. both of Good Silver & full weight, will advance about 7$^d$ or 7$^d$ ½ more then now they doe.

"Every 12$^d$ then to be 2 peny weight and halfe.

6$^d$ one peny weight 6 graines.

3$^d$ 15 graines.

2$^d$ 10 gr.

"The same fyneness to be kept, & Put a new date.

"Let the Coynage & wast be as by the last settlem$^t$.

---

[1] Archives, vol. c, p. 245.

"obj. 1. from the difficulty of making Paym^ts.

"Ans. 1. Let all money debts above six monthes old be Paid one halfe in new money & the other halfe in old money at its Present & former value, or the debtor & Creditor equally bear the loss between them.

"2. All debts not six monthes old be Paid in new money, or the old as advanced, unless any Perticuler Contract Positively Express otherwise.

"If all the Bullion of the Countrey be Coyned at the Publique charge, it will reduce it to a Certain fineness, & being weight for weight the merch^ht may as well transport the Coyned money as the bulion, and then you may have noe money left in the Countrey."

A writ of *Quo Warranto* was issued, June 27th, 1683,[1] against the Governor and Company of Massachusetts. This was followed, June 2d, 1684, by *Scire Facias*, which "setts forth  *  *  *  The s^d. Gov^r. & Company in their Geñall Court held at N. E. vizt. at Westm^r in Middx, Haue made & published certaine Laws," and gives the substance of the laws relating to the mint; and another paper, headed "Briefe of the Lawes vpon which the Second Breach is Assigned," does the same. These it will be useless for us to repeat, as those laws have already been given in full. We will, however, copy a note relating to the list of grievances enumerated in the *Scire Facias:*

"It is doubted the Breaches assigned ag^t the def^ts are true in fact.

"But it is as true That,

"(1). Noe money has been Raysed but by Generall Consent of the Company.

"(2). They were long vnder the Burthen of an Indian warr without any Assistance from abroad, which put them at the End thereof into a debt of 100,000^li, which is not yet cleared.

"(3). There is none of the Company, none that bore any of the Taxes Complained of that are agreiued; they Saw the necessity of the Charge and bore it cheerefully, and now find the effect of the lasting Peace procured by it.

"As to the Mint.

"That was set vp in 1652, a time of Licence, and Is a Conveniency to all without detrim^t to any, and if the erecting of it be a fault,[2] It is presumed

---

[1] Drake states, (Hist. Boston, p. 449,) "The judgment was rendered at Trinity-term [June 18th,] 1684, but an official copy of it was not received in Boston till July 2d, 1685."

[2] Chalmers says, (Annals, p. 182, 1780,) "At a subsequent period the general-court gravely justified this irregularity by reversing the maxim: that ignorance of law shall not excuse."

to be noe more then a Bare Trespass, and not to be offered to avoyd the Charter.

"As to the Imposeing of Oathes.

"It is hoped any Legall Society may Secure their mutuall quiett by agreeing on an Oath to be taken by their members.

"And where It is imposed on Strangers they may avoyd it by giueing Security for their good abearance to the Governm$^t$.

"Soe Pray vpon the whole matter what is fitt to plead to the Severall Breaches assigned [by the *Scire*] *fac$^s$* ag$^t$ : the Def$^{ts}$ of their Charter."

In a tract written in 1688, entitled "New England Vindicated," [1] we find this defence of the colonists :

"As to what is objected about Coyning, many Goldsmiths in London can testifie that the Money Coyned in New England is as good as that of England, and not of a baser Alloy, (as is suggested.)

"It was formerly customary for private Persons in England to Coyn Farthings for their own Use, and the Coyning in Massachusetts Colony was little more than that, and with Design to prevent the great Injuries Merchants and others sustained by base Spanish Money. And the Mint was set up in 1652, when there was no King in England, but the Government out of Course; and when the ancient Government of England was resettled, and the King's mind to the contrary signified to them, they resolved to comply therewith, though many wayes disadvantageous to themselves. Was not the Value of Coyn altered in Pensilvania? Did not the Lord Baltimore in Maryland Coyn Money with his own Image on one side, and his Coat of Arms on the other? Did not the East India Company? But when they understood their Error they petitioned the King for liberty of Coynage, and pardon of what was past, and it was granted them. Why, then, should New England be esteemed more criminal than other Plantations?"

With one other quotation we will conclude our history of the Massachusetts coinage. This interesting account of the system of trade in the early days, is found in Lambert's Colony of New Haven :

"On account of a deficiency of money, wages and taxes were paid in produce or country payment, and nearly all the merchandise of the colony was transacted by the same medium. A correct idea of that method of trade in old times, may be gathered from the following extract from the travels of

---

[1] Andros's Tracts, vol. ii, p. 115.

Madam Knight, a lady of rank, of such remarkable courage as to make the tour from Boston to New York, about 1695.

"'They give the title of merchant to every trader who rate their goods according to the time and specie they pay in, viz., pay, money, pay as money, and trusting. Pay is grain, pork, and beef, &c., at the prices set by the general court that year; money is pieces of 8, ryals, or Boston or Bay Shillings, (as they call them,) or good hard money, as sometimes silver coin is called by them; also wampum, viz., Indian beads wch. serves for change. Pay as money is provisions as aforesaid, one third cheaper than as the Assembly or generall court sets it, and trust as they and the merchant agree for time. Now when the buyer comes to ask for a commodity, sometimes before the merchant answers that he has it, he sais, is your pay ready? Perhaps the chap replies, yes. What do you pay in? sais the merchant. The buyer having answered, then the price is set; as suppose he wants a 6$^d$ knife, in pay it is 12$^d$, in pay as money 8$^d$, and hard money, its own value, 6$^d$. It seems a very intricate way of trade, and what 'Lex Mercatoria' had not thought of."

Having given the records referring particularly to the moneys current in Massachusetts in the seventeenth century, we will, in order to complete the action of the State upon the subject, next place the few papers having reference to the coin circulating in or proposed for this State, early in the eighteenth century.

The first of these acts may have been issued partly on account of those pieces now known as the "New Yorke Token," which is found in brass and tin, and the "New England Stiver," in copper. This prohibition, if it did apply to the tokens just named, would, if issued soon after their appearance, account for the extreme rarity of specimens of these issues, — but a single one being known of the "Stiver," and four, two in each metal, of the "New Yorke Token."

We know of no other pieces likely to have been struck about this period for circulation in America, or of any more likely than these to be among those here interdicted. Sufficient unauthorized coin was evidently in circulation to cause some difficulties in trade and call forth the following act:

"Province of the Massachusetts Bay.

"An Act against the making or passing of base or Counterfeit money.

"Whereas some persons, for private gain, have of late presumed to Stamp and Emit peices of brass and Tin at the rate of a penny each, not regarding what loss they thereby bring on others, which, if not timely remedyed, may prove greatly detrimental to his Ma^tys Subjects, and embolden others to be so hardy as to attempt the doing of the like,

"For Prevention whereof,

"Be it Declared and Enacted by the Lieu^t Governo^r, Council, and Representatives in General Court Assembled, and by the Authority of the same, That any person or persons who after the publication of this Act shall presume to make or Stamp any such peices as afores^d, or others of like or different mettal, matter, or forme, and to Emit, utter, or put off the same for pence, or at a greater or lesser value, and be thereof convicted, Every person so Offending shall be punished by Fine and Imprisonment, at the discretion of the Court where the prosecution shall be, not exceeding the Sum of Fifty pounds Fine, nor Six months Imprisonment for one offence. And shall further Forfeit and pay in currant lawful money of this Province Treble the value of all such peices as he shall have Emitted or uttered after the highest rate they have passed at; One halfe of said Fine and Forfeiture to be unto his Majesty for & towards the Support of the Government within this Province, and the other halfe to him or them that shall Informe and Sue for the same in any of his Maj^tys Courts within the Province.

"And be it further Enacted by the Authority afores^d That every person or persons that have or shall Offend as aforesaid, shall Exchange and pay in currant lawful money of this Province the full value of all such peices haveing his Stamp or marke thereon, unto any person or persons that shall bring the same to him, according to the rate they have passed at.

"So as such peices be brought and offered to him to be exchanged at any time or times within the space of three months next after the publication of this Act, And in case of refusal so to do, he shall be compelled thereto by Order of the General Sessions of the Peace within the same County, or of one Justice of the Peace, where the value exceeds not Forty Shillings.

"And no person or persons whatsoever shall hereafter offer to put off, utter, or take any such base or Counterfeit money.

"In Council. Feb^r 21^st, 1700-1. Read a 1^st and 2^ond time and Voted to be Engrossed, and sent down for Concurrance.

Is^a Addington, Secry.

"In the House of Representatives. Feb^ry 21, 1700. Read a first time. 28^th, Read a 2^d time. march 12: 3^rd time, and Resolved a Concurrence.

John Leverett, Speaker."

We next find a report of a committee advising the regulation of the value of coins of gold and silver, and the coinage of "Provinc penc," of copper.

"March 3, 170$\frac{0}{1}$:

"The Comitte appoynted by this Present Gen$^{rl}$ Court to consider of the proposals about puting a Vallue upon Gold, And to make other proposals for Supplying the Scarcity of Mony, as they shall see cause, and make Report to this Court,

"Report as followeth,

"1) That Pistoles of fouer peny waight Eaight grains do pass Curant in all payments for twenty *fouer* Shilings, And that small pieces of fforaigne Gold waying two peny waight *Six* grains, & not Inferior in goodnes to pistoles, do pass at *twelve* Shilings a p$^s$. [2]

"2) That p$^{cs}$ of $\frac{8}{8}$ that are either more or less then seventene peny wait do pass at seaven Shilings p ounce Troy waight, in all payments of ten pounds & upward.

"3) That Provinc penc be made of Copper & pass Curant for change of Mony.

"4) That a Sutable Number of Meet persons, with their Associates, their Heirs, &c., for the Space of      years, be allowed, appoynted, & Impowred, To Erect & Set up a Bank of Credit & to make & Emit Bills of Credit, at their owne proper cost & charge, from two Shiling Bills to three pound Bills, in such proportion as they see meet, to any Vallue, and not to take more then Three p Ct p Anñ for Interest.

"That all other persons be Inhibeted making any of the Like Bills of Credit, or Seting up Such Bank dureing s$^d$ Terme.

"That no Person shal or may buie any of s$^d$ Bills under the Value therein Exsprest, on penalty of forfiting the Vallue of the same, so Exsprest in s$^d$ Bill or Bills.      Elisha Hutchinson, p

         ord$^r$ of y$^e$ Comitte.

"Read In Council, March 6$^{th}$, 1700, and sent down.

"In the House of Representatives, Mar: 8$^{th}$: 1700.

"Read, 1$^{st}$ time; 12$^{th}$: 2$^d$ time, & a 3$^{rd}$.      Ordered, That a Bill be drawn

---

[1] Archives, vol. ci, p. 184.    [2] The words in italics, in sect. 1, were amended by side notes to six, four, and thirteen.

pursuant to the first and 3ᵈ Paragraphs of the above Report: (P.¹ Paragraphs being accepted, the Rest Rejected.)   Sent up for Concurrence.

John Leverett, Speaker.

"March 13th, 1700.     In Council.

   "Read, and the Question being put for a Concurrance, it was carried in yᵉ Negative.                                         I. Addington, Secry."

On the eighteenth of June, 1704, a proclamation was issued by Queen Anne, for reducing to one uniform rate the coins circulating in different parts of America.   We find a copy of this proclamation in the "American Journal of Numismatics,"² which we here insert.

"[ARMS OF GREAT BRITAIN: MOTTO, SEMPER EADEM.]

By the Queen.

# A   PROCLAMATION

For settling and ascertaining the current rates of Foreign coins in her Majesties colonies and plantations in America.

ANNE, R.

WE having had under our consideration the different rates at which the same species of foreign coins, do pass in our several colonies and plantations in America, and the inconveniences thereof, by the indirect practice of drawing the money — from one plantation to another, to the great prejudice of the trade of our subjects; And being sensible that the same cannot be otherwise remedied, than by reducing of all foreign coins to the same current rate, within all our dominions in America; and the principal officers of our mint, having laid before us, a table of the value of the several foreign coins, which usually pass in payments in our said plantations, according to their weight, and the assays made of them in our mint, thereby shewing the just proportion which each coin ought to have to the other, which is as followeth, Sevill pieces of eight, Old plate, seventeen-peny-weight, twelve grains, four shillings and sixpence; Sevill pieces of eight, new plate, fourteen peny-weight, three shillings seven pence one farthing; Mexico pieces of eight seventeen peny-weight twelve grains, four shillings and sixpence.   Pillar pieces of eight, seventeen peny-

---

¹ The first and third paragraphs are marked "Passed," the others, "Rejected."   ² Vol. vii, p. 94.

weight — twelve grains, four shillings and sixpence three farthings. Peru pieces of eight, Old plate, seventeen peny-weight, twelve grains, four shillings and five pence or thereabouts; Cross dollars, eighteen peny-weight, four shillings and four pence, three farthings; Duccatoons of Flanders twenty peny-weight and twenty one grains, five shillings and sixpence; Ecu's of France or silver Lewis, seventeen peny-weight twelve grains, four shillings and sixpence; Crusadoes of Portugal, eleven peny-weight four grains, two shillings and ten pence, one farthing; Three gilder pieces of Holland twenty peny-weight and seven grains five shillings and two pence one farthing; Old Rix dollars of the empire, eighteen peny-weight and ten grains, four shillings and sixpence; The half, quarters and other parts, in proportion to their denominations, and light pieces in proportion to their weight.

"We have therefore thought fit for remedying the said inconveniences, by the advice of our Council, to publish and declare, that from and after the first day of January next ensuing the date hereof, no Sevill, Pillar, or Mexico pieces of eight, though of the full weight of seventeen penyweight and an half, shall be accounted, received, taken, or paid, within any of our said colonies or plantations, as well those under proprietors and charters, as under our immediate commission and government, at above the rate of six shillings per piece current money, for the discharge of any contracts or bargains, to be made after the said first day of January next, the halfs quarters and other lesser pieces of the same coins to be accounted, received taken, or paid in the same proportion: And the currency of all pieces of eight of Peru, dollars, and other foreign species of silver coins, whether of the same or baser alloy, shall, after the said first day of January next, stand regulated, according to their weight and fineness, according and in proportion to the rate before limited and set for the pieces of eight of Sevill, Pillar, and Mexico; so that no foreign silver coin of any sort be permitted to exceed the same proportion upon any account whatsoever.

"And we do hereby require and command all our Governours, Lieutenant Governours, Magistrates officers and all other our good subjects, within our said colonies and plantations, to observe and obey our directions herein as they tender our displeasure.

"Given at our Castle at Windsor, the eighteenth of June 1704. In the third year of our reign.

GOD SAVE THE QUEEN."

The Queen's proclamation was communicated to the Council on the 28th of November, 1704, as we find this entry upon the Council Records of that date: "His Excell^y communicated to the Council a Letter from the R^t Hon^ble the Lords Commissioners for Trade and Plantations, accompanying Her Maj^tys Royal Proclamation of the 18^th of June past, for setling and ascertaining the curr^t Rates of Foreign Coynes in Her Maj^tys Colonys and Plantations in America, and ordered the s^d Proclamation to be printed & published in solemn manner."

This proclamation called forth the ensuing action by the authorities here, on the third of March, 170$\frac{4}{5}$.[1]

"Ordered,

"That there be forthwith a proclamation Issued,

"That no Money shall pass by Tale but what is of due weight according to her Majestyes proclamation and the laws of the province.

"& That all other light Money & plate of sterling alloy shall pass & be good in payments *at seven shillings* by the ounce Troy pro rato, *& no More* untill* *further provision be made by the assembly at their next session.*

"March 3^d, 1704.     In Council.

Read and pass'^d.          Is^a Addington, Secry.

"Sent down for concurrance.

"In the House of Representatives.

"Die p̄dict.   Read,

And Pass'd a Non-Concurrence.          Ja^s Converse, Speaker.

"In Council, march 3^d.   Passd w^th the amendment.

"Sent down[2] concurrance.                    Is^a Addington, Secry.

"In the House of Representatives.

"Die p̄dict.   Read & Pass'd w^th y^e amend^mt annex'd.

Jam^s Converse, Speaker."

* "untill the end of the session of this Court in may next, when further consideration shall be had thereof.

"march 3^d.   Agreed to In Council."

The amendment mentioned above is upon a slip of paper sealed upon the sheet, and is intended to take the place of the line in italics ; whether the other italicised words were intended to be omitted, is uncertain.

In accordance with the last order the ensuing proclamation was issued :

---

[1] Archives, vol. ci, p. 286.     [2] *Sic.*

[SEAL.]

"By his Excellency Joseph Dudley, Esq^r, Captain General and Governour in Chief in and over Her Majesties Province of the Massachusetts Bay in New Engl^d.

## A PROCLAMATION.

"Whereas Her Majesty, by Her Royal Proclamation For Settling and ascertaining the current rates of Foreign Coins in Her Ma^tys Colonies and Plantations in America, Given at Her Ma^tys Castle at Windsor, the Eighteenth day of June, In the Third year of Her Reign, hath Published Her Royal Pleasure, That all foreign Coins be reduced to the same current rates within all Her Dominions in America, according to their weight and Value and just proportion which Each Coin ought to have to the other, as in the s^d Proclamation is particularly set forth and express'd. But forasmuch as, by the corrupt, wicked practices of some ill men, the running coins within this Province are so debased and Impaired by rounding and clipping, (Notwithstaing the good and wholesome Laws made against the same,) To the rendring of Her Maj^tys Royal Intention impracticable. And will be of pernicious and fatal Consequence to Her Ma^tys good Subjects, unless it be speedily prevented.

"For Remedy whereof,

"I do, by and with the Advice and Consent of Her Maj^tys Council and of the Representatives in General Court assembled, Declare and Order, That from and after the Publication hereof, no money shall pass by Tale but what is of one weight, according to Her Ma^tys Proclamation and the Laws of this Province; That all other light money and Plate of Sterling Alloy shall pass and be good in payments by the ounce Troy pro rato, until the End of the Session of this Court in May next, when further Consideration shall be had thereof.

"And the Sheriffes of the several County's are hereby Commanded to Publish this Proclamation within the same.

"Given at the Council Chamber in Boston, the Third day of March, 1704, In the Third year of the Reign of our Soveraign Lady Anne, by the Grace of God, of England, Scotland, France, and Ireland, Queen, Defender of the Faith, &c.                                    J. Dudley.

"By Order of the Govern^r, Council, and Assembly.

Is^a Addington, Secry.

GOD SAVE THE QUEEN."

Thus affairs remained until June 1st, 1605, when this order[1] was passed:
"1st June, 1705.   In Council.

"Ordered, That Elisha Hutchinson, W[m] Browne, Sam[l] Sewall, Eliakim
Hutchinson, Samuell Legg, Esq[rs], with the Secretary, be a Committee of the
Board to joyne with such as shall be named by the Representatives, to consider and Report what they shall thinke proper to be done by this Court *for
the annexing of Penaltys on such as shall offer money by tale, under Due
weight, and further for the reforming of the money.*

"Sent down for concurrance.                    Is[a] Addington, Secry.

"In the House of Representatives,
     June 1[mo] 1705, Read.   5: Read.

"7th Pass'd a Concurrence with the amendm[t] annex'd, & That Capt Sam[ll]
Checkley, Capt. Stephen French, Maj[r] Sam[ll] Brown, M[r] Nath[ll] Knolton, Maj[r]
Jam: Converse, Cap[t] Tho[s] Oliver, M[r] Sam[ll] Clapp, M[r] Ephr[m] Pierce, M[r] Sam[ll]
Knowles, & Cap[t] Preserved Clapp, be a Comittee to Joine with the Comittee
of the Board in the affair above mentioned.

                              Thomas Oakes, Speaker.

     "Agreed — In Council.                    Is[a] Addington, Secry."

The amendment is "for the reforming of the money & rendring the law
effectuall to Prevent the Debasing thereof." The italics denote the words
erased for the substitution of the amendment.

The committee appointed by the last order report, June 8, 1705, and the
action relating to their recommendation is recorded with their report.[2]

(Attached to the ensuing report is a copy of the preceding proclamation,
printed in Old English type, and headed by the British coat-of-arms.)

"June 8th 1705.

"That this Proclamation be revived and continued without Limitation.

"That the Treasurer and Receiver General of the Province, The Treasurers of the several Countys, Towns, and all Constables, Collectors, and Subordinate Receivers under either of them.

"All Judges, Jurors, and Publick Officers whatsoever be Commanded
Strictly to Conform themselves accordingly. Saving all pas't particular
Contracts.

"That some skilful persons be appointed to calculate a Table of the due proportion of Coines and Silver of Sterling alloy by the Ounce Troy to the weight of a peny, and that Copy's thereof be printed.

"That some other skilful person be appointed to make weights of brass of the Ounce Troy to the least denomination with such Stamps thereon as the Governo.<sup>r</sup> and Council shall direct.

"All which is humbly Submitted by      Elisha Hutchinson, by order
"June 9.<sup>th</sup> 1705.                          of the Committee.

"Read in Council.

"June 11.<sup>th</sup> 1705.     Read and Pass'd an acceptance w.<sup>th</sup> this Addition, Viz.<sup>t</sup>

"Provided, That for all pas't bargains and Debts except by Special Contract, If the Debtor shall tender Satisfaction to his Creditor in y.<sup>e</sup> bills of Publick Credit on this Province, all process in the Law shall be stayed against every such Debtor by the space of twelve months next comeing and then proceed.  Sent down for concurrance."

No further action appears to have been taken upon this report.

We have discovered nothing further in relation to coin or coinage until the issue of silver and copper was proposed in 1786.  In the interim attention was directed to the project of issuing "Bills of Credit," as paper money was then called.  With one order relating to these, not having met with it in print, we will finish this department of our subject:

"Nov.<sup>r</sup> 26.<sup>th</sup> 1706.  In Council.

"Ordered, That a Plate be forthwith provided, and the Eight several Stamps or blazons affix'd to the Bills of Publick Credit on this Province respectively, be Engraven thereupon; And That the Committee for Imprinting of the Bills, do forthwith Imprint *one* [Three] Thousand *or more* [proportionably to the sum they pay in the publick Tax,] of them, to be dispersed and Transmitted to the several Towns within the Province, for the better Information of Her Ma.<sup>tys</sup> good Subjects of the different form's of the said Stamps, and to which of the Bills respectively they belong ; The figure of the Sum of the Bill to be placed in the middle of the Stamp ; for discourageing and preventing the Designs and Endeavours of ill men to alter and increase the Sum of the Bills.                          Is.<sup>a</sup> Addington, Secry."

"Sent down for Concurrance.

"In the House of Representatives.  Nov.<sup>r</sup> 26, 1706.  Read and concurr'd, with y.<sup>e</sup> amendments annex'd.                          Thomas Oakes, Spe.<sup>r</sup>

"In Council, Agreed."

# MARYLAND.

———•—•———

The charter of Maryland, which had been prepared for George, the first Lord Baltimore, not having been perfected, owing to some delays in the completion of the necessary formalities before his death, which occurred April 13th, 1632, it was, according to Ogilby, passed in favor of his son Cecil, the second Lord Baltimore, "under the Great Seal of England, bearing Date June 20, 1632. in the eighth Year of His said Majesties Reign, with all Royal Jurisdictions and Prerogatives, both Military and Civil in the said Province, as Power to Enact Laws, Power of pardoning all manner of Offences, Power to confer Honors, &c." It is probable that, although the power of coining money was not specified, Cecil considered the powers therein conveyed as ample to justify him in such a proceeding, especially as that power had been granted to Virginia in the terms of her patent of April 10th, 1606.

In relation to the coinage of Lord Baltimore, for Maryland, little is known in addition to the information furnished by S. F. Streeter, in his "Sketch" before referred to. We shall, therefore, upon the subject of this coinage, quote largely from that paper :

"The principal production of Maryland, as well as of Virginia, for a long period after their first settlement, was tobacco; and this also formed their principal article of currency. While settlers and servants were few in number, and the price of the article was high, there was but little difficulty; but as the population, and consequently the production, increased, and the value of tobacco suffered a marked diminution, the resources and comforts of the colonists were seriously abridged, and their progress impeded.    *    *    *

"Maryland, from the first period of her settlement, suffered similar difficulties, in reference to a circulating medium, to those experienced in Virginia. Indeed, the establishment of a new settlement engendered an additional competition, which tended to depress the value of tobacco, and thus made it less available than before as an article of currency. The amount of money, therefore, which found its way into the colony, or which remained there, was but small; the rents of land being payable in tobacco at a fixed value, and traffic for goods being carried on in the same article, or with such furs as were obtained by traders licensed to deal with the Indians.

"During one period of great distress and civil difficulty, his lordship's cattle were made to fulfil the office from which one of our terms indicating money is derived, and discharged a pecuniary obligation due to certain soldiers, who were somewhat mutinous on account of not receiving their pay; and in 1650, instead of a money tax, a levy of half a bushel of corn per poll was made upon the inhabitants of Ann Arundel, St. Mary's, and Kent counties, for the support of Governor William Stone. Powder and shot were also common articles of currency, and formed, as in Virginia, almost the only medium in which ship duties were paid; when, at the suggestion of some of the leading colonists, his lordship began to entertain the idea of providing a currency for his colony, which would greatly diminish the obstacles then existing in the way of trade, and, it was hoped, prove profitable to him, as well as advantageous to the colony.

"He accordingly had the dies prepared in London, and specimens of the coins which he proposed to put in circulation struck off, which, with letters to the governor and council, and to his brother, Philip Calvert, he despatched on the 12th of October, 1659. The nature of the communications will appear from the following extracts from the original records of the council: —

"'At a Councell held at Bushwood, Mr. Slyes howse, in St. Mary's County, on Saturday, the 3ᵈ of March, 1659–60.

"'Present, — The Gov. Josias Fendall, Esq.; Philip Calvert, Esq., Secretary; Thomas Gerrard, Esquier, Coll. John Price, Robert Clarke, Esqr., Col. Nathaniell Utye, Baker Brooke, Esqr., Doctor Luke Barber.

"'Then was read his L'd'ps Letter, directed to his Lieutenant and Councell, dated 12th of October, and directed to the Secretary, touching the Mint, as followeth, viz: —

"'After my hearty commendations, &c. Having with great paines and charge, procured Necessaries for a particular coyne to be currant in Maryland, a sample whereof, in a peece of a shilling, a sixpence, and a groate, I herewith send you, I recommend it to you to promote, all you can, the dispersing it, and by Proclamation to make currant within Maryland, for all payments upon contracts or causes happening or arising after a day to be by you limited in the said Proclamation: And to procure an act of Assembly for the punishing of such as shall counterfeit the said Coyne, or otherwise offend in that behalfe, according to the form of an act recommended by me last year to my Governour and Secretary; or as neere it as you can procure from the Assembly, and to give me your advice next year touching what you think best to be further done in that matter touching coyne; for, if encouradgemnt be given by the good success of it this yeare, there wilbe abundance of adventurers in it the next yeare.'

"With this communication was also forwarded the following letter to his brother Philip, then Secretary of State:

"'To my most affectionat loving brother, Philip Calvert, Esqr., at St. Mary's, in Maryland.

"'I sent a sample of the Maryland money, with directions for the procuring it to pass, because I understood by letters this yeare from the Governor and you and others that there was no doubt but the people there would accept of it, which if we find they do, there wilbe meanes found to supply you all there with money enough; but though it would be a very great advantage to the Colony that it should pass current there, and an utter discouradgment for the future supply of any more, if there be not a certain establishment this yeare, and assurance of its being vented and currant there, yet it must not be imposed upon the people but by a Lawe there made by their consents in a Generall Assembly, which I pray faile not to signify to the Governor and Councell there together from me, by showing them this Letter from

Your most affectionat Brother        C. BALTEMORE.
"'London, 12 October, 1659.'

"Ten days after the reception of his lordship's letters, and the discussion in council of the question of the best mode of introducing his new coinage among the people, Governor Fendall, with a part of the council, attempted to revolutionize the province, and, throwing off all dependence upon Lord Baltimore, to concentrate all power in themselves. They were probably incited to this by the unsettled state of affairs in England; but they soon found there was no hope of success, and were glad to give in their submission to the newly-restored king, and to Lord Baltimore as the lawful proprietary of the province.

"The confusion that followed this wild attempt of Fendall and his party, of course, rendered it impossible to carry out the proposed plan in reference to a specie currency. According to his Lordship's prudent and just instructions, the coins were not to be forced upon the people; on the contrary, he would not consent to their introduction, until the people, by their representatives, had not only expressed their assent, but had even invited their emission.

"Philip Calvert received his commission to act as governor, in November, 1660, and complied as promptly as possible with the wishes and instructions of his brother. In April following, an assembly was held in St. John's, and, at his instance, an act was drawn up and passed, 'for setting up a mint within the Province of Maryland.'"

There are preserved among the papers at Annapolis, Md., three draughts of the act referred to above, of which the two following are from certified copies; the other, being a repetition of the second of these, we omit.

"An Act concerning the setting up of a mint.

"Forasmuch as money being the rule & measure of y$^e$ value of Comodities, no trade or commerce can be well managed w$^{th}$out it. & the want of it in this Province is a main hinderance to y$^e$ advancement of this Colony in trades, Manufactures, Towns, & all other things w$^{ch}$ conduce to y$^e$ flourishing & happy Estate thereof, Wee the ffreemen of this Province Assembled in this present gen$^{all}$ Assembly doe humbly pray y$^e$ L$^d$ Prop$^r$ of this Province to take order for y$^e$ setting up of a mint for coyning of money w$^{th}$in this Province & consent that it may be enacted. And

"Be it enacted by y$^e$ L$^d$ Prop$^{ry}$ w$^{th}$ y$^e$ consent of the upper and Lower houses of this present gen$^{all}$ Assembly that y$^e$ money so coyned or w$^{ch}$ shall be coyned in the said mint shall be as good silver as the currant coyn of English sterling money. And that y$^e$ weight of every shilling so coyned as afores$^d$ shall weigh above nine pence in such silver as afores$^d$, & soe proportionably for other peeces of money coyned in said mint. And

"Be it further enacted that every offence of Clipping, scaling, Counterfeiting, washing or any way diminishing any Coyne soe to be made within this Province shall suffer pain of death, & forfeit his or her Lands, goods &

Chattles w^th^in this Province, to the Lord Prop^ry^ of this Province, & his heirs Lords & Prop^rs^ of the same.   And

"It is further enacted by y^e^ autho. afores^d^ that y^e^ L^d^ Prop^r^ & his heires Lords & prop^rs^ of this Province shall take & accept y^e^ s^d^ coyne in payment for his Rent, Arreares of rent, & all other engagem^ts^ due unto him y^e^ s^d^ Lord Prop^r^ & his heires Lords & Prop^rs^ of this Province, according to this Act."

"'An Act concerning the setting up of a mint within the Province of Maryland.

"'Forasmuch as money being the Rule and measure of the value of Comodities, noe trade or Comerce can be well managed without it, And the want of it in this Province is a main hinderance to the advancement of this Collony in trades, Manufactures, Townes, and all other things which Conduce to the flourishing and happy Estate thereof, Wee, the freemen of this Province Assembled in this present Generall Assembly doe humbly pray the Lord Proprietary of this Province to take order for the setting up of a mint for the Coyning of money within this Province, And Consent that it may be Enacted, And Be it Enacted by the Lord Proprietary, with the Consent of the upper and lower house of this present Generall Assembly, that the money soe Coyned, or which shall be coyned in the said mint, shall be as good silver as the Currant Coyne of English sterling money, And that the weight of every shilling soe coyned as aforesaid, shall weigh above nyne pence in such silver as aforesaid, and soe proportionably for other peeces of money Coyned in the said mint.   And bee it further Enacted that every offence of Clipping, Counterfeiting, scaling, washing, or any way diminishing any Coyne soe to bee made within this Province, or of wittingly importing into this Province any Coyne Counterfeiting any sort of Coyne which shall be made in the said mint, or that shall be by the Lord Proprietaryes Authority and the Authority of this present Assembly made Currant, shall be deemed and adjudged Fellony, And every offender thereof convicted according to the Law of this Province, shall suffer payne of death and forfeite his or her lands, goods and chattles within this Province, to the Lord Proprietary and his heires, Lords and Proprietaryes of this Province.   And itt is further Enacted by the Authority aforesaid that the Lord Proprietary and his heires, Lords and Proprietaryes of this Province, shall take and accept the said Coyne in payment for his rent, Arrears of Rent, and all other Engagements due unto him the said Lord Proprietary and his heires, Lords and Proprietaryes of this Province, according to this Act."   The foregoing act was passed May 1st, 1661.

"These proceedings were transmitted to the proprietary in England; upon the receipt of which he prepared to send to the colony a sufficient quantity of coin to supply its wants. The main object was now to throw a considerable amount at once into circulation; and to this end the aid of the Assembly was again invoked."

Bacon, in the Laws of Maryland, says, referring to an act passed April 12th, 1662, "This Act was to put the Coin (struck under the Act of 1661, ch. 4,) in Circulation; and enacted that every Householder and Freeman in the Province, should take up Ten Shillings per Poll of the said Money, for every Taxable under their Charge and Custody, and Paý for the same in good Casked Tobacco, at 2d. per Pound, to be paid upon Tender of the said Sums of Money, proportionably for every such respective Family, &c. For 3 Years, &c."

Of the last mentioned act no copy can now be found in the Archives at Annapolis.

"The effect of this measure was to cause a forced exchange of sixty pounds of tobacco by every tithable for ten shillings of the new coinage; and, as there were at least five thousand tithables then in the province, this act alone, if it were carried fully into effect, must have thrown into circulation coin to the amount of twenty-five hundred pounds sterling. It is probable that the new emission proved acceptable to the people, as it must have greatly facilitated exchanges; yet it by no means superseded tobacco as an article of currency. That still continued largely in use, especially in important transactions; and many of the public dues were still collected in tobacco, and not in coin. What was the amount of this new currency in circulation at any time after, we have no means of ascertaining, neither do we know when it began to be disused."

Ogilby states in his work[1] published in London, in 1671, speaking of Maryland, that "The general way of Traffick and Commerce there is chiefly by Barter, or Exchange of one Commodity for another; yet there wants not, besides English and other foraign Coyns, some of his Lordships own Coyn, as Groats, Sixpences, and Shillings, which his Lordship at his own Charge caus'd to be Cóyn'd and dispers'd throughout that Province; 'tis equal in fineness of Silver to English Sterling, being of the same Standard, but of somewhat less weight, and hath on the one side his Lordships Coat of

---

[1] "Description of the New World," p. 188.

Arms stamp'd, with this Motto circumscrib'd, *Crescite & Multiplicamini*, and on the other side his Lordships Effigies, circumscrib'd thus, *Cæcilius Dominus Terræ-Mariæ, &c.*"

Oldmixon, whose work was published in 1708,[1] says, "The Lord Proprietary had a Mint here, to coin Money, but it never was much made use of." * * * [2] "Tobacco is their Meat, Drink, Cloathing, and Money: Not but that they have both Spanish and English Money pretty plenty, which serves only for Pocket-Expences, and not for Trade, Tobacco being the Standard of that, as well with the Planters and others, as with the Merchants."

"From the title of the act of assembly of 1661, in Bacon's Laws of Maryland, some have inferred that a mint was established, and that the coinage was actually done in Maryland; but it appears more probable that the coins were struck in England, under the supervision of the lord proprietary, and transmitted to the governor, as circumstances made it necessary or convenient. The operation was a profitable one, inasmuch as the shilling contained but about seventy-five per cent. of its nominal value in silver, and was exchanged, in the first instance, for tobacco at the ordinary price.

"Specimens of this coinage, so interesting in the commercial and pecuniary history of Maryland, have been placed in the cabinet of the Maryland Historical Society, through the liberality of George Peabody, Esq., of London, one of its honorary members."

The fact of this coinage having been done in England is satisfactorily established by the action of the authorities, as recorded in the orders of the Council of State[3] in England.

"Tuesday, 4 Octobr, 1659.

"Ld Baltimore to be apprehended. Upon Information given by Richard Pight, Clerke of the Irons in the Mint, that Cicill Lord Baltamore and diverse others with him, and for him, have made and transported great Sums of mony and doe still goe on to make more,

"Ordered, That a warrant be issued forth to the said Richard Pight for the apprehending of the Lord Baltamore and such others as are suspected to be ingaged w^th him in the said offence, and for the seizeing of all such moneys, stamps, tooles, & Instrum^ts for Coyning the same as can be met w^th, and to bring them in safe Custody to the Counsell."

---

[1] Vol. i, p. 204.    [2] Ibid, p. 206.    [3] State Papers, London, vol. cvii, p. 646.

"Wednesday, 5 Octob<sup>r</sup>, 1659.[1]

"Ld Baltimore        The Councell being Informed that a great quantity of
to attend.           Silver is coyned into peeces of diverse rates & values,
and sent into Maryland by the Lo. Baltamore or his Order,

"Ordered, that the said Lo. Baltamore be Sumoned to attend the Comittee
of the Councell for Plantaçõns, who are to inquire into the whole business
and to report the State thereof to the Councell."

We have been unable to ascertain what action, if any, was taken upon
these orders.

The Maryland Shilling has upon the

OBVERSE,

Device — A bust of Lord Baltimore, to left, slightly draped.
Legend — CÆCILIVS : DÑS : TERRÆ-MARIÆ : &CT · ✤
Mint Mark — A cross patée or formée, — ✜

REVERSE.

Device — A lozenged shield, surmounted by a crown, and dividing the
numerals X   II
Legend — CRESCITE : ET : MVLTIPLICAMINI ·

Plate III, No. 1, and Fig. 25.

The Sixpence and Groat do not differ from the Shilling in any important
particulars, the most noticeable variation being in the legends, — those upon
the Sixpence being CÆCILIVS : DÑS : TERRÆ-MARIÆ : &C. ✤ and CRESCITE : ET :
MVLTIPLICAMINI

[Plate III, No. 2, and Fig. 26.]

Of the Groat we find two varieties. That most frequently met with has

---

[1] State Papers, London, vol. cvii, p. 653.

the head and shield larger than the other; its legends are CÆCILIVS: DN̅S: TERRÆ-MARIÆ. &c ✠ and CRESCITE : ET : MVLTIPLICAMINI · The other variety is extremely rare; its legends are CÆCILIVS: DN̅S: TERRÆ MARIÆ . &c ✠ and CRESCITE · ET · MVLTIPLICAMINI ·

[Plate III, Nos. 3 and 4.]

The numerals upon the Sixpence are VI, and on the Groat, IV. The punctuation marks upon the reverses of both the Sixpence and Groats are so light as to be almost imperceptible upon the plate.

The device upon the reverses of the silver coins of this series is the family coat-of-arms of Lord Baltimore.

The shield may properly be described as, Paly of six sable and argent, a bend counterchanged.

In the collection of Dr. Clay, of Manchester, England, was an impression in copper, from Shilling dies, which differed slightly from any we have seen in silver, the colon after MARIÆ being omitted. There are also in the British Museum impressions in copper both from Shilling and Sixpenny dies, but we have no knowledge as to their varieties.

A coinage of copper seems also to have been intended by Lord Baltimore, although we find no record referring to an issue of copper coin; but, if we may judge from the fact that but a single specimen is known of his coin in that metal, no large amount of it could have been put in circulation.

The obverse of the Penny is of the same design, and very similar to that of the Sixpence; the reverse bears, as a device, a ducal coronet, from which fly two pennants; its legend is DENARIVM : TERRÆ-MARIÆ ✠ [Fig. 27.]

Rev. Henry Christmas, of London, says of this piece, "The Maryland Penny was successively in the collections of Mr. Hodsol and of Mr. Martin; it is now no longer in this country, having been purchased at the sale of the last-named collection for the large sum of £75, and sent to America." It was in the celebrated collection of J. J. Mickley, Esq., of Philadelphia, and at the sale of that collection was purchased at $370 for an unknown buyer.

It may be seen that in the copy, [Plate III, Nos. 19 and 20,] striking errors appear in the legend, which there is CÆCILIVS : DNS : TERRÆ MARIÆ : &CT ✠

The borders of all these coins are milled, and their edges plain; the size of the Shilling is 17; the Sixpence, 13½; the Groat, 11, and the Penny, 13.

The weight of those in silver is respectively, 66, 34, and 25 grains. One specimen, however, of the Groat, in the collection of the writer, is upon a very thick planchet, and, although pierced and much defaced, bearing evidence of having been worn as an amulet, weighs 40 grains; this piece, we conclude, must have been struck as a trial piece in testing the dies.

Various acts for regulating the coin current in Maryland were passed and repealed between 1662 and 1694. The only one the terms of which are given by Bacon, is that here following, which was passed November 19th, 1686, and entitled "An Act for the Advancement of Coins."

"This Act sets forth in the Preamble, the great Want of ready Money, whereby the Trade of the Province, and Settlement of Handicrafts and Tradesmen therein was much impeded, and enacts:

"(1.) That New England Shillings and Sixpences shall pass as Sterling, (viz. at the Advance of 3$^d$ in each Shilling,) French Crowns, Pieces of Eight, and Rix Dollars, to pass at 6$^s$. Ducatoons at 7$^s$ 6$^d$, and all other Coins of Silver or Gold, foreign or not foreign, (except base Coin,) to be taken and received with the Advance of 3$^d$. Sterling, in the Value of 12$^d$. Sterling.

"(2.) All such Coins so advanced, to be received in all Payments contracted for in ready Money, or the Persons refusing so to accept thereof, to lose such Debt, never to be recovered in any Court, &c.

"(3.) Persons exporting such Coins so advanced, to forfeit the same, Half to his Lordship, and Half to the Informer.

"(4.) This Act not to affect his Lordship's Rents, &c., nor extend to protested Bills of Exchange.

"(5.) Officers Fees, and Ordinary Keepers Accommodations, to be payable in such Coin so advanced, at the rate of 6s. for every 100 lb. Tobacco, if tendered in ready Money: otherwise to be paid in Tobacco, as usual before this Act, &c."

The last act was "To endure 3 Years, or to the End of the next General Assembly," and another, with the same limitations, which settled the rates in the same manner as that, was passed June 9th, 1692, but repealed October 18th, 1694.

# CANADA.

————◄ ●•● ►————

Another series of coins struck for use in America, although not strictly included in our original plan, seems next to require notice.

These were coins of silver and copper, issued by Louis XIV. of France, in 1670, for circulation in Canada.

We are more fortunate in the existence of an authentic record of the authority by which these coins were issued, than in the preservation of the coins themselves, as we have met with but one denomination of the silver pieces, that of five sous, of which we have seen only two specimens, and these from dies very slightly differing. For the opportunity to illustrate it we are indebted to the kindness of Mr. William S. Appleton.

### OBVERSE.

Legend, — LVD · XIIII · D · G ◉ FR · ET · NAV · REX

Device, — Bust of the king, to right, laureated. Above the head, a small figure of the sun.

### REVERSE.

Legend, — GLORIAM · REGNI · V · TVI · DICENT · 1670 ℞

Following the date is an unknown character, resembling that given above.

Device, — The French coat-of-arms, crowned. Beneath the shield the Paris mint mark, A shown in the line of the legend, inverted.

Borders, milled; edge, plain; size, 13; weight, 35 grains.

[Plate III, No. 5.]

Although we find no genuine specimen of the copper coin of this series, we have been favored by M. Jules Marcou, of Cambridge, with a copy of one, which is represented on Plate III, No. 6.

### OBVERSE.

Device, — A large Roman L, dividing the date, 16  70   Above is a crown, and beneath, the Paris mint mark, A

Legend, — LVDOVICVS · XIIII · D · GR · FRAN · ET · NAV · REX

### REVERSE.

Inscription, in four lines, —  DOVBLE  DE · LA  MERIQVE ·  FRANCOISE
Under the legend is the mint mark, A with a fleur de lis at each side and one beneath it.

Borders milled; size, 14½.

We quote from The American Journal of Numismatics[1] an extract relating to these coins:

"'COLONIAL COINS OF COPPER. — AMERICA. — CANADA. — In Le Blanc's Historic Treatise on the Coins of France it is mentioned, on p. 304, that under Louis XIV.'s government were struck for Canada — which is well known to have once belonged to France, and not to have been ceded to England till 1763, — special coins, namely: in silver, fifteen-sous and five-sous pieces, recognizable by the inscription, GLORIAM REGNI TUI DICENT; and, of pure copper, Doubles, or pieces of Two Deniers, which bear the inscription DOUBLES DE L'AMERIQUE FRANCOISE. The silver pieces are of the year 1670, and familiar. Unknown, on the contrary, are the Doubles, and a more exact description of them would be highly interesting'.

"On page 388 of our edition of Le Blanc's 'Traité Historique des Monnoyes de France,' Paris, 1703, we read, 'In order to facilitate commerce in Canada, the king caused to be struck a hundred thousand livres' worth of Louis of 15 sous, and 5 sous, and Doubles of pure copper. These coins were of the same value, weight and fineness with those of France. On the silver Louis of 15 sous and 5 sous, in place of *Sit nomen Domini benedictum*, there was *Gloriam regni tui dicent;* and, on the Doubles, *Doubles de l'Amerique Francoise*'."

---

[1] Vol. iv. p. 65.

# THE "ST. PATRICK" OR "MARK NEWBY" HALFPENCE.

———◄•••►———

Upon the 19th of November, 1681, there arrived in New Jersey a party of emigrants from Dublin, Ireland, Mark Newby[1] and his family being among them. He brought with him a quantity of the pieces known as St. Patrick's half-pence, which, owing to the scarcity of small money there, were, in the ensuing May, made current in that State under certain conditions expressed in the act by which they were authorized. This act is found in the "Grants, Concessions and Original Constitutions of the Province of New-Jersey,"[2] under date of May 8th, 1682, and is as follows:

"Section VI.

"And for the more convenient Payment of small Sums,
"Be it Enacted by Authority aforesaid:

"That Mark Newbie's half-pence, called Patricks half-pence, shall, from and after the said Eighteenth Instant, pass for half-pence Current pay of this Province, provided he, the said Mark, give sufficient Security to the Speaker of this House, for the use of the General Assembly from Time to Time being, that he the said Mark, his Executors and Administrators, shall and will change the said half-pence for pay Equivalent, upon demand: and provided also, that no Person or Persons be hereby obliged to take more than five Shillings in one Payment."

The date and origin of these pieces are enveloped in mystery, and various

---

[1] "Newby lived on the farm in Newton since owned by Jos. B. Cooper, Esq., where many of the Patrick half-pence have been ploughed up."—*Mickle's New Gloucester.*    [2] Vol. iii, p. 445.

opinions have been expressed upon these points, which we will briefly mention, substantially as recorded by Dr. Aquilla Smith.[1]

Evelyn gave the first published account of them in 1697, thinking them Irish coins, referring probably to those struck in silver, as he described them among the silver medals of Charles II.

Thoresby next describes them, in 1715, placing them among the coins of Charles II., and he presumes that those in copper were originally current for half-pence and farthings.

Bishop Nicholson, in 1724, placed them among the coins of Charles I., stating that they "'are still common in Copper and Brass,' and 'are current for half-pence and farthings.'"

Leake makes mention of them, in 1726, with the opinion that they were struck in the time of Charles I., "'by the Papists, when they rebelled in Ireland, and massacred the Protestants'".

In Harris's edition of Sir James Ware's works, 1745, they are noticed as bearing the arms of the city of Dublin, and are assigned to the time of Charles II. It is also said here, "'John Putland, Esq., has among his curious Collections the two before-mentioned Pieces struck in Silver, no way differing but in the Metal, and that they are milled, which Copper Money never is; and this proves that they were struck in Silver for Medals, as Mr. Evelin thinks, and not as Proof Pieces.'"

Simon, 1749, considered them as coins of the rebels, struck about the year 1642, during the reign of Charles I., and says of the silver pieces, "'it is thought that they were struck as medals, but for my part I think they were struck upon the same occasion, and intended by the Kilkenny assembly to pass for shillings.'"

It is noticeable that Simon refers to but one size in silver, while Smith had both in that metal, and a proof in lead of the smaller size. One of the smaller pieces, somewhat worn, weighed 108 grains, and the larger, which was in the same condition, weighed 176½ grains. From these relative weights it is difficult to decide upon their intended value, if designed for coins.

Dr. Robert Cane concludes "'That it was minted upon the Continent for the use of the Confederate Assembly,' and 'was transmitted to Kilkenny to be there distributed.'" He proposed to call it the "'Rinunccini Confederate money,'" as it "'is in some parts of its design exceedingly in keeping with

---

[1] Proc. Kilkenny & S. E. Arch. Soc., 1854. See Am. Numis. Journal, vol. vii, pp. 9 and 25.

the opinions and sentiments of the Nuncio, Rinunccini.'" Dr. Cane states it as decidedly his opinion "'that they are foreign coins, and not coined in these kingdoms, but brought over by Rinunccini, for the use of the Confederate army.'"

Dr. Smith, after summing up the evidence of all the preceding, concludes that these pieces were private tokens, and "issued in Dublin at some time between the Restoration (1660) and the year 1680, when regal copper halfpence were coined for Ireland."

Not presuming to "decide where doctors disagree," we can only add, that, judging from the fact that Mark Newby brought with him, in 1681, a quantity of these tokens sufficient to call for an act to legalize their currency, it would appear that they must have been at that time of a comparatively recent issue.

The great number of varieties existing of these pieces, indicates that they must have been issued in considerable quantities. Of the large pieces in copper we find four obverse and six reverse dies.

This size we have never seen in silver.

### OBVERSE.

Device, — A crowned king, kneeling, facing left, and playing the harp. Above the harp is a crown in brass.

Legends, variously punctuated, —

| ···FLORE AT REX· | ··FLOREAT· ·✳· ·REX· |
| · FLOREAT · ··✳· ·REX· | ··FLOREAT ·✳· :REX· |

The letters of the third obverse legend, ··FLOREAT· ·✳· ·REX· are much smaller than any of the others.

### REVERSE.

Device, — St. Patrick, with a trefoil in his right hand and a crozier in his left, surrounded by a crowd of people. At his left is a shield charged with three castles, on some resembling six flaming altars.

Legends, —

| · ECCE GREX 2 | ECCE : GREX 1 |
| · ECCE · GREX 2 | : ECCE · GREX 1 |

[Plate III, Nos. 7 and 8.]

The figures following the legends indicate the number of dies of each variety.

Upon the smaller size we find twenty-two dies of the obverse, and twenty-three of the reverse, in copper, and two of each in silver.

The obverse of this piece is of a design similar to that of the larger, with legends, —

| | | | | | |
|---|---|---|---|---|---|
| FLOREAT | : REX | 1 | FLOREAT · : REX : | 1 |
| FLOREAT | REX : | 3 | FLOREAT : REX : · | 3 |
| FLOREAT | : REX : | 13 | FLOREAT ✶ REX ✶ ✶ ✶ | 1 |

Upon some specimens a bird, sometimes accompanied by three small circles, is found beneath the figure of the king.

The first example we have noticed only in silver, and the fifth in both silver and copper; all the others in copper only.

Upon the reverse is St. Patrick, with his right hand outstretched, as if driving away the serpents and reptiles represented beneath it, probably alluding to the belief, as expressed in an old Irish song, that

"He gave the snakes and toads a twist,
And banished all the varmint."

In his left hand he carries a double or metropolitan cross, and at the extreme right is a church.

The legends of the reverse vary thus, —

| | | | | |
|---|---|---|---|---|
| QVIESCAT PLEBS | 9 | QVIESCAT PLEBS : | 3 |
| QVIESCAT PLEBS · | 2 | QVIESCAT : PLEBS : | 1 |
| QVIESCAT · PLEBS . | 1 | QVIESCAT PLEBS : · | 2 |
| QVIESCAT · PLEBS · | 1 | QVIESCAT : PLEBS : · | 1 |
| QVIESCAT : PLEBS | 2 | QVIESCAT✶ PLEBS ✶ | 1 |

Of the reverses we have found the first in silver and copper, the third in silver only, and all others in copper only.

[Plate III, No. 9.]

Although it is said by Sir James Ware that the silver pieces differ from the copper, in being "milled, which Copper Money never is," it is necessary for us to state that we have seen none in either metal without milled edges.

In size the large pieces vary from 17 to 20, and the small are about 16.

The heaviest specimens we have weighed of the large, in copper, contain 144 grains ; the small copper, 98 grains, and the small silver, from 98 to 114 grains.

# PROPOSALS FOR COINAGE.

The scarcity of small coin in America at the end of the seventeenth and beginning of the eighteenth centuries, induced several schemes, ostensibly for the good of the colonies, but actually for the profit of the projectors. Of the first of these we know nothing beyond what we are told by Ruding,[1] which is this :

" 1700. On the 5th of July, in this year, the Board of Trade took into consideration the state of the coin in the plantations. A memorial by Mr. John Fysack was then read, proposing the erection of a mint in some of the plantations on the continent of America, as a means to remedy many inconveniences in the trade of those parts. And he being further heard in what he had to offer, their lordships, after full consideration of the matter, did not think fit that any mint should be erected there. But esteeming it generally convenient that all coins current in the plantations should pass in all places at one and the same rate, they resolved, in the first convenient opportunity, to consider the difficulties that occur therein, and in what manner it may be best effected; but I do not find that they proceeded any further."

Another plan was soon devised for supplying the want of small change, as shown by the two papers which follow. These were found by a search among the unarranged papers in one of the State Paper Offices in London, and include all known to us in relation to this project, which probably resulted

---

[1] Annals of the Coinage of Great Britain, vol. ii, p. 59.

in nothing at that time, although some of its features seem to have been adopted in Wood's patent, a few years later.

The first of these papers is endorsed,

"Proposalls to the Lords of the Treasury, relating to the Coining of small money in America.

"Cock Pit, Treasury Chambers, 21 May, 1701.

"from Samuel Davis to officers of ye Mint."

"To the Right Hon[ble] the Lords Commissioners of the Treasury.

"The humble proposall of Samuel Davis.

"The least piece of Money Comonly Current in the Islands and Colonys upon the Continent of America is Seven pense halfe penny, being an 8[t] part of a piece of Eight, which puts ye Inhabitants to ye necessity of Carrying Sugar and Tobacco upon their Backs to barter for little Comon Necessarys.

"This Inconveniency cannot be remedyed by Sending such farthings and half pence as are used in England, because they will be picked up and sent back for Returns, Especially from the Continent, where Returns of goods often fall Short, and 30 p Cent will be got by sending back such farthings and half pence, the value of English money being so much more than the value of American Money upon the Continent.

"The proper remedy is to Coin halfe pence and pence of Copper or a Mixed Metall, and of halfe ye value the English Small Money is made, with severall Mottoes or Devices for ye Severall Colonys, and to Order them to pass only in the respective Colonys for which they shall be Appointed, viz. one Sort for all the Colonys upon the Continent, another sort for the Island of Barbadoes, a 3[d] sort for Jamaica, and a 4th Sort for all the Leeward Islands.

"This Method will keep this Money within the respective Colonys, and otherwise they will be sent from the Continent to ye Islands, and hinder the Exportation of the Naturall product of the Continent to the Islands.

"If his Majesty will please to order the Coining such half pence and pence, and to enforce the passing of them by a proclamation, It will be a great accommodation to all the plantations, and be a grievance to no body.  The Proposer is ready to shew how the King may vent them presently to a profit that shall more then double the value of ye Charge, and humbly prays a Third part of the profit for his discovery.

"All which is most humbly submited to yo[r] Lord[ps]."

"To the Rt Honorable the Lords Commissioners of His Majesties Treasury.

"May it Please your Lordships

"In Obedience to your Lordships order of Reference Signified to us by Mr Lowndes, 21ˢᵗ May Last, upon the Proposall of Mr Samuel Davis for coining Small Money in the Plantations, Wee are humbly of Opinion that the Plantations in America are in great Want of Small Money, but that the coynage of it Should be made, as near as may be, to the intrinsick value which the Metall bears in the Severall Plantations, including the charge of Coynage; and that such Small Money be made of Coarse Copper, Such as the halfpence are coyned of here, that there may be less temptation to counterfeit it, And that the quantity necessary to be coyned be settled. As also that the pieces have different markes upon them to prevent their coming back into England as is mentioned In the said Proposall.

"All which is humbly Submitted to your Lordships great Wisdom by

J Stanley<br>Is Newton

"Mint Office the 9ᵗʰ July 1701." Jn Ellis.

A reference to another scheme of this kind is found in a letter to the General Court, from Jeremiah Dummer, who writes thus from Whitehall, April 5th, 1715:

"Sʳ My last to you for the General Court was by the Solebay Man-of-war, which I hope you have long before this time. In the mean while I have receiv'd the three instructions agreed on the last October Session, which I shall carefully observe. Onely that, which commands me to oppose any attempts that may be made here to incorporate a private Bank in New England, is what there will probably be no occasion to make use of. For the Gentlemen who have bin desir'd from Boston to Sollicit this buisness, have not yet mov'd in it, & I'm inform'd by one of 'em, that they don't design to Stirr in it at all. Some other people having heard of it, & of the Exigency which the Countrey was reduc't to for want of money, or some other medium of trade, have started a project for the coining base money here, (that is to Say, one third copper, and the rest silver) to pass in New England, which they pretend will answer all the necessities of trade, tho' in truth it will answer nothing but their own private gain, which they propose

---

[1]Archives, vol. li, pp. 273-4.

by it.  Upon the first notice I had of this project, I waited on Several of the Ministry in order to speak to 'em of the destructive consequences of it, if it Should take Effect, but their Lord^pps would not hear me upon it;  for they were so clear in it, that they assur'd me at once that no such thing should be done.

     \*   \*   \*   \*   \*   \*                    Your most Obed^t ser^t

Mr Secretary Addington.                                                  Jer: Dummer."

The scheme here alluded to must have met with the fate of its predecessor, as we find no reference to it elsewhere.

We find in Lyson's Environs of London this notice of Sir Alexander Cuming, who conceived a project for supplying coin for New England and Carolina, from England:

"S^r Alexander Comyns, Bar^t, pensioner in the Charter-house, buried Aug. 28, 1775.  He was son of Alexander Cuming, of Coulter, created a baronet in 1695.  \*   \*   \*   In 1729 he was induced by a dream of Lady Cuming's to undertake a voyage to America, for the purpose of visiting the Cherokee nations.  He left England on the 13^th of September, and arrived at Charles-Town on the 5th of December.  \*   \*   \*   Sir Alexander says, in his journal, that whilst he was in America in 1729 he found such injudicious notions of liberty prevail, as were inconsistant with any kind of government, particularly with their dependence on the British nation.  This suggested to him the idea of establishing banks in each of the provinces dependent on the British exchequer, and accountable to the British parliament, as the only means of securing the dependency of the colonies.  But it was not till 1748 (as it appears) that he laid his plans before the minister, who treated him as a visionary enthusiast, which his journal indeed most clearly indicates him to have been."

We have obtained from the State Paper Office, at London, a copy of his proposal, which here follows:

"To the Right Hon. Henry Pelham, Esq. etc.   The humble Memorial of Sir
Alexander Cuming, Bart. July 14, 1748, sheweth

"That in order to preserve the dependency of the British Plantations on great Britain their Mother Country, as being their natural and true interest, and as being the surest means to secure their rational liberties and properties against all invaders whatsoever, it is humbly proposed, that the current specie of great Britain may be made the current lawful money of the said Plantations, as the proper Measure of property in all countries depending on the British crown and nation.

"It is also humbly proposed, that 200,000l. sterling may be coined at the Tower of London for that purpose, to be lent upon good and sufficient securities in the said provinces, at the present legal interest there.

"It is also humbly proposed, that the said sum should be made the foundation of a provincial bank for all the British Plantations in America; that the said bank should issue out bank notes to the value of the said sum, and that the planters should be obliged to pay their quit-rents in such bank notes as are authorized by the British Exchequer for the said purpose; which notes, being payable by the said provincial bank in gold and silver specie on demand, cannot fall under any discount so long as the managers act agreeably to their several trusts.

"It is humbly conceived, that this regulation is requisite to abolish the paper money in New England and Carolina, and for setting aside the currency of the clipt Spanish money in Jamaica or elsewhere. And as altering or debasing the lawful money of this kingdom is truly high treason, and as the paper money of the above-mentioned provinces does really alter the value of what ought to be the current lawful money of these countries as subjects to the Crown of great Britain, so these regulations would remove many temptations they are now under to commit high treason."

The next proposal for a coinage for this country was for Carolina, and regarding this proposition all we can learn is the information given by Snelling, which we next quote:

"In 1754 a proposal was sent over here for approbation, from Arthur Dobbs, Esq., Governor of North Carolina, for to coin copper money for that colony, to consist of pieces of the value of two-pence, one penny, and an half penny of their currency, which was in proportion to that of England as four to three; the quantity proposed to be coined to be such as the Governor and Council of Carolina should think proper, but not to exceed 50 tons, they delivering the copper into the mint, paying all expenses and fees attending the coinage, and to have such a device on them as should be thought proper. His letter with the proposals were sent down from the Treasury, June 24, to the officers of the mint to consider of them, and give their opinion on the most proper method to put them in execution; in answer to which it was proposed, that one half of what should be coined should be in halfpence of such a size, that 61 pieces was to make 1 lb weight avoir. one fourth should

consist of two penny pieces, and the other fourth of penny pieces, of a pro-
portional weight to the halfpence, the remedy to be $\frac{1}{45}$ part of a lb. wt. avoir-
dupoize, and this not by design, but accident; to perform them at the same
price as those for Ireland, five-pence per lb. wt. for the master, and 20s. per
hund. to the deputy comptroller; the proportion as to the number of each
sort to be kept, as an increase in the number of halfpence, would increase
the expence, one side to have the king's effigies with GEORGIUS II. REX. on
the reverse the arms of North Carolina, inscribed, SEPT . CAROLINA, and under
it the date of the year; we apprehend it rested here, and was never put in
execution."

We find no reference to a coinage for Carolina in any of the records,
but another plan seems to have been devised for a supply of coin for that
State, if a paragraph in the Massachusetts Centinel, of October 18, 1786, may
be taken as evidence:

"Charleston, S. C., Sept. 29.

"Government has received information that Mr. Borel has compleated his
contract of coinage for this State, in Switzerland, and may be soon expected
here by the way of London.  The stipulation was for 30,000 l. in silver and
copper, to be exchanged for the paper medium."

If this contract was carried into effect the results thereof have entirely
disappeared, as no specimen traceable to that source is to be found in any of
our cabinets.

# THE ROSA AMERICANA SERIES.

The various plans for furnishing a small coinage for America appear to have culminated in the project of William Wood, who obtained patents, very similar in their terms, for coining "tokens" for America and Ireland, both patents bearing the same date, July 12, 1722. That for America appears to have taken precedence, as it is the one first recorded upon the Patent Rolls, it being "Pat. 8, Geo. I. part 4, No. 1;" that for Ireland, "Part 5, No. 5."

It is said that George I. was, upon his journey from Hamburg to England, previous to his coronation, accompanied by a German baroness, a frail beauty, who, having captivated that monarch, was raised to the peerage and favored with several titles, among which that of the "Duchess of Kendal" is the one best known to us. She possessed unbounded influence over the king, and as her favor was esteemed a sure means of gaining his, she was induced to espouse the cause of Wood in his application for the grant of his patents.

Coxe states that "the emoluments arising from the disposal of the patent for supplying Ireland with copper coin, were given by Sunderland to the duchess of Kendal, who sold it to Wood." We have no information as to whether the same disposition was made of the profits of the patent for America, but presume both to have been procured under similar circumstances.

Four pattern pieces of much interest, in our estimation, have recently for the first time been brought into notice in this country, which were, in all probability, made by William Wood, in or about the year 1717, with the design of their adoption in his American coinage. These are in a mixed metal, resembling Wood's metal, having a head of George I., with legend as upon the Rosa Americanas,—the letters D. G. omitted from the smaller or half-penny size.

It seems not unreasonable to believe that Wood must have been engaged in experiments in coining as early as 1717, the date of the twopenny piece, as his preparations must have been well forwarded at the time his patents were granted, or he would hardly have been able to strike so great a quantity of his coin in the first year of their existence, the year of their date being already half expired at the time of their issue.

It appears certain that these were patterns for his coinage for America, as they bear striking points of agreement with the design ordered by the patent for that coinage, although, as will be seen, this order was not final, but was followed by provisions by which it might be changed or a different design adopted; while they bear no resemblance either in weight, composition, or valuation, to any known coin of England or her dependencies, but agree in their valuation with the coins proposed for America, being evidently de-signed for twopenny, penny, and halfpenny pieces.

Snelling, in his "Miscellaneous Views," &c., in his remarks upon Wood's coinage, says, "We have a piece much like the penny in size, struck in the same metal, the head also nearly the same, inscribed, GEORGIUS D. G. [M: BRI:] FRA. ET HIB. REX. and on the reverse the figure I crowned between two laurel branches, inscribed, BRUN ET LUN DUX SA ROM MI ARC THE ET PR. ELEC." He expresses no opinion regarding it, but evidently considered it a piece belong-ing to America, and the production of William Wood. The letters in brackets and the punctuation marks were omitted by Snelling.

In the style of their workmanship and in their composition these patterns strongly resemble the Rosa Americana series.

The head of the king, as well as the legend upon the obverses of the larger pieces, is nearly the same with that upon the corresponding Rosas, and the effigies bear so strong a resemblance to those of that series as to leave no room for doubt that they were the work of the same artists.

In the metal of which they are composed may also be noticed a great similarity,—three of these being of the brassy composition frequently found in those; the other, mostly resembling copper, but with flecks of brass scat-tered through it,—a peculiarity met with, so far as our observation extends, only in coins of the Rosa Americana series.

# PLATE III.

THESE BELOW ARE COPIES

PLATED PATENT

Mr. Bushnell wrote of the largest of these pieces, (the others being then unknown in this country,) "This pattern is undoubtedly one of Wood's, and from its striking similarity to the Rosa Americana pieces, there is every reason to suppose it to be a rejected pattern for an American coinage. Besides this, there is no English coin to which it bears the least resemblance.

"The Halfpenny was the highest denomination of the copper coinage issued at that period for England; but as Twopences were coined for America, in brass, and as the pattern in question is of the same metal and workmanship, and having II to denote its value, I cannot imagine it to have been any thing else than a pattern for an American coin."

The largest has for its obverse a well-executed laureated head of George I., facing right, with the legend, GEORGIVS · D : G    M : B : FR : ET · H : REX. Reverse, the Roman numerals II surmounted by a crown, above which, in the circle of the legend, is the date, 1717 ·  Legend, MAG · BRIT · FRA · ET · HIBER · REX : ·   The legend is between two plain circles; the borders are milled, as are all the others.  Edge plain; size, 17½; weight, 107 grains.  Plate III, No. 10.

Two of the smaller size, 16½, bear obverses alike, having a head of the king, as in the preceding, but rather larger, and the legend, GEORGIVS · D : G : M : BRI : FRA : ET · HIB : REX ·

Reverse No. 1.  The Roman numeral I surmounted by a crown, and encircled by the legend, DAT · PACEM · ET · NOUAS · PREBET · ET · AUGET · OPES ·   Edge plain ; size, 16½ ; weight, 96 grains.  Plate III, No. 11.

Reverse No. 2.  Numeral, crowned as in the last, but having at each side a branch, the stems of which cross below.  Legend, BRVN : ET · LVN : DVX · SA : ROM : MI : ARC=THE : ET · PR : ELEC ·   Edge, plain; weight, 109 grains.

The last is that described by Snelling.  It is singular that this piece should weigh more than the larger one of double its value, but such is the case.  Plate III, No. 12.

The obverse of the smallest, size 13½, has the head of the king to right, with the legend, GEORGIVS · REX ·

Reverse, ½ under a crown.  Legend, · DAT · PACEM · ET · AUGET · OPES · Edge, plain ; size, 13½ ; weight, 72 grains.  Plate III, No. 13.

These pieces are all of the highest degree of rarity, no duplicate being known of either.  One other impression is known from the dies of that having branches upon the reverse, but it is in the composition resembling brass.

This set, with the exception of the piece in brass, last mentioned, is in the collection of the writer.  No other impression is known in any metal.

A slight digression from the subject of this chapter is necessary here, to introduce an issue of parchment money for small change, which, although not a coinage, approached as nearly to one as could well be devised in that material, and shows the conditions of trade, in Massachusetts at least, to have been such as would favor the introduction of coin of the denominations proposed by Wood.

We will present copies of the records[1] to relate the history of this parchment money:

June 15th, 1722. "In Council the Board, taking into Consideration the Great Inconvenience arising to the affairs, & Trade of the Province, for Want of Small Money for Change (the Copper half pence being Sent out of the Province) & thereupon, Ill Minded people have presumed to Splitt or tare, the New Small Bills of Credit of the Province, not withstanding the Proclamation to the Contrary, to the Great dishonour of the Government, & prejudice of the Province: Voted, that Penn Townsend, Thomas Hutchinson & Jonathan Belcher Esq[r], with Such as the Honb[le] House of Representatives shall Appoint, be a Committee, to think of & report to this Court what may be proper to be done in that affair; In the House of Representatives; Read & Concurred, & Voted that M[r] Clarke, M[r] Tay M[r] Chambers & M[r] Remington, be added to the Committee."

"Committees Report for makg. Small Bills."[2]

"In Obedience to the Order on the other Side, the Committee propose, that there be printed, in Parchment, to the Value of Five hundred pounds, of the Following Denomination Vizt.

| 40—001 | Penny Bills | - | - | - | - | £ 166 : 13 : 5 |
| 20—000 | Two penny Bills | - | - | - | 166 : 13 : 4 |
| 13—333 | Three penny Bills | - | - | - | 166 : 13 : 3 |
| | | | | | £ 500 : — : — |

"And that the Said Bills be delivered to the Treasurer of the Province, by him to be Exchanged for other Bills of this Province, to Such persons as Come for the Same, but not less at One Time than Twenty Shillings, and that there be an Act pass,d for their Being Accepted by the Treasurer and Receivers Subordinate to him, in all publick payments, as other the Bills of

---

[1] Court Records, vol. xi, p. 327 ; [2] Ibid, vol. xi, p. 343.

this Province are, and that the Five hundred pounds Exchanged for those Bills be burnt.

"All which is humbly Submitted.
" June 26ᵗʰ 1722.        By Order of the committee.

Penn Townsend.

" In Council, Read & Accepted, & Ordered that the Committee appointed to Consider of a Remedy for the want of Small Money for Change be desired to take Care of the Making & Imprinting the Small Bills, agreeable to their Report, and that they prepare the draught of a Bill accordingly.  In the House of Representatives Read and Concurred.

Consented to,        Samˡˡ Shute."

The following act was accordingly passed at the session of May, 1722 :
" Chap. V.
"An Act for Emitting Five Hundred Pounds in Small Bills of several Denominations, to be Exchanged for larger Bills by the Province Treasurer.

" Whereas great Inconveniences and Difficulties have arisen to the Affairs and Trade of this Province, for want of small Money for change :
For Remedy whereof :
" Be it Enacted by His Excellency the Governour, Council and Representatives in General Court Assembled, and by the Authority of the same, That there be forthwith Imprinted on Parchment, the sum of Five Hundred Pounds in Pennies, Two Pences and Three Pences of the following Figures and Inscriptions: viz. Forty Thousand and One Pennies, to be Round, Twenty Thousand Two Pences, Four Square, Thirteen Thousand Three Hundred and Thirty-three [Three] Pences, Sex-angular.

" And that the Committee already appointed by this Court for that purpose, are hereby Directed and Impowred to take Effectual Care for the Making and Imprinting the said Bills; and that the said Bills be delivered to the Treasurer of the Province, by him to be Exchanged for other Bills of this Province, to such persons as come for the same; but not less than Twenty Shillings at any one time; and that the said Bills be Accepted by the Treasurer and Receivers subordinate to him in all Public Payments, as other the Bills of this Province are, and that Five Hundred Pounds in Bills Exchanged by the Treasurer for these Bills, shall be burnt to Ashes by a Committee to be appointed for that purpose.

"And be it further Enacted by the Authority aforesaid, That whosoever shall presume to Forge, Counterfeit or Utter any Bill or Bills (knowing the same to be False and Counterfeit) of the Figures or Inscriptions of those mentioned in this Act, or any ways in Imitation thereof; or that shall Counsel, Advise, Procure or any ways Assist, in Forging, Counterfeiting, Imprinting or Stamping of any such false Bills: Every person and persons so offending being thereof Convicted, shall be Punished for the first Offence as in Case of Forgery, and for the second Offence as those that Counterfeit the other Bills of this Province." [1]

Illustrations of the intended bills were inserted in the act, in place of which we have given representations, copied from the bills actually issued. The cuts there given closely resemble these, with the exception of the ornamental borders, which are there omitted. We have supplied the word "Three", in brackets, it being evidently an omission in the original.

In returning to our subject, that which first claims our attention is the patent granted to William Wood, Esq., for coining "Tokens * * * to go for half pence pence and Two pences," of such an alloy "that a mass or peice of fine metal made of such mixture or Composicõn and weighing Twenty ounces Averdupoiz doth contain one penny weight Troy of fine virgin Silver ffifteen Ounces Averdupoiz of fine Brass, and the Remainder of the said peice of Twenty ounces Averdupoiz is made of the said double refined linck, otherwise called Tutanaigne or Spelter".

We have obtained copies of both of the Patents granted to Wood, which are still preserved in the State Paper Office in London: that referring to America being the only one of interest in this connection, we next present to our readers.

---

[1] Laws of Massachusetts, vol. i, p. 299.

Wm Wood Ar' Grant } This Indenture made the day of in the year of the Reign of our Sovereign Lord George by the Grace of God of Great Britain ffrance and Irēland king Defender of the ffaith &c Annoq Dñi one thousand seven hundred twenty two Between our said Sovereign Lord the king of the one part and William Wood of Wolverhampton in the County of Stafford Esquire of the other part Whereas our said Sovereigne lord hath received Information that Within his Majesties Islands Dominions and Territories in America there is a great Want of small money for making small payments to such as would voluntarily accept the same and that Retailers and others do suffer by reason of such Want and Whereas the said William Wood hath humbly represented to his Majestie that he the said William Wood hath Invented a certain Composicon or mixture consisting partly of fine virgin Silver partly of superfine Brass made of pure Copper and partly of double refined linck otherwise called Tutanaigne or Spelter so that a mass or peice of fine metal made of such mixture or Composicon and weighing Twenty ounces Averdupoiz doth contain one penny weight Troy of fine virgin Silver ffifteen Ounces Averdupoiz of fine Brass and the Remainder of the said peice of Twenty ounces Averdupoiz is made of the said double refined linck otherwise called Tutanaigne or Spelter A Standard peice whereof weighing Twenty Ounces Averdupoiz hath been humbly presented to his Majesty by the said William Wood in Order to be delivered to the Comptroller or king's clerk to be appointed as hereinafter menconed for trying the fine metal to be made for coynage of such moneys hereinafter prescribed and the small moneys to be made with the same metal And the said William Wood hath humbly proposed to his Majestie vpon the Terms and Condicons herein after expressed to make small moneys of such Composicon or Mixture as aforesaid for the Service of his Majesties Subjects in America who will voluntarily accept the same as aforesaid Now this Indenture Witnesseth That our said Sovereign Lord by virtue of his Prerogative Royal and of his Speciall Grace certain knowledge and meer mocon and in Consideracon of the Rents Covenants and agreements hereinafter contained and expressed on the part and behalfe of the said William Wood his Executors Administrators and Assignes to be paid done observed and performed hath given and Granted and by these presents for himselfe his heirs and Successors Doth Give and Grant unto the said William Wood his Executors Administrators and Assignes full free sole and absolute power Priviledge lycence and Authority That he the said William Wood his Exec-

utors Administrators and Assignes by himselfe or themselves or by his or
their Servants Workmen and Assignes (and no other Person or Persons whatsoever) shall and may from time to time during the Term of ffourteen yeares
to be reckoned and accounted from the ffeast of the Annuncia͂on of the
Blessed Virgin Mary one thousand seven hundred and twenty-two Coyne or
make and cause to be Coyned or made at his and their own proper Costs and
Charges at some publick and convenient Office Within his Majesties City of
London or the Suburbs of the same or such other place as shall be approved
by the Com̄issioners of his Majesties Treasury or high Treasurer for the time
being to be Provided from time to time by him the same William Wood his
Executors Administrators or Assignes any Number or Quantity of Tokens or
peices of such mixt metal or Composiͭon as is before described to go for half
pence pence and Two pences and to be from time to time after the coyning
thereof transported or carried into his Majesties Islands Dominions and Territories in America or some of them and may be uttered or dispersed there
and not elsewhere Provided allways that every such Office for Coyning such
halfpence pence and Two pences (before any such coyning therein) shall be
Notified by the said William Wood his Executors Administrators or Assigns
in the London Gazette and by a Writing to be openly affixed vpon the Royal
Exchange in London Provided also that the Whole Number or Quantity to be
Coyned by virtue of such his Majesties letters Patent do not exceed in the said
Whole Term the Quantity to be made of Three hundred Tunns of such mixt
metal or Composiͭon as before described Provided likewise that the Number
or Quantity (part of the said whole Quantity) do not exceed in the first four
years of the said Term the Quantity to be made of Two hundred Tunns of
such mixt Metal or Composiͭon as aforesaid and do not exceed for any one
year for the last Ten years of the said Term the Quantity to be made of Ten
Tons of the said mixt Metal or Composiͭon   And so as all the mixt Metal or
Composiͭon of Which the said half pence pence and two pences shall be made
do consist of such Ingredients and in such Proportions as are above described
and so as all the said halfpence and two pences be of such size and bigness
That Twenty ounces Averdupoiz Weight of such mixt Metal or Composiͭon
shall not be converted into more half pence pence or two pences than shall
make sixty pence by tale and so as all the said half pence Pence and Two
pences be made of equal Weight in themselves or as near thereunto as may be
being allowed a Remedy not exceeding one penny over or under in each Weight
of them holding Twenty Ounces Averdupoiz And so as the said Metal or

Composicõn for making the said half pence pence and Two pences be from time to time before the making thereof assayed and so as the half pence pence and Two pences be made therewith from time to time before the uttering the Coyned half pence pence and Two pences from such Office be assayed and tryed for their Weight and ffineness and an Account be taken of the Tale in the manner hereinafter prescribed And that he the said William Wood his Executors Administrators and Assigns shall and may at his and their own Wills and pleasures from time to time during the said Term after the said half pence pence and two pences shall have been so assayed and tryed for their Weight and ffineness and an Account taken of their Tale as aforesaid Transport and Convey or cause the same to be transported and Conveyed unto the said Islands Dominions or Territories belonging or to belong to his Majestie his heirs or successors in America or any of them and shall and may utter and disperse them to his and their best advantage and profit to pass and be received as Current money by such as shall be Willing to receive the same Within the said Islands Dominions and Territories or any of them and not elsewhere  And the said William Wood for himselfe his Executors Administrators and Assignes doth Covenant promise and Grant to and with our said Sovereign lord his heires and Successors by these presents That he the said William Wood his Executors Administrators and Assignes shall and will make the said half pence pence and Two pences of such fine Metal or Composicõn as aforesaid When the same shall be cast into Barrs or ffillets and which when heated red hot will spread thin under the hammer without Cracking and shall and will out of the same Coyn the said Two pences pence and half pence of such a bigness that thirty Two pences sixty pence and one hundred and twenty half pence may weigh sixteen ounces Averdupoiz being allowed a Remedy as aforesaid and shall and will when any Quantity of such money shall be Coyned permit and suffer such person or persons as the Commissioners of the Treasury of his Maisty his heires and Successors for the time being shall in Writing under their or his hands or hand from time to time or at any time or times Constitute and appoint to mix the same in an heap and to assay the same by Counting out Thirty Two pences Sixty pence or One hundred and Twenty half pence and there by to Estimate the value of the whole heap and of every part thereof according to its Weight and shall and will permit and suffer such person or persons to be appointed to assay such half pence and Two pences in fineness by taking some peices of the money heating them red hot and battering them to see if they will spread thin under the hammer and shall and will permit and suffer such Person or Persons as the said Commissioners of the Treasury or the high Treasurer for the time being shall by any Warrant or Warrants from time to time constitute and appoint to see the said mixed Metal or Composiƈon in Barrs or ffillets for making the said money from time to time and to keep an Account of the severall Parcels thereof and shall and will permit and suffer such Person or Persons to see the Assays performed and the money Weighed and to take one or more peices out of every parcell of money assayed to be kept in a Box under his or their key and a key of the said William Wood his Executors Administrators and Assignes to be tryed annually in Weight and fineness before whom the said Commissioners of the Treasury or the high Treasurer for the time being shall appoint  And it is hereby declared and agreed that the Person or Persons to be appointed as afforesaid for assaying or trying the said mixt metal or Composiƈon and the small moneys to be made thereof and taking the Tale of such monies shall be and be called the king's Clerk and Comptroller of the Coynage of the halfe pence pence and two pences to be Coyned for the Service of the Islands Dominions and Territories be- longing or to belong to his Majestie his heirs or Successors in America and may be impowered to Execute such Trust by himself or themselves his or their sufficient Deputy or Deputies from time to time  And the said William Wood for himselfe his Executors Administrators and Assignes Doth hereby Covenant and agree at his and their own proper Costs and Charges to allow and pay to such Comptroller for the time being a Salary after the rate of Two hundred pounds per Annum to be paid Quarterly at the four usual ffeasts in the year by equal porƈons during his continuance in the said Trust and to be Computed and paid by the day for any broken part of a Quarter in Which such Deputy or Deputies shall execute the same Trust Provided nevertheless That in Case the said Commissioners of the Treasury or the high Treasurer for the time being shall not constitute and appoint a Person or Persons to Assay and take Account of the said mixt Metal or Composiƈon or of the small monies to be made therewith as aforesaid or in case of the Death of such Person or Persons that shall be appointed The said William Wood his Executors Administrators or Assignes shall not be molested hin- dered or deprived of the benefit of making and coyning the said half pence and Two pences but shall and may proceed therein in manner aforemenƈoned So as the said William Wood his Executors Administrators or Assignes or his or their Agent or Agents make Oath if required of the Quantity and Goodness of the said halfe pence pence and Two pences and of the Metal or Composic͠on whereof the same shall have been made And it is his Majesties will and pleasure And he doth by these presents for himselfe his heires and Successors Grant and Authorize and appoint That the said halfe pence pence and Two pences of such mixt metal or Composic͠on as aforesaid shall and may be made and Coyned with Engines or Instruments having on the one side the Effigies or Portraiture With the name or Title of his Majestie his heires or Successors and on the other side the ffigure of a Crown With the Word America and the year of our lord and any other marks or Addi-c͠ons as may be proper or the said Engines or Instruments for Coyning the said half pence pence and Two pences may have any other Inscripc͠ons as by any Warrant or Warrants to be obtained under the Royal Sign Manual of his Majestie his heirs or Successors shall be allowed and approved And that the said half pence and Two pences being made and coyned as afore-said shall pass and be Generally vsed between Man and Man or between any persons that shall and will voluntarily and willingly and not otherwise pay and receive the same as Tokens or peices of and for the respective values of half pence pence and Two pences of money of Great Britain With the customary allowance for Exchange within the said Islands Dominions and Territories belonging or to belong to his Majestie his heires or Successors in America or any of them and not elsewhere And to the intent the said William Wood his Executors Administrators and Assignes may have and obtain the full benefit and profit intended vnto him and them by this present Grant his Majestie doth by these presents for himselfe his heires and Suc-cessors strictly prohibit and forbid all and every person and persons What-soever (other than the said William Wood his Executors Administrators and Assignes and his and their Servants Workmen and Assignes before menc͠oned) to make Coyne or Counterfeit such half pence Pence or Two pences of such mixt Metal or Composic͠on as aforesaid or of any other Metal or Composic͠on Whatsoever or to make or vse any Engines or Instruments for the making of any Two pences Pence or halfe pence to pass or go within his Majesties said Islands Dominions and Territories or any of them or to Import or bring into the said Islands Dominions or Territories or any of them from any his Majesties Dominions or from any fforeign parts to be vttered vended or dis-persed in the said Island Dominions and Territories or any of them any Two pences Pence or half pence or any Engines or Instruments for making of the same at any time or times during the said Term of fourteen yeares vnder pain of incurring his Majesties Displeasure and such Corporal Pecuniary or other Punishments as by law may be inflicted upon any such Person or Persons in such Case or Cases Offending  And his Majestie doth by these presents for himselfe his heires and Successors Give and Grant vnto the said William Wood his Executors Administrators and Assignes full power and Authority so far as his Majestie can lawfully Grant That the said William Wood his Executors Administrators or Assignes by himselfe or themselves or by his or their Deputy or Deputies for Whom he or they will be Answerable from time to time and at all times during the said Term Granted (taking a Constable or other Officer to his or their Assistance) and in the Day time shall or may enter into any Ship vessell house or other place Within the said Islands Dominions and Territories belonging or to belong to his Majestie his heires or Successors in America Where he or they may reasonably suspect that any Counterfeit half pence pence or Two pences are or shall be made or are or shall be brought or imported from any other of his Majesties Dominions or from any fforeign parts and by all lawfull Ways and means to search for the same and vpon finding of any such Counterfeit half pence pence or Two pences or any Tools or Instruments for making thereof to Arrest seize carry away detain and keep such Counterfeit half pence Pence and Two pences Instruments and Tools to the proper vse and behoofe of him the said William Wood his Executors Administrators and Assignes Without any Account to be therefore rendered to his Majestie his heires or Successors for the same To have hold Exercise and Enjoy all and Singular the aforesaid Powers liberties priviledges lycences Grants Authorities and other the premisses vnto the said William Wood his Executors Administrators and Assignes from the ffeast of the Annunciation of the Blessed Virgin Mary one thousand seven hundred Twenty two vnto the full end and Term of fourteen yeares from thence next Ensueing and fully to be compleat and ended yeilding and paying therefore And the said William Wood for himself his Executors Administrators and Assignes doth hereby Covenant promise and Grant to and with his Majestie his heires and Successors at the Receipt of the Exchequer of his Majestie his heires and Successors the yearly Rent or Sume of one hundred pounds (over and above the Comptrollers Salary before menc̃oned) at two of the most usual ffeasts or days of payment in the year that is to say at the ffeast of St. Michael the Archangel and the Annunciac̃on of the Blessed Virgin Mary by even and equal Porc̃ons The first payment thereof to begin and be made at the ffeast of Saint Michael the Archangel next ensueing the date hereof Provided always and these presents are and shall be vpon this express Condicõn That if it shall happen that the said yearly Rent or Sume of one hundred pounds to be behind and vnpaid in part or in the Whole by the space of Thirty days after any of the said ffeasts or Days of payment on which the same ought to be paid as aforesaid That then and from thenceforth it shall and may be lawfull to and for his Majestie his heires and Successors by any Instrument vnder his or their Royall Signe Manual to revoke determine and make void these presents and all and every the Powers benefits and Advantages thereby Granted to the said William Wood his Executors Administrators and Assignes any thing therein contained to the contrary notwithstanding And further his Majestie for the Consideracõns aforesaid hath Given and Granted And by these presents for himself his heires and Successors of his more Special Grace certain knowledge and meer mocõn Doth Give and Grant vnto the said William Wood his Executors Administrators and Assignes all such Profit Gains benefit Benefits Emoluments and Advantages as shall from time to time be made gotten obtained or raised by the making Issuing uttering or vending of the said half pence Pence and Two pences which during the said Term of fourteen years are hereby authorized to be made transported vttered vended and dispersed as aforesaid The same to be had taken and received by him the said William Wood his Executors Administrators and Assignes to his and their only vse and behoof Without any account or other matter or thing (other than the said yearly Sume of one hundred pounds to be therefore rendered to his Majesty his heires or Successors and other than the said Salary to be paid to the said Comptroller as aforesaid) And the said William Wood for himself his Executors Administrators and Assignes doth Covenant promise and Grant to and with his Majestie his heires and Successors by these presents That he the said William Wood his Executors Administrators and Assignes shall and will at his and their own proper Costs and Charges from time to time during the said Term in pursuance of the Powers Granted to him and them as aforesaid make and Coyn or Cause to be made and Coyned and Transported into the said Islands Dominions and Territories belonging or to belong to his Majestie his heires or Successors in America or some of them and to be vttered and vended there as aforesaid at or under the respective values as aforesaid such and so many Two pences pence and half pence of such mixt metal or Composicõn as aforesaid of the goodness and bigness and of the form before mencõned as shall be sufficient for the use and accomodacõn of the

Subiects of his Majestie his heires and Successors in those parts in and for the Change of their small moneys and in relaō̄n as their retailing Trade and other Com̄erce and business in Which the Subiects of the Crown of Great Britain there shall or may have occasion to vse them But not to exceed in any one year the Quantities before menō̄ned   And further That the said William Wood his Executors Administrators and Assignes shall and will from time to time in the making *the making* the said Two pences Pence and half pence in England and in Transporting the same from time to time to the said Islands Dominions or Territories in America or any of them and in vttering vending disposeing or dispersing the same there and in all his and their Doings Accounts concerning the same submit himselfe and themselves to the Inspecō̄n Examinaō̄n Order and Comptroll of his Majestie his heires and Successors and of his and their Com̄issioners of the Treasury and high Treasurer for the time being and of such Person or Persons as shall be appointed as afore said And our said Sovereign lord for himselfe his heires and Successors doth hereby Covenant promise and Grant to and with the said William Wood his Executors Administrators and Assignes That he the said William Wood his Executors Administrators and Assignes paying the Rent and performing the Covenants herein reserved and contained on his and their part and behalf to be paid done and performed shall and may peaceably and quietly have hold and enioy all the Powers Authorities Priviledges lycences Profits and Advantages and all other matters and things hereby Granted and every part thereof for and during the said term of fourteen years Without any let Suit Trouble Molestaō̄n or Denyal of his Majesty his heires or Successors or of or by any of his Majesties or their Officers or Ministers or any Person or Persons Claiming or to Claim any lawful Power or Right by from or under his Majesty his heires or Successors Provided always that if the said William Wood within six Months after the making hereof Doth not give good and sufficient Security to his Majestie his heires or Successors for the payment of the said yearly Rent hereby reserved and for the performance of all the Covenants Clauses and Agreements herein contained on his and their parts and behoof to be done and performed (Which Security is to be such as the Com̄issioners of the Treasury or any three or more of them or the high Treasurer for the time being of his Majestie his heires or Successors shall approve Then all and every the Grants hereby made to the said William Wood his Executors Administrators and Assigns shall cease determine and be vtterly void any thing herein contained to the contrary notwithstanding   And his Maiestie doth hereby for himselfe his heires and Successors Will Require and Covenant All and every the Governours Deputy Governours and all the Persons Who are or shall be entrusted With the Care or Administraçõn of the Government in all and every or any of the said Islands Dominions or Territories belonging or to belong to his Maiesties his heires or Successors in America and all Judges Justices and other Officers and Ministers Whatsoever of his Maiestie his heires or Successors in Great Britain or in the said Islands Dominions or Territories in America or elsewhere to be aiding and assisting to the said William Wood his Executors and Assignes in the Execuçõn of all or any of the Powers Authorities Direcçõns matters and things to be executed by him or them or for his or their benefit and Advantage by virtue or in Pursuance of these presents in all things as becometh In Witness &c whereof our selfe at Westminster the Twelfth day of July.

By Writt of Privy Seal".

In addition to the patent we find a paper entitled
"Mʳ Wood    Lycence.

"A Lycence unto William Wood of Wolverhampton in the county of Stafford Esqʳᵉ his Extᵒʳˢ Admʳˢ and Assigns to Coyn or make at his and their own propper Costs and charges at Some Publick Office within the City of London or Suberbs thereof or such other place as shall be approved by his Majᵗⁱᵉˢ Com̄issioners of the Treasury or High Trearer for the time being to be provided from time to time by the Said William Wood his Extʳˢ Admʳˢ or Assigns any Number or Quantity of Tokens or Pieces of a certain Mixt Metall or Composition as in the Bill Described to go for halfe-pence, Pence, and Two pences to be from time to time after the Coyning thereof Transported or Carryed into His Majᵗⁱᵉˢ Islands Dominions and Territories in America or Some of them, and to be uttered and Dispersed there, and not else where during the Terme of Fourteen years to Commence from Lady Day 1722 Under the Yearly Rent of £100 and paying a Yearly Sallary of £200 to His Majᵗⁱᵉˢ Comptroller during the Said Term Provided that every Such Office for Coyning Such halfe-pence Pence and Twopences (before any Such Coyning) be Notified by the Said William Wood his Extᵒʳˢ Admʳˢ or Assigns in the London Gazette and by a Writing to be openly affixed upon the Royal Exchange in London. And also that the whole Number or Quantity to be Coyned by Virtue of this His Majᵗⁱᵉˢ Lycence do not exceed in the said whole Term the Quantity to be made of 300 Tons of the said mixt metal or composition and such other Provisoes et in Oibus ut ante."

We have caused search to be made in the files of the London Gazette for the notice required by the license to be published, but no such notice is there to be found. All we can learn as to the place of their coinage is the mention made by Snelling, who wrote thus : "We have also been informed that Kingsmill Eyres, Esq ; Mr. Marsland, a Hardwareman in Cornhill, and several others were concerned in the scheme, the last mentioned person had great quantities of them in his cellar, was ruined by it, and died housekeeper at Gresham College, the dyes were engraved by Mr. Lammas, Mr. Standbroke, and Mr. Harold, some of which were in the possession of Mr. Winthorpe, who went to New-York, his father lies buried at Beckingham ; they were struck at the French Change, in Hogg Lane, Seven Dials, by an engine that raised and let fall an heavy weight upon them when made hot, which is the most expeditious way of striking Bath metal, which was the sort of metal they were made of."

Sir Isaac Newton was the comptroller first appointed, but afterwards his nephew, Mr. Barton, was, at his request, appointed in his stead. This was for the inspection of his Irish coinage, but it is supposed that the same officers performed the duties of that office for that for America also.

Immediately upon the appearance of Wood's coin in Ireland, great objections were raised to it, and soon appeals were made to the king to protect the people from the dangerous results feared from it.

Lord Walpole, in a letter to Lord Townsend, in October, 1723, says of Lord Carteret, "He slurs the duke of Grafton, he flings dirt upon me, who pass'd the patent, and makes somebody (probably the Duchess of Kendal,) uneasy, for whose sake it was done."

So great a disturbance was created on account of this coin, Dean Swift being a leading spirit in arousing and keeping active the discontent of the people, that the king reduced the amount to be coined from £100,000 to £40,000 ; but the clamor not subsiding, Wood was induced, in 1725, to surrender his patent in consideration of a pension, to which we find the following reference by Sir Robert Walpole, in a letter to Lord Townsend :

" (London, October 12—21, 1725.)

"His majesty, before he left England, signed a warrant for granting a pension of 3,000 *l.* per annum, on the establishment of Ireland, to Thomas Uvedale, esq. which was to him in trust for Mr. Wood, for the surrender of his patent. That warrant is still in my hands, and is not to be given out till all difficulties in the parliament of Ireland are over. Mr. Wood has now been with me, to desire that the pension of 3,000 *l.* per annum to Mr. Uvedale, may be turned into three pensions of 1,000 *l.* per annum, for the same number of years, which he desires, for the greater conveniency of disposing of it to the best advantage, finding it very difficult, and almost impracticable to part with the whole in one sum, which being divided into three parts, may be easily had. I therefore send your lordship three warrants of 1,000 *l.* per annum, each for eight years, which I desire your lordship will present to his majesty to be signed; and upon the return of them, I will cancel the former warrants, and keep these in my custody, until it shall be proper to give them out."

These pieces have usually been known as the Penny, Halfpenny, and Farthing ; but as the patent designates "two pence pence and half pence", as the value of the pieces to be issued, we take that as our authority for deviating from the common nomenclature.

### ROSA AMERICANA TWOPENCE OF 1722.

#### OBVERSE.

Device, — Head of George I. to right, laureated.

Legend, — GEORGIUS · D : G : MAG : BRI : FRA : ET · HIB : REX ·

#### REVERSE.

Device, — A full double rose, from which project five barbs.

Legend, — · ROSA · AMERICANA · 1722 · in the superior half of the field; and upon a label beneath the rose, UTILE · DULCI

Size, 20; weight, 255 grains.

[Plate IV, No. 1.]

### PENNY.

#### OBVERSE.

Device, — Head of George I. to right, laureated.

Legend, — GEORGIUS · DEI · GRATIA · REX ·

#### REVERSE.

Device, — A full double rose, from which project five barbs.

Legend, — ROSA · AMERICANA · UTILE · DULCI · 1722 ❊ This legend encircles the piece.

Size, 16 to 18; weight, 139 grains.

[Plate IV, Nos. 2, 3, 4, and 5.]

## HALFPENNY.

Same devices and legends with the Penny, but with some variations which will be noted. Size, 13 to 14 ; weight, 75 grains.

[Plate IV, Nos. 6, 7, and 8.]

Of the Twopence with rose uncrowned we find four varieties, two of which are without date. The legends upon these dateless varieties are GEORGIVS · D : G : MAG : BRI : FRA : ET · HIB : REX Reverse: · ROSA · AMERICANA · · UTILE · DULCI · and GEORGIVS · D : G : MAG : BRI : FRA : ET · HIB : REX · Reverse : · ROSA · AMERICANA · UTILE · DULCI These pieces are respectively, size 14, weighing 270 grains, and size 20, weighing 244 grains.

[Plate III, Nos. 14 and 15.]

The first of these is the unique specimen known as the "Iron Rosa Americana." Why it is called "iron" we cannot divine, as it is clear copper. The most striking feature of this piece, aside from its size and the rudeness of its impression, (it apparently having been struck as a trial piece,) is that the motto, · UTILE · DULCI · is upon the field, and not upon a label, as is usual.

We find, also, two varieties of the Twopence of 1722, with legends, — GEORGIUS · D : G : MAG : BRI : FRA : ET · HIB : REX and GEORGIUS · D : G : MAG : BRI : FRA : ET · HIB : REX · The reverses of these are from different dies, both punctuated as already specified.

Of the Penny there are many dies, differing so slightly as to be difficult to describe. The principal varieties may be recognized by their legends and punctuations. The most marked variety is GEORGIVS · DEI · GRATIA · REX · Reverse : ROSA · AMERICANA ❋ VTILE · DVLCI · 1722 ❋ This reverse has also the obverse GEORGIUS · DEI · GRATIA · REX · upon two dies, in one of which the letter G is under the lower lock of hair ; in the other, the letter E occupies that position. Other less marked varieties are,

1 — GEORGIUS · DEI · GRATIA · REX ·
      Reverse : ROSA · AMERICANA · UTILE · DULCI · 1722 ·
2 — GEORGIUS · DEI · GRATIA · REX ·
      Reverse : ROSA · AMERICANA · UTILE · DULCI · 1722 ❋
3 — GEORGIUS · DEI · GRATIA · REX
      Reverse : ROSA · AMERICANA ❋ UTILE · DULCI · 1722 ❋
4 — GEORGIUS · DEI · GRATIA · REX
      Reverse : ROSA · AMERICANA ❋ UTILE · DULCI · 1722 ❋

# PLATE IV.

Of these we find but one pair of dies each of Nos. 1 and 3, specimens from which are very rarely met.with. Of Nos. 2 and 4 we find impressions from about a dozen pairs of dies of each, and they are of nearly equal rarity.

The varieties of the Halfpenny are,

1 — GEORGIUS · DEI · GRATIA · REX ·

Reverse : ROSA · AMERI : VTILE · DVLCI · 1722 ·

2 — GEORGIUS · D : G : REX ·

Reverse : ROSA · AMERI : UTILE · DULCI · 1722 ·

3 — GEORGIUS · DEI · GRATIA · REX ·

Reverse : ROSA · AMERICANA · UTILE · DULCI · 1722 *

Of Nos. 1 and 2 we find one pair of dies of each, both rare, — No. 1 especially so, — and of No. 3 six pairs.

ROSA AMERICANA TWOPENCE OF 1723.

OBVERSE.

Device, — Head of George I. to right, laureated.

Legend, — GEORGIUS · D : G : MAG : BRI : FRA : ET · HIB : REX ·

Size, 19 to 21; weight, 220 grains.

REVERSE.

Device, — A full double rose with barbs, surmounted by a crown.

Legend, — ROSA · AMERICANA · 1723 · in the superior half of the field; and upon a label beneath the rose, UTILE · DULCI

[Plate IV, Nos. 9 and 10.]

PENNY.

OBVERSE.

Device, — Head of George I. to right, laureated.

Legend, — GEORGIUS · DEI · GRATIA · REX ·

REVERSE.

Device, — A full double rose with barbs, surmounted by a crown.

Legend, — ROSA · AMERICANA · 1723 and upon a label beneath the rose, UTILE · DULCI This legend nearly encircles the device.

Size, 16 to 18; weight, 148 grains.

[Plate IV, Nos. 11 and 12.]

We have one specimen, probably a trial piece, measuring $20\frac{1}{2}$, and weighing 185 grains.

### HALFPENNY.

This is usually found with the same devices and legends with the Penny, and in four slightly differing pairs of dies, all quite scarce. Size, 14 ; weight, 64 grains.

[Plate IV, No. 14.]

An extremely rare variety of the Halfpenny is that of 1723 with rose uncrowned, as on those of 1722. Of this we find one obverse and two reverse dies. Its legends are GEORGIUS · DEI · GRATIA · REX · Reverse: ROSA · AMERI-CANA ✸ UTILE · DULCI · 1723 ✸ Size, 14 ; weight, 51 grains.

[Plate IV, No. 13.]

It should be stated that the words UTILE DULCI are never found upon a label on the uncrowned Pennies or Halfpennies.

The varieties in the legends of the Twopence of 1723 are,

1 — GEORGIUS · D : G : MAG : BRI : FRA : ET · HIB : REX

Reverse : ROSA · AMERICANA · 1723    UTILE · DULCI

2 — GEORGIUS · D : G : MAG : BRI : FRA : ET · HIB : REX

Reverse : ROSA · AMERICANA · 1723 · UTILE · DULCI

3 — GEORGIUS · D: G : MAG: BRI : FRA : ET · HIB : REX ·

Reverse : ROSA · AMERICANA · 1723    UTILE · DULCI

Of Nos. 1 and 2 we find one pair of dies each, No. 2 being very rare. Of No. 3, eight pairs.

We have noticed no difference in the punctuation of the dies of the Penny, of which we find impressions from twenty pairs, or in that of the Halfpenny. The difference in the positions of the points we have not considered sufficient to specify as denoting varieties.

The Penny is found, but very rarely, with the date of 1724, it being similar in design to that of 1723. Two varieties of it are known, which are,

1 — GEORGIUS · DEI · GRATIA · REX

Reverse : ROSA : AME    RICANA · 1724    UTILE · DULCI

2 — GEORGIUS · DEI · GRATIA · REX ·

Reverse : ROSA : AME    RICANA · 1724    UTILE · DULCI

The cross upon the crown divides the legend between E and R, as indicated. One owned by Mr. Bushnell is of copper. Size, 18; weight, 125 grains.

[Plate IV, No. 15.]

The weights here given are from the heaviest specimens we have found.

The figure 1 upon all the preceding issues resembles the letter **J.** The borders of all are beaded, and their edges plain.

Wood's coinage for America seems to have received his earliest attention, as coins of that series, with the date of 1722, are very much more common than are those dated 1723 ; while the rarity of the dates of the Irish pieces is the reverse of this, these coins with the former date being extremely scarce, while those of 1723 are quite common.

Dr. Clay writes of the pieces without date, "I feel convinced that this dateless type preceded the dated types; if so, the Rosa Americanas will have to be considered as preceding the 'Wood' money, both in design as well as issue in the American States. This appears the more evident from the fact that the second type of Rosa Americanas bears a date quite as early as the earliest 'Wood' money. Ruding makes a great mistake on this subject by asserting that the dates of the Rosa Americanas are 1720 and 1722, whereas the real dates are 1722, 1723, and 1733, unless he means to prove that there was a mintage of these coins in 1720, but which does not satisfactorily appear unless we suppose (and it is not improbable,) that the pieces bearing *no date at all* might have been minted in 1720 ; if so, the priority of the Rosa Americanas over those called 'Wood' money would be fairly established."

Swift says in his third Drapier's Letter, "He (Wood) hath already tryed his Faculty in New England, and I hope he will meet at least with an Equal Reception here ; what That was I leave to publick Intelligence."

The author of a pamphlet entitled "A defence of the conduct of the people of Ireland in their unanimous refusal of Mr Wood's Copper Money," says, "Mr Wood obtained a Patent for Coining small Money for the English Plantations, in pursuance of which, he had the Conscience to make Thirteen Shillings out of a Pound of Brass. This Money they rejected in a Manner not so decent as that of Ireland. But he has never called it Popular Fury, and we hear Nothing of the Patent it self. Our Traders suffered prodigiously, and for a long Time by our former Coinage of Copper. For it is not here as in England where if they be overstocked with Halfpence, it is only sending them to the English Plantations, where they pass for Pence. Halfpence there are a good Commodity. We had this Trade once, which freed us from the Load of Copper Money which we laboured under. But that Trade is now over, for our Halfpence will not pass above their Intrinsick Value in the Plantations."

We learn no particulars in confirmation of the above statement regarding the reception of Wood's coinage in America, although we have no reason to suppose it a success as a speculation.

Although Wood surrendered his right to coin tokens for Ireland, it does not appear that he at once discontinued his efforts to introduce them here, as we find in the Massachusetts Archives, [Vol. 52, p. 305,] the following letter from the Duke of Newcastle :

"Sir                                          "Whitehall 29ᵗʰ Octʳ 1725.

His Majesty having been pleased to grant to Mʳ William Wood his Letters Patents for the Coyning of Halfpence, pence and Two Pences of the Value of Money of Great Britain for the Use of His Majᵗʸˢ Dominions in America, which said Coyn is to receive such additional Value as shall be reasonable and agreeable to the customary allowance of Exchange in the several parts of those His Majᵗʸˢ Dominions, as you will see more at large by a Copy of the Patent, which will be laid before you by the person, that delivers this Letter to you ; I am to signify to you His Majᵗʸˢ pleasure, that, in pursuance of a Clause in the said Patent by which all His Majᵗʸˢ Officers are to be aiding & assisting to Mʳ Wood in the due Execution of what is therein directed and in the legal Exercise of the several Powers and Enjoyment of the Privileges and Advantages thereby granted to him, you give him all due Encouragement and assistance, and that you and all such other of His Majᵗʸˢ Officers there, whom it may concern, do readily perform all legal Acts, that may be requisite for that purpose ; This I am particularly to recommend to your Care ; and to desire your Protection to Mʳ Wood and to those he shall employ to transact this affair in the Provinces under your Government.   I am

                              Sir
                         Your most humble Servant
                                   Holles Newcastle.

" Govʳ of the Massachusets Bay
and New Hampshire."

The only early reference we find to the Twopence of 1733, is that of Snelling, who says, " We never heard of any proposals made about the year 1733, for an American Coinage; however, No. 28 has the appearance of a pattern piece for some such scheme; it has the king's head laureat, inscribed, GEORGIUS II . D . G . REX . and on the reverse a leafed rose crowned, inscribed, ROSA AMERICANA 1733 — UTILE DULCI.   The only piece we know of, is in the collection of Thomas Hollis, Esq; we have also seen a proof of the head in steel, said to be struck on that metal to shew how malleable they could make it by smelting it with pit coal, by a scheme then on foot."

It seems unnecessary to seek far for the origin of this piece, as it is reasonable to suppose that Wood, the term of whose patent was unexpired, still entertained hopes of reaping some advantage from it, and intended to throw another issue into circulation; but, judging from its extreme rarity, only a very small quantity could have been struck, probably no more than a few patterns.

### THE TWOPENCE OF 1733.

#### OBVERSE.

Device, — Head of George II. to left, laureated.

Legend, — GEORGIVS · II · D · G · REX ·

#### REVERSE.

Device, — A rose branch, bearing at its top a full-blown rose, a stem at the left bearing four leaves, another at the right three leaves and a bud.

Legend,—ROSA · AMER ICANA · 1733 · The motto, UTILE DULCI · is upon a scroll-like label, beneath the rose. The crown divides the word Americana, as indicated. Size, 21; Weight, 266 grains.

[Plate IV, No. 16.]

The only specimen we have seen is in the collection of the writer; another, as well as an obverse in steel, is said to be in the British Museum. Two other impressions of the obverse, in steel, are known.

### THE ROSA : SINE : SPINA.

We insert this piece, not because we consider it as strictly belonging to this series, but because it has been confounded with the Twopence of 1733, to the reverse of which it bears some resemblance.

A piece is engraved on the second additional plate to Simon, [No. 28,] the obverse of which is nearly identical with this, its reverse having for device, a sceptre and trident crossed, interlaced with a three-looped cord, with tassels pendant; legend, REGIT ❂ VNVS ❂ VTROQVE ❂ 1724 ❂ also one of half the size and of the same description. These are there called "a sort of jettons". But a single specimen of one of these pieces has come to our knowledge; this is one of the larger size, in the collection of William S. Appleton. Its size is $17\frac{1}{2}$; weight, 127 grains.

A medal is represented on plate IX of "Thirty Three plates of English Medals By the late Mr. Thomas Snelling", the reverse of which has the same device and legend with that last described : its date is 1628. Another reverse much resembling it is given upon the same plate.

The Rosa Sine Spina doubtless belongs to the same class of pieces with those described by Simon, and both designs may have been intended as patterns, but of this there is no evidence.

OBVERSE.

Device, — Head of George I. to right, laureated.
Legend, — GEORGIUS · DEI · GRATIA · REX ·

REVERSE.

Device, — A rose bush springing from the ground, bearing at its top a full-blown rose, below which are two stems, each bearing a closed bud, and a bud half opened.
Legend, — ROSA : SINE : SPINA ·
Size, 16½ ; Weight, 120 grains.
We have been favored by Matthew A. Stickney, Esq., of Salem, with the use of the specimen in his cabinet, for illustration.

[Plate III, No. 16.]

This piece is eagerly sought by collectors of American coins, but is met with in very few cabinets. Of the only specimens we have seen beside the one mentioned above, one is in the collection of Chas. I. Bushnell, Esq., and the ownership of the other is unknown to us.

# PENNSYLVANIA.

———◆·◆———

Pennsylvania passed no act authorizing a coinage, but as some early action occurs regulating the circulation of copper coin in this State, as well as a petition to the State authorities for the privilege of coining, we next give it a place.

We find in Watson's Annals of Philadelphia, the following paragraph: "18 June 1741.—C. Hasel, Mayor. The Board having taken into Consideration the Currency of the English Half pence and the Disquiet that is among the Inhabitants, occasioned by some persons refusing to take them, thought proper that a Declaration should be made publick by the Board, that the sd halfpence shd be taken at fifteen to the shilling, which is adjudged to be nearest to such value, as might discourage too great a quantity being Imported, and at the same time prevent their being carried away, and a Proclamation for that purpose was ordered to be drawn, and that the same should be published in the City by the Beadle."

We are indebted to Dr. Edward Maris, of Philadelphia, for our copy of the action here referred to, as well as for the order prohibiting halfpence of base metal, soon to be given.

From the Pennsylvania Gazette, June 18, 1741. "Printed by B. Franklin, Postmaster, at the New Printing Office near the Market."

" *By the Mayor and Commonalty of the City of* Philadelphia.

"WHEREAS the Currency of English Half-pence in this Province, has long been found convenient for the Use of the Inhabitants, for small Change;

but the Value or Rate at which they should pass not having been settled by any Authority, they have been often received at too high a Value, by Reason whereof great Quantities of Half-pence were imported from the Neighboring Colonies, and exchanged for our Gold and Silver.

"And whereas at a late General Meeting of the Merchants and others, it was agreed that the said Half-pence should be received at Fifteen for One Shilling, current Money of this Province, which was judged to be the nearest to such a Value as might discourage too great a Quantity being imported, and at the same Time prevent their being carried away.

"And Whereas some uneasy and ill-disposed Persons, without any Authority or Consent of the trading Part of the Province, are now endeavouring to lessen the Value or Rate at which the said Half-pence were lately agreed to pass ; which tends very much to interrupt the Trade of the Province, and to breed Disquiet among the Inhabitants: And the Mayor and Commonalty having taken the same into their Consideration, and being willing, as far as they may, to prevent the Inconveniencies that may happen by Reason of such a Proceeding; *Do declare*, That until the Value or Rate at which English Half-pence were lately agreed to pass, be alter'd by some lawful Authority, or general Agreement among the trading Persons and Inhabitants of the Province, any Person or Persons who shall refuse to receive English Half-pence in small Payments, at the Rate of Fifteen English Half-pence for One Shilling, ought to be deemed a Disturber of the Publick Peace of the Province.

"*Philadelphia, June* 18, 1741."

The next action of this State appertaining to our subject was an act against counterfeiting, passed on the 21st of February, 1767, and found in the book of laws, at date.

"And be it further enacted, That if any person or persons within this province, after the publication of this act, shall falsly forge and counterfeit any coin of gold or silver, which now is or shall be passing, or in circulation, in this province, every such person or persons so offending, and being thereof lawfully convicted, shall suffer death, without the benefit of clergy; and every person or persons, who shall pay, or tender in payment, any such forged and counterfeited coin of gold or silver, knowing the same to be so forged and counterfeited, and being thereof legally convicted in any court of record in this province, such person or persons shall be sentenced to the pillory[1] for the space of one hour, and to have both his or her ears cut off, and nailed to the pillory, and be publickly whipped, on his or her bare back, with twenty-one lashes, well laid on; and, moreover, every such offender shall forfeit the sum of one hundred pounds, lawful money of this province, one half to the use of the Governor, and the other half to the discoverer, with costs and charges of prosecution."

We have found nothing more of interest in the records of Pennsylvania, until 1781, when an order was passed for the purpose of suppressing the quantity of base halfpence with which the State was flooded, as indicated by the following order of Council.

PILLORY.

[1] It is not our intention to give all acts relating to counterfeiting, but we have inserted this as an example of the severity with which such offences, and indeed many of much less enormity, were punished in olden times. An instance of the use of the pillory in 1679, is thus recorded in Drake's History of Boston, p. 437.

"Peter Lorphelin, a Frenchman, was accused of uttering 'rash and insulting speeches in the time of the late conflagration, thereby rendering himself justly suspicious of having a hand therein, was seized and committed to the Goale in Boston;' his chest and writings were examined. In his chest were found two or three 'crusables, a melting pan, a strong pair of shears to clip money, and seuerall clippings of the Massachusets money, and some other instruments.' He denied having ever made use of these things, but said they were given him by a privateer. But, on being remanded to jail, he made up another story, by which he hoped to clear himself. All, however, to no purpose. He was 'sentenced to stand two hours in the Pillory, have both ears cut off, give bond of £500 (with two sureties), pay charges of prosecution, fees of Court, and to stand committed till the sentence be performed.' The annexed engraving represents an ordinary constructed Pillory of the time."

STOCKS.

An item of interest relating to the Stocks, another instrument of punishment used in olden times, is thus related by Drake: "Edward Palmer had been employed to erect Stocks in which to punish offenders. Having brought in his bill for the woodwork, amounting to £1, 13s. & 7d, the Court decided that it was exorbitant; and, instead of drawing an order on the Treasurer for its payment, they ordered him to be set in said Stocks for an hour and to pay a fine of £5. It is difficult at this day to understand on what ground Edward Palmer was subjected to an ignominious punishment. He probably found the materials for the Stocks, and not less than two days must have been taken up in making them."

We are indebted to the kindness of Samuel G. Drake, A. M., for the use of the engravings upon this page.

## ORDER OF COUNCIL.

Philadelphia, Saturday July 14th 1781

The following proclamation being read and Considered, the same was agreed to and ordered to be published, vizt: By his Excellency JOSEPH REED, Esquire, President, and the Supreme Executive Council of the Commonwealth of Pennsylvania:

## A PROCLAMATION.

WHEREAS, Divers ill-disposed persons have manufactured or imported into this State quantities of base metal, in the similitude of British half-pence, but much inferior in value and weight to genuine British half-pence, to the great depreciation of that coin, the injury of the community in general, and the poor in particular, such practices having a natural tendency to raise the necessarys of life and introduce new confusion in the currency of the Country: We have, therefore thought proper to prohibit, and do hereby strictly enjoin all officers employed in the receipt of taxes or other publick dues, not to receive such base coin in any payments whatsoever; and do earnestly recommend to all the faithfull inhabitants of this State to refuse it in payment, and by all other lawful ways and means discourage the currency thereof; and we do in a special manner direct and enjoin all Magistrates, Sheriffs, Constables and other civil officers within this State, to make due inquiry after offenders in the premises, that they may be brought to speedy and condign punishment.

Given by order of the Council, under the hand of his Excellency JOSEPH REED, Esquire, President, and the less seal of the State, at Philadelphia, this fourteenth day of July, in the year of our Lord one thousand seven hundred and eighty one.

JOSEPH REED, President.

These base halfpence were, in the opinion of Dr. Maris, and we think all will agree with him, those bearing various legends, many of which appear intended to be taken for Georgius II. or III. Rex. and Britannia or Hibernia, while others merely imitate the general design of the English or Irish halfpence, without any evident attempt to mislead by the legends.

Among the legends are found, CORNWALLIS IND. Rev.—DELECTAN DOS 1000; GEORGE RULES — BRITAINS ISLES · 1730 ; GLORIOVS IER · VIS.—BRITAN RULE 1771; BRUTUS SEXTUS—BRITANNIA · 1771; GREGORY · III · PON.—BEL \* ONA 1771; GLORIVS. PIT · SEX.—BONNY GIRL . 1779

On most of these the head resembles one of the Georges, and the reverses have a figure of Britannia; similar pieces are found of the farthing size.

The four following have similar heads, but a harp upon the reverse: GEORGE RULED.—BRITAINS ISLES. 1756; GRUM'RUIS · ITI NEX—HIRARMIA · 1776; CORNWALLIS IND — HIBERIA 1776; GREGORIVS · III · PON.—HEBRIDES 1781

The above will serve as examples of this class of pieces, of which many others are found. The light pieces of brassy composition, with devices similar to English and Irish coins, but without legends, sometimes called "Carolina" or "Georgia" cents, we should class among these; and also the pieces with

OBVERSE. { Device, — A female, seated, facing left, with a harp at the right.
Legend, — NORTH AMERICAN TOKEN
In exergue, — 1781

REVERSE. { Device, — A ship, sailing to the left.
Legend, — COMMERCE

The trouble from base halfpence seems to have continued up to the time of the mint, as we find in the American State Papers, Vol. 7, p. 101, this notice regarding them:

"The coinage of copper is a subject that claims our immediate attention. From the small value of the several pieces of copper coin, this medium of exchange has been too much neglected. The more valuable metals are daily giving place to base British half-pence, and no means are used to prevent the fraud. This disease, which is neglected in the beginning, because it appears trifling, may finally prove very destructive to commerce. It is admitted that copper may, at this instant, be purchased in America at one-eighth of a dollar the pound.

"British half-pence, made at the Tower, are forty-eight to the pound. Those manufactured at Birmingham, and shipped in thousands for our use, are much lighter, and they are of base metal. It can hardly be said that seventy-two of them are worth a pound of copper; hence it will follow, that we give for British half-pence about six times their value. There are no materials from which we can estimate the weight of half-pence, that have been imported from Britain since the late war, but we have heard of sundry shipments being ordered, to the nominal amount of one thousand guineas; and we are told that no packet arrives from England without some hundred weight of base half-pence. It is a very moderate computation which states our loss, on the last twelve months, at 30,000 dollars, by the commerce of vile coin."

The following petition for the privilege of coining was presented to the Assembly of Pennsylvania; and we are indebted to Chas. I. Bushnell, Esq., for a certified copy. The original is on the files of the House of Representatives at Harrisburg, Pa.

"Petition of Tho⁵ Smyth, Jr. and Thomas Harwood.   Read 1ˢᵗ time Apl 5, 1786.
"To the Hon'ble, the General Assembly of Pennsylvania.

"The Petition of Tho⁵ Smyth Jr. and Tho⁵ Harwood 3ᵈ both Citizens of the State of Maryland —

"Humbly Sheweth, That your Petitioners are possessed of Mines which will produce large quantities of Silver and Copper, and that as there is throughout the United States a distressing scarcity of Specie, They Humbly Conceive that those Mines may be made use of much to the advantage of the Public, by a part of their produce being Coined. For which purpose they are induced to Solicit your Hon'ble body for a law giving them an exclusive right of Coinage either to a certain amount or length of time, as your honors may deem most expedient.

"Your Petitioners will be ready to give you Satisfactory Security for Coining one fourth as much Silver as Copper, equal in purity and weight to any of the like Kind now circulating in America, and the Copper equal, if not Superior, to those made at Tower Hill, London, as well as the performance of every other Obligation, it may be necessary for them to enter into.

"Your Petitioners flatter themselves, that Your Honors will readily percieve the benefits, the State must derive from an acceptance of their proposition, and that their Application will meet with the Approbation of Your Honorable Body, And your Petitioners, as in duty bound, will ever pray, &c &c          Tho⁵ Smyth Jr.   Tho⁵ Harwood 3ᵈ."

It does not appear that this petition received any other attention than a single reading, as we discover no reference to any further action thereupon; neither do we learn of any subsequent attempt to establish a coinage in this State.

# NEW HAMPSHIRE.

———•—◀—•———

New Hampshire was the first of the States which, subsequent to the declaration of independence, considered the subject of a coinage of copper.

Soon after that event, she authorized such a coinage, and designated the devices and legend to be placed upon it; it is supposed, however, that although patterns were prepared, little, if any, of the proposed coin was put into circulation. We are indebted to the Hon. Charles H. Bell, of Exeter, N. H., for our copy of the original record of this act, as well as for draughts of the designs sketched upon it, from which our engravings have been made. The design for the reverse is found upon the back of the original, and not on the face as we have placed it.

"in the House of Representatives Mar: 13ᵗʰ 1776.

"Voted that a Committee be chose to Joyn a Committee from the Honᵇˡᵉ Board, to confer upon the expediency of making Copper Coin & make a report to this House.

Voted, that Capᵗ Pierce Long Jonathan Lovell Esqʳ & Deacon Nahum Balden be the Committee for the above mentioned purpose. Sent up for concurrence.

P White Speaker.

In Council *Eodem Die* Read & Mʳˢ Clagett & Giles added on the part of the Board.

E. Thompson, Secy.

"The Committee humbly report that they find it expedient to make Copper Coin, for the Benefit of small Change, and as the Continental and other Bills are so large that William Moulton be impowered to make so many as may amount to 100ˡᵇ wᵗ subject when made to the Inspection and Direction of the General Assembly, before Circulation. Also we recommend that 108 of said Coppers be equal to one Spanish milld Dollar: That the said Coin be of pure Copper and equal in Wᵗ to English halfpence, and bear such Device thereon as the Genˡ Assembly may approve. Wyseman Claggett, Chairman."

A copper piece has recently been discovered in Portsmouth, N. H. (it having been there exhumed by a laborer in removing a bank of earth, the accumulation of many years,) which, from the initials upon its reverse, it would appear probable was either a card or a pattern issued by the William Moulton mentioned in the report of the committee. It is still in the possession of the finder, who refuses to part with it except at a price so excessive that no purchaser has yet been found. This piece is much corroded and defaced, but is well represented by the wood cut, Fig. 28—A.

In Force's "American Archives" we find that in the New Hampshire House of Representatives, it was, on the 28th of June, 1776, "Voted, That the Treasurer of this Colony receive into the Treasury, in exchange for the Paper Bills of this Colony, any quantity of Copper Coin, made in this Colony, of the weight of five pennyweight and ten grains each, to the amount of any sum not exceeding £1,000 lawful money; three of which Coppers shall be received and paid for two pence, lawful money, in all payments; which Coppers shall have the following device, viz: A Pine tree, with the word American liberty on one side, and a harp and the figures 1776 on the other side."

A copper coin in the collection of Matthew A. Stickney, Esq., corresponds with the description given in this vote, but exceeds the weight there specified, as this, though much worn, weighs 155 grains. It is represented as clearly as its condition will admit, on Plate VI., No. 3. We have seen one specimen similar to the last in its design, but with the date 1776, barely legible, not struck in dies, but engraved, probably as a pattern of the time; this is owned by Charles M. Hodge, of Newburyport. It is shown in Fig. 28—B, and its obverse on Plate VI., No. 4. Size 18½, weight 127 grains.

Belknap states, [Hist. N. H., 1791,] that "the names of streets which had been called after a King or Queen, were altered; and the half-pence, which bore the name of George III., were either refused in payment or degraded to farthings. These last have not yet recovered their value."

# VERMONT.

———— ▸•◂ ————

The first State that can be said to have issued a coinage of copper, was Vermont, — not one of the original thirteen States, neither was she then considered one of the "United States of America," not being admitted to the Union until 1791.

A petition was presented by Reuben Harmon, Jr., probably June 10th, 1785, as we find recorded in the Journal of the House, —

"Friday June 10, 1785 Two o'clock P. M.

"A petition signed Reuben Harmon Jun, praying for leave to coin a quantity of copper, &c. being read, was referred to a Committee of three, to join a Committee from the Council, to take the same under consideration, state facts, & make report of their opinion to this House.

"The members chosen, Mr. Tichenor, Mr. Strong, and Mr. Williams." Mr. Ira Allen was added to this committee from the Council.

A Bill was brought in June 15th, "and sent to the Governor and Council for perusal & proposals of amendment."

The Bill was as follows:

"An act Granting to Reuben Harmon Jun.ʳ Esq.ʳ a right of coining Copper, and regulating the same.

"Whereas Reuben Harmon Junior Esq.ʳ of Reuport, in the County of Benington, by his Petition has represented that he has purchased a quantity of Copper, suitable for coining, and praying this Legislature to grant him a right to coin Copper, under such regulations as this assembly shall think meet; and this assembly being willing to encourage an undertaking that promises so much public utility, therefore

"Be it enacted and it is hereby enacted by the Representatives of the Freemen of the State of Vermont in General assembly met and by the authority of the same, that there be and hereby is granted to the said Reuben Harmon Junior Esq, the exclusive right of coining Copper within this State for the term of two years from the first day of July, in the present year of our Lord, one thousand seven hundred and eighty five: and all Coppers by him coined, shall be in pieces of one third of an ounce, Troy weight each, with such Devices and Mottos as shall be agreed upon by the Committee appointed for that purpose by this assembly.

"And be it further enacted by the authority aforesaid that the said Reuben Harmon before he enter on the business of coining, or take any benefit of this act, shall enter into a bond of five thousand pounds, to the Treasurer of this State, with two or more good and sufficient sureties, Freeholders of this State, conditioned that all the Copper by him coined as aforesaid, shall be of full weight as specified in this act, and that the same shall be made of good and genuine Metal."

This record of the passage of this bill occurs upon the same day: — "A bill entitled An act granting to Reuben Harmon Jun. Esq<sup>r</sup>: a right of coining copper and regulating the same, being concurred by Council, was read, and passed into a law of the State."

In accordance with the clause in the bill requiring bonds from Harmon before the commencement of coining, this Bond was given: —

"Know all men by these Presents that we Reuben Harmon Jun<sup>r</sup> Esq<sup>r</sup> & David Sheldon of Rupert, Abraham Underhill & Benjamin Baldwin of Dorset all in the County of Bennington & State of Vermont are Held & firmly Bound in the Penal sum of Five Thousand Pounds L. M.y, to Ira Allen Esq<sup>r</sup> Treasurer of the State of Vermont & his successor in said office the sd. Harmon as Principle & the sd Sheldon, Underhill & Baldwin as sureties to which Payment well & Truly to be done we Bind ourselves our Heires Executors & Administrators firm by these Presents.

"In Testimony whereof we have hereunto set our Hands & Seals this 16<sup>th</sup> day of June 1785 in Presents of

"The Condition of this Bond is such that the above Bound Reuben Harmon as Principle & the sd Sheldon Underhill & Baldwin as Sureties Be

Responcible to sd Treasurer that sd Harmon will agreeable to an act Intitled 'an Act Granting to Reuben Harmon Jnᴿ Esqᴿ a Right of Coining Copper & Regulating the same' that all the Coppers by sd. Harmon Coined shall be in Pieces of one third of an ounce troy wait each & that the same shall be made of good & genuine metal —

"Provided sd Harmon should at any time Coine Coppers of Wait Mettle or Motto's Contarary to said Act then this Bond is forfit —

"In witness whereof we have hereunto set our Respective Hands & Seals in Presents of —

|  |  |  |
|---|---|---|
| N. Chipman | Reuben Harmon, Junᴿ | [L.S.] |
| John Strong | David Sheldon | [L.S.] |
|  | Abraham Underhill | [L.S.] |
|  | Benj: Baldwin | [L.S.] " |

Finding that their coins were required to contain more copper than those current in the "United States of America," an act was soon passed reducing the weight, to bring them more nearly to the standard there adopted :

"An Act in Addition to and Alteration of an Act entitled 'an Act granting to Reuben Harmon Junᴿ Esqᴿ a right of Coining Copper and regulating the same.'

"Whereas, an Act was passed by this Assembly at their session in June last granting to Reuben Harmon Esqᴿ Junᴿ of Ruport in the County of Bennington the privilege of coining Copper for the time therein Specified in pieces of one third of an ounce each, which is found to exceed in weight the Copper Coins used in the United States of America, Therefore

"Be it enacted and it is hereby enacted by the Representatives of the freemen of the State of Vermont in General Assembly met, and by the authority of the same ; that all Coppers coined by the said Reuben Hermon Esq. shall be of genuine Copper in pieces weighing not less than four pennyweight fifteen grains each and so much of the aforesaid act as regulates the weight of said Coins, is hereby repealed — And the Treasurer is directed to deliver up the bond entered into by said Hermon in pursuance of said Act on his the said Harmon entering into another Bond with Sureties, in the same sum conditioned for making said Coin agreeable to the regulations in this Act."

This Act was passed on the 27th of October, 1785. We find no proof that the bond was changed in accordance with its terms.

The coins issued by Harmon under this act were of the following descriptions, and constitute the first type of the Vermont coins:

OBVERSE.

Device, — The sun rising from behind a range of wooded mountains, a plough in the field beneath.

Legend, — VERMONTS . RES . PUBLICA · 1785 ·

REVERSE.

Device, — An eye within a small circle, from which issue twenty-six rays, thirteen long, their points intersecting a circle of thirteen stars, and thirteen short, between the stars and the centre.

Legend, — STELLA . QUARTA . DECIMA ·

Borders beaded or milled, edge plain ; size, 17 ; weight, 111 grains.

[Plate IV, No. 18, and Fig. 29.]

Of this there are two pairs of dies : on one, one ray of the sun points at the period after RES; in the other, a rarer variety, it points to the right of the period. On the last die a short dash or break usually follows the figure 5, as shown in the cut. A slight break follows DECIMA, on its reverse.

The reverses may be distinguished by the ray nearest the letter Q, which in the first variety points at Q, and on the second, more towards the U.

The next variety has the legend, VERMONTIS . RES . PUBLICA · 1785 · It has no marked peculiarity beyond the legend itself. One ray upon the reverse points at the left part of the Q.

Size, 17 ; weight, 117 grains.

[Plate IV, No. 19, and Fig. 30.]

Each of the pieces just described has eight trees on the obverse, and the rays upon the reverses are all cuneiform, or wedge-shaped.

From another pair of dies we have seen but one impression, which is owned by J. Carson Brevoort, of Brooklyn. It is too much worn to represent satisfactorily. The legend on the obverse encircles the device and date; the hills appear to be thickly wooded, the sun rises at the left — on all others it is at the right — and a line separates the date from the device. Instead of an eye in the centre of the reverse, this has the face of a sun: the rays are single pointed, and composed of fine lines of unequal length. Legends, — VERMONTIS RES PUBLICA and STELLA QUARTA DECIMA.

We have seen two specimens, apparently counterfeits of that last described, but cast, and of very rude workmanship.

### 1786.

The third variety of this type has the legend, VERMONTENSIUM · RES · PUBLICA · 1786 · and that of the reverse, STELLA · QUARTA . DECIMA ·
Size, 17 ; weight, 123 grains.

[Plate IV, No. 20, and Fig. 31.]

This variety is found with three obverse dies, and two of the reverse. Of these, one has seven trees, and the U of PUBLICA double-cut below ; another, nine trees, the U double-cut at the left, and the date close under the ploughshare ; the third has nine trees, and the figure 1 of date double-cut at the right, but much to left of ploughshare. The reverses both have thirteen rays of many fine lines ; one ray of that found with the first obverse, pointing just right of Q, on the other, found with the two other obverses, it points full to left of that letter, and the legend reads, — QUARTA ·· DECIMA · STELLA ·

Before the expiration of the right first granted him, Harmon sent in a petition for an extension of his privilege, which we next present:

"To the Honorable General Assembly of the State of Vermont now setting
    at Rutland —

"The Petition of Reuben Harmon Jʳ. of Rupert in the county of Bennington humbly sheweth — that the legislature of this State did at their Session
held at Norwich in June 1785 grant him the sole right of coining Copper
within this State for the term of two years — that he your Petitioner has
been at a very great expence in erecting works and procuring a quantity of
genuine copper for that Purpose — that said Term is nearly expired — and that
your Petitioner, by reason of the shortness of said Term, will be unable to
indemnify himself for said expences — farther your Petitioner conceives that
in the present scarcity of a circulating medium the coining of coppers within
this State may be very advantageous to the Public —   Your Petitioner therefore prays this Honorable assembly to grant him the priviledge of coining
copper for a farther term of ten years or such other Term and under such
regulations and restrictions as to your Honours in your wisdom shall seem
meet —          And as in Duty bound shall ever pray
    "Rutland, Octʳ. 23, 1786.                    Reuben Harmon, Junʳ "


                                        "In General Assembly, Oct. 23ᵈ, 1786

"The above petition was read and refered to a Committee of three to
join a Committee from the Council to take the same under consideration
state facts and make report — The members chosen, Mr. Chipman, Mr.
Bridgman & Mr. Goodrich"

Mr. Walbridge was joined to this Committee by the Council.


The report of the Committee last appointed was as follows :
"Rutland, Octʳ. 24, 1786 —

    "To the General Assembly now sitting —

"Your committee to whom was referred the consideration of the within
Petition beg leave to report as their opinion that the sole priviledge of coining
copper be granted to the said Reuben Harmon Jr. for the Term of eight years
from the experation of the former grant under the following regulations viz —
that he procure bond to the Treasurer as is provided in the former grant —
that the first three years the said Ruben shall enjoy the said priviledge free
that for the remaining five years he shall pay two & one half pr. cent to the
State on all the coppers he shall coin and give security for the payment —
that the device be in future a head on one side with the motto 'Auctoritate

Vermontensium' abridged — on the reverse a woman representing the Genius of America with the Letters INDE-ET . LIB. for Independance and Liberty — All which is Humbly submitted by

Eben.ʳ Walbridge for Committee "

"In General Assembly, Oct. 24ᵗʰ, 1786 The above report was read and accepted and leave given to the petitioner to bring in a bill accordingly —
attest Ros. Hopkins, Clerk."

The following bill was then presented, and passed the same day :
" An Act granting to Reuben Harmon Jun.ʳ Esq.ʳ the right of coining copper within this State, for a farther term of eight years.

" Whereas, the Legislature of this State did, at their sessions at Norwich, in June 1785, grant to Reuben Harmon Jun.ʳ Esq.ʳ of Ruport, in the County of Bennington, the exclusive right of coining copper within this State, for the term of two years from the first day of July in the aforesaid year of our Lord 1785 : And whereas, the said Reuben has, by his Petition represented to this assembly that he has been at great expence in erecting works and procuring a quantity of Copper for the purpose of carrying on said business of coining, and that, by reason of the shortness of said term, he will be unable to idemnify himself for his said Expence ; and praying this Assembly to grant him said privilidge of coining Copper for a longer term ; and this Assembly willing to encourage an undertaking that promises a considerable public utility, Therefore

" Be it enacted by the General Assembly of the State of Vermont that there be and hereby is granted and confirmed to the said Reuben Harmon Jun.ʳ Esq.ʳ the exclusive right of coining copper within this State, for a farther term of eight years from the first day of July in the year of our Lord 1787 ; and that all copper by him coined, shall be in pieces weighing not less than four penny weight, fifteen grains each ; and the device for all coppers by him hereafter coined shall be, on the one side, a head with the motto auctoritate Vermontensium, abridged — on the reverse, a woman, with the letters, INDE: ET: LIB: — for Independence and Liberty.

" And be it further enacted by the authority aforesaid ; that the said Reuben shall have and enjoy the aforesaid priviledge of coining coppers within this State free from any duty to this state, as a compensation therefor, for the full term of three years from the first day of July, in the year of our Lord

1787; and that from and after the expiration of the said three years, he the said Reuben shall pay for the use of this State, two and one half per cent, of all the copper he shall coin for and during the remainder of the aforesaid term of eight years : and the said Reuben, before he take any benefit of this act, shall enter into a bond of five — thousand pounds, to the Treasurer of this State, with two or more good and sufficient sureties, Freeholders of this State, conditioned that all the copper by him coined as aforesaid, shall be of full weight, as specified in this act, and of genuine metal, and that from and after the expiration of the aforesaid three years, he will well and truly render an account of the sums by him coined by virtue of this grant, and pay over all such sums as shall, on account of said coinage, become due to this State, at such times and in such manner, as this or a future assembly shall direct."

In accordance with the last act, this Bond was given :

" Know all Men by these Presents that we Reuben Harmon of Rupert in the County of Bennington & State of Vermont as Principle & Nathaniel Chipman of Tinmouth and Lemuel Chipman of Pawlet both of the County of Rutland and State aforesaid Esquires as sureties Are held and firmly bound unto Samuel Mattox Esquire Treasurer of said State of Vermont & his successors in said office in the full sum of Five Thousand pounds Lawful Money to be paid to the said Samuel or his successors in said office of Treasurer.

" For the True payment whereof we Bind ourselves Heirs & Assigns Firmly by these Presents   In witness whereof we have hereunto set our hands and seals 23ᵈ Day of Febʸ, A. D. 1787 —

" The Conditions of the above Obligation is such that whereas the above Bounden Reuben Did on the 24ᵗʰ of Octʳ 1786 obtain Licence from the General Assembly of the State of Vermont, to Coin Copper under Certain Regulations & Restrictions which are Particularly set forth in a Certain Act Granting Licence to the said Reuben as aforesaid on the above 24ᵗʰ of October now if the said Reuben shall strictly and Punctually attend to all the Rules Regulations Direction & Restrictions or Limitations which are set forth or Injoined in said Act then this obligation to be Void otherwis to remain in full force & Virtue.

" Signed, Sealed & Delivered in presence of

| John A. Graham | | Reuben Harmon | [L.S.] |
| David Russell | } | Nathⁱ Chipman | [L.S.] |
| | | Lem. Chipman | [L.S.] " |

The Legislature having by the terms of the last grant designated new devices and legends to be placed upon the coins, those next issued constitute another type, of which also there are several varieties.

### TYPE No. 2. OBVERSE.

Device,—A head, on some facing to the right, on others to the left.

Legend,—VERMON AUCTORI or AUCTORI VERMON

### REVERSE.

Device,—The goddess of liberty, seated, facing left, with olive branch and staff.

Legend,—INDE ET LIB

In exergue,—The date,— 1786  1787  or  1788

Borders serrated, edges plain.

### TABLES OF VARIETIES OF VERMONT COINS.

| OBVERSE. | | | | | 1786. | REVERSE. | | | |
|---|---|---|---|---|---|---|---|---|---|
| No. Facing. | Legends and Punctuation. | Rarity. | No. of Dies. | With Rev. | No. | Legends and Punctuation. | Rarity. | No. of Dies. | With Obv. |
| 1 Right. | AUCTORI :   VERMON : | R³ | 1 | C | A | INDE ✣ ETLIB | R⁴ | 1 | 2 |
| 2 Left. | VERMON :   AUCTORI : | R⁴ | 1 | A | B | INDE : ✄ ETLIB : | R⁶ | 1 | 3 |
| 3 do. | VERMON :·   AUCTORI | R⁶ | 1 | B | C | INDE · ✄ ET : LIB : | R³ | 1 | 1 |

| OBVERSE. | | | | | 1787. | REVERSE. | | | |
|---|---|---|---|---|---|---|---|---|---|
| No. Facing. | Legends and Punctuation. | Rarity. | No. of Dies. | With Rev. | No. | Legends and Punctuation. | Rarity. | No. of Dies. | With Obv. |
| 1˙ Right. | VERMON   AUCTORI | C | 2 | A, C | A | INDE   ET LIB | C | 1 | 1. 2 |
| 2 do. | VERMON·   AUCTORI· | C | 1 | A | B | INDE : ✄ ET LIB : | R⁶ | 1 | 3 |
| 3 Left. | VERMON :·   AUCTORI | R⁵ | 1 | B | C | BRITAN NIA· | C | 1 | 1 |

| OBVERSE. | | | | | 1788. | REVERSE. | | | |
|---|---|---|---|---|---|---|---|---|---|
| No. Facing. | Legends and Punctuation. | Rarity. | No. of Dies. | With Rev. | No. | Legends and Punctuation. | Rarity. | No. of Dies. | With Obv. |
| 1 Right. | VERMON   AUCTORI | R² | 3 | A, D | A | INDE   ET LIB | C | 5 | 1, 2, 3 |
| 2 do. | VERMON·   AUCTORI· | C | 2 | A | B | INDE × ET · LIB× | R³ | 1 | 3, 5, 6 |
| 3 do. | VERMON×   AUCTORI × | R³ | 1 | A, B | C | INDE ∗ ET LIB ∗ | R² | 1 | 4 |
| 4 do. | VERMON ,   AUCTORI ∗ | R² | 1 | C | D | ∗ ET LIB ∗ ∗ INDE | R⁶ | 1 | 1 |
| 5 do. | VERMON ∗   ∗ AUCTORI | R⁵ | 1 | B | | | | | |
| 6 do. | ∗ VERMON ∗   ∗ AUCTORI ∗ | R⁵ | 1 | B | | | | | |

In size these coins range from 16 to 17, the heavier specimens varying in weight from 120, to 141 grains, and by far the larger portion of them, when but little worn, exceeding the stipulated weight of 111 grains.

[Plate V, Nos. 1, 2, 3 and 4, and Figs. 32, 33, 34, and 35.]

No. 1, of 1786, is known as the "baby head." See Fig. 32. Nos. 2 and 3 have heads much like the common varieties of the Connecticut cents. For No. 2 see Plate V, No. 1. Fig. 33 represents its obverse only.

There is little peculiarity to be noted in the coins of 1787, except in No. 3, the obverse of which is from the same die with No. 3 of 1786. Its reverse has a break nearly obliterating the date. For No. 2 see Plate V, No. 2, and Fig. 34.

The coins of 1788 are also much alike, with the exception of those punctuated with stars, most of which are quite rare. For No. 2 see Fig. 35.

We have seen one specimen of No. 4 in brass. Plate V, No. 3.

Reverse B, of 1788, is found with one of the Connecticut obverses of 1787. See Plate V, Nos. 4 and 24.

A very rare piece, the origin of which is unknown to us, has for its obverse a die similar to the more common dies of this mint, but with reverse,

Device,— The goddess of liberty, seated, facing right, with scales of justice extended in her left hand ; the staff, with liberty cap and flag, in her right.

Legend, — IMMUNE COLUMBIA ·

In exergue, — 1785 .

This piece may have been produced by muling a discarded die of the Vermont mint, with the Immune Columbia. It is accurately represented above.

PLATE V.

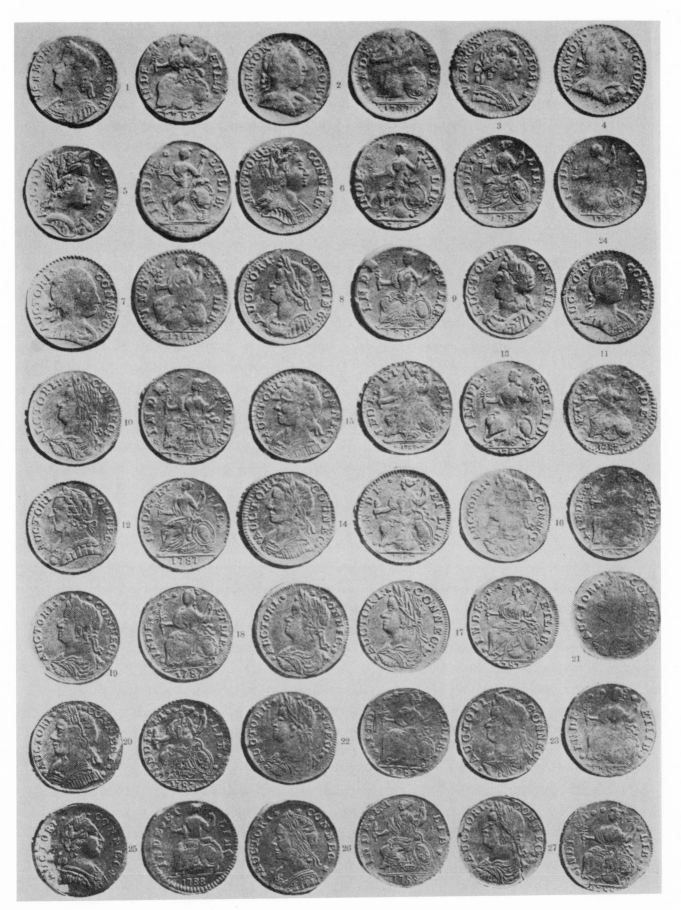

The coins of this mint, and, in fact, those of most, if not all, of the other State mints, are frequently found struck upon other coins, — most commonly British halfpence, though frequently Nova Constellatios, or coins of some other State, producing curious combinations of letters without adding value to the specimens. Upon some of these, the legends and dates of both dies appear.

They are also occasionally found incused, as if one coin being retained in the die after striking, was, by the next motion of the screw, forced into the planchet placed for striking another.

Another feature, rarely seen, is, that some pieces are found bearing upon both sides of a *solid* planchet, impressions from the same die: this is probably caused by the coin last struck becoming by some means turned over upon the planchet next to be struck; thus the planchet would protect it from one die, becoming itself incused, while the other die would impress the other side of the planchet upon which it had before acted.

A piece in the cabinet of the writer, has upon each side an impression of the " Vermontis " obverse, one side having in addition an incused impression from the reverse of one of the same coins.

Double impressions from the same dies will sometimes extend or contract a letter or a word, thus changing a v to a w, causing an R to resemble a K, or creating a " Deima," a " Coonnec," etc.: no observing collector will readily be deceived by these.

We have been favored by Chas. I. Bushnell, Esq., of New York, with extracts from his correspondence upon the Vermont coinage, which we next present :

Extract from a letter from B. H. Hall, of Troy, to Charles I. Bushnell of New York City, dated March 3d, 1855.

" Reuben Harmon, Jr., came from Suffield, Conn., in company with his father, Reuben Harmon, Senr., about the year 1768, and settled in the North East part of Rupert, Vt. He was a man of some note and influence while there. At a meeting of the inhabitants of the N. H. Grants, held at Dorset, Sept. 25, 1776, initiatory to their Declaration of Independence, Mr. Reuben Harmon, (probably Jr.,) was one of the representatives from Rupert. He was representative in the Vermont Legislature from Rupert in 1780, was justice of the peace from 1780–90, and held several minor offices. In the year 1790 or thereabouts, he left Rupert, for that part of the State of Ohio called New Connecticut, and there died long since.

" His Mint House was located near the north-east corner of Rupert, a little east of the main road leading from Dorset to Pawlet, on a small stream of water called Millbrook, which empties into Pawlet River. It was a small building, about 16 by 18 feet, made of rough materials, sided with unplaned and unpainted boards. It is still standing, but its location and uses are entirely different from what they were originally. Its situation at present is on the border of the adjoining town of Pawlet whither it was long since removed, and what was once a coin house is now a corn house.

" Colonel William Cooley, who had worked at the goldsmith's trade in the city of New York, and who afterwards removed to Rupert, made the dies and assisted in striking the coin."

From B. H. Hall to Charles I. Bushnell, dated July 18th, 1855. [The information contained in this extract was obtained by him from Abel Buel Moore, a grandson of Abel Buel.]

" The Sun dial, or ' Mind your business' copper coin, common in New England at the close of the last and at the commencement of the present century was first manufactured by Abel Buel at New Haven, Conn., the original dies having been designed and cut by himself. Not long after this, his son William Buel, removed the manufactory to the town of Rupert, Bennington Co., Vt., and in connection with a Mr. Harmon established the mint-house on what is known as Mill Brook. William had taken with him the original dies used by his father at New Haven, and continued at Rupert the coinage of the coppers above referred to, until the coin had depreciated so much in value as to be worthless or nearly so, for circulation. The remains of the dam which rendered the waters of Mill Brook eligible, are still to be seen, and pieces of copper and specimens of the old coin are still occasionally picked up on the site of the old mill and in the brook below.[1]

" William Buel fled from New Haven and went to Vermont under the

---

[1] The statement concerning the "Sun dial" coins, contained in the above letter, has been doubted, as the law under authority of which Harmon acted, strictly prohibited him, under severe penalties, from striking any coin, other than that authorized and described therein, or that designated by "the Committee appointed for that purpose." Still it may be that his allowing Buel to strike coins authorized by the United States, was not considered an infraction of the law, causing the forfeiture of his bond. If it be true that many of these coins have been found in that locality, it appears strongly to favor the opinion that some part of this coinage was performed at this mint, though it is unlikely that any large proportion of it emanated from this source.

following circumstances. Having occasion to use Aquafortis, he had procured a quantity in a jug from a druggist and was returning to his residence, when he was accosted by some Indians who insisted upon drinking from the jug what they assumed to be rum. He told them that he had no rum, but that his jug contained Aquafortis, and that it would poison them. The Indians supposing this a mere pretence, took the jug from him, and one of them having swallowed a portion of its contents, died soon after from the effects. Buel was then accused of killing the Indian who had fallen by his own rashness, and in accordance with their notions of justice his savage companions claimed that the life of the jug-owner was forfeit and sought every opportunity to take it. To escape their animosity Buel sought refuge, privately, in the then newly settled, and unacknowledged State of Vermont. Enveloped with this, you will find a letter from Julian Harmon, grandson of Reuben Harmon, Jr. * * * * Some of the statements which it contains are mixed, yet I think, with the knowledge you already are in possession of, on the subject, you will understand them. I have heard many stories about Abel Buel, think I have seen them in print. You are probably aware of his genius as a mechanic, of his skill in invention, of his pecuniary troubles, and of his successful imitation of the Continental Bills which little freak was not the pleasantest in which he was engaged."

Copy of Julian Harmon's letter, above referred to:—

"Warren, O., June 14, 1855.

"Sir,

"Your letter of April 27th was duly received, and an answer was designed at once, but has thus far been neglected. I write you on behalf of my father to whom your letter was addressed. He gives me answers to your questions as follows. 'Does not know what year precisely, but thinks about 1760, his father came to Vt., in company with *his* father, from Sandisfield, Mass. He was justice of the peace several years and a member of the Assembly. No likeness extant to his knowledge. Has no copy of the act referred to. Has none of the coins or dies. Thinks Wm. Buel of N. Haven, cut the dies. The Mint House stood on Pillet River, three rods from his father's house — story & a half house, not painted — a furnace in one end for melting copper & rolling the bars, &c.; in the other (west) end, machinery for stamping, — in the centre that for cutting &c. The stamping

was done by means of an iron screw attached to heavy timbers above, &
moved by hand through the aid of ropes. 60 per minute *could* be stamped,
although 30 per minute was the usual number. Wm. Buel assisted in
striking the coins. 3 persons were required for the purpose, one to place
the copper, and 2 to swing the stamp. At first, the coins passed 2 for a
penny, then 4 — then 8, when it ceased to pay expenses. The British imported
so many of the 'Bung Town Coppers,' which were of a much lighter color.'
My father, Dr. John B. Harmon, also thinks there was a plough upon one
side of the coins of his father, who removed to Ohio in 1800, & engaged
in making salt, at the 'Salt Spring Tract,' in Weathersfield Township, Trum-
bull Co., which he continued to his death, Oct. 29th, 1806, in his 56th year.
Excuse my delay in this reply. I regret not being able to give fuller
answers to your enquiries. I add that Reuben Harmon, Jr., kept a store also,
in connection with his other business in Vt.     Yours Truly,

                                                     "Julian Harmon."

B. H. Hall to Charles I. Bushnell, dated June 4th, 1856.

"On the north side of Mill Brook the 'old Copper House' was first
erected. * * * * From this location, in the town of Rupert, the 'Mint
House' was afterwards removed to and placed on the eastern bank of Pawlet
River, in the same town. Here also it was used for minting purposes. When
the manufacture of coins was abolished, it was allowed to remain on Pawlet
River for several years, but we could not learn to what uses it was put.
Its third removal was to a spot north of the house of John Harwood, Esq.,
in the town of Rupert, on the east side of the main road. While here it
was occupied as a residence by a family named Goff. It was again removed
from its third location to a site nearly opposite, where it remained until its
final journey which took place many years ago. This placed it on the
farm of William Phelps about a mile north of John Harwood's residence
in 'the edge' of the town of Pawlet. Here it stood until last winter, when
it was blown down."

In 1787, a manufactory of "hardware," known as Machin's Mills, was
established at New Grange, Ulster County, now Newburgh, N. Y., the
principal purpose of which is supposed to have been the coinage of copper.

This mint had no legal connection with that of Vermont, but its
managers had business relations with the persons conducting the coinage of
that State, and the little known of its history is so interwoven with that of

the coiners of the Vermont money, that we know of no place more appropriate than this to introduce the papers relating to it.

Eager writes, (History of Orange County,) "Orange Lake * * * * was also called Machen's Pond. Captain Machen first opened the outlet of the pond, and erected a manufactory to make coppers for change and circulation. The outlet composes a large part of Chamber's Creek, which supplies the New Mills and other manufacturing establishments with water. This outlet was originally the place where the waters of the pond ran off at high water. The natural one is further west at a place called Pine Point, and the stream from the pond crosses the turnpike just east of Mr. Nathaniel Brewster, between five and six miles from Newburgh.

"Capt. Machen, we believe, was an Englishman, and came out before the Revolution as an officer in the British service. During the war he entered the American army as an engineer, and was employed by Congress in 1777, in erecting fortifications in the Highlands, and in stretching the chain across the river at West Point. After the war he came and located at the pond. His operations there, as they were conducted in secret, were looked upon at that time with suspicion, as illegal and wrong."

Mr. Bushnell supplies some interesting information relative to this coining establishment which we here introduce: —

"The Mint House at Newburgh, Ulster County, N. Y., was situated on the east side of Machin's Lake or Pond, about one eighth of a mile distant from the pond. The building was erected in 1784, by Thomas Machin, and was still standing in 1792, at which time the rollers, press and cutting machine were taken out. The coins were struck by means of a large bar loaded at each end with a 500 pound ball, with ropes attached. Two men were required on each side, making four in all, to strike the pieces, besides a man to set the planchets. The metal of which the coins were struck, was composed of old brass cannon and mortars, the zinc from the copper being extracted by smelting in a furnace. About sixty of the coins were struck a minute. The sloop 'Newburgh,' (Capt. Isaac Belknap,) carried for a number of years the coining press, as part ballast. The coins were made by James F. Atlee. Many of them bore the obverse 'GEORGIUS III.' and rev. 'INDE ET LIB.' Others bore the figure of a plough on one side. The mint ceased operations in the year 1791."

It is supposed that the coins here mentioned as bearing the figure of a plough, were some of the Vermont coins with that device, and there is strong reason to believe that Atlee, who is said to have made the dies of all the coins struck at Newburgh, made dies for others of the Vermont coins.

The pieces with the obverse GEORGIVS III. are of two varieties: the head upon the first of these closely resembles that upon the more common varieties of the Vermont coins; its legend is, GEORGIVS · III · REX ·

The reverse is from the die represented on plate V, No. 4. This die is found upon coins attributed both to Vermont and Connecticut.

The other, a more common variety of this piece, has a smaller head, and the legend GEORGIVS III. REX.

The reverse of this is identical with that found upon two pieces classed as Connecticut coins. The legend is INDE * ET * LIB *

We have found this reverse die in its perfect condition, used with the obverse just described: it next appears, with cracks across I and B, with an * AUCTORI. CONNEC * face to right, until this obverse die became useless by reason of a break; it is again found, and in a still more defective condition, now having breaks in E of ET, at the foot of the goddess, and a slight crack at her chin, used with the GEORGIVS III. REX., and lastly, as proved by the extension of the breaks already noted, particularly that at the foot of the goddess, it is found with obverse ⁕ AUCTORI.⁕ ⁕ CONNEC.⁕ face to left. Here its endurance seems to have been exhausted, as the break last mentioned is so extended as to render it probable that it could have been of little further service.

It is probable, judging from the facts just noted, that many pieces now classed as Connecticut coins, are counterfeits from this mint; and it is not unlikely that the VERMON AUCTORI with reverse BRITANNIA · as well as many of the counterfeit halfpence of George III., formed part of the "hardware" manufactured here.

The articles of agreement between the proprietors of Machin's Mills, and those between them and the coiners at Rupert, Vt., copies of which have been furnished us by Mr. Bushnell, are contained in the documents next ensuing.

These copies are exact, even to their orthographical errors.

This Indenture of six parts made the eighteenth day of April one thousand seven hundred and eighty-seven: Between Samuel Atlee of the City of New York of the first part: James F. Atley of the same place of the second part: David Brooks of the same place of the third part: James Grier of the same place of the fourth part: James Giles of the same place of the fifth part: and Thomas Machin of the County of Ulster of the sixth part: Witnesseth, that the said parties for the affiance, trust and confidence which each of them hath, and doth repose in the other, have concluded and agreed to become copartners and joint traders together in such trades, and merchandizing as well within this State of New York, as elsewhere where the said parties shall think to trade and merchandize for their most benefit, advantage, and profit, and that for, and during the space of seven years, to be computed from the day of the date hereof, from thence next ensuing and fully to be complete, and ended, there shall be such joint trade.   And to that end and purpose the parties shall add and put together on or before the first day of June next, a joint stock, to be employed in, and about the said joint trade; that is to say the sum of three hundred pounds of current money of New York; to wit the said Samuel Atlee for his part fifty pounds; the said James F. Atlee for his part fifty pounds; the said David Brooks for his part fifty pounds; the said James Grier for his part, fifty pounds; the said James Giles for his part fifty pounds; and the said Thomas Machin fifty pounds more: being the remainder of the three hundred pounds.   Which said stock shall be occupied and employed together upon an account of sixths both in profit and loss, the whole in six equal parts to be divided; whereof the said Samuel Atlee his executors and administrators is, and are to have and bear for his and their parts one sixth part thereof both in profit and loss; the said James F. Atlee his executors, and administrators one sixth part thereof, for his and their part both in profit and loss; the said David Brooks his executors and administrators, one sixth part thereof for his and their part both in pofit and loss; the said James Grier, his executors and administrators, one sixth part thereof, for his, and their part both in profit and loss, and the said James Giles, his executors and administrators another part thereof both in profit and loss; and the said Thomas Machin his executors and administrators the other sixth part thereof both in pofit and loss, for his and their parts, according to the true intent and meaning thereof.   And the said Samuel Atlee, and James F. Atlee being possessed of certain implements for carrying on said trade, do agree to lend them to the parties to these presents for and during the continuance of their copartnership without any fee or reward for the same.   And the said Thomas Machin being possessed of certain mills, doth hereby agree to let the parties to these presents have the free use of them for and during the continuance of their copartnership (for the purpose of carrying on their joint trade) without any fee or reward for the same. And the said David Brooks, James Grier and James Giles, do agree to advance the further sum of ten pounds each towards finishing and completing the works for carrying on said trade And it is further agreed between the parties to these presents that the said James Giles have the sole receiving, keeping and charge of all the cash and money during the said copartnership; and also of the charge of the writing, true keeping and custody of the Books to be kept for the said copartnership. And that the said James F. Atlee and Thomas Machin shall equally manage, act and perform that part of the trade which concerns the manufactory of hard-ware; and the other joint business, is to be equally acted and performed by the said Samuel Atlee, David Brooks and James Grier. And it is further agreed by and between the parties to these presents, that they shall once every four months during the said copartnership; to wit, on the first day of February, on the first day of June, and on the first day of October in every year, come to a plain, fair and perfect account and reckoning with each other of, for and concerning all matters relating to the said copartnership; to the intent it may appear how, and in what state and condition they then stand in referrence to their said copartnership and joint stock. And it is agreed that after the said account is made up, each of the said parties shall, and may deduct, and take out of the profits neat produce, and increase of the said trade, to and for his own particular use, such sum and sums of money as shall be mutually agreed upon by and between the parties to these presents. And it is hereby further agreed that no advantage of survivorship shall be taken by the said parties; but on the death of either of them the executor or executors or administrator of the party so dying, giving security to the survivors to indemnify them, shall and may receive the share or interest in the said joint stock of the party so dying. And it is mutually agreed by and between the said parties that in case either of them shall at any time during the said term of seven years, be minded to break off and dissolve the said copartnership, they shall either of them be at liberty so to do, on giving six months notice to the others of them in writing of such his intention to dissolve the same; and the party giving such notice paying the others of them, one hundred pounds out of his sixth part of the said joint stock and produce thereof, as the same shall be appraised; but the same copartnership to exist as to the other parties who continue notwithstanding. And further that it shall and may be lawful to and for the parties to these presents or any of them, at his or their will, and pleasure, to have liberty, ingress, egress and regress into, out of, and from the compting house, store house or room where the same Thomas Machin and James F. Atlee may be employed in the manufactory aforesaid; also into, out of, or from the dwelling house of the said James Giles for the time being, and shall and may freely as occasion may require as well view the works where the said Thomas Machin and James F Atlee may be employed; as also view and peruse the said Books of account, as also all wares, goods, and merchandizes, and other things whatsoever, relating to the said joint trade, in the hands, custody or posession of the said Thomas Machin and James F. Atlee, and James Giles. And it is further agreed between the parties to these presents that if any doubt, question, controversy, or difference shall happen or arise, between the said parties concerning their said copartnership the same shall be determined by a majority of the copartners. And it is further agreed by and between the said parties to these presents, that neither of the said parties shall make any charge for his or their labour in carrying on the designs, or transacting, doing or acting any particular branch of the copartnership; but that all such costs and charges and expenses as may be disbursed by any of the parties hereto, in carrying into execution the intent of this copartnership, other than such as have been already mentioned, shall be equally borne by the parties to these presents. And it is further agreed by and between the parties to these presents that if either or any of them during the continuance of their copartnership, should get or procure in his or their name, or names, any grant for coinage of money from the United States of America in Congress assembled or from the Legislature of any of the United States, or shall enter into a contract or contracts with such other persons who may have the privilege of coinage from the Congress aforesaid, or any of the Legislatures aforesaid, That then, and in such case, the profits and losses of such grant of coinage or contract aforesaid shall be had, and borne and shared between the parties to these presents share and share alike. And further it is concluded and agreed by and between the said parties to these presents and their true intent and meaning is, that none of the said parties, nor the executors or administrators of any of them shall at any time or times, be charged, or chargeable, by virtue of these presents, further than for his own poper offence or breach of covenant, and not for the offence or breach of covenant of any other of the said parties, his executors, or administrators, anything before mentioned notwithstanding. And lastly it is agreed That none of the said parties, shall or will, at any time or times hereafter make, do, commit or omit to do any act, deed or device whatsoever, with an intent to defet or make void in part, or in all the true intent, and meaning of these presents; and for the true and punctual performance hereof, the parties to these presents bind themselves, their heirs, executors and administrators each unto the other, their executors and administrators, severally and not jointly in the penal sum of Five hundred pounds.

"In Witness whereof, the parties to these presents have hereunto interchangeably set their hands and seals, the day and year first above written

"Sealed and delivered ⎰
   In the presence of ⎱

"[The words ' The Parties' between the 10, & 11, line of the first page, 'and' between the 21, & 22, line of the same page, 'doing or acting' between the 28 and 29, lines of the Second page, first interlined before the executors hereof]

   A. Blacklye
"Jos. McIlvaine

| | |
|---|---|
| Sam¹ Atlee | [L.S.] |
| James F. Atlee | [L.S.] |
| D. Brooks | [L.S.] |
| James Grier | [L.S.] |
| James Giles | [L.S.] |
| Thomas Machin | [L.S.]" |

The second agreement is a formidable legal document, evidently intended to cover an extensive business: the expectations of the parties thereto were probably greatly disappointed in the extent of the business transacted under it, which there is reason to believe was of no great amount.

"This Indenture of ten parts made the seventh day of June in the year of our Lord One Thousand seven hundred and eighty seven Between Reuben Harmon of the County of Bennington in the State of Vermont Esqʳ of the first part William Coley of the same place of the second part, Elias Jackson of Litchfield County in the State of Connecticut of the third part, Daniel Van Voorhis of the City of New York, Goldsmith, of the fourth part, Samuel Atlee of the same place, Porter Brewer, of the fifth part, James F. Atlee of the same place of the sixth, David Brooks of the same place of the seventh part, James Grier of the same place of the eighth part, James Giles of the same place, Atty at Law, of the ninth part, and Thomas Machin of the County of Ulster, in the State of New York, of the tenth part: Wheras the said Reuben Harmon by virtue of an act of the Legislature of the State of Vermont is entitled to the Privilege of the Coinage of Copper Coin for the use of the said State, and wheras the said Reuben Harmon subsequent to the Passing of the said act, hath admitted the said William

Coley, Elias Jackson and Daniel Van Voorhis into a full participation with him in the Privileges of the Coinage of Copper for the Purpose aforesaid, upon full and equal shares, share and share alike. And whereas the said Samuel Atlee, James F. Atlee, David Brooks, James Grier, James Giles and Thomas Machin by their Articles of Copartnership, bearing date the eighteenth day of April One Thousand seven hundred and eighty seven have become Copartners & Joint Traders together in such Trades and Merchandize, and in the coinage of Coppers, as shall be for their most Benefit and Advantage and Whereas the said Reuben Harmon, William Coley, Elias Jackson, & Daniel Van Voorhis, have agreed to admit the said Samuel Atlee, James F. Atlee, David Brooks, James Grier, James Giles & Thomas Machin into a full Participation of all benefits, Privileges & advantages arising from the Coinage of Copper for the State of Vermont upon such Conditions & in such manner, as shall be hereinafter expressed. Now This Indenture Witnesseth, that the said parties to these Presents for the affiance, trust & confidence which each of them hath and doth repose in the other, have concluded & agreed to become Copartners & Joint traders together, in such trades & Merchandizing and in the Coinage of Copper for the State of Vermont aforesaid as well within the States of Vermont, Connecticut & N. York as elsewhere, where the said Parties shall think fit to Trade & Merchandize for their most benefit advantage & profit, and that for & during the term of eight years to be Computed from the first Day of July next being the term allowed by the Legislature of Vermont to coin as aforesaid, and to that end and purpose the said Samuel Atlee, James F. Atlee, David Brooks, James Grier, James Giles & Thomas Machin shall add and put together, on or before the said first Day of July, a Joint Stock to be employed in and about the said trade That is to say, the sum of three hundred pounds Current mone of New York, & also that they the said Sam¹ Atlee, James F. Altee, David Brooks, James Grier, James Giles, and Thomas Machin, shall add & put together on or before the first Day of November next the further sum of Two hundred pounds like money as part & share of the said Reuben Harmon, William Coley, Elias Jackson, and Daniel Van Voorhis to compleet the sum of Five hundred pounds which is intended to be the Joint stock in trade of the Parties to these presents, which said stock shall be employed & occupied together upon an account of Tenths, the Whole in ten equal parts to be Divided, Whereof the said Reuben Harmon his Executors & Administrators is & are to have and bear for his and their parts on tenth part thereof both in profit & Loss.

The said William Coley his Executors & Administrators, one tenth part thereof both in Profit & Loss. The said Elias Jackson his Executors & Administrators One tenth part thereof both in Profit & Loss the said Daniel Van Voorhis, his Executors & Administrators, one tenth part thereof both in Profit & Loss. The said Samuel Atlee, his Executors & Administrators one tenth part thereof both in profit & Loss, the said James F. Atlee his Executors & Administrators one tenth part both In Profit & Loss, the said James Grier his Executors & administrators one tenth part thereof for his and their part both In profit and Loss. The said David Brooks his Executors & administrators one tenth part thereof for his & their part both In Profit and Loss. The said James Giles his Executors & administrat⁵ one tenth part thereof, for his & their part both In Profit & Loss, and the said Thomas Machin his Executors & Administrators the other tenth part thereof, for his & their part both In Profit and Loss, According to the True Intent & meaning thereof, & the said Samuel Atlee, James F. Atlee David Brooks, James Grier, James Giles & Thomas Machin having by their several Obligations bearing even date with these Presents bound themselves for the payment of four hundred pounds in the whole New York Currency to the said Reuben Harmon, William Coley, Elias Jackson & Daniel Van Voorhis, payable in two years from the date hereof which said sum of Four hundred pounds Together with the said sum of two hundred Pounds to be put into the stock aforesaid by the said James Atlee, James F. Atlee, David Brooks, James Grier, James Giles and Thomas Machin as the Part & Share of the said Reuben Harmon William Coley, Elias Jackson & Daniel Van Voorhis to be Employed in the stock as abovesaid, making in the whole six hundred pounds, Which said sum of six hundred pounds is Considered by the said Reuben Harmon, William Coley, Elias Jackson & Daniel Van Voorhis as a full and ample Compensation to them for admitting the said Samuel Atlee, James F. Atlee, David Brooks, James Grier James Giles & Thomas Machin into a full and equal share agreeably to the Proportions before mentioned, that is to say each of the Parties to these Presents, one tenth part, share and share alike of all the Privileges, Profits & Advantages arising from the Coinage of Copper for the State of Vermont, persuent to the Act aforesaid, during the Continuance of the Term aforesaid, and it is further agreed by the parties of these Presents that the said Samuel Atlee, James F. Atlee, David Brooks, James Grier, James Giles & Thomas Machin, shall on or before the said First day of July next Compleat at their own Proper Cost & Charges the Works now

Errecting at the Mills of the said Thomas Machin near the Great Pond in the County of Ulster aforesaid, so as to Enable the parties to these presents to Carry on their Joint Trade, & also that the said Reuben Harmon, William Coley, Elias Jackson & Daniel Van Voorhis shall on or before the said first day of July next at their own proper Cost & Charges, Compleat the Works they are now Errecting at Rupert in the County of Bennington aforesaid for the purpose of Coining aforesaid, so as to enable the parties to these presents to Cary on their Joint Trade, and that when the Works errecting at the said Thomas Machin's Mills & those at Rupert aforesaid shall be Compleated for the purpose aforesaid that then & from thence forward during the Continuance of the Copartnership all Repairs or Alterations which shall be deemed necessary to the said Works shall be made & born by the parties to these presents, share & share alike. And it is further agreed between the parties to these presents that the said James Giles shall have Charge of the Writing True Keeping & Custody of the Books to be Kept for the said Copartnership & that the said Reuben Harmon & William Coley shall equally manage act & perform that part of the trade which Concerns the Coinage of Money at Rupert aforesaid, & that the said Thomas Machin and James F. Atlee shall equally manage & perform that part of the Trade which Concern the Coinage of Money & Manufacuring Hard Ware at the Mills of the said Thomas Machin in the County of Ulster aforesaid and that the said James Grier shall be the Cashier of the Money Coined at Rupert aforesaid & the said Daniel Van Voorhis Cashier of the Money Coined at the Mills of the said Thomas Machin & that the said James Grier & Elias Jackson shall have the General management of the Expenditures of the Money Coined at either places last Mentioned in the Purchase of such Articles as shall be for the most Benefit and advantage of the Copartnership, and that the other Joint Business shall be equally acted and performed by the said David Brooks & Samuel Atlee, and also it is agreed that a Certain Book shall be Kept by the said James Giles, which shall be called & Known by the name of the Book of Resolutions in which Book such Resolutions shall be made and Entered as the Majority of the Copartners shall determine for the better Regulating the Concerns of this Copartnership Provided such Resolutions are not Contrary to the True Intent & meaning of this Copartnership and it is further agreed by & between the parties to these Presents that they shall once every four Months during the said Copartnership to wit, on the first Day of Feb^y on the first Day of June and on the first day of

October in every year, Come to a plain fair and perfect account & Reckoning with each other of for and Concerning all Matters Relating to the Copartnership, to the Intent it may appear how, & in what State & Condition they then stand in Refference to their said Copartnership & Joint Stock, & it is agreed that after the said Account is made up, each of the said parties shall & may deduct & take out of the profits Nett Produce & Increase of the said trade to & for his own Particular use such sum & sums of money as shall be Mutually agreed upon by & between the Parties of these Presents, & that the place of Meeting for the purpose of settling the said account shall be at Rynbeck in the State of New York, unless otherwise Determined by a Majority of the Copartners to be expressed in their Resolution Book, And Whereas it may be Inconvenient for all the parties to these presents to Meet at the time above mentioned, it is therefore hereby agreed that such of the parties who cannot attend that then & in such case he or they may authorize and appoint either of the others of the said Parties to transact, doo, & perform in his or their name or names, the necessary Business of such Meeting & the dooing or acting of such Person so appointed shall be binding on the person or persons so appointing him and which authority for so acting shall be in the words following, to wit, I —— do hereby authorize and appoint you —— for me & in my name to negotiate & settle on my account all matters Relating to the Copartnership in which we are connected for the Coinage of Copper &$^c$ for the State of Vermont &$^c$, and if case should require to sign my name to any Resolution that may be made for the Government of the Copartnership and for which this shall be your warrant dated this —— day of —— 17— which authority or Letter of Attorney shall be equally binding on the party giving it as tho' he had given a Regular Letter of Atty, Perscribed by the forms of Law, And it is hereby further agreed that no advantage of Survivorship shall be taken by the said parties but that on the Death of either of them the Executors or Administrators of the Party so dying giving security to the Survivors to Indemnify them shall and may Receive the share or Interest in the said Joint stock of the Party so Dying, and it is Mutually agreed by and between the said parties that in Case either of them shall at any time during the said term of eight years be minded to break off & quit the said Copartnership they shall either of them be at Liberty so to do on giving six months notice to the others of them in Writing of such his Intention to quit the same, but the same Copartnership to Exist as to the other Parties who remain Notwithstanding. And further that it shall and may be lawful to & for the Parties to these Presents or any of them at his & their will & Pleasure to have Liberty, ingress, egress and regress into, out of and from the Compting house, store House & Room where either of the Parties to these presents may be employed, in the Coinage & Manufactury aforesaid, & shall & may freely as occation may require as well View the Works as also view & peruse the said Book of Accounts as also all Wares, Goods & Merchandise & other things whatsoever relating to the said Joint Trade in the hands Custody or Possession of either of the Parties to these Presents; And it is further agreed between the Parties to these Presents that if any Doubt Question, Controversy or difference shall happen or arise between the said Parties Concerning their said Copartnership the same shall be Determined by a Majority of the Copartners or by a Referrence of Indifferent Persons if either of the Parties shall think fit which reference shall not consist of more than three Persons, and those Refferees to be chosen in the Usual maner in which Referrees are chosen that is, one on either side, & the third by the two Chosen if an Umpire should be necessary. And further it is Concluded and agreed by and between the said parties to these presents and their true Intent and meaning is that none of the said Parties, nor the Executors or Administrators of any of them shall at any time or times, be Charged or Chargable by Virtue of these presents further than for his own proper offence or Breach of Covenant, & not for the Offence or breach of Covenant of any of the other of the said parties his Executors or Administrators, anything before or hereinafter to be mentioned notwithstanding; and it is further agreed by and between the said Parties to these presents that neither of the said parties shall make any Charge for his or their Labour in carrying on the design or transacting doing or acting any particular branch of the Copartnership except all such costs and charges & expenses as may be Disbursed by any of the parties hereto when abroad from their Habitations in transacting the Business of the Copartnership or unless by a Resolution of the Majority of the Copartners to be expressed in their Resolution Book, which shall be Equally born by the parties to these presents and it is further agreed by & between the parties to these presents that if either or any of them during the Continuance of their Copartnership shall get or Procure in his or their name or names any Grant for Coinage of Money from the United States of America in Congress Assembled or from the Legislature of any of the United States or shall enter into a Contract or Contracts with such other persons who may have the Privilidge of Coining from the Congress as aforesaid or any of the Legislatures aforesaid that then & in such Case the Profit & Losses of such Grant of Coinage or Contract aforesaid shall be had and born & shared between the parties to these presents share and share alike, and lastly it is agreed that none of them the said parties shall and will at any time or times hereafter do Commit or Omit to do any act, Deed or Device whatsoever with an Intent to defeat or make Void in part or in all the true Intent or meaning of these presents, and for the true and punctual Performance hereof of the parties to these Presents Bind themselves, their Heirs, Executors and Administrators, each unto the other, their Executors & administrators, Severally & not Jointly in the pennal Sum of One thousand pounds. In Witness Whereof the Parties to these presents have hereunto Interchangeably set their Hands and Seals the Day and year first above written.

"Sealed & Delivered
in the Presence of

[Here is inserted a long list of additions, erasures, etc., as in the previous agreement. These it will not be necessary to print, as they probably have all been incorporated into the body of the paper; and had they not, the lines in print not corresponding with those of the original, it would be impossible correctly to place the alterations.]

Amasa Sprague
" Henery Evens

Reuben Harmon [L.S.]
William Coley [L.S.]
Elias Jackson [L.S.]
Dan¹ Van Voorhis [L.S.]
Sam¹ Atlee [L.S.]
James F. Atlee [L.S.]
D. Brooks [L.S.]
James Grier [L.S.]
James Giles [L.S.]
Thoˢ Machin [L.S.] "

Simms, in the History of Scoharie County, gives some account of this copartnership, concluding with these remarks: "Whether the long firm of money makers ever coined coppers enough to fill the pockets of all the Green Mountain boys; or whether they found the business profitable, is uncertain; but from Mr. Machin's papers, I am led to conclude they never effected much. At his mills perhaps a thousand pounds of copper was manufactured, as appears by the papers, in the year 1789; previous to which little seems to have been done. 'What is everybody's business is nobody's;' and the saying seems to have been verified in the doings of this copper firm: for in a letter from J. F. Atlee to Mr. Machin, dated Vergennes, October 14, 1790, he expresses a wish that the concern might arrive at a settlement on equitable terms, and compromise their matters without a tedious and expensive law suit."

# CONNECTICUT.

––––•–•––––

The attention of Connecticut was, at an early period, called to the regulation of a coinage now unknown to us, or, if known, not recognized under the name by which it is here introduced, as we learn from the records, that as early as May 25th, 1721, this vote was passed by the Upper House, in that Colony:—"An act sent from the Lower House that the coin called black doggs pass at 2ᵈ pᶜᵉ was dissented to at this board."

We can gain no clue as to what coins were here referred to under the name of "black doggs," but conclude, from the value placed upon them, that they must have been composed of copper, or some alloy of that metal.

At this time Connecticut had, in common with other colonies, adopted the practice of issuing paper money. Considerable sums of this money were emitted between 1709, when the first was authorized, and 1780, which was the date of the last. A remedy for the evils produced by these rapidly depreciating bills was soon proposed.

In 1739, a petition was presented by John Read, of Boston, to the General Court of Connecticut, praying their aid in obtaining a Patent from the Crown, for the coinage of copper money from the metal produced from the native ores of that State. The profits of this coinage were to be secured to him, he defraying all expenses incident to the attempt, whether successful or otherwise.

This petition, and a letter from Read referring thereto, are preserved by the Connecticut Historical Society, at Hartford, Conn. We here acknowledge our indebtedness to the Hon. Charles J. Hoadly, of that city, for copies of these two papers, which are next presented.

The first of these is the petition of John Read, and is endorsed:—

"Mr. John Reeds of y^e 15 Oct^r 1739 come to not untill No^r 21^t 1739."

"To the Honble the Gov^r Council & representatives in Gen^l Court assembled at New-haven 10 Oct^r 1739.

" The Memorial & Petition of John Read of Boston Gent.

"May it please your hon^r & this honble Court

" The Province of the Massachusets Bay are sending home Mr. Christopher Kilby lately chosen by the house of Representatives their Agent at the British Court to allow them to make Province bills as in times past as the only & necessary means of carrying on their trade as well as defending their frontiers: while the Governour loudly tells them their attempt will be utterly fruitless.

" The Colony of Rhode-Island are from time to time multiplying their bills after the old manner, & we take them & are glad of them, tho' they are still declining in value, & now one ounce of Silver is 28^s of them or any others of New England old tenor bills & will doubtless grow worse & worse.

" The King & Council at home are concerned at our pitiful moans & are privately inquiring what bills are out in New England & what hath been out & called in, & consulting the merch^ts that trade hither to find out some means to establish the value of our money or bills, & give no farther relief than shall be found necessary.

" Hearing & perceiving these things without inquiring, & whether I will or not, I have considered & apprehend the present & best expedient will be the Coining of English half pence & farthings out of the Copper produced in Connecticut of Sterling value, make that the Standard of all your money, call in all y^e old bills & emit so many new only as at y^e different value shall equal those called in, make a bank of the new bills & Copper money payable on demand one half in bills now to be renewed & redeemable at y^e periods you have already set (which then shall be redeemed with copper money) & the other half in Copper money, which in a short compass of time may be effected & will establish & for ever preserve the value of your bills against all factors Stock-jobbers & chances whatsoever. This will immediately supply a lasting money of Intrinsick value & effectually supply us with small change, & bring in Silver also. For mens pockets are locked up now that have any silver, because men cannot trade in it for want of knowing y^e value tis now of & the value twill be of to morrow in comparison with our bills, and so are afraid to part with it for fear of losing, but if they can once find the paper established & y$^r$by y$^e$ silver men will as soon part with that as with copper or paper.

"Now there are no people can expect to be favoured with a Patent from y$^e$ Crown to Coin Copper in New-England upon so good grounds as Connecticut & I doubt not but you might obtain it, for

"Connecticut hath been the most innocent in the point of paper money of any part of New-England, your stock being reduced very low before the New London Society's presumption obliged you for y$^e$ sake of saving innocents imposed upon by their bills to make a quantity for y$^e$ calling in of theirs & to be paid for by them. And this is a great point at y$^e$ British Court.

"Connecticut is the Native Soil that produceth this Copper & furnisheth a strong argument for you at Court therefore to gain this patent that you may improve your own natural production & manufacture.

"Connecticut will be the first that finds an expedient to rectify y$^e$ value of our money & establish the value of it which will be a strong inducement to the Courts favour.

"And this is the luckiest juncture you can possibly appear in it as appears by the premisses laid down & publickly known; I have heretofore for two years past had this very thought in my mind for substance. I have several times occasionally moved discourse upon it, and at last seem to be pretty much alone in my sentiments: but this juncture has made me the more Confident of the success if y$^e$ matter be prudently managed.

"Now therefore if it will be deemed a real publick benefit to have money produced & multiplied among us of a certain value & steady continuance, I offer this honble Court to take upon me the management of this affair, to procure a pattent from y$^e$ Crown to this Government to Coin Copper money. I will only desire their orders to their agent to petition & use all his diligence to obtain it, and particularly under my directions, also an authentick account under the Province Seal of the sums & time of Emitting & calling in your bills, a ballance drawn shewing how much was outstanding at the time of your last Emission for y$^e$ New London Society & y$^e$ occasion of that Emission, & the account continued down to this time to show what is now out, & I will give all necessary directions to your Agent touching it, at y$^e$ same time I will furnish your Agent with all the Sterling Cash to pay him for all his trouble attendance & disbursements, and the condition is that if I do not procure any pattent nor fruit of my labour & expense in y$^e$ attempt I will stand to & bear the loss all myself & such as I shall join with me if any body do join with me, & on y$^e$

other hand if I do procure such a patent or such like fruit of my attempt as the publick will reap y^e benefit of a good supply I shall have all the benefit that may lawfully arise from it to the undertakers.   And this I desire may be insured to me by y^e Government as my Incouragem^t to pursue it at this time which I look upon to be the happiest that can well be.

"This proposal of mine requireth secresy & dispatch, that no man but whom I trust may know it, till it rest in your agents hands at home in England. And if you send any agents from hence (as I suppose you are about no such thing) they may know Nothing of it.

"I am may it please y^r honour & this honble Court

Y^or most humble Serv^t

"Boston 15 Oct^r 1739.                                    Jn^o Read."

Mr. Read, having written twice, (his second letter we have been unable to trace,) but failing to elicit a reply, writes a third time to this effect :—

"12 Nov^r 1739.

"S^r I have writ two letters to you at New-haven that I judged it of great importance to Connecticut to procure the King's patent to coin the copper of your own production: That I had desired Mr. Woodbridge of Simsbury to intimate this to you: That the mine adventurers Mr. Cradock & others communed with me about procuring it: That we had done, & if the Colony would give me their name to their Agent, I would procure one at my own expense but to my own profit.   I wrote the first Monday after October Gen^l Court met & the next Monday after, both by the post, but never received one word of answer, therefore only desire to know if you had them, proposed them &c. or not, for I never had any answer touching the premises.

"My service to all friends.

"I am y^r honours

"Most humble serv^t

Jn^o Read."

"To the honble Joseph Talcott Esq^r

From the coincidence of dates, it appears probable that Higley, who was coining coppers upon his own account in 1737—1739, was connected with Read in this attempt to secure the right of coinage, particularly as his own proceedings in that business were without the sanction of law: he probably

was one of those referred to by Read as, "such as I shall join with me."
Deferring the subject of Higley's coinage, as unauthorized, and on that
account not properly belonging in this chapter, we proceed to the copper
coinage of this State, as introduced by the petition of Samuel Bishop, James
Hillhouse, John Goodrich, and Joseph Hopkins, dated at New Haven, October 18th, 1785.

"To the Honorable General Assembly of the State of Connecticutt now
sitting at New Haven in said State

"The Petition of Samuel Bishop James Hillhouse & John Goodrich all
of New Haven in New Haven County and Joseph Hopkins of Waterbury
in said County humbly sheweth That there is a great & very prevalent
scarcity of small Coin in this State, in consequence whereof great inconveniences are severely felt by all orders of men in the Article of making
Change, especially by the laborious Class, who are indeed the Stay & Staff
of every Community that our late Enemies conscious of this, & unrestrained
by any Law, are countirfeiting in vast abundance, that others even of our
Countrymen, &, your Memorialists are sorry to say some, even of their fellow
Citizens have attempted the same nefarious Business, and are now Coining &
stamping a Copper Coin much under standard weight and Endevouring to
Impose the same upon the Inhabitants of this State manifestly to the injury
of the Credit of our Copper Currency and to the great Damage, in point of
fraud and imposition, of the honest & unsuspicious Citizens of this State—

"Your Memorialists conceive that the Right of Coining Copper is in
this Honorable Legislature, that it is of high importance that it be not
tolerated but by their permission, & under their superintendency, & that the
State ought to derive some pecuniary advantage from such a toleration—

"It must be very needless to suggest arguments to the Wisdom of your
Honors in support of this proposition the Justice thereof being obvious to
every one who hears it made—Impressed with these ideas your Memorialists
beg leave to address your Honors on this subject, and to propose to your
Honor's Consideration the Expediency of granting to them for the term of
ten years from the rising of the Assembly, the Right & power of establishing
a Mint in this State to be under the inspection of such Committee consisting
of three persons to be appointed by your Honors from time to time as there
shall be occasion, for the purpose of Coining Coppers of good metal of the
standard & weight of British half pence commonly called coppers, five per

Cent. however of all the Coppers thus coined to be paid by them half yearly to the Treasurer of this State to and for the use of this State & that no other persons, but by permission of this Honorable Assembly, to have right to Coin within this State any Copper Coin under the Penalties by Law to by inflicted on persons who counterfeit any of the Gold or Silver Coin current in this State —

"On these terms or such as may suggest themselves to the Wisdom of your Honors, your Memorialists are wiling and desirous of establishing a Mint for coining Coppers and to be under Oath to account with the Treasurer of this State for one twentieth part of all Coppers by them Coined, and that a Committee appointed by your Honors from time to time shall at the Expence of your Memorialists inspect the quality & weight of all Coppers coined by them previous to their being put off for Circulation and on the Principles suggested in this Memorial they Humbly pray your Honors that they may be permitted to establish a Mint for the purpose of coining Coppers and they as in duty bound will ever pray   New Haven October 18th 1785 —

Sam[l] Bishop<br>
James Hillhouse<br>
Joseph Hopkins<br>
John Goodrich "

" In the Lower House (Oct 19th)   The Prayer of this Memorial is Granted & Liberty for a Bill in Form &c                Test J Strong Clerke "

" In the upper House

" The further Consideration of this Memorial is referred to the Gen[l] Assembly of this State to be holden at Hartford on the 2[d] Thursday of May next                              Test George Wyllys Secrety "

On the back of the above document is the following: —

" In the Lower House

" Col Wadsworth & Mr Ingersol are appointed a Comm[ee] to confer with such Gentlemen as the hon[l] upper House shall appoint on the different Votes of the Houses on this Memorial        Test James Davenport Clerke "

" In the upper House Joseph Platt Cook Esq[r] is appointed to confer with the Com[tee] of the lower House on the differing Votes of the Houses on this Memorial                              Test George Wyllys Secrety "

" In the Upper House

On Report of the Committee and Reconsideration granted on this Memorial that the Memorialist have Liberty to establish a Mint for coining Coppers as prayed for to an Amount not exceeding ten Thousand Pounds— and that a Bill &c                    Teste George Wyllys Secrety "

" In the Lower House on Reconsideration Concurred
                    Test Jedediah Strong Clerke "

The bill first drawn up having undergone some slight changes by amendment in the Assembly, was again presented, in the form which follows :

                              "Oct. 1785.

" Upon the Memorial of Samuel Bishop, Joseph Hopkins James Hillhouse and John Goodrich praying for Liberty to Establish a mint for coining Copper in this State under the Direction and Superintendance of the General Assembly they paying one Twentieth part of all Copper by them Coined into the Treasury of this State to and for the Use of this State as p.ʳ memorial on File &c—

" Resolved by this Assembly that said Samuel Bishop, Joseph Hopkins, James Hillhouse & John Goodrich have Liberty, and Liberty and Authority is hereby Granted to them to Establish a Mint for Coining and manufacturing Coppers, not to exceed the amount of Ten Thousand Pounds lawful money in Value of the Standard of Brittish half pence, to weigh Six penny weight, and to bear the following Impression or Stamp (Viz) a mans head on the one side with a Circumscription in the Words or Letters following (Viz) AVCTORI : CONNEC : and on the other side the Emblem of Liberty with an olive branch in her hand with a circumscription in the Words and Figures following (Viz) INDE : ET . LIB : 1785 : — Which Grant is to continue during the pleasure of the General Assembly, the Mem.ᵗˢ paying into the Treasury of this State, at the end of every six Months, one twentieth part of all Coppers by them Coined or manufactured at said Mint—The mem.ᵗˢ are not however to put off or into Circulation any Coppers by them Coined untill the same shall have been Inspected and Approved by the Hon.ᵇˡᵉ Roger Sherman and James Wadsworth Esq.ʳˢ David Austin Esq.ʳ and Mess.ʳˢ Ebenezer Chittenden & Isaac Beers or the major part of them who are hereby appointed a Committee for that purpose, or such other Committee as the General Assembly shall from time to time appoint such Inspection to be made at the Expence of the Mem.ᵗˢ —

"Provided nothing in this Act shall be construed to make such Coppers a legal Tender in payment of Any Debt, *except for the purpose of making even Change, for any sum not exceeding three Shillings*

"Pass^d in the upper House

Teste George Wyllys Secrety"

"In the Lower House

"Concurred with the following alterations & exclusions Viz. with the Addition of the Words *not exceeding five years* next after the Word *Assembly* in the 22^nd. Line of the Bill—and exclusive of what follows the word *Debt* in the last Line save two of the Bill.

Test Jedediah Strong Clerke"

"Concurr^d in the upper House

Teste George Wyllys Secrety"

The final passage of the bill is thus recorded:—

"Thursday Afternoon 20 Oct^r. 1785—

"Passed a Bill in Form on Memorial of Samuel Bishop &c granting Liberty to coin Coppers under the Inspection of the Hon. R Sherman & Ja^s Wadsworth Esq^rs David Austin Esq^r & Messrs Eben^r. Chittenden & Isaac Beers"

We are permitted to give the following extract from Mr. Bushnell's Numismatic Notes in manuscript, in relation to this coinage:

"Hon. Henry Meigs, late of this city, (New York,) deceased, informed me in Sept. 1854, that Connecticut coins were made in a building situated under the Southern Bluff, near the centre of the north shore of the harbor in New Haven, west of the Broome and Platt houses. Mr. Meigs lived at the time, between the latter residences, at a short distance from the mint house. He visited it frequently, and saw the press in operation. The building was a small frame house, and he thinks was painted red. Messrs. Broome and Platt, who had formerly been merchants in the city of New York, and were men of fortune, he thinks must have had a sub-contract for the manufacture of the State coinage, as Mr. Broome superintended the mint, and gave orders to the men, not more than three of whom were seen at work at one time. Both members of the firm would sometimes distribute some of the coins among the boys, among whom was my informant. Mr. Meigs said he saw the mint in operation in 1788, and it had been in operation some considerable time before that.  The coins were struck by means of a powerful iron screw.  Mr. F. Kingsbury thinks that the house described by Mr. Meigs was probably at a place at Morris Cove, now so called, which is on the right hand side of the harbor going up, and about two miles above the light house.  The firm of Broome and Platt was composed of Samuel Broome and Jeremiah Platt.

"I have understood from another source that a building at Westville, at the foot of West Rock, about two miles inland of New Haven, was likewise used for the coinage of Connecticut coppers.  At the time the old building was last seen, it contained an old coining press, and the remnants of copper castings.

"The dies for the Connecticut coins were made by Abel Buel, of New Haven."

The coins struck in accordance with the foregoing acts consist of but a single type, comprising a great number of varieties which we have endeavored to tabulate in a condensed, and yet in an intelligible manner.  The tables may be found on the two following pages.

A single description will suffice for the coins of the four years, 1785 to 1788 inclusive.

OBVERSE.

Device, — A head, laureated, on some facing left, on others, right.

Legend, — AUCTORI CONNEC

REVERSE.

Device, — The goddess of liberty, seated, facing left, an olive branch extended in her right hand, the liberty staff supported by her left.

Legend, — INDE ET LIB

In exergue, — The date, — 1785, 1786, 1787, or 1788

Borders, — on some serrated, on others milled.

Edges, — plain; size, 17 to 18.  For weights see notes following the tables.

Our tables of varieties are not so satisfactory as we could wish, since in tables based upon the differences of punctuation, it is impossible to describe the peculiarities of each die.  This might be accomplished by a system of classification, but as such tables would be too extended to come within the limits of this work, we are compelled to accept the more simple though less scientific method.

# TABLES OF VARIETIES OF CONNECTICUT COINS.

## 1785.

### OBVERSE.

| No. | Facing. | Legends and Punctuation. | With Reverse. |
|---|---|---|---|
| 1 | Right. | AUCTORI. CONNEC. (1st colon clear of head) | E |
| 2 | do. | AUCTORI: CONNEC: (colon close on head) | A |
| 3 | do. | AUCTORI: CONNEC: (colon partly on head) | B, C, F |
| 4 | do. | AUCTORI: CONNEC: (colon partly on head) | B, D, F, H |
| 5 | do. | AUCTORI: CONNEC: (colon half on head) | F, H |
| 6 | do. | AUCTORI: CONNEC: (colon and I part on head) | A, F, G |
| 7 | Left. | AUCTORI: CONNEC: | D |
| 8 | do. | AUCTORI: CONNEC: | D |

### REVERSE.

| No. | Legends and Punctuation. | No. of Dies. | With Obverse. |
|---|---|---|---|
| A | INDE: ETLIB: | 1 | 2, 6 |
| B | INDE: ETLIB: | 2 | 3, 4 |
| C | INDE: ETLIB: | 1 | 3 |
| D | INDE: ETLIB: | 1 | 4, 7, 8 |
| E | INDE: ET · LIB · | 1 | 1 |
| F | INDE: ETLIB: | 5 | 3, 4, 5, 6 |
| G | INDE: ET · LIB: | 1 | 6 |
| H | INDE: ET · LIB: | 3 | 4, 5 |

## 1786.

### OBVERSE.

| No. | Facing. | Decoration. | Legends and Punctuation. | With Reverse. |
|---|---|---|---|---|
| 1 | Right. | Mailed. | AUCTORI CONNEC | A |
| 2 | do. | do. | AUCTORI · CONNEC · | A |
| 3 | do. | do. | AUCTORI: CONNEC: | D |
| 4 | Left. | do. | AUCTORI: CONNEC | G |
| 5 | do. | do. | AUCTORI: CONNEC: | { B, C, E, F, / G, H, I |
| 6 | do. | Draped. | AUCTORI: CONNEC: | K |
| 7 | do. | do. | AUCTORI: ★ CONNEC: ★ | K |

### REVERSE.

| No. | Legends and Punctuation. | No. of Dies. | With Obverse. |
|---|---|---|---|
| A | ETLIB | 1 | 1, 2 |
| B | INDE ET LIB | 1 | 5 |
| C | INDE ET LIB: | 1 | 5 |
| D | INDE ET LIB: | 1 | 3 |
| E | INDE: ET LIB: | 1 | 5 |
| F | INDE: ET · LIB: | 1 | 4, 5 |
| G | INDE: ET · LIB: | 4 | 5 |
| H | INDE: ET · LIB: | 3 | 5 |
| I | INDE: ET · LIB: | 1 | — |
| K | INDE: ET · LIB: | — | 6, 7 |

## 1787.

### OBVERSE.

| No. | Facing. | Decoration. | Legends and Punctuation. | With Reverse. |
|---|---|---|---|---|
| 1 | Right. | Mailed. | AUCTORI CONNEC | A, C, L |
| 2 | Left. | do. | AUCTORI CONNEC | B |
| 3 | do. | do. | AUCTORI CONNEC · | G |
| 4 | do. | do. | AUCTORI · CONNEC · | L |
| 5 | do. | do. | · · AUCTORI · CONNEC · | P |
| 6 | do. | do. | · · AUCTORI · CONNEC · | M |
| 7 | do. | do. | AUCTORI · CONNEC: | I |
| 8 | do. | do. | AUCTORI · CONNEC: ∴ | N, O |
| 9 | do. | do. | + AUCTORI + CONNEC + | D, E, R |
| 10 | do. | do. | + AUCTORI + + CONNEC + | E |
| 11 | do. | do. | ★ AUCTORI + ★ CONNEC ★ | E, K |
| 12 | do. | do. | AUCTORI . ★ CONNEC ❋ | Q |
| 13 | do. | do. | ★ AUCTORI ★ CONNEC · ★ | D |
| 14 | do. | do. | ↑ AUCTORI ↓ CONNEC · ↓ | H |
| 15 | do. | do. | ❋ AUCTORI ❋ CONNECT ❋❋ | F*, R, S |

### REVERSE.

| No. | Legends and Punctuation. | No. of Dies. | With Obverse. |
|---|---|---|---|
| A | ETLIB INDE | 1 | 1 |
| B | INDE ET LIB | 1 | 2 |
| C | INDE ● ET LIB · | 1 | 1 |
| D | + INDE + ET + LIB · + | 1 | 9, 13 |
| E | + INDE ❋ ET + LIB · ★ | 1 | 9, 10, 11 |
| F* | ❋ INDE ❋ ET ❋ LIB · ❋ | 1 | 15 32 |
| G | INDE ★ ET · LIB · ★ | 1 | 3 |
| H | INDE: ↑ LIB · ↓↓ | 1 | 14 |
| I | INDE: ❋ ET LIB · ★ | 1 | 7 |
| K | ★ INDE ★ ET · LIB · ★ | 1 | 11 |
| L | INDE: ★ ET · LIB · | 1 | 1, 4 |
| M | INDE: ❋ ET · LIB · ❋ | 1 | 6 |
| N | INDE: ★ ET LIB · ★ | 1 | 8 |
| O | INDE: ★❋ ETLIB · ★❋ | 8 | 8 |
| P | · INDE · ❋ ET · LIB · | 1 | 5 |
| Q | · IN DE · ETLIB · ❋ | 1 | 12 |
| R | + IND + + ET + LIB · + + | 1 | 9, 15 |
| S | ❋ INDL ● ET ❋ LIB · ? ❋ | 1 | 15 |

## OBVERSE. — 1787.

| No. | Facing | Decoration | Legends and Punctuation | No. of Dies | With Reverse |
|---|---|---|---|---|---|
| 16 | Left | Draped | AUCTORI: CONNEC: | 4 | L, M, N, O |
| 17 | do | do | AUCTORI: -CONNEC: | 1 | G |
| 18 | do | do | AUCTORI: + CONNEC: | 1 | G |
| 19 | do | do | AUCTORI: + CONNEC: | 1 | G |
| 20 | do | do | AUCTORI: * CONNEC: | 1 | A |
| 21 | do | do | AUCTORI: + CONNEC: | 1 | G |
| 22 | do | do | AUCTORI: + CONNEC: | 1 | C |
| 23 | do | do | -+AUCTORI: -+ CONNEC: | 5 | A |
| 24 | do | do | -+AUCTORI: -+ CONNEC: | 2 | F, G |
| 25 | do | do | **AUCTORI: * CONNEC: | 1 | B |
| 26 | do | do | +AUCTORI: × CONNEC: | 1 | D, B, K |
| 27 | do | do | AUCTORI: + CONNEC: | 1 | A |
| 28 | do | do | AUCTORI: * CONNEC: | 2 | M, N |
| 29 | do | do | AUCTORI: * CONNEC: | 1 | N, P |
| 30 | do | do | AUCTORI: * CONNEC. | 3 | X, H |
| 31 | do | do | AUCTORI: * CONNEC: | 6 | R, G, |
| 32 | do | do | AUCTORI: * CONNEC: | 40 | F*, V, X, A, H |
| 33 | do | do | AUCTORI: ⇑ CONNEC: | 1 | L, Q, R, S, ; T, W, Z, H |
| 34 | do | do | AUCTORI: ⇑ CONNEC: | 1 | F |
| 35 | do | do | AUCTORI: ⇑ CONNEC: | 1 | |
| 36 | do | do | AUCTORI: ⇑ CONNEC: | 3 | K, L, |
| 37 | do | do | AUCTORI: + CONNEC: | 11 | E, G, H, I ; K, C, D, E |
| 38 | do | do | AUCTORI: ⇑ CONNEC: | 1 | G, L |
| 39 | do | do | AUCTOPI + CONNEC. | 2 | H, E. F |
| 40 | do | do | AUCTOPI: * CONNEC. | 1 | I |
| 41 | do | do | AUCTORI. * CONNEC. | 1 | K |
| 42 | do | do | AUCTORI. * CONNFC. | 1 | Y |
| 43 | do | do | | 1 | |

## REVERSE.

| No. | Legends and Punctuation | No. of Dies | With Obverse |
|---|---|---|---|
| A | INDE: · ETLIB: | 3 | 20, 23, 27 |
| B | INDE: · ETLIB: | 1 | 25 |
| C | INDE: · ETLIB: | 1 | 22 |
| D | INDE: · ETLIB: | 1 | 26 |
| E | INDE: · ET LIB: | 1 | 37 |
| F | INDE: · ET-LIB: | 1 | 24 |
| G | INDE: · ET-LIB: | 5 | 17,18,19,21 ; 24,37,38 |
| H | INDE: × ET-LIB: | 2 | 37,39 |
| I | INDE: · ET-LIB: | 1 | 37 |
| K | INDE: · ET-LIB: × | 4 | 36, 37 |
| L | INDE: · ET-LIB: ⇓ | 4 | 16,33,36,38 |
| M | INDE: · ET-LIB: * | 1 | 16, 28 |
| N | INDE: · ET-LIB: * | 2 | 16, 28, 29 |
| O | INDE: · ETLIB | 1 | 16 |
| P | INDE: · ETLIB | 1 | 29 |
| Q | INDE: · ETLIB: | 1 | 33 |
| R | INDE: · ET-LIB: | 4 | 31,33 |
| S | INDE: · ET-LIB: | 3 | 33 |
| T | INDE: · ET LIB: | 2 | 33 |
| V | INDE: · ET LIB: | 1 | 33 |
| W | INDE: · ETLIB: | 3 | 33 |
| X | INDE: · ETLIB: | 4 | 30, 32 |
| Y | INDE: · ETLIB: | 1 | 43 |
| Z | INDE: · ETLIB: | 23 | 33 |
| A | INDE: · ET-LIB: | 1 | 32 |
| B | FNDE: · ET-LIR: | 1 | 26 |
| C | INDE: · ET-LIR: | 2 | 37 |
| D | INDE: · ET-LIR: | 1 | 37 |
| E | INDE: · ET-LIR: | 2 | 37, 39 |
| F | INDE: · ET-LIR: | 1 | 34, 35, 39 |
| G | INDE: · ETLIR: | 1 | 31 |
| H | INDE: · ETIIB: | 2 | 30, 32, 33 |
| I | INDE: · ETIIB: | 2 | 41 |
| K | INDE: · ETIIB: * | 2 | 26, 40, 42 |

## OBVERSE. — 1788.

| No. | Facing | Decoration | Legends and Punctuation | No. of Dies | With Reverse |
|---|---|---|---|---|---|
| 1 | Right | Mailed | AUCTORI CONNEC | 1 | I |
| 2 | do | do | AUCTORI . CONNEC * | 1 | D* |
| 3 | do | do | AUCTORI * CONNEC * | 1 | B |
| 4 | do | do | AUCTORI * CONNEC * | 1 | B, K |
| 5 | do | do | AUCTORI * CONNEC * | 1 | B |
| 6 | do | do | AUCTORI * CONNEC * | 1 | H* |
| 7 | Left | do | AUCTORI * CONNEC * | 1 | E |
| 8 | do | do | AUCTORI * CONNEC * | 1 | K |
| 9 | do | do | AUCTORI * CONNEC * | 1 | E |
| 10 | do | do | AUCTORI * CONNEC * | 1 | C |
| 11 | do | do | AUCTORI * CONNEC * | 2 | G |
| 12 | do | do | AUCTORI * CONNLC * | 1 | C, E, F |
| 13 | do | do | AUCTORI * CONNEC * | 2 | A* L |
| 14 | do | Draped | AUCTORI * CONNEC * | 2 | L, M |
| 15 | do | do | AUCTORI * CONNEC * | 2 | D* H* L |
| 16 | do | do | AUCTORI . * CONNEC . * | 5 | N, O |

## REVERSE.

| No. | Legends and Punctuation | No. of Dies | With Obverse |
|---|---|---|---|
| A* | INDE * ET * LIB * | 2 | 13, 14 |
| B | INDE * ET * LIB * | 1 | 3, 4, 5 |
| C | INDE * ET * LIB * | 1 | 10, 12 |
| D* | INDE * ET * LIB * | 1 | 2, 16 |
| E | INDE * ET * LIB * | 1 | 7, 9, 12 |
| F | INDE * ET * LIB * | 1 | 11 |
| G | INDE . * ET * LIB * | 1 | 6, 16 |
| H* | INDE . × ET * LIB . * | 1 | 1 |
| I | INDE . * ET * LIB × | 1 | 4, 8 |
| K | INDE . * ET * LIB . * | 2 | 14, 15, 16 |
| L | INDE . * ET * ETLIB . | 1 | 15 |
| M | IN DE . * ET * LIB . | 1 | 16 |
| N | INDL . ET * * LIB . * | 1 | 16 |

NOTES ON THE TABLES OF CONNECTICUT COINS.

The Connecticut coins of 1785 all have mailed busts, most of them facing the right. We have found but two dies facing the left, both extremely rare.

No. 1 is quite rare; the fillet ends are long, ending between the bust and the legend. It has a wreath of seven leaves and three berries.

The heads upon most of Nos. 2, 3, 4, 5 and 6, are much alike; in No. 2, the fillet ends point at A. One die of No. 4, is the "African head"—a large head with wreath of six leaves [Plate V. No. 5]; another has a wreath of seven leaves, much like heads of wheat.

In two dies of No. 6, the fillet ends point at A; in the other, they are long, as in No. 1. [Plate V. No. 6.]

Nos. 2 to 6, inclusive, are punctuated alike; but we have, for greater convenience, separated them according to the position of the first colon.

Of Nos. 7 and 8, which face to left, we know of but one specimen each; these much resemble the more common heads of 1786.

The weights of the coins of 1785 show a greater degree of regularity than do those of any other year; the extremes we have noticed in well preserved specimens, being that of a No. 3 weighing 132 grains, and specimens of Nos. 1 and 6, 153 grains each.

Judging from the number of specimens we have seen of each variety, we should rate the rarity of coins of 1785 as given below :— $r^6$, indicating that we know but one specimen from the dies; $r^5$, two or three; $r^4$, about six; $r^3$, ten; $r^2$, fifteen; $r^1$, twenty; $r$, thirty, and $c$, a greater number.

No. 1, $r^4$: 2, $r^3$: 3–B, $r^2$: 4–F, $r^3$: 5–H, $r^4$: 6–G, $r^4$: 7 and 8, $r^6$. All the others are more common.

1786.

No. 1 is a rudely cut die, with small head, heavy features and double chin. The wreath has seven leaves.

No. 2, also a small head, but much better work; eight leaves in wreath.

Nos. 1 and 2 are small, light pieces, both having the same reverse die, with legend, ETLIB INDE We much suspect the genuineness of these two varieties, partly on account of the great difference in their execution from that of other Connecticut coins, and partly on account of their light weight, specimens which are but little worn, weighing respectively, 84, and 102 grains.

No. 3, the largest head of this year; wreath of seven leaves. [Plate V. No. 7.]

No. 4, head to left, without punctuation ; wreath of four pairs of slender leaves.

Nine of the dies of No. 5 present few points by which to be distinguished from each other, except in the relative positions of the parts, and the size of the colons. Wreaths of eight serrated leaves. [Plate V. No. 8.]

The tenth die of No. 5, is the "Hercules" — a deeply cut head, with a scowling face ; the same die is found in 1787. Wreath of seven leaves. [Plate V. No. 9.]

The busts of all the preceding are mailed; those which follow are draped.

Of No. 6, we have seen no impression sufficiently sharp to show the wreath ; it has a large button at the throat, and the fillet ends very near the letter C.

No. 7. Head resembles No. 6, but has no button, and the fillet ends are near the colon ; the wreath has seven laurel leaves, and three large berries. [Plate V. No. 10.]

The weights of this year's coinage, (disregarding Nos. 1 and 2, before noted,) vary much, some fine specimens weighing but 116 grains, others, 173 grains ; few are found, however, which do not reach the legal weight of 144 grains. No. 3 is the heaviest variety, and a No. 5, the lightest.

No. 1, $R^5$: 2, $R^4$: 3, $R^4$: 4, $R^3$: 5–F and 5–E, $R^5$: 6 and 7, $R^5$. All the others more common.

### 1787. MAILED BUSTS.

The three dies of No. 1 of this year, include the largest and the smallest of the heads found upon coins of this State, if, indeed, both really belong to this State, as we suspect that with the small head to be a counterfeit ; it is of light weight, 104 grains only, and in execution is more like coins of other States, than those of Connecticut. The legend upon the reverse is ETLIB INDE [Plate V. No. 11.]

The largest head is known as the "mutton head." It has a wreath of eleven medium leaves, and is very seldom found in fine condition. The other die of this variety has a medium sized head with wreath of seven broad leaves. We have seen only one specimen of it, which is owned by E. Maris, M. D., of Philadelphia.

No. 2 is the only head to left without punctuation. Twelve leaves, in triplets.

No. 3, a smaller head, and very rare ; nine leaves and four berries. [Plate V. No. 12.]

No. 4 is usually found with a break from the bust, whence it is called the "horned bust." Wreath of ten leaves and two berries. Its reverse is from the same die with that of the rarest variety of No. 1.

No. 5. The head resembles that of No. 2 ; twelve leaves, in triplets. This die is of the greatest rarity ; the only specimen we know, is owned by Dr. Maris.

No. 6. The more common of these dies is known as the "laughing head ;" it is a small head with nine broad leaves, very sharply outlined. The head upon the other die has a very simple expression. The first of these is not very rare, but of the last we have seen but two impressions.

No. 7. The "Hercules" head ; the same die with No. 5 of 1786. [Plate V. No. 13.]

No. 8 is curiously punctuated. It has six leaves and three large berries.

No. 9 has a peculiar wreath of twelve leaves, in triplets, with knots, and five small berries. It is punctuated with crosslets (⋅), the last one being very near the C.

No. 10, also with crosslets. Wreath of twelve, in triplets, but no berries.

No. 11. Head much like 10. Stars of five points (∗). [Plate V. No. 14.]

No. 12. Wreath of twelve, in triplets. Same die with No. 8 of 1788.

No. 13. A childish face. Nine leaves and four berries ; stars of six (∗).

No. 14. Head much like 11. Upon the reverse of some specimens a small pheon, or heraldic spear-head (↣), appears after ET. The date has a pheon at each side; this character is found in no other die. [Plate V. No. 15.]

No. 15. The CONNECT. Head similar to that of No. 11, but with six berries in the wreath. It is found with three reverses, that usually found having eight cinquefoils(✳). [Plate V. No. 20.] We have seen but one specimen each with the other reverses, one of these being an IND ET LIB with eight crosslets ; the other, an INDL ET LIB with probably eight cinquefoils, one of which was destroyed by a break in the die ; but five appear in the table, as one is in doubt, and two are with the date — one at each side. Instead of the branch or sprig usually held by the goddess, on these she appears to hold a bouquet. [Plate VI. Nos. 1 and 2.]

No. 1–A, $R^3$: 1–C, $R^4$: 1–L, $R^6$: 2, $R^4$: 3, $R^5$: 4, $R^2$: 5, $R^6$: 6, $R^3$, and $R^5$: 7, $R^4$: 8–N and 8–O, $R^5$: 9–D and 9–E, $R^4$: 9–*R*, $R^5$: 10, $R^4$: 11–E and 11–K, $R^3$: 12, $R^5$: 13, $R^4$: 14, $R^3$: 15–F*, $R^4$: 15–*R* and 15–*S*, $R^6$.

The italics denote mis-spelt legends, and the asterisks, reverse dies used with both mailed and draped obverses.

## 1787. DRAPED BUSTS.

These, though much more common than are the mailed busts, furnish several specimens of extreme rarity. It will not be necessary to note every variety of them, but only some of those which are not often seen, or which present marked peculiarities.

No. 16. This variety is not common, and from one die we have seen but one impression.

No. 18 is illustrated on Plate V. No. 16.

No. 20 has peculiar punctuation and large letters ; it is seldom found.

No. 25 is very curiously punctuated, and quite rare. [Plate V. No. 17.]

No. 32. Most dies of this are common, but from one, we have seen but one impression ; its letters are large, and the die shows many cracks. Its reverse is from the die most frequently found with the CONNECT.

No. 33 is the most common variety, and it is found with so many dies, and in so many combinations, that at least seventy-nine pieces are required to represent all which have been discovered. Of these, seventy-one are in the collection of Mr. J. Carson Brevoort, of Brooklyn, N. Y. [Plate V. No. 19.]

No. 34 is the only die upon which we have found large fleurons ($\Leftarrow$).

Nos. 35, 36 and 37, have small fleurons ($\Leftarrow$), and are not difficult to obtain.

No. 38. The AUCIORI. It is found with two reverses. [Plate V. No. 21.]

No. 39. The AUCTOBI. It is found in three dies, with three reverse dies, two of which have the legend INDE ET LIR. [Plate V. No. 22.]

Nos. 40, 41 and 42. All AUCTOPI. The reverses of these are from three different dies, all having the legend INDE ET IIB. [Plate V. No. 23.]

No. 43. AUCTORI CONNFC. The punctuation of its reverse is peculiar. [Plate V. No. 18.]

No. 16–L and 16–M, R²: 16–N, R⁶: 17, R³: 18, R³: 19, R³: 20, R⁴: 21, R⁴: 22, R⁴: 23, R⁴: 24–F and 24–G, R³: 25, R⁵: 26–D and 26–B R⁴: 26–K, R⁵: 27, R⁴: 28–M and 28–N, R⁴: 29–N, R⁶: 29–P, R⁴: 30–X, R: 30,–H, R¹: 31–G, R¹: 32–F*, R⁶: 33–L, R⁵: 33–Q, R³: 33–T, R⁵: 33–H, R³: 34, R⁴: 35, R³: 36–K and 36–L, R²: 37, C: 38–G and 38–L, R⁴: 39, R⁵: 40, R⁴: 41, R⁴: 42, R⁴: 43, R⁴.

The coins of 1787, omitting No. 1, previously noted, vary in weight, from 117 grains, — a No. 4, to 184 grains, — a No. 9. Most of the mailed busts exceed the legal weight, though some fall much below it; the draped busts show less variation, few of them much exceeding that required, and many of them, when slightly worn, falling a little short of it.

## 1788. MAILED BUSTS.

No. 1 of 1788, is identical with No. 1 of 1787, and in its reverse with B of the Vermont coins. [Plate V. No. 24.] This also is a light piece, unique, so far as we know, weighing but 89 grains. Its lettering agrees closely with that of some of the Vermont coins, many of the New Jersey, the first of the GEORGIVS · III · REX · (page 192,) and with others, which will be noted later.

No. 2 is punctuated with mullets(*); wreath of seven leaves and three berries. Its reverse is from the same die with that of the second variety of the GEORGIVS III. REX.

No. 3. A very rare variety, with small head, five leaves and two berries.

No. 4. Another rare variety; wreath of seven leaves. [Plate V. No. 25.]

No. 5. The head much like that of No. 4; wreath of seven leaves.

No. 6. Head larger; seven leaves and three berries; extremely rare.

No. 7. Head to left; twelve leaves in triplets.

No. 8. The same die with No. 12 of 1787.

No. 9. Wreath of seven leaves and three berries.

No. 10. Twelve leaves, in triplets. An extremely rare variety.

No. 11. Twelve leaves, in triplets, and six berries.

No. 12. Twelve leaves, in triplets; one die with three berries, the other has none. [Plate V. No. 26.]

No. 13. AUCTORI CONNLC; leaves and berries in triplets.

No. 1, $R^6$; 2, $R^3$: 3, $R^6$: 4–B and 4–K, $R^5$: 5, $R^6$: 6, $R^6$: 7, $R^3$: 8, $R^5$: 9, $R^4$: 10, $R^6$: 11, $R^3$: 12, $R^3$: 13, $R^4$.

## 1788. DRAPED BUSTS.

No. 14. In one die the letters are closely, in the other widely spaced.

No. 15. In one, the last cinquefoil is below the shoulder, in the other, it is above it.

No. 16. Four of these dies are much alike. The other has both letters and characters larger, and the reverse is INDL ET LIB. [Plate V. No. 27.]

No. 14, $R^4$: 15, $R^4$: 16–D*, $R^3$: 16–H*, $R^2$: 16–N, $R^5$.

The coins of 1788 average of lighter weight than those of any other year, few of them being up to the standard. The extremes, (omitting No. 1,) are 108, and 168 grains, both specimens of No. 12.

We have not fixed the rarity of all combinations of any year, but have intended to give that of at least one of each variety, those not given being more common. Numbers 31, 32, 33, and 37, are the most common varieties.

It is very difficult correctly to estimate the rarity of the different varieties, as it sometimes happens that one which is very rare in one section of the country, is not so in another. Possibly the entire coinage of some dies may have been sent to distant parts, and there remained until thrown out of circulation: thus many specimens from these dies might be found in those localities, though almost if not quite unknown elsewhere. These remarks will equally apply to the coins of all the States.

In Dickeson's tables of these coins, we find recorded nine "types" of 1785. Thirteen varieties of these are said to face left, twelve of which are rated as of only the first and second degrees of rarity. We have been unable to find dies corresponding with more than four of these "types," and of those facing left, we have found but two specimens, these being of the two rarest varieties.

Of the coins of 1786, he records eleven "types": — we find but seven.

Of 1787, he gives ninety-three, we find but forty-three; and of 1788, thirty-five, while we find but sixteen.

The discrepancy in these numbers is so great as to require some notice.

Probably Dr. Dickeson, (the second edition of whose work, — from which these numbers are taken, — was published in 1860,) had unequalled facilities for obtaining varieties, there being then quantities of colonial coins sent to the mint at Philadelphia, where he resided, and he, we have been informed, had every opportunity to examine and to select such as he desired ; few other collectors were then interested in procuring varieties, and he probably obtained some not now to be found. Yet the fact that nine of those upon his table for 1787 are duplicated, justifies us in the opinion that errors were also made in the examination of specimens, and that the numbers upon his tables were thereby much increased.

The numbers duplicated are, No. 2, by Nos. 75 and 76: 27, by 32: 28, by 79: 29, by 80: 49, by 85: 51, by 52 and 87: and 89, by 90.

But to return to the record: —

The next step was the passage of a bill for preventing the coining of copper by any person, other than those authorized.

"October 1785.

"An Act to prohibit the Coining of Copper without permission first had and obtained of the General Assembly—

"Be it enacted by the Governor Council and Representatives in General

Court Assembled and by the authority of the same that no person whatever shall Coin or Manufacture any Copper Coin of any description or size without permission first had and obtained from the General Assembly on pain of forfeiting for each offence the sum of one hundred pounds lawful Money which forfeiture shall be if sued for by a private person one Moiety thereof to the use of the person prosecuting to Effect and the other Moiety thereof to the Treasurer of this State to and for the use of this State and shall be recoverable by Action of Debt or Information before any Court proper to try the same —

"Passed in the Lower House

"Test Jedidiah Strong Clerke"

"Concurred in the Upper House

"(Oct 1785)                                    Test George Wyllys Secret'y"

The record of the passage of the above is : —

"Monday Afternoon 24ᵗʰ Octʳ 1785

"Passed a Bill to prevent Coining Coppers without Licence from the General Assembly."

An act was soon proposed, for the remedy of the evils produced by counterfeit coin; this was passed in the Lower House, but defeated in the Upper.

"(May 1786)

"Whereas great Quantities of base and Counterfeit Copper Coin are already imported & circulating in this State and there is great Danger of further Importations thereof, to the great Loss & Injury of the Citizens of this State — Which Mischief to prevent — Be it enacted by the Governor, Council and Representatives, in General Court Assembled & by the Authority of the same — that whatever Person shall import into this State any Copper Coin of any Description or Size, to a greater number than fifty, except such as shall be coined & put forth by the Authority of Congress or some one of the united States and of equal Value with the Copper coined in this State by lawful Authority — shall on Conviction thereof before any one Assistant or Justice of the Peace, pay a fine of Ten Pounds lawful Money for each Offence  Provided always, that Liberty of an Appeal to the next County Court shall be allowed, from the Determination of such Assistant or Justice of the Peace on the Party so appealing becoming bound with sufficient Surety to prosecute such appeal to effect & answer all Damages in Case he make not his Plea good —

"And be it further enacted by the Authority aforesaid, that all such Copper Coin so imported into this State, shall be treated & disposed of in the same manner as counterfeited Coin —

"Passed in the Lower House

"Test Jedidiah Strong Clerke."

"Dissented to in the upper House

"Teste George Wyllys Secret'y"

In accordance with the acts already printed, the coinage of copper was commenced in 1785, and continued, if we may rely upon the records as evidence, until 1789, although we find no coins bearing date later than 1788. But in January, 1789, a committee was appointed to inquire into the proceedings in this business. It was then : —

"Resolved by this Assembly, that Daniel Holbrook & James Wadsworth Esquires be & they are hereby appointed to enquire into the conduct of those Persons who were by Resolve of Assembly in October A D 1785 authorized to coin & manufacture Coppers & report to the next General Assembly whether said Resolve of Assembly has been complied with, by coining the Coppers equal in value to British Half pence & by paying into the Treasury of this State one Twentieth part of all Coppers by them Coined and they are directed to give such further information to s^d Assembly respecting the transactions of those persons who have been concerned in the Manufacture of Coppers by virtue of said Resolve of Assembly as they may Judge proper.

"Passed in the Lower House

"Test James Davenport Clerk"

"(Jan. 1789)

"Concurr^d in the upper House

"Test George Wyllys Secret'y"

This committee met on the 7th of April, 1789, and thus reported to the Assembly at their session in the following May.

"To the Honourable General Assembly of the State of Connecticut to be Holden at Hartford on the Second thursday of May next —

"We, your Honours Committee appointed at your Sessions in January Last to enquire into the Conduct of those Persons Who Were by a Resolve of Assembly in Octob^r 1785 authorized to Coin and manufacture Coppers take Leave to Report — that haveing notefyed the Parties to Meet at the Dweling House of John Smith Inholder in New Haven on the 7^th Day of

April 1789 Samuel Bishop James Hilhouse and Mark Leavenworth Esq$^{rs}$ and John Goodrich attended, and haveing examined touching the Premises We find that on the 12$^{th}$ Day of Novb$^{r}$ 1785 Samuel Bishop James Hilhouse John Goodrich & Joseph Hopkins the Origonal Grantees named in s$^{d}$ Resolve of Assembly entered into Articles of Agreement With Pierpoint Edwards & Jonathan Ingersol Esq$^{s}$ and Abel Bewil and Elias Shipman and formed a Company by the name of the Company for Coining Coppers and thereby became Joint Owners of the Right of Coining Coppers and equal Sharers of the Profit … or Loss arising therefrom and under equal Obligations to Conform to the Regulations of s$^{d}$ Resolve that they Jointly pursued s$^{d}$ Business untill Feb$^{r}$ 1786 when s$^{d}$ Ingersol Sold 1/16 Part of s$^{d}$ Company's Right to s$^{d}$ Goodrich, in March 1786 s$^{d}$ Hopkins Sold 1/16 Part of s$^{d}$ Company's Right to s$^{d}$ Goodrich—in April 1786 s$^{d}$ Edwards & Shipman, sold 2/8 Parts and s$^{d}$ Ingersol 1/16 Part of s$^{d}$ Company's Right to James Jarvis Who Still Continued s$^{d}$ Business until Some Time in the Summer following When want of Stock Obliged them to Desist—that on the 10$^{th}$ of Sep$^{r}$ 1786 The Company leased s$^{d}$ grant & Apparatus for Coining Coppers to Mark Leavenworth Esq$^{r}$ Isaac Baldwin & William Leavenworth for Six Weeks or So many days Over as the Works Should be Useless by Reason of the Failure of Any of the Implements takeing their Bond to Conform to s$^{d}$ Resolve of Assembly under Which lease they improved the Apparatus about eight weeks—

"That on the first of Nov$^{r}$ 1786 the Company Agreed by A Certain Writing under their hands for the greater Advantage of Carrying on s$^{d}$ Coinage to improve s$^{d}$ Apparatus Seperately by Certain Periods of time Agreed upon—that on the 17$^{th}$ of Nov$^{br}$ 1786 s$^{d}$ Goodrich Sold to s$^{d}$ Mark Leavenworth Isaac Baldwin and William Leavenworth 1/8 part of s$^{d}$ Company's Right—that in Jan$^{y}$ 1787 s$^{d}$ Hopkins sold to s$^{d}$ Goodrich 1/16 Part of s$^{d}$ Comp$^{ys}$ right—that about the 1$^{st}$ of June 1787 s$^{d}$ Bishop & s$^{d}$ Goodrich Sold to s$^{d}$ Jarvis 2/8 Parts of s$^{d}$ Comp$^{ys}$ Right.

"That the Presint Owners are James Jarvis 4/8 & 1/16 Parts

"James Hilhouse Esq$^{r}$ 1/8                        Part

"Mark Leavenworth Esq$^{r}$ 1/8                    Part

"Abel Buel 1/8                                       Part

"& John Goodrich 1/16                               Part

Who carryed on the Coinage of Coppers until About the 1$^{st}$ day of June 1787 Since which Time they have ceased to Carry on s$^{d}$ Business—and on Examination s$^{d}$ Bishop Hilhouse Leavenworth and Goodrich Declared that they had not put of or into Circulation any of s$^d$ Coppers Except they had been Inspected —

" We further find by A Certificate from three of the Inspectors that there had been Inspected by the Com$^{tee}$ of Inspection twenty eight Thousand nine Hundred and forty four Pounds Weight of Coined Coppers — that the One Twentieth Part thereof is 1447$^{lb}$ 3$^{oz}$ Which being estimated at 18 Coppers for One Shilling amounts to One Hundred Ninety two Pounds nineteen Shilling & 2$^d$ — That it appears from the Treasurers Receipts that he had rec$^d$ One Thousand three Hundred & Eighty Six Pound & one oz — of Coined Coppers Delivered into the Treasury at Various times which being Estimated at Eighteen Coppers for One Shilling Amounts to One Hundred Eighty four Pounds Sixteen Shillings & /2$^d$ which leaves a Ballance Due the State of Sixty one Pound & two oz$^s$ of Coined Coppers Which at the rate Above s$^d$ amounts to Eight Pound three Shillings — We do not find that s$^d$ Comp$^y$ have permited any Person to coin Coppers in the Works belonging to s$^d$ Company exept those Coppers herein before Mentioned — We further find from the Information of Maj$^r$ Eli Leavenworth that he has Made blank Coppers the Last fall had them Stamped in New york With Various Impressions — Some few of them With an Impression Simular to the Impresion of the Coppers Coined by the Aforementioned Comp$^y$ — We further find that Abel Bewel has Gone to Europe that previous to his Departure he gave his Son 'Benjamin Bewel Liberty to coin Coppers Which Bussiness he is now pursuing and has Just began to Stamp them All which is humbly submitted by your Honors most obedient humble Servants

" James Wadsworth<br>" Daniel Holbrook — "

" New Haven April }
      9$^{th}$ 1789   }

" In the House of Representatives

" The foregoing Report having been read is accepted & approved

" Test James Davenport Clerk "

" In the Uper House

" Concured in Accepting this Report With addition that it be transmitted to the Treasurer's Office —

" Teste George Wyllys Secret'y "

" In the House of Representatives

" On reconsideration Concurred

" Test James Davenport Clerk "

In consequence of the report of the Committee of investigation, the Assembly passed this resolve, suspending the coinage from the 20th of June, to the end of the next session : —

"Whereas this Assembly did at their Sessions holden at New Haven in Oct[r] 1785 granted Liberty and Licence to Samuel Bishop Esq[r] and others to Manufacture or Coin Copper under the Authority of this State during the pleasure of this Assembly not exceeding five years —

"Resolved by this Assembly that all further proceedings by Virtue of or Under said Grant be and the same are hereby suspended from and after the 20th day of June 1789 untill the rising of the General Assembly to be holden at New Haven on the 2[d] Thursday of Oct[r] next and that the Proprietors to and all Persons Interested under said Grant be notified to appear before said General Assembly and shew Reason if any they have why said Grant should not case — And the publication of this Resolve in one of the News Papers in the City of New Haven on or before the 15th day of June 1789 shall be sufficient Notice to such Proprietors —

"Pass[d] in the upper House

"(May 1789)                              Test George Wyllys Secret'y

"Concurred in the House of Representatives

                                    "Test James Davenport Clerk"

This was in effect the conclusion of the business of this mint.

The preceding documents are copied from the originals preserved in the State Library at Hartford, — "Miscellaneous," Vol. III. pp. 243 to 251.

The latest records we find having reference to this subject relate to the disposal of the coin belonging to the State, as its share in the coinage of this mint. The first of these is dated December, 1790. "Resolved by this Assembly that the Treasurer be and he is hereby authorized and directed to sell and dispose of the Copper Coin in the Treasury of this State for the Liquidated notes or Securities of this State provided he can obtain two shillings in said Notes or Securities pr pound weight for said Coppers."

The other is dated, "May Session 1791," and is as follows : —

"Resolved by this Assembly that the Treasurer be and he is hereby authorized and directed to dispose of the Coppers now in the Treasury and the property of this State to the best advantage and Report make of his proceedings in said Business."

# MASSACHUSETTS.

## COPPER CURRENCY.

As Massachusetts was the only colony that established a mint for the coinage of silver, so also was she the only one known to have considered a proposal for the importation of a supply of copper coin for small change; in fact, her attention seems to have been almost unremittedly directed toward some project for furnishing a supply of money, either of metal or paper.

Of the proposition of William Chalkhill, we have no knowledge other than that supplied by the ensuing records.[1]

March 17th, 1702–3, "A Memorial of William Chalkhill, One of the Monyers of Her Majesties Mint in the Tower of London now resident in Boston Proposing That if the Government think fitt, He would undertake to bring over hither Ten Thousand Pounds in Copper Money, at Such Prices and Values as shall be Agreed upon, Was Sent up from the House of Rcpresentatives, and read"

March 19th. "Proposals Offered by William Chalkhill, One of the Moneyers of Her Maj^ties Mint in the Tower of London to furnish the Province from England with Small Money of Copper to the Value of Ten Thousand pounds Sent up from the Representatives, were read  And

"Resolved

"That John Walley, Penn Townsend, and Andrew Belcher Esq^rs be a Committee of the Board to joine with Such as shall be Named by the House of Representatives to Consider of the said Proposals, And to make their report thereupon — Which Resolve being Sent to that House for their

---

[1] Court Records, Vol. vii., pp. 370, 373, 378, and 381.

Concurrance, Was returned Agreed to, And M$^r$ Nehemiah Jewett, Capt Samuel Checkley, and Capt Samuel Phips Named to be of the Committee for that Affair "

March 26th, 1703. " The Report of the Committee upon the Proposals Offered by M$^r$ William Chalkhill, was brought in by John Walley Esq$^r$ Chairman and read, and laid upon the Table. The said report being in favour of an Agreement for £5000 only and y$^t$ in Pence."

March 27th, 1703. " The Report of the Committee upon the Proposals offered by M$^r$ William Chalkhill for Furnishing of the Province with small Money of Copper was sent down to the Representatives at their Desire, & return'd again from that House with their Resolve thereupon ; Viz.

" That the Report of the Committee be Accepted, And John Walley Andrew Belcher & Samuel Legg Esq$^{rs}$ & Cpt. Samuel Checkley be appointed & Impowered a Committee forthwith to draw Articles of Agreement with the said M$^r$ Chalkhill accordingly, And the Covenants . . . & Engagements of the said Comm$^{tee}$ in this Affair shall be ratified and made good by this Court;

" W$^{ch}$ Resolve being read at the Board, & the Question put, for Concurrence It was not Consented to, But refer'd to Consideration at the next Court, if then Offered."

Felt says, " This appears to have been accomplished," but as we find no mention of the affair subsequently, we infer that no further action was taken upon the subject.

Probably the largest importation of specie that was made during the colonial period was that of the money voted by the Parliament of Great Britain for the reimbursement of the expenses incurred by Massachusetts on account of the expedition against Cape Breton.

The amount of the expenses of that expedition which it was estimated had been defrayed by this Province was £183,649 2 7½ sterling. It was decided by Parliament, that this amount should be repaid, and a large quantity of silver and copper coin was therefore procured, and forwarded to Boston for that purpose.

According to the invoice, the silver amounted to six hundred and fifty thousand ounces, requiring two hundred and seventeen chests to contain it, while the copper halfpence and farthings weighed ten tons, for the transportation of which one hundred casks were purchased.

The arrival of this remittance is thus mentioned on the Council records: —
"Monday Sept<sup>r</sup> 18<sup>th</sup> 1749."

"His Majesty's Ship the Mermaid Cap<sup>t</sup> —— Montague Commander being this Day arrived in the Harbour of Boston from Great Britain with the Money allowed by Parliament to this Province for defraying their Charges in the late Expedition against Cape Breton: — William Bollan Esq<sup>r</sup> one of the Agents for this Province for receiving the said Money being arrived in the said Ship, was admitted into Council, & gave the Board a general Account of his Proceedings in that & other Affairs of the Province in his Management.

"Captain Montague being also admitted into Council, informed the Board that he was now ready to deliver the abovesaid Money sent hither by his Majesty's Ship Mermaid as soon as the Treasurer, was ready to receive it."

"Septem<sup>r</sup> 19<sup>th</sup> 1749 . . . The Secretary laid before the Board a publick Letter subscribed by the Hon<sup>ble</sup> Sir Peter Warren & William Bollan Esq<sup>r</sup> surviving Agents for this Province for receiving the Money allowed by Parliament for the Charges on the Expedition against Cape Breton, & informing the Government of their Proceedings as to the receiving and Shipping the said Money, with an Invoice thereof, & an Account Currant, containing Charges in the said Affair."

The possession of so considerable an amount of money seems to have been the source of much anxiety to the authorities, and they at once set themselves about finding a place where it might be securely deposited; their action upon this point is related in the records as follows : —

"Voted, that Ezekiel Lewis & Samuel Danforth Esq<sup>rs</sup> go with M<sup>r</sup> Treasurer Foye to his House in King's Street, & see if there be any convenient Place for Lodging the publick Money there, & treat with the Tenant about her Removal in Order to the Treasurer & his Familys Removing thither.

"M<sup>r</sup> Lewis reported thereupon that the Committee had viewed the House (which they found well accommodated for receiving the said Money) & discoursed with the Tenant, who could by no Means be persuaded to remove out of it.

"Voted thereupon, That a Brick Arch be built in the Cellar of the House where the Treasurer now dwells for the Reception of the Province Money from on board his Majesty's Ship Mermaid as soon as may be, & that Samuel Danforth & Andrew Oliver Esq<sup>rs</sup> assist the Treasurer in the said Affair."

The following extracts are from the invoice of the agents : —

"Invoice of Silver and Copper purchased by Order of the Honourable the Great and General Court of His Majesty's Province of the Massachusetts Bay in America by the Hono^ble Sir Peter Warren, Knight of the Bath and William Bollan Esquire, shipped on board His Majesty's Ship Mermaid, Captain John Montague Commander, bound to Boston for Account and on the Risque of the said Province to be delivered to the Treasurer of the Same for the Time being. Viz^t.

" M. B
N^o 1 @ 206 Chests each containing 3000 Ounces of milled $\overline{pss}$ of $\frac{8}{8}$ in Bags . . . . . . . . . . . . . . . . . . . . . . . 618,000

207 @ 214 containing each 3000 Ounces Pillar $\overline{pss}$ of $\frac{8}{8}$ . . 24,000

215 containing Halves D^o . . . . . . 3,000

216 containing 1000 oz Halves D^o . . . . . ⎫
  876¾ mixt D^o     281¼ milled . . . . . ⎬ 3,000
  423½ D^o Half    418½ D^o Small . . . . . ⎭

" 217 containing milled $\overline{pss}$ of $\frac{8}{8}$ . . . . . . 2,000
——————
" Total Six hundred and fifty thousand Ounces . . . . 650,000 "

" Copper coined in Halfpence & Farthings bought at His Majesty's Mint. Viz^t.

Tons Cwt
7 : 18 of Halfpence @ £10 11 4 ℘ Cwt . . . . 1699 10 8
2 : 2 of Farthings @ £10 10 4 ℘ Cwt . . . . 441 14 0
——————
10 Tons cost . . . . . . . . . . 2111 4 8 "

Among the expenses are : —

" Paid for 100 Casks @ 1/9 each . . . . . 8 15 0
Paid to Porters for loading them . . . . . 10

" Paid Fees at the Custom House, to the Searchers and for Officers⎫ 9 5 0
  attendance at the Bank . . . . . . .⎭

Paid George Clark, Carrier, for Carriage of the Silver and Copper⎫
  from Southwark to Portsmouth, and for the Hire of Vessels to⎬ 157 1 0
  carry it on board the Mermaid . . . . .⎭

Paid the Escort of a Sergeant and twelve Men who guarded the⎫ 24 13 6
  Money to Portsmouth . . . . . . .⎭

Paid Charges upon the Road and at unlading at Portsmouth . 3 10 10
Paid the Searchers at Portsmouth . . . . . 10 6 "

Many collectors have noticed the frequent appearance of fine specimens of English halfpence and farthings dated 1749; the presence of these may be accounted for by this importation.

This specie was appropriated to the redemption of the bills of credit, or paper money of the Province; and by means of it the greater part of the issues then outstanding, were taken up.

The first document we find relating to the coinage of copper in Massachusetts, is the petition presented by Seth Reed of Uxbridge, asking liberty to coin copper and silver, which he represented to be the product of native ores. The original petition, which we next present, with the action of the two Houses as entered thereupon, is preserved in the Senate archives.

"To the honorable the Senate and House of Representatives in General Court assembled. March 1786—

"The memorial of Seth Reed—

humbly represents that it is in his power to obtain a considerable quantity of copper & silver from bodies of ore within the United States—that he has in his possession and is ready to produce to the honorable Court samples of the ore and of the production of the same, both of silver and copper, when wrought ; which he conceives will evince the genuineness of the metal—he supposes that by coining the same, the public may be greatly benefitted, especially when the present scarcity of a metallic medium is considered, and that an increment of the medium in this way, will much better answer the wishes of the citizens in this Commonwealth at large, than an emission of paper currency.—he conceives that the extracting the metal from the ore in its crude state, will be attended with great expence and trouble as also the coining it, yet believes it may be done without loss to the adventurer—your memorialist is willing to make an attempt of this kind, if he may be so happy as to meet with the approbation of this honorable Court, they granting to him the exclusive right of coining for this Commonwealth during such time as shall be deemed necessary, to save him harmless from the expence which he must unavoidably be at to accomplish the business ; with this restriction that in case he shall not coin, at any future time, (within the term, for which such exclusive right shall be granted) so much, as by Government he may be permitted to do, he would not wish to be Entitled to the privilege.

"Your memorialist, in this proposal, would have it understood, that he wishes & expects to be under the direction of the Government, as to devices, weight, size and other matters relative to coinage.

"Seth Reed."

"In the House of Representatives March 8, 1786   Read and committed to M\. Ely, M\. Merrick & M\. Folger with such as the Honble Senate may join.   Sent up for concurrence

"A. Ward Speaker."

"In Senate March 9ᵗʰ 1786 — Read & concurred, and Hugh Orr & Richard Cranch Esqˢ are join'd —

"Samˡ. Phillips junʳ. Presidᵗ"

A petition was soon presented by James Swan, for the right of coining copper only; this also is preserved in the Senate Archives, and is as follows:

"To the Honbˡᵉ the Senate & House of Representatives of the Commonwealth of Massachusetts.

"The Petition of James Swan — Humbly Shews

"That your Petitioner with the Community at large very sensibly feeling the want of a Circulating Medium, which may neither depreciate, be exported, or hoarded by the Rich, applies to this Honourable Court for leave, by Patent to be granted for the purpose, to Coin and utter Twenty thousand Pounds Value in Copper under the following restrictions, or such other as you may lay him under.

"1. The Coin to be of such size and impression, as three or such other number of persons to be appointed by the General Court, shall determine.

"2. The same persons shall be judges of the quality of the metal.

"3. The Value of the Coin to be determined by the proportion it shall bear in weight, to the British halfpence, or to the French sols.

"4. The petitioner shall establish the mint in this Commonwealth, at his own expence & Cost.

"For which your Petitioner will engage on condition that all foreign Copper Coin of whatever denomination be declared illegal — to pay into the Treasury of the Commonwealth, five & one half ℔ Cent on all that shall be Coined, for the benefit of the publick, which shall be in lieu of Impost and every other dutie whatever.

"The proposed Coin, will never be in danger of being exported, and consequently will ever continue in circulation: — at the same time that it will have that happy effect, it must be agreeable to the views of the Legislature as much as in their power, to spread a medium which can without loss or depreciation communicate freely amongst the poor, & which may tend to retire the base coin that is so plenty amongst us.

"To urge farther reasons to actuate your Honors to grant this Patent—

must be needless; or to mention that the States of New-Jersey & Connecti-cut have given similar ones — Your Petitioner rests on the reasonableness & utility of the thing, and on your wish & constant exertion to promote the public good.   He therefore

" Prays the Honb! Court to grant him a Patent for Coining & uttering Twenty thousand Pounds Value of Copper, within such space of time, & under such restrictions as to Your Honors shall seem meet: and as in duty bound shall ever Pray

" Boston 15 March 1786.                                            Jam. Swan."

" In the House of Representatives March 16, 1786.

" Read & committed to the Committee of both Houses on the petition of a like nature from S. Reed Esq!

" Sent up for concurrence                              A. Ward Speaker "

" In Senate March 16, 1786 —   Read and concurred

" Sam! Phillips jun! Presid! "

The statement in Swan's petition, that New Jersey had granted a similar right, appears premature, as no records are found indicating any action upon this subject in that State, until the 23d of May following.

The following is the report on the petition of Seth Reed: no attention appears to have been paid to that of James Swan.

" The Committee of both Houses to whome was committed the Petition of Seth Reed Esq! have attended that Service, and beg Leave to report as their Opinion, that it is expedient that a more particular Account of the Oars mentioned by him in his said Petition, and larger Samples of the same, should be exhibited to this Court, than those that have been already pro-duced ; and also that the Petitioner bring sufficient Evidence that the same Oars are the Produce of Mines that are situated within the Limits of this State.

" And the Committee further report as their Opinion, that the said Peti-tion be referred over to the next General Court, to give the Petitioner an Opertunity of producing the Samples and Evidence aforementioned.

" In Senate March 24th 1786 —   Read & accepted —

" sent down for concurrence          Sam! Phillips jun! Presid! "

" In the House of Representatives March 24, 1786

" Read & concurred                              A. Ward. Speaker."

On the day preceding that of the action last noted, another plan was introduced in the House of Representatives: the papers relating thereto will next be given.

March 23d, 1786. "Ordered that Mr. Hitchbourn, Mr. Grout & Mr. Williams of Salem be a Committee to Consider of the expediency and practicability of coining a quantity of copper or Silver money & report."

The committee reported this resolve, which was accepted "as taken into a new draft."

"Resolved that His Excellency the Governour and the Hon'ble Council be & hereby are requested

"To consider the best Method to be adopted by this Commonwealth for the Coining of Silver & Copper, to determine the Value of the several Sorts of Coin, togather with the Quantity that it will be expedient to issue, with proper Devices therefor, and what Advantages may accrue to the Commonwealth thereby, and to make Report to the General Court at their next Session."

The following is a copy of the paper referred to as a "new draft": —

"Commonwealth of Massachusetts

"In the House of Representatives March 24<sup>th</sup> 1786

"Whereas application hath been made to this Court by divers Persons praying for a Right of coining Copper in this Commonwealth

"Resolved that his Excellency the Governour and the Honble the Council be & they are hereby requested to consider of the Expediency of coining silver and Copper in this Commonwealth, and if in their Opinion it is expedient that either be coined, that they consider what Quantity it will be convenient to coin, in what Mode the Business should be conducted, the proper Devices to be used, and the Advantage that may accrue from such coining to this Commonwealth, and to make such Communications on this Subject to the General Court at the next Session as they may think conducive to the Interest of the State — "

This resolve was then brought before the Council, as entered on their records, Saturday March 25th, 1786.

"His Excellency was pleased to communicate to Council a Resolve requesting the Governor with advice of the Council to consider the best method to be adopted for the coining of Silver & copper of the several sorts of Coin, passed the twenty fourth instant & asked the Advice of Council thereon what steps were expedient to be taken — Advised that the said Resolve be committed to His Honor the Lieut. Governor & Honble M! Adams to confer with the persons who have applied for a right of coining coppers in this Commonwealth, & to consider what mode is necessary to be adopted respecting the subject of said Resolve & Report — "

June 7th, 1786, the committee reported as follows : —

"The Committee appointed by the Governor & Council to consider the expediency of coining silver & copper, & if expedient, what quantity it will be convenient to coin, in what way the business should be conducted, the proper devices to be used, & what advantage will accrue to the Commonwealth, have attended the service & take leave to report, That your Committee did not enter particularly into the consideration of the Coinage of Silver, as they apprehended it would be most convenient if the Alloy & value of Silver Coins of the several denominations were the same throughout the United States which cannot be effectually accomplished unless Congress previously consider & determine upon the subject. With respect to the coinage of coppers, your Committee have received proposals from James Swan Esq! who has offered to pay into the Treasury of this State for the benefit of the publick the sum of Eleven hundred Pounds lawful money or in case the sheeting of Copper is practicable in this State, twenty two hundred pounds, in consideration of this Government's granting him a patent for the exclusive right of coining & uttering twenty thousand pounds lawful money value in copper, under certain restrictions, or he will lend the Government fifty thousand pounds for a term of years for the benefit of the Privilege aforesaid — M! Swan's several proposals & estimate accompany this report. — Your Committee have entered into a further investigation of the charges that must accrue in conducting this business of coining — Provided Government should establish a mint for coining & manufacturing of coppers at their own expence, & under their own immediate direction & upon the best estimate they can form, they find the costs of the copper, necessary for coining Twenty thousand pounds lawful money value in coppers

"Will amount to . . . . . . . £8,250
"And that work houses, furnace, Presses Plating Mill, & other apparatus, together with the fuel & wages of the Workmen & others imployed in the business will cost . . . } 1,950
———
10,200
consequently that the profits arising to Government by this business will amount to at least the sum of . . . } 9,800
——— 20,000 0 0

as appears by the estimates herewith exhibited — Your Committee further report, that in the prosecution of this business, Government will not be obliged
to advance a great sum to set it a going, as the publick have a large quantity
of copper oar suitable for the business by them, if they choose to imploy it
that way, but if they should not incline to do that, they may purchase old
copper enough at two or three months credit, to be paid for in coppers as
soon as it is coined — Your Committee further report, that in case the Government should establish a mint at their own expence, it would be most convenient for the Commonwealth to have copper coined of the several following
denominations viz$^t$ ... Of the value of one penny, one half penny, & one
farthing lawful money & in such proportions of each as shall be thought
most beneficial.  That the coining of copper to the amount of Twenty thousand Pounds lawful money would be sufficient for the present year — That
the business should be conducted by an honest skilful man, well acquainted
with the art, he to be under the controul & direction of a Committee consisting of three, who should superintend the business, keep the keys of the
coining apparatus & stamps &c & see that no more copper was coined &
emitted than ordered by the Court.

   The Devices to be on one side  .   .   .   .
   on the other   .  .  .  .  .  .  .

" As the Governor & Council may think proper.  The value of the coin
to be determined by the proportion it shall bear in weight to the British
halfpence —

" The Committee after having stated these facts are of opinion that it
will not be for the interest of the Public to grant a Patent to any particular
person to Coin & utter a certain sum of money in coppers but that a mint
should be established for the purpose at the cost & expence of the Commonwealth —

     " All which is submitted

          Thomas Cushing ℈ order "

" In Council – – Read & accepted —

" Estimate of the expence of coining Twenty thousand pounds of Coppers each 2/8 to weigh one pound —

| | |
|---|---:|
| " It will take at least 165,000$^{lb}$ of Copper to make £20,000 lawful money in Coppers . . . . . . . | £8250 |
| Work house, furnace & other apparatus will cost . . . | 250 |
| 4 Presses at £60 will amount to . . . . . . | 240 |

"1 Plating Mill, apparatus &c will cost . . . . . 160
Fuel for melting copper &c will cost . . . . . 250
8 hands one year their Wages £60 ℔ Ann . . . . 480
_____
9,630
"other incidental unforseen charges . . . . . . 20
"The undertaker or Superintendant's Salary ℔ Ann . . . 250
Government's Committee to inspect to consist of three Persons at ⎱ 300
£100 ℔ Ann . . . . . . . . . ⎰
_____
£10,200

"S. Holten
"Edward Cutts"

The original draft of this report of the Committee shows these erasures and alterations. After the words, "take leave to report", are erased the words, "That as to the coinage of silver, the profits attending of it will be so small as not to be worthy the attention of the public." The phrase "most convenient for the Commonwealth," referring to the denominations to be coined, originally stood, "most for the interest of the Commonwealth", and the opinion of the Committee was first set down as, "The Committee after having stated these facts, leave it with the Governour and Council to consider and determine whether it will be most for the interest of the public to grant a Patent to any particular person for such valuable consideration as they shall think proper, to coin and utter a certain sum lawful money value in Copper, or to establish a mint for this purpose at their own cost and expence."

Mr. Swan's papers next follow : —

"Calculation by James Swan
"One pound weight of sheet Copper thinned to the size or thickness of Coppers ⎱ £ money
℔ Certificate of M$^r$ Inman or M$^r$ Brimmer — 1/4$^d$ Sterling . . or . ⎰ -.1 9$\frac{4}{12}$

"Note. If that price should be higher than it can now be purchased at — there is to balance it the loss or Waste in the clippings or Corner pieces formed in stricking off every Copper and which are not so valuable as in Sheets by one half ; on the Waste on new melting those clippings & running them again out in to sheets — and on exporting, sheeting & importing them again (for it can't be done in America) : on the outlay for several years of the sum to be advanced Government ; and on the risque by the Coppers not being made a tender, of a great loss on forcing them into circulation — all of which will fully make $\frac{1}{5}$th or 20 ℔Ct

"Commissions 5 ℔ ct on the purchase, & other charges in Europe till on ⎱ — — 1$\frac{6}{12}$
board 1 ℔ ct is 6 . . . . . . . . ⎰

"Insurance to America — 3 ℔ ct . . . . . . — — $0\frac{8}{12}$

"Freight to America, Trucking charges, Storage &$^{ca}$ . . . . — — 1

"Interest of money, allowing to be but 1 year in replacing advances — ⎫
 6 ℔ c$^t$ . . . . . . . . . ⎬ $1\frac{6}{12}$

"Loss on difference of exch$^a$ in replacing money in Europe 7½ ℔$^c$ . . — — $1\frac{8}{12}$

"State dutie 5½ ℔ ct . . . . . . . . — — $1\frac{6}{12}$

"Expences in building the mint, Support of Committee on Coining the Cop- ⎫
 per making & renewing dyes &$^c$ — 10 ℔ C$^t$ . . . . ⎬ $2\frac{6}{12}$

"For advancing money, my own trouble &$^c$ 12 ℔ Cent . . . — — 3

                 £– 2 $10\frac{1}{3}$

"The Value of 1$^{lb}$ Coined Copper, agreeable to the Standard of ⎫
 British halfpence — is . . . . . . . ⎬ – 2 8

"Excess to be charged to the purchase of Copper . . . . £– – $2\frac{1}{3}$"

## "2$^d$ Proposal.

"To the Honb$^!$ Committee, to whom is referred the consideration of the subject of Coining Copper.

"Finding it the belief of many, that they can Sheet Copper and still preserve its mallabilitie, altho' I never could get any to demonstrate it to me, I make an additional offer, upon the sheeting of Copper being practicable here, of *five and one half* ℔ *Cent* more, to Government on all that they shall think proper to allow me to Coin, the same to be paid into the Treasury in Gold or Silver at the end of the first Session of the General Court, next after the mint shall have began to opperate : the first five & half to be paid on granting the Patent.—

"Boston 29 May 1786.           Jam. Swan"

## "3$^d$ Proposals

"To the Honb$^{le}$ Committee to whom is referr'd the Consideration of the Subject of Coining Copper.—

"If neither the first or second proposal I have made, should be accepted, I offer the following —

   "That the General Court grant Liberty to me to Coin Fifty Thousand pounds in Copper, within five years — to be of the Standard of British half pence & of pure Copper.

## "For which —

"I will lend Goverment Fifty Thousand pounds, that is to Say, Five thousand pounds in Silver & Gold, to be paid £1000, at the End of the first Session of the General Court, £2000, at the End of the Second & £2000, at the End of the third;

"Twenty thousand pounds in Copper Coin to be deliver'd half yearly in a proportion of two fifths of what shall then be coined, and Twenty five thousand pounds in Consolidated Securities of the Commonwealth that are now due, or become due this year — The whole to be new funded by Ten Treasurers notes on Interest for £5000, each, the first to be payable three years hence, & so on untill I receive my principal in thirteen years — The principal & Interest to be paid in Specie only, out of the Excise duties, which duties shall be by a special resolve or Act, continued for the term of 13 years & appropriated, to this purpose. I mention Excise only, as I suppose the present Impost dutie will Cease, as soon as the Continental Imposts opperates. —

"Jam. Swan"

On the 12th of June, 1786, this message from the Governor was received:—
"Gentlemen of the Senate and Gentlemen of the House of Representatives —

"By a Resolve of the General Court of the 24th of March last, the Governour and Council were requested to consider the expediency of coining Silver and Copper in this Commonwealth, the quantity it would be convenient in that case to coin; in what mode the business should be conducted; the proper devices to be used; and the advantage that would accrue to the Commonwealth from such a coinage.

"I laid the resolve before the Council, and after a discussion of the subject, a Committee was appointed to consider it more fully. The Committee have reported; and their report, having been accepted by the Council, is now with the papers to which it refers, laid before you for your consideration —

"Upon the subject of a coinage I have had a letter of the 18th of May from one of our Delegates in Congress, the honorable Mr. Gorham, enclosing the report of the Treasury Board, relating to the establishment of a Mint: which Report it was expected would in a few days be considered by Congress.

"Mr. Gorham taking notice, that according to the News-papers, proposals had been made to the Legislature of Massachusetts, relative to a Copper Coinage, observes, that it is apprehended, it will be attended with great inconveniences if the States should act in this matter separately; that after Congress had agreed upon a plan, which they will soon do, there might be, and it would be of great utility, there should be, an uniformity in the money throughout the Union; and that Massachusetts and any other State, after knowing the terms, on which the Board of Treasury would conduct this business, could more advantageously act upon it, than before: and therefore seems to suppose, that it would be adviseable to suspend the coinage, until we are notified of the proceedings of Congress upon that head.

"These reasons, without mentioning others that might be given, may induce you, Gentlemen, to suspend this business accordingly.

"The report made to Congress[1], relative to the establishment of a mint for the United States, accompanies the Papers abovementioned —

"Council Chamber                                        James Bowdoin"
"June 12th 1786

"In Senate June 12th 1786.   Read, & with the papers accompanying, committed to Richard Cranch and Oliver Phelps Esqs. With such as the Honble may join.                    Sent down for concurrence.

"Saml. Phillips junr. Presidt. "

"In the House of Representatives June 12. 1786
"Read and concurred & Mr. Titcomb, Mr. Cross & Mr. Jarvis are joined
"Artemas Ward Speaker —"

July 6th, 1786, the committee reported as follows: —

"The Committee of both Houses to whom was committed the Governor's Message of the 12th of June 1786, on the Subject of a Coinage, have attended that Service, and ask Leave to report as their Opinion — That it is adviseable to suspend the further Consideration of that Subject untill the Proceeding of Congress, relating to the Establishment of a Mint, shall be made known to the several States.

"Which is humbly submitted,                    Richard Cranch, pr Order."

Notwithstanding the suggestion of the Governor, and the report of the committee advising that this business be suspended, the Representatives soon appointed another committee to forward it; and on Monday, July 3d, they "Ordered that Mr. Jarvis Mr. Davis, & Mr. Sargent be a Committee to Consider of the Expediency of Coining Money & report."

The committee reported the following resolve: —

"In the House of Representatives, July 7th 1786
"Resolved — That his Excellency the Governour be & he is hereby requested to write to the Delegates of this Commonwealth in Congress: informing them,

---

[1] This report is not to be found, but probably was that considered by Congress, August 8th, 1786.

that it is the earnest Wish of the Legislature of this Commonwealth that a mint for coining Silver & Copper, to serve as a Currency throughout the United States, be established as soon as may be —"

This report was considered by both Houses, and accepted, "as taken into a new draft" — which was as follows: —

"Commonwealth of          In the house of Representatives
    Massachusetts.                      July 7$^{th}$ 1786

"Ordered that his Excellency the Governor be, and he hereby is, requested to write to the Delegates of this Commonwealth in Congress, informing them that it is the earnest wish of the Legislature of this Commonwealth to obtain a quantity of copper and silver Coin to be struck off, for the use of this Commonwealth, and desiring them to acquaint him with the situation of the mint proposed for the service of the United States — when it may probably be ready for striking off Coin, and what the Expence of coining copper — or silver will be — and of any other circumstance relative thereto which his Excellency may think proper."

The preceding report seems more in favor of hastening the establishment of a mint for the United States, than that of a State mint; but obtaining no relief from Congress, the State soon passed an act authorizing a mint of her own; the consideration of the act afterward passed, immediately followed the report just presented.

The paper next in order is endorsed, "Act respecting the coinage of money, July 8, 1786, referred to next session."

"Commonwealth   }      In the year of our LORD one thousand seven
  of Massachusetts. }            hundred & eighty six.

"An Act authorizing and empowering the Governor with advice of Council to coin a certain Quantity of Copper and to erect a Mint for that Purpose

"Whereas the coining of a Quantity of Copper and bringing the same into Circulation may be productive of great Advantages to the Commonwealth —

"Therefore Be it enacted by the Senate & House of Representatives in General Court assembled and by the Authority of the same, That the Governor and Council be and they are hereby authorized and empowered to erect for the Use of the Commonwealth a Mint for the Coinage of Copper and therein to coin a Quantity of Copper into Pieces of different Denominations of the Value                      each and in such Proportions with such Device or Devices and descriptive Marks as they shall judge proper, the whole not to exceed Twenty Thousand Pounds and the Mint so erected shall be under the Management & Direction of the Governor & Council untill otherwise determined by the General Court " —

The following order was passed by the Representatives, July 8th, 1786: —

" Ordered that Mr Breck, Mr Ward of Salem & Mr Bowdoin with such as the Hon Senate may join be a Committee to devise further ways and means in the recess of the General Court for discharging the interest and principal of the public debt of this Commonwealth, and of its proportion of the fœderal debt & to report at the next Session of the Legislature "

The Senate concurred, and added to the committee Messrs. Phillips and Tufts. The connection of this committee with our subject is explained by the ensuing records: —

" In Senate Oct. 4, 1786 Ordered that a Committee of both Houses appointed the 8th of July last to devise further ways and means for discharging the interest and principal of the public debt of this Commonwealth, and of its proportion of the federal debt, be instructed to consider of a proper mode for regulating the Current Copper Coin, and the expediency of Coining gold, silver & Copper, and also to Consider a regular system for supplying the Treasury with specie & report. Sent down for Concurrence Read and concurred."

Wednesday, Oct. 11th 1786,

" The Hon. S. Baker Esqr. brought down a report of the Committee appointed 8th of July last, to Consider the expediency of Coining gold &c., ' That it will be highly advantageous to the Commonwealth to erect a Mint as soon as may be, in the Town of Boston for the Coinage of Gold, Silver & Copper, and that a bill be brought in for establishing a Mint, and for empowering the Governor, with the advice of Council to appoint some suitable person or persons to erect the same, and when completed, to inspect the business of the said Mint, the Committee ask leave to sit again

" In Senate Oct. 11, 1786. Read & accepted. Sent down for Concurrence Read and concurred."

Omitting the dry details of the several readings of the bill for the establishment of the mint, which occupied much of the time between the 11th and the 17th of October, we proceed to the bill, which was passed on the day last mentioned. The following is a copy of the engrossed bill: —

"Commonwealth of Massachusetts.

"In the year of our LORD one thousand seven hundred and eighty six

"AN ACT for establishing a Mint for the coinage of Gold, Silver and Copper —

"WHEREAS the United States in Congress assembled, by their Resolve of the eighth day of August in the present year, have regulated the Alloy and Value of Coin, and whereas the want of a sufficient circulating medium, renders it expedient, that a Mint should be erected and a quantity of Coin be struck.

"Therefore be it enacted by the Senate and House of Representatives in General Court assembled and by the authority of the same, That there shall be a Mint erected within this Commonwealth, for the coining of Gold, Silver and Copper; and that all the Coin that shall be struck therein, shall be of the same weight, alloy and value and each piece bear the same name, as is by the said Resolve of Congress fixed & established.

"And be it further enacted by the authority aforesaid, that there shall be a quantity of Copper Coin struck, equal to the amount of seventy thousand Dollars, in pieces of the two different denominations mentioned in the said resolve, and in convenient proportions; one of which to have the Name — *Cent* — stamped in the Center thereof, and the other — *Half Cent* — with such inscriptions or devices as the Governor with the Advice of Council may think proper; and the said Coin, when struck, shall be received in all payments in this Commonwealth —

"And be it further enacted, That the Governor with the advice of Council be and he is hereby authorized and empowered to appoint some suitable person or persons, to procure all the necessaries requisite to the compleating of the said Mint, fit for coining, and to take due care that the same be compleated as soon as may be, and also to procure an able Assay Master, Stock, Workmen and whatever may be necessary for the actual coinage of Gold, silver and Copper as before directed; and the Governor with advice of Council is hereby farther empowered to appoint some suitable person or persons to have the oversight and inspection of the said Mint when completed, and to see to the coinage of the Copper aforementioned and of the Gold and Silver that may be brought[1] in for Stock or brought in for coining — And the Governor with the advice of Council is hereby further empowered

---

[1] In the bill as passed to be engrossed, this word is "bought."

to establish proper rules and regulations, respecting the well ordering and managing the business of the said Mint, for the safe keeping the stock and Coin that may be kept therein and for securing the fidelity of all employed in the said Business—And the Inspector or Inspectors appointed as aforesaid, shall, before he or they enter on the business of said appointment, give bonds for the faithful discharge of the duties of the appointment with sureties to the Treasurer of this Commonwealth in such sum or sums as the Governor with advice of Council shall direct.—

"And be it further enacted, That all the Gold, silver and Copper belonging to the Commonwealth that may from time to time be coined in the said Mint, so often as the same shall amount to the value of one thousand Dollars, shall be delivered by the said Inspector or Inspectors into the Treasury of this Commonwealth, he or they taking duplicate receipts therefor, one of which shall be lodged in the Secretary's Office —

"And be it further enacted that the charge of erecting and completing the said Mint, of Stock, Workmen, Officers and all other disbursements for carrying on the said business of coining, shall be defrayed out of the said Coin, by warrant from the Governor with advice of Council; the Accounts relating to the said Mint and the business thereof, having been first attested by the Inspector or Inspectors, and laid before the Council examined & approved. And if there should remain any sum or sums of money arising from the said coinage, more than is necessary for the payment of the aforesaid expences, the same shall be appropriated to the purchase of Stock for the said Mint unless the General Court shall otherwise order.

"And be it further enacted, that the Inspector or Inspectors of the said Mint, shall from time to time lay before the Governor and Council an account of their doings, and state of the said Mint, that the same may be laid before the General Court. —

"In the House of Representatives October 16th 1786. —
"This Bill having had three several Readings passed to be Enacted.
"Artemas Ward Speaker.—

"In Senate October 17th 1786 —
"This Bill having had two several readings, passed to be Enacted
"Saml Phillips junr Presidt

"By the Governour
"Approved
"James Bowdoin"

The next proceedings in this business were the appropriation of money for the necessary expenses, and the providing of a supply of metal for coining; the papers relating to this we copy from original drafts, on file at the office of the Secretary of State :—

"Commonwealth of Massachusetts }  In the House of Representatives Oct 22.ᵈ 1786

"Resolved,

That there be paid out of the Treasury of this Commonwealth, The sum of Six hundred pounds for the use of the Governour & Council to Enable them to prosecute the business of Coinage agreeably to an Act passed this present session, they being accountable for the same

"Resolved,

That the Commissary General be, and he is hereby authorized and directed, to deliver to the order of the Governour & Council such quantity of Copper as he may have on hand for the purpose of Coinage, and the said Commissary General is hereby further directed, to call on All persons who have Copper in their hands belonging to this Commonwealth and deliver the same to the order of the Governour & Council for the purposes above mentioned "

This was approved Nov. 11th, " as taken into a new draft," which follows:—

"Commonwealth of Massachusetts }  In the House of Representatives Octob. 22. 1786 —

"Resolved, That the Governor with Advice of Council, be and He is hereby empowered to draw a Warrant on the Treasurer of this Commonwealth, for the Sum of Two Hundred Pounds, to be applied to the carrying into Execution, An Act, for establishing a Mint for the Coinage of Gold Silver & Copper, passed the present Session.

"Resolved, That all Persons having in their Possession any Copper, belonging to this Commonwealth, Be and they are hereby directed to deliver, the same, to the Commissary General, who is hereby directed to deliver, to the order of such Person or Persons as may be appointed by the Governor with Advice of Council Inspector or Inspectors of the mint, such Copper as He may receive as aforesaid, together with what He may now have on Hand, and is useful for Coinage, taking duplicate Receipts therefor, one of which shall be lodged with the Secretary — "

On the 23d of October, 1786, we find this entry upon the Council Records:

"His Excellency laid before the Council an Act of the General Court of the seventeenth instant establishing a mint for the coinage of Gold, silver & copper & asked the advice of the Council thereon — Advised that the said Act be committed to His Honor the Lieut. Governor, Mr Spooner & Austin to report a system for carrying the said Act into execution—"

On the 9th of November, Hon. Nathan Dane was requested to appear before the Representatives, and though no record of his speech is found upon the Journal of the House, the Independent Chronicle of the week following gives an abstract of it, from which we quote the part relating to coinage :—

"Hon. Nathan Dane, a Delegate to Congress from Mass." appeared before the State Legislature, and made a statement of the situation of public affairs. Speaking of the U. S. Mint, he said 'that no great pecuniary advantages could be expected from it at present, but he conceived the measure of considerable importance, as it tends to give us a national feature, to render our circulating medium more pure, and gradually to increase it ; that much skill and attention is required in assaying the materials, mixing in the alloy, and in providing against counterfeiting the coins of the States or Union; that it may be doubtful whether the States will have full confidence in the coins struck by each other, and when they are struck at several mints in the Union, the probability being, that more base money may get into circulation.  For these considerations, and to save expence, it is to be wished that the coinage of money, at the federal mint, may be made as extensive as conveniently may be."

No progress appears to have been made during the winter, toward forwarding the business of the mint, as we find no further reference to it until the report of the committee last appointed, which was not sent in before the next Spring, when the following report was rendered :—

"May 2ᵈ 1787.

"The Committee appointed to carry into effect the act passed last fall for establishing a Mint for the Coinage of Gold, Silver & copper beg leave to report — That they have attended the service & upon enquiring what articles it would be necessary to procure for compleating said Mint, they find it was necessary to erect a furnace, & the clay with which the bricks were to be made for erecting of the same could not be procured nor the bricks made until this Spring— That they have fully conversed with Capt Joshua Wetherle upon the subject of establishing a mint for the coinage of copper & find he is a suitable person to procure the necessaries requisite to compleat the same & to conduct the business & is ready, if he should be appointed for this purpose, immediately to proceed upon the business as soon as he shall have an order for such copper as now belongs to this Commonwealth — And the Committee further report that Capt Joshua Witherlee be appointed to the business accordingly & be furnished with an order on the Commissary General for the copper belonging to this Commonwealth he giving bond with sureties for the faithfull discharge of the duty of his appointment & that the copper he may be furnished with shall be appropriated to the business of coining copper —

"His Excellency was pleased to nominate Capt Joshua Wetherle as a person suitable to be employed in the mint for the coinage of copper & asked the advice of the Council — The Council thereupon Advised that Joshua Wetherle be appointed to conduct the said business of coinage —"

"Thursday May 3ᵈ 1787

"Advised that His Excellency be requested to order the copper now in the hands of the Honble Hugh Orr esqʳ to be delivered to the Commissary General for the purpose of carrying into execution a resolution of the General Court passed November 11ᵗʰ 1786, & also to direct the Commissary General to deliver the said copper to Joshua Wetherle esqʳ appointed to carry on the business of coinage together with what he may now have on hand & is useful for coinage taking duplicate receipts therefor one of which to be lodged with the Secretary of this Commonwealth — "

Next follows a memorandum of the copper available for coining : —

"Bridgewater May 10ᵗʰ 1787

"We Weighed off Thirty four hundred & thirty four pound net weight of Copper, and Six hundred & fifty weight of Sprews (so Called) belonging to the Common Wealth of Massachusetts, now in the possession of the Honˡᵉ Hugh Orr Esqʳ at his Store in Bridgewater.

"David Kingman } Comᵗᵉᵉ
"Hugh Orr      } appointed for
               ( that purpose

"There is Also One Ten Inch Mortar Two Eight & half Dᵒ, four Cohorn Morters unfinished, now on hand, also Two four pound Brass Cannon that are to be run Over Again and a Ten Inch Mortar that failed in the Casting Supposed to weigh 12 or 14 Cwᵗ together with a Brass rack belonging to the Machine for boring Cannon, the Above together with the Above mentioned, are under my Care Witness my hand —                          Hugh Orr "

"A true Copy Richᵈ Devens Comʸ Gen."

In the House of Representatives, on Friday, June 1st, 1787, it was "Ordered that M.<sup>r</sup> Jones of Boston, M.<sup>r</sup> Dawes & M.<sup>r</sup> Bowdoin be a Committee to examine what measures have been taken respecting the coinage of copper and the assaying of minerals, and report." . . . . "A petition from James Swan praying to be allowed to coin twenty thousand pounds in copper on certain conditions therein mentioned. Read & ordered that the said petition lie till the committee appointed to enquire what measures have been taken on the subject of coinage report." On Monday, June 4th, "The House reconsidered their vote of the 1.<sup>st</sup> inst.<sup>t</sup> on the petition[1] of James Swan and committed the same to the Committee appointed to consider what measures have been taken respecting the coinage of copper."

June 11th, "The committee appointed to examine what measures had been taken with respect to the coinage of copper reported verbally that in their opinion, it would be best to continue that business in the hands of the Lieu.<sup>t</sup> Governour & Council and that James Swan Esq.<sup>r</sup> have leave to withdraw his petition upon this subject. Report accepted & ordered accordingly."

Another committee was appointed by the Representatives, on Saturday, June 23d, 1787, when it was "Ordered that M.<sup>r</sup> Davis, M.<sup>r</sup> Clarke, & D.<sup>r</sup> Kilham be a Committee to consider the expediency of coining silver at the mint now establishing in this Commonwealth, & report."

On Wednesday, June 27th, the Council designated the devices, &c., for the copper coin, in these words :—

"Advised that the device on the copper coin to be emitted in this Commonwealth be the figure of an indian with a bow & arrow & a star on one side, with the word 'Commonwealth,' the reverse a spread eagle with the words—'of Massachusetts A. D. 1787'—"

The coins show a slight variation from this order, in the legend upon the reverses, only the word Massachusetts and the date being there found.

Still another committee was named by the Senate, it being on the 30th of June, "Ordered that Tristam Dalton, Joseph B. Varnum and Isaac Stearns be a Committee to enquire, what progress has been made in the coining of Gold, Silver & Copper—"

We next find a resolve, probably reported by the committee of June 23d; this was passed by the Representatives, but rejected by the Senate.

---

[1] This petition was probably the same which had been previously presented, and has already been given on p. 230.

"Commonwealth of Massachusetts

"In the House of Representatives July 2ᵈ 1787.

"Whereas the Governour and Council have taken measures for the establishing a Mint for the Coinage of Copper, pursuant to an Act of the General Court passed the 17 day of October 1786; and whereas it is necessary, that provision should also be made for the receiving of Silver and for coining the same, therefore

"Resolved, that the Governour and Council be, and they are hereby empowered and requested, to take such measures as they may judge necessary, for the receiving into the said Mint all such Silver Bullion as may be brought in by any person or persons for the purpose of coining; with such Devices, of such weight and under such regulations, as are established by a Resolve of the United States in Congress assembled, passed the 8ᵗʰ day of August 1786, and by an Act of the General Court passed the 17ᵗʰ day of October in the same year.

"Sent up for concurrence              J Warren Spkʳ"

"In Senate July 5ᵗʰ 1787
          "Read and nonconcurred          S. Adams Presidᵗ"

The coins of Massachusetts are all of one type, consisting of several varieties of both cents and half cents, and may be described as follows : —

### OBVERSE.

Device,—An Indian standing, facing left, holding in his right hand a bow, and in his left, an arrow ; between the top of the bow and his head, is a mullet.

Legend,—COMMON WEALTH.

### REVERSE.

Device,—An eagle, displayed, on his breast a shield argent, six pales gules, a chief azure; on the chief, the word CENT ; in his right talon is an olive branch, and in his left a bundle of arrows.   Legend, —MASSACHUSETTS.

In exergue,—The date—1787 or 1788.

Borders,—Milled.   Edge,—Plain.   Size, 16½ to 19.

Weight,—From 146 to 165 grains.

The half cents are of the same description, except that the shield bears the words HALF CENT instead of CENT.   The Size of these is from 15 to 15½, and the weight of those of 1787 from 75 to 83 grains ; those of 1788, usually 76 grains.

Tables of the varieties will be found on the two pages following.

## CENTS, 1787. OBVERSES.

| Point of Arrow below Tunic | Bow. | | One Ray of Mullet Points | End of Arrow under | Number. | With Reverse | Rarity. |
|---|---|---|---|---|---|---|---|
| | Top rises to | Lower end | | | | | |
| Twice the length of arrow head. | ¾ height of letters. | Left of foot. | At chin. | Middle of E. | 1 | B | R⁶ |
| | ½ height of letters. | Near foot. | At collar. | Upright of E. | 2ᵃ | F | R⁵ |
| | Same die. | Recut, heavy | At collar. | Upright of E. | 2ᵇ | A, C, E | C |
| | ½ height of letters. | Near foot. | At forehead. | Upright of E. | 3 | G | R |
| | ½ height of letters. | Left of foot. | Below collar. | Left part of E. | 4 | C, D | R³ |
| One and one half lengths. | ⅓ height of letters. | Left(?),light. | At chin. | Left part of E. | 5 | I | R⁶ |
| One length. | ½ height of letters. | Left,medium | Above collar. | Upright of E. | 6 | G | R² |
| | ¾ height of letters. | Left, light. | At mouth. | Upright of E. | 7 | H | R⁶ |

## CENTS, 1788. OBVERSES.

| Point of Arrow below Tunic. | Top of Bow rises to | One Ray of Mullet Points | End of Arrow under | Number. | With Reverse. | Rarity. |
|---|---|---|---|---|---|---|
| Full two lengths of head . . . . | Top of letters. | Below collar. | Upright of E. | 1 | D | C |
| | ¾ height or letters. | Above collar. | Right part of E. | 2 | B | R³ |
| | Top of letters. | At throat. | Left part of E. | 3 | A, E | R |
| | Top of letters. | At nose. | Right part of E. | 4 | G | R² |
| | ½ height of letters. | Below collar. | Left part of E. | 5 | H | R⁶ |
| | ¼ height of letters. | At collar. | Upright of E. | 6 | N | R |
| | ¾ height of letters. | Above collar. | Upright of E. | 7 | M | R |
| About one and one half lengths. . . | Top of letters. | At mouth. | Upright of E. | 8 | C | R² |
| | ½ height of letters. | At forehead. | Left part of E. | 9 | M | R⁵ |
| | ¾ height of letters. | Above collar. | Upright of E. | 10 | L | C |
| | Top of letters. | At throat. | Upright of E. | 11 | C, E, F | C |
| One length . . . . | ½ height of letters. | Above collar. | Left part of E. | 12 | H, I, K, M | C |

## HALF CENTS, 1787. OBVERSES.

| Head of Arrow | | Feather End under | One Ray of Mullet points | Defects. | Grass. | Number. | With Reverse | Rarity. |
|---|---|---|---|---|---|---|---|---|
| Below tunic | Small. | Middle of W. | At collar. | None. | None. | 1 | D | R⁴ |
| | Large. | Right foot W. | At eyebrow. | Inside right leg. | Thin. | 2 | A | R³ |
| | Small. | Between W and E. | At collar. | None. | Thicker at right. | 3 | A | R⁵ |
| | Small. | Left part E. | At mouth. | Over right foot. | Very thin. | 4 | B, C | C |
| Half below tunic. | Large. | Right foot W. | Above collar. | Inside left leg. | Light. | 5 | A | R² |
| | Large. | Between W and E. | At throat. | From left top of E. | High, light. | 6 | D | R⁵ |

## HALF CENTS, 1788. OBVERSE.

| Arrow Point | Arrow Head | Feather End under | One Ray of Mullet points | Grass. | Number. | With Reverse. | Rarity. |
|---|---|---|---|---|---|---|---|
| Just below tunic | Medium, joining tunic | Left part of E. | At nose. | Very light. | 1 | A, B | R |

### CENTS, 1787.  REVERSES.

| Dash. | Leaves on Branch. | Point of leaves turn | Arrows. Number barbed. | Arrows. Pointing below wing. | Figures and Spacing. | Upper stroke of Dash. | Number. | With Ob-verse. | Rarity. |
|---|---|---|---|---|---|---|---|---|---|
| Double. | Four. | Up. | 10, spread. | 5 | Medium. | Short, light. | A | 2$^b$ | C |
| | | Straight. | 6, medium. | 2 | Wide. | Long, light. | B | 1 | R$^6$ |
| | Five. | Up. | 7, spread. | 5 | Medium. | Long, light. | C | 2$^b$ 4 | C |
| | | 1st 2 down, others up. | 9, spread. | 3 | Medium. | Long, heavy. | D | 4 | R$^2$ |
| | | 1st down, others up. | 6(?) spread. | 3 | Close. | Light, close. | E | 2$^b$ | R$^6$ |
| | | Last down, others up. | 5(?) close. | None. | Small, close. | Long, heavy. | F | 2$^a$ | R$^5$ |
| | | | | | | Dash single. | | | |
| Single. | | Up. | 6, spread. | 2 | Medium. | Light. | G | 3, 6 | R |
| | | 1st 2 down, others up. | 8 close. | 5 | Large, wide. | Medium. | H | 7 | R$^6$ |
| | | Up. | 7 close. | 2 | Large, heavy. | Heavy. | I | 5 | R$^6$ |

### CENTS, 1788.  REVERSES.

| Punctuation. | Dash. | Form of S. | Last S from tip of Wing. | Number of Arrows. | Figures. | Number. | With Obverse | Rarity. |
|---|---|---|---|---|---|---|---|---|
| Point after legend | Upper stroke of dash heaviest. | S narrow, like figure 8. | Entirely below. | 7, close. | First 8 low. | A | 3 | R |
| | | | $\frac{3}{4}$ below. | 8, close. | Spread. | B | 2 | R$^3$ |
| | | | $\frac{1}{2}$ below. | 7, close. | 1 high. | C | 8, 11 | R |
| | | | $\frac{1}{3}$ below. | 7, close. | 78 low. | D | 1 | C |
| | | | Well above. | 7, close. | 78 low. | E | 3, 11 | C |
| | | | Just above. | 7, close. | First 8 low. | F | 11 | R$^5$ |
| | | | Just above. | 8, close. | 88 wide. | G | 4 | R$^2$ |
| | Lower stroke of dash heaviest. | S wide and open. | $\frac{1}{2}$ below. | 10. medium. | Light. | H | 5, 12 | R |
| | | | $\frac{1}{2}$ below. | 6, medium. | 88 low. | I | 12 | R$^5$ |
| | | | $\frac{1}{2}$ below. | 7(?), medium. | 1 small. | K | 12 | R |
| | | | $\frac{1}{2}$ below. | 8(?), medium. | 78 wide. | L | 10 | C |
| | | | $\frac{1}{2}$ below. | 7, spread. | 1 low. | M | 7, 9, 12 | C |
| No point | | | $\frac{1}{2}$ below. | 10(?), close. | 17 close. | N | 6 | R |

### HALF CENTS, 1787.  REVERSES.

| Dash | Outer Leaves turn | Barbed Arrows. | Pointing below Wing. | Upper Stroke of Dash. | Figures. Spacing. | Figures. Proportions. | Number. | With Obverse | Rarity. |
|---|---|---|---|---|---|---|---|---|---|
| Double . . | Up. | Five(?). | Two. | Very light. | Wide. | Medium. | A | 2, 3, 5 | R |
| | Down. | Six. | Four. | Light. | Medium. | Heavy. | B | 4 | R$^5$ |
| | | | | Arrows. | | | | | |
| Single . . | Up. | Seven. | Two. | Spread. | Close. | Heavy. | C | 4 | C |
| | Up. | Eight(?). | Three. | Close, irregular. | Wide. | Light. | D | 1, 6 | R$^2$ |

### HALF CENTS. 1788.  REVERSES.

| Dash | Outer leaves | Barbed Arrows. | Pointing below Wing. | Dash. | Figures. | Number. | With Obverse | Rarity. |
|---|---|---|---|---|---|---|---|---|
| Single . . . | Nearly straight. | Four. | One. | Tapers to ends. | 88 high, medium. | A | 1 | R$^6$ |
| | Turn up. | Five. | One. | Straight. | 78 low, medium. | B | 1 | R |

### NOTES ON THE TABLES OF MASSACHUSETTS COINS OF 1787.

No. 1 is among the most peculiar of the coins of this State. The Indian has an aged face, a prominent chin, and his body is slightly bowed ; the only specimen of it we have seen, is owned by Mr. J. Carson Brevoort, of Brooklyn, N. Y. It is on a small planchet, measuring but 16½.

No. 2ᵃ we find only with reverse F ; the tops of the letters, and the lower end of the bow are very light, (Plate VI, No. 5.) but in 2ᵇ they seem to have been recut more heavily ; the last with reverse C, is R⁵.

No. 3 has a defect like a period before C.  [Plate VI, No. 6.]

No. 4 is the " bowed head ; " it has a tassel near the top of each boot, and no grass near the feet.

No. 5 we have seen only in the cabinet of Chas. I. Bushnell, Esq: the Indian is stout, and slightly bowed.

No. 6.  Upon this, as well as on Nos. 2, 3, and 7, the Indian stands erect.

No. 7.  Another stout Indian ; the die badly broken.  [Plate VI, No. 7.]

In reverse A, the period is under the head of the right hand arrow, and the sixth arrow from the right joins the tip of the wing.  From a break like a horn over the eagle's head, this is called the " horned eagle."

B, period large, and very near S ; the third arrow is nearest tip of wing.

C, period joins the point of the first arrow, the fifth, nearest tip of wing.

D, period nearer point of second arrow, the fourth, joins tip of wing.

E, period near first arrow, the third, nearest wing ; many arrows joined.

F.  This deserves particular notice.  The eagle grasps the arrows in his right talon (at observer's left,) and the olive branch in his left.  The second and third leaves from the right join the wing.  But four specimens of this are known.

G, period under point of first arrow, the third, joins tip of wing.

H, period very large; all arrows with small and distinct heads.

I, period large, arrows all with heads.

Of the cents of 1788 few notes will be required; we will, however, mention some points necessarily excluded from the tables.

In Nos, 1, 6, 8, 9 and 11, the lower point of the bow is very near the foot of the Indian ; but in 2, 3, 4, 5, 7, 10 and 12, it is about 1-32d of an inch to the left of the foot, and in No. 9 is slightly double.

The points of the two outer leaves turn upward, except in I, where the first leaf, in K, the second, and in M and N, both, turn downward.

The half cents are so fully illustrated on Plate VI, only one die being there omitted, that no notes will be required, other than references to the numbers

# PLATE VI.

upon the plate, where No. 12, represents 1–D : No. 9, 3–A : No. 13, 4–B : No. 14, 4–C : No. 10, 5–A : No. 11, 6–D, of 1787, and Nos. 16 and 15, respectively, 1–A and 1–B, of 1788. The last is often found broken through the last 8. As the plates were printed before the tables were arranged, the numbers do not stand in their proper sequence.

In the tables of reverses of the cents of 1788, F, should be enclosed by the lower brace in the dash column, the lower stroke being heaviest.

The Massachusetts coins are represented by the cuts below ; the chief of the shield upon all, should be like that of No. 37.

Most of the dies for this mint were made by Joseph Callender,[1] whose place of business was in 1789 at "Half-square, State-street," (nearly where Brazier's Building now stands,) but as appears in the report of the mint-master, the cost of his dies was so great, (£1. 4s. each,) that another engraver was employed as soon as one could be found, who was to receive but one per cent of the coin struck from his dies ; this probably was Jacob Perkins of Newburyport, to whom the mint accounts show that payments were made at different times.

It appears to us certain that a clue by which the dies cut by these engravers can be distinguished, exists in the letter S, upon the reverse dies. In all those of 1787, and in six of those of 1788, this letter is broad and open : while in seven

---

[1] The Directory of 1789 says, "Callender, Joseph, engraver, Half-square, State-street." Half Square Court was, as nearly as it can now be located, about where Congress Square now is. Drake records it, " ' From King-st. (State st.) by the house of Isaac Addington Esq., with the return into Pudding-lane,' (Devonshire st.) 1708. In 1732, ' from Maccarty's cor. turning into Pudding-lane.' "

of the cents and both of the half cents of 1788, it is narrow, and the points so connected with the curves, as to resemble a figure 8.

Callender's bill specifies three dies repaired, and thirty-nine new dies ; curiously enough, the dies with the open S, and the obverses found with them according to the tables, number thirty-eight.

The three sums paid to Jacob Perkins amount to but £3. 18s. 10d., while Callender's bill was for £48. 12s. from which it would appear that his work must have much exceeded that of Perkins.

On Thursday, September 13th, 1787, the Governor submitted to the Council these instructions to the Master of the Mint :—

"His Excellency laid before the Council an act for establishing a mint for the coinage of gold, silver & copper passed October 17th 1786 & submitted to their consideration some proper rules & regulations respecting the well-ordering & managing the business of the said Mint — The Council took the subject matter of said act into consideration & thereupon Advised that Mr Wetherle the master workman of the mint purchase the copper suitable for coinage at as reasonable a price as possible until further order — That Mr Wetherle procure the workmen for the mint at as cheap a rate as possible — That the Master Workman of the mint be & hereby is authorized to judge of the quality of copper suitable for coinage previous to the purchase — That the Master workman of the mint have full power to discharge any person under his care without making application to Government & shall also have full power to make such regulations for the workmen from time to time as he shall think it necessary for carrying on the business with despatch — That the Committee appointed the twenty third of October 1786 to report a system to carry the act for establishing a mint into execution be empowered to give such further rules & regulations respecting the well ordering & managing the business of the said Mint as they shall judge expedient 'till the next meeting of the Council — * * * * *

"His Excellency suggested to the Council the expediency of appointing some suitable persons to have the oversight & inspection of the Mint & to see to the coinage of the copper & whether it was necessary that two inspectors of said mint should be appointed passed in the negative — The opinion of the Council was then asked whether from the declaration of the Master Workmen of the mint this day it was necessary to come to the choice of one inspector for the mint passed in the affirmative —

"The Council took under consideration the sum that was necessary to be given to the said inspector for his services & thereupon Advised that one hundred & twenty pounds be paid to the said inspector for his services yearly, & that he give bonds previous to his entering on the business of his appointment for the faithful discharge of his trust with sureties to the Treasurer of this Commonwealth in the sum of one thousand pounds —

"His Excellency was pleased to nominate Ebenezer Hancock esq". to be inspector of the mint established for the coinage of copper which nomination the Council did advise & consent — "

"Friday September 14th 1787

"Mr. Hancock inspector of the mint mentioned to the Council for their consideration Benjamin Hichborne esq". & Edward Blanchard both of Boston as his sureties for the faithful discharge of his trust — who were approved of by the Council —"

The Governor, in his speech of Oct. 18th, 1787, remarked upon the mint : — "In consequence of an act made October 1786, a mint has been erected for coining cents, and a very considerable quantity of copper will soon be ready for circulation. I wish your attention to the subject, and that a law may be made to prevent the daily frauds and impositions arising from the circulation of foreign copper coin in this Commonwealth."

A committee was therefore appointed to consider the troubles complained of.

"Commonwealth of
    Massachusetts                              In Senate Oct". 22d 1787 —

"Ordered that Cotton Tufts Esq". with such as the Honble House may join, be a Committee to consider what is necessary to be done respecting the Copper coined in the Mint, and for preventing frauds & impositions from the circulation of foreign Copper Coin, and the future importation of it —

sent down for concurrence,                              S Adams Presidt "

"In the House of Representatives October 22d 1787

"Read and concurred and Mr. Bowdoin and Mr. Parsons are joined

                                        J Warren Sp'kr "

The name of Mr. Parsons was afterwards erased, and that of Mr. Lithgow substituted.

The above named committee returned this report : —

"The Committee of both Houses appointed to consider what is necessary to be done respecting the Mint, for preventing Frauds & Impositions arising from the Circulation of foreign Coin & the future Importation of it, ask leave to report a Bill in Addition to an Act against counterfeiting or uttering counterfeit Coin — and the following Resolve —

Cotton Tufts p.ʳ ord.ʳ ”

"Commonwealth of Massachusetts —

"Resolved, That such of the Copper coined in the Mint of this Commonwealth, as shall be lodged in the Treasury (whenever the Payment of the Expences provided for in the Act for establishing the said Mint shall be compleated) Two Fifths thereof be and it is hereby appropriated to the sole Purpose of paying the Members of the Gen.ˡ Court from Time to Time in such Proportion among them as the Sum in the Treasury shall admit off, and the remaining Three Fifths to the purchasing of necessary Stock for carrying on the Business of the said Mint, and defraying the Charges thereof—

"And It is further Resolved That The Governor and Council be and they are hereby requested to *to* lay before the Gen.ˡ Court at their next Sitting an Account of the Cost & Charges of erecting the said Mint and the whole Amount of Expenditures whether for Stock or any other Purpose —

"In Senate November 22.ᵈ 1787, Read and accepted and Resolved accordingly —

sent down for Concurrence    S Adams Presid.ᵗ ”

This paper is on file in the House archives endorsed: —

"Report & Resolve respecting the Mint, Nov.ʳ 22, 1787 read and ordered to lie."

In the House, it was on the 25th of October, 1787, "Ordered that D.ʳ Taylor General Brooks M.ʳ Dawes D.ʳ Manning and M.ʳ Freeman be a Committee to make enquiry whether silver can be obtained at such rate and in such quantity as will be for the interest of Government to *to* coin the same. — and report."

"The Committee Appointed to Make enquiry whether Silver can be Obtained at Such Price and in Such Quantity as it will be for the Interest of Government to Coin the Same —— have attended that Service and ask leave to Report as their Opinion that Such Quantity of Silver may be purchased and at Such price that in case Government can now advance one Thousend pounds for the purchase of Silver and do Appoint a proper Person to purchase and assay the Same and Order it Coined as Soon as may be that there will a very Considerable Revenue arise therefrom to Government ; beside the almost Infinite advantage of greatly

Increasing the Circulating medium the want of which has greatly Injured thousends.

"if the profits arising from the abovementioned thousend pounds is Sacredly appropriated for the Sole purpose of purchaseing Silver and So on from time to time we hope a full medium may be Soon Obtain'd and no one Injured : but every Individual and the publick at large greatly Releived from there present Embarresd Situation.

your Committee are further of Opinion that every person lodging Silver of a good Quallity with the Assay Master Shall receive nine tenths the weight thereof in money as Soon as Coined

John Taylor p<sup>r</sup> order "

Thursday, November 8th, "The Commitee appointed to make enquiry whether Silver can be obtained at such Price and in such Quantity as it will be for the interest of the Government to coin the same made report

"Read and Recommitted and the Committee are directed to bring in a Bill or resolve if they judge it necessary."

They consequently, on Nov. 14th, reported the following resolve : —

"The committe appointed to make enquiery whether silver can be obtained at such price and in such Quantity as it will be for the interest of Government to coin the same —— have attended that service and report as their Opinion, That it will not be expedient for Government at present to undertake the purchasing silver for coining : but as your committe are of Opinion That it will be of public utillity That provision be made for the coining of silver The property of private person therefore Report the following Resolve

"Commonwealth of Massachusetts in the House of Representatives Nov,r 14<sup>th</sup> 1787

"Resolved That His Exel<sup>y</sup> the Governor with The advice of council be & Hereby are requested as soon as may be to procure all the requisites for the mint necessary for coining small silver of such Value as they shall think most for the advantage of such individuals as shall bring their silver to be coined — and all persons who shall chuse to have their silver coined, shall receive nine Tenths of the weight of all the pure silver they shall offer to be assayed for coining when The same shall be coined —

"and it is further resolved that the Governor and council in making provision for the coining silver agreeably to these resolves govern themselves by a law of this commonwealth Made and passed on the seventeenth day of October in the year of our Lord one Thousand seven Hundred & eighty six —

"and it is further resolved that the tenth part of all the silver offered to be assayed in order for coinage, shall when coined be applied (as far as shall be found necessary) to pay for assaying: preparing the mint for coining of silver: and all other necessary Expence of coinage

Sent up for Concurrence

J Warren Spk[r] "

This resolve was not passed by the Senate, but is endorsed, "Nov 1787 Refer'd "

The Council, finding that the mint did not furnish a supply of coin as speedily as was expected, soon instituted an inquiry into the state of its affairs, and ordered the mint-master to report thereupon. Their orders, and the report elicited by them are next presented.

Wednesday, January 16th 1788. "Ordered that M[r] Wetherle be directed to exhibit his account to this time in order for a settlement & that the Secretary state an Account of all the charge attending the coinage of the copper —

"Ordered that M[r] Hutchinson, Colonel Dawes & M[r] Sullivan be a Committee to direct M[r] Wetherle's attendance to know of him what the situation of the copper mint is at present the number of Workmen imployed in the service of said Mint &c & that his attendance be directed at 12 o'clock to-morrow noon "

January 17th, "M[r] Wetherle attended agreeably to the direction of yesterday & was admitted before the Council & after questioning him upon several matters respecting the Coinage of copper he was directed to make a representation of his proceedings on Monday next, & to point out particularly the obstacles he has met with relative to said Coinage — "

In compliance with this order of the Council, Mr. Witherle submitted a written report, which we copy from the Archives, Vol. 140, p. 319: —

"May it please your Excellency, and the Hon[ble] Councill.—

"In May 1787, I Receivd Orders from Government to Erect necessary Buildings, and prepare Machines suitable for the Purpose of Coining Copper Cents &c, agreeable to an Act of this Commonwealth, which was immediately begun to be put into Execution, and no Pains was spared to procure every Article that might be thought necessary — The Iron Furnaces which I was oblig'd to depend on for several Articles which I could not do without, were so nearly out of Blast, that I could not get the Patterns made for the Rollers, and sundry other Articles that were necessary, done so as to answer the Purpose intended in the Spring, therefore was obliged to go on as well as I could, and after spending some Time, and great Pains in making the Rollers, which I had Cast, answer the Purpose expected, was obliged to have a pair of Rollers. made of wrought Iron, which have been made Use of to this Time, and are yet good. —

"The Dies, with which the Coin is struck, have been the means of great Delay in the Business, as it was not in my Power to procure Steel of a proper Quality to receive the proper Degree of Hardness which is so absolutely necessary to sustain the great Force of the Machine in making the Impression on the Coin. — I have now procur'd Steel of that Quality, which appears to answer the Purpose very well. — In addition to this, it must be supposed that some Time would be spent to Instruct Persons in a Business which has not been practised in this Country. —

"The Moulds which I proposed to Cast the Copper into when melted, so as to have it in a proper Situation for the Rolling Mill, without any further Expence or Trouble, was a Matter of great Consequence in the Business ; therefore I took the Advice of all those Persons that might be supposed to have good Judgment in a Matter of this kind ; who unanimously agreed that it was not only a cheap but very expeditious Way of doing the Business ; therefore I pursued the Plan, as soon as the first Furnace that I could hear of was in Blast, to get such a number of them as would be sufficient to prove the Experiment which took some Time and Trouble to have them in proper Order for the Business proposed ; when this was done, it appeared that the above Plan would not be a means of saving Money and Expediting Business as was Expected, but would really injure the Mettal, employ more Hands, and destroy more Fuell, than Casting it in much larger Pieces, and Drawing it with a Trip Hammer, which might be made, and fixed to the Mill at Dedham, which is now almost ready to Opperate ; but before I began to fix the above Hammers, I fully prov'd the Experiment by having about a Thousand Weight drawn at Newton —

"Thus far I have given a general Account of the Matter to this Time, and have Surmounted every Difficulty that commonly Occurs in any new Business, more especially in one of this Nature, without any Expence to, or Assistance from Government, than Thirty five Hundred Pounds of rough Copper, receiv'd from Hugh Orr Esq. ; and at your next Meeting shall lay before you a more particular Account of the State of the Mint. —

"Boston Jan.ry 22.d 1788.—                              Joshua Witherle"

Friday June 13th 1788, "His Excellency communicated to the Council a resolution of the General Court requesting the Governor & Council to lay before the two branches of the Legislature an account of the cost of erecting & compleating the mint, of the expences of carrying on the business of said Mint, of the quantity of coin already struck & what may be expected to be struck in the course of the present year & in general the state of the said Mint & asked the advice of the Council Advised that Mʳ Wetherle, master workman of the Mint be directed to attend the Governor & Council on Tuesday next & lay a true statement of the mint before them agreeably to said resolution — he was directed accordingly — "

Wednesday June 18th 1788 "Mʳ Wetherle attended the Council & laid before them a statement of the mint & made answer to the several particulars mentioned in the resolve of thirteenth instant, but as he could not accurately give the whole cost of erecting & compleating the mint for the reasons mentioned by him in his statement — The Council thereupon Ordered that Mʳ Witherle make a true statement agreeably to the said resolution of the thirteenth instant & that he cause a settlement of all the accounts by the first of July next & that at the end of every month after he lodge in the Secretarys office a true statement of the mint — "

Mr. Witherle's statement was as follows : —

"May it Please your Exelency & the Honˡᵉ Council

"Having laid before you the accounts of expences for erecting the mint &c. to the 3ʳᵈ of November. 1787 the Amount being £411 1 3¾. likewise the state of said mint to the 22ⁿᵈ of January 1788 ; — In which statement you was informed that the works at Dedham were Nearly compleated : But the severity of the season being such that it was found Impracticable to proceed any further untill spring, by reason of the ice &c. — therefore I was under the necessety of haveing the copper Drawn at Newton, or to stop the works ; in which case I humbly conceive that I should not have been able to had the works in so Good a situation as they are at present, nor the workmen capeable of Rendering one half the service to Government as they are Now.

"The Dies which was mentioned in the former Statement, which was the Occaison of great Delay are now brought to that state of perfection not onley as it Respects their Quality & stability, but also the Expence which I esteemed to be Great at that time. Yett it was unavoidable, untill some other person could be found, to cure this difficulty — therefore a person was sought for and is now procured to provide and supply the mint with Dies for copper coin, at the reasonable rate of one p.r Cent without any other expence to Government ; The saveing made in this particular will fully appear by M.r Callenders Account laid before you Respecting this article : —

"The cost of erecting & compleating the mint, with the expences that have attended the same, cannot be accurately given at this particular time as there are several accounts handed in that appear to be erroneous and must be corrected, and Others, which it is not in my Power to colect and adjust so as to Give them in now but such account as could be collected & adjusted are laid before you —

"The quantity of coin, already struck will appear by the Treasurers Receipts lodged in the Secretary's Office by the Inspector : the amount being 2500 Dollars

"With respect to the quantity of Coin that may be expected to be struck in the course of the present year (if copper coin onley is ment) will depend on the Quantity of stock that Government can supply the mint with, if a sufficient Quantity can be supplied about fifty dollars p.r Day may be coined, with those Machines that are now compleated ; But if it is the Intention of Government to have Gold & silver coin struck, — agreeable to their act for that purpose, which the mint was erected & calculated for as well as for copper coin, it be performed with a small addition of expence to that which is necessary for coining Copper only ; as the Machines now Erected are capable of executing any coin under the size of a Dollar. —

"The expence of carrying on the business of the mint as near as can be calculated may amount to about £1100. — p.r Annum.  Including all Charges; and about 15000 Dollars may be struck in copper coin in that time provided there can be about six tons of Copper supplied, which may cost about £600 — which it is supposed will enable the mint to go on with business and discharge the expences that have or may occur. — the quantity of coper now on hand is about 2500 pound weight —

"A General & Particular Statement of the Mint with a proper Distinction between the cost of erecting & the expence of carrying on the business will be laid before you as soon as all the accounts Can be collected & adjusted —

"Boston 17. June 1788                         Josh.a Witherle "

Thursday, June 19th, 1788.  "The Secretary brought down the following Message from His Excellency the Governour viz.

" Gentlemen of the Senate and Gentlemen of the House of Representatives.

"Agreeably to the request of the two Houses of the 12th instant a particular inquiry has been made into the state of the mint, the result of which is, that from the many unsettled accounts M[r] Wetherle, the Master Workman, is unable to ascertain with any considerable degree of exactness the expense of erecting the buildings &[c]. The accounts which he has closed amount to about six hundred pounds. That from the various delays which have attended the business there has been coined the value of twenty five hundred dollars only, which has been delivered to the Treasurer, but that the works are now in such a state, that with a full supply of stock, which will cost about six hundred pounds the business may be carried on with such dispatch as that the value of fifteen thousand dollars may be struck off in one year. That the expense of doing this exclusive of the copper will amount to eleven or twelve hundred pounds.

"That we have on hand about twenty five hundred pound of copper after the coining of which, the business must cease or be prosecuted with loss to the Commonwealth unless the sum of six hundred pounds beforementioned shall be advanced, for with a less stock than can be procured with that sum it cannot be pursued with any advantage to the State. The master-workman is called upon to settle immediately all his accounts, and to lay them before the Governour and Council on the first day of July next, with a particular account of all the expenses of buildings, &[c] and make a full representation of the state of the mint, which will be communicated to you.

"Signed,

" Council Chamber                                " John Hancock
    " Boston
    " June 19th 1788 "


Friday, July 18th, 1788, the Council "Advised that M[r] Wetherle have a further time allowed him to make a true statement of the whole cost of erecting & compleating the mint, & that he cause a settlement of all the accounts by the fifth of August next — that he then lodge the same in the Secretary's office — "

Tuesday, August 5th, 1788. "Ordered that the attendance of M[r] Wetherle be directed this afternoon with his accounts of the expence of the Mint agreeably to the order of the Governor & Council of the eighteenth of July last — * * * * *

"M.ʳ Wetherle attended this afternoon agreeably to order & exhibited sundry accounts amounting to Five hundred eighty nine pounds eighteen shillings & three pence ½ respecting the cost of erecting & compleating the mint for coinage of copper & made answer to the several questions asked him & informed the Council that he was unable to render an account of the whole amount of the cost for want of two or three accounts which he would lay before them as soon as he can obtain them — The Council directed him to make a complete statement of the whole amount of cost & of the sum coined & to render the same at the time the Secretary shall inform him — "

Tuesday, September 9th, 1788. "In pursuance of the order of the Council of the fifth of August last M.ʳ Wetherle Master Workman of the Massachusetts Mint exhibited the remainder of his accounts of the cost of erecting & compleating the Mint, of the expences of carrying on the business of the said Mint of the quantity of Coin already struck & what may be expected to be struck in the course of the present year & in general the state of the said Mint agreeably to the order of the two branches of the Legislature of the thirteenth of June last which being laid before the Governor & Council was read & committed to His Honor the Lieut. Governor & the Honble M.ʳ Phillips to arrange in order to their being laid before the General Court at their next Session."

On Friday, September 12th, 1788, a warrant was drawn on the Treasury for "Three hundred & ninety Pounds in favor of Capt Joshua Wetherle, Master Workman of the Mint to be paid in Cents — he to be accountable for the same — "

A statement of the expenses of the mint was rendered Nov. 4th, and :— "The Council having taken the above statement into consideration, thereupon Advised that His Excellency lay said statement before the General Court with the papers supporting the same in order that they may take such measures as they judge shall be expedient "

Wednesday, November 5th, 1788, "The Secretary brought down the following Message from His Excellency the Governour viz.

" Gentlemen of the Senate and Gentlemen of the House of Representatives.

"Enquiry has been made into the State of the Mint ; from which it appears that

"The expenses of the buildings amount to   .   .   .   .   .   £ 677 11 2½
Expences of conducting the business   .   .   .   .   .   1026 15 4½
Amount of Stock expended   .   .   .   .   .   431 19 0

                        2136 5 7

"Amount of Coin struck off   .   .   .   .   .   .   939

which leaves a balance against the Commonwealth   .   .   .   1197 5 7

as will appear by the papers which I have directed the Secretary to lay before you in order that you may take such measures as you may judge expedient.

                              " (Signed)     John Hancock
   "Council Chamber
   "Nov<sup>r</sup>. 5. 1788.

"Read again and committed to M<sup>r</sup>. Mason, M<sup>r</sup>. Choate & M<sup>r</sup>. Spooner, with the papers accompanying"

Friday, November 21st, 1788. "The Committee on the Governour's message respecting the Mint made report. Recommitted in order for a Resolve to be brought in to appoint a Committee to receive proposals from individuals for Coining, in the recess of the General Court, & to report at their next setting"

We next present the Report mentioned above.

"The Comm<sup>ttee</sup> Appointed upon the Governors Message, upon the state of the Mint, Have attend<sup>d</sup> that service & ask leave to Report as follows —viz.

"It appears by the Statements in his Excellency<sup>s</sup> Message that a Ballance is due from the Commonwealth of .   .   .   £ 1197 5 7
"From wich ballance deduct the Cost for the Buildings & tools for carry<sup>g</sup> on the Business amount<sup>g</sup> to .   .   .   677 11 2½

                        £ 519 14 5½

"The above ballance of £519 14 5½ appears to have been lost in carri<sup>g</sup> on the business as will appear by the following statement —

"To Expence of coining   .   .   .   .   .   .   £ 1026 15 4
"To cost of stock   .   .   .   .   .   .   431 19 —

                        £ 1458 14 4

"Deduct for amount of Coin struck off   .   .   .   939 — —

                        £ 519 14 4½

"your comm<sup>ttee</sup> are of Opinion that if the Mint had been suppli<sup>d</sup> with a sufficient stock for the carr<sup>g</sup> on the business its probable the loss woo<sup>d</sup> have been much less and perhaps *no* loss might have ensue^d — and considering the state of our Finances the comm^ttee submit to the Hon^ble House wether it woo^d not be more for the Interests of the common wealth to contract with some Person or Persons for the purpose of compleat^g the sum to be coin^d mention^d in the s^d act, than to continue it on the present establishment"

November 21st, 1788. "The Committee on the Governours message, respecting the Mint reported a Resolve for appointing a Committee to be joined by such as the Hon Senate might appoint to receive proposals for coining copper, agreeably to order. Read & the blank being filled with the names of Jonathan Mason and Samuel Breck Esquires the same was accepted and sent up for concurrence."

"Saturday November 22^d 1788"

"In the House of Representatives — Whereas it is expedient, that some new measure should be adopted for rendering the coinage of copper in the mint more advantageous to the Commonwealth : — Resolved that Jonathan Mason & Samuel Breck esq^rs with such as the honorable Senate may join be a Committee to receive proposals from any person or persons who may offer to contract to carry on the coinage of copper within this Commonwealth, and to report such propositions, with their opinion respecting the same, and what may be necessary further to be done, the whole to be laid before the General Court at their next sitting. — And it is further Resolved that the Governor and Council be and hereby are requested to cause all the copper now on hand to be coined as soon as may be and when compleated to discharge all the persons now employed in that business untill the further order of this Court.

"In Senate read and concurred        Approved by the Governor"

Witherle, having been notified of this action of the Court, writes to John Avery, secretary of the Council : —

"Sir                                  "Boston 29^th Dec^r 1788 —

"Agreeable to your Request to me of the 27^th Instant I would now Inform you, that the Quantity of Copper in the mint not Coined, is about 900^lb — about 350^lb of which is in hand to be Coined, & will leave about 550^lb uncoined, which is too small a quantity to proceed any further, without an addition of more Copper. As soon as the above Copper in hand to be Coind is finished, shall Immediately Render in the whole accounts of the mint —

"I am Sir your Verry Hum^bl Ser^t

"John Avery Jun^r Esq^r                        Joshua Witherle "

To which Avery replies,

" Sir                                                Boston Dec. 30ᵗʰ 1788

" Your fav. of Yesterday respecting the Quantity of Copper uncoined I have communicated to his Excellency the Governour and I have it in charge from him to inform you that as soon as you have compleated the Business of coining the copper on hand that you make an immediate return to him thereof and render in the whole Accounts of the mint and that you will be as speedy as possible in the completion of the Business

" I am Sir your hum Sevᵗ

" Mʳ Joshua Witherle                                      J. A "

The Committee appointed on the 22d of November report as follows :—

" The Committee of both Houses appointed to receive Proposals for carrying on the Coinage of Copper in this Commonwealth, having attended that Service and received Proposals from Mʳ Jonathan Pierce & from Col. John May are of opinion that those made by Mʳ May are best calculated to promote the Interest of the Commonwealth  But the Committee being in doubt respecting the Power of the General Government to contract this Business submit the said Proposals to the Court for their Consideration —

" Cotton Tufts pʳ ordʳ "

" Mr Jonᵃ Peirces Proposals — for Coining Coppers "

" Salem 18ᵗʰ December 1788

" Proposals for Coining Copper for the Commonwealth of Massachusetts vizᵗ

" First  I will engage to give the State for the exclusive right Ten per Cent —

" Secondly  I will find my own Stock, on Governments taking the Coin, when a certain quantity is made, which shall be agreed on, so as to enable me to purchase Stock from time to time as it is expended

" Jonathan Peirce "

The following paper is unsigned, but endorsed " John May Esqr Proposals."

" Boston December 31ˢᵗ 1788 —

" To the Honoᵗ Committee of both houses of the Commonwealth of Massachusetts, appointed for the purpose of Contracting with some person or persons for the Coining of Copper agreeably to an act of the Legislature of the Said Commonwealth —

" Proposals of John May of Boston, for takeing the Mint and works now erected on the Lands of Major Joshᵃ Whetherle together with the roleing mills at Dedham, and all the apparatus allreddy provided by the Commonwealth, for the purpose of makeing Cents & half Cents agreeable to y.ᵉ ordinance of Congress, untill the Sum stipulated by government shall be Compleeted —

"The Said May will undertake this Buisness and Carry it on in the most expeditious manner, he will at his Own expence furnish the Stock & pay the Expences of mint.ᵍ and will further pay to the order of the Commonwealth for the exclucive right of Coining the sum required and the Use of all the materials that are allreddy provided, Eleven Cents for every hundred Cents, coined until the sum required is made to Compleet the Sum of Seventy Thousand Dollars, deducting however the Sum allreddy made by said Wetherlee, and the Said May will further agree that from and after the Signing his Agreement with the Hon.ᵒ Committee afforesaid, he will exempt the Commonweath from every charge of rents, for Said Land, Untill the expiration of said Contract. —

"And it is further Understood by Said May & these proposials are made on this express Condition, that the Legislature or the Hon.ᵒ Committee shall indemnify the S.ᵈ May against any resolve of the New Federall Governmt that Shall tend to deprive him of the right of Coining Cents & half Cents, as the Federall Convention have Stated in the first Article 8.ᵗʰ Sec.ⁿ of the Said Constitution it being by that Article expressed that No State has Right to Coin money &c, on there own Accompt.

"of these Circumstances however the Hon.ᵒ Committee are the best Judges — "

The following proposition has neither date or signature: we insert it as one of the plans presented for consideration.

"If the legislature will pass a law to the following effect, the State may form a contract, for the performance of which the most satisfactory security shall be given

"The Treasurer of the State and — Mess. A. & B. to be jointly authorized to contract for the coining of £        L'f' M'y, in copper coin to be delivered into the treasury of the State within eighteen months from the first day of Jan'y 1789.

"The treasurer, on the rec.ᵗ of said coin or any part thereof not less than 10 ⅌ Ct of the whole amount, to give engagemts to be paid in gold or silver, and subject to no deduction whatever, that the same shall be paid by the state to the contractor in five equal and yearly payments with 6 ⅌ Ct in.ˢᵗ in gold or silver, untill the principal shall be discharged —

"On the contract's being formed and good security given for the performance the treasurer of the state shall deposit into the hands of such person as shall be deemed sufficient by himself and Mess. A. & B. double the am.ᵗ of the copper coin, in the funded debt of the United States of America, as a security for the fulfilment of the contract on the part of the State, & which said am.ᵗ of the deposit shall be lodged with the contractor, after the coin is delivered to the treasurer to be returned by him when he shall have rec.ᵈ payment for the coin, in gold or silver ; and in the same state as to principal and interest, as when rec.ᵈ by him —

"The debt that the State have incurred by their coinage to be paid, & the apparatus purchased at a fair appraisement, by the contractor & to be paid in an additional sum in copper coin — "

The next action of the authorities was as follows : —

"Commonwealth of Massachusetts        In Senate Jan.ʸ 22.ᵈ 1789 —

"Ordered that Eben.ʳ Bridge Esq.ʳ with such as the honorable House may join be a committee to contract with John May Esq (A) for the coining of Cents to the amount of Seventy thousand Dollars including what is already coined, upon such terms as shall be for the interest of the Commonwealth —

"And that upon like terms, they contract (B) with the said May for the use and improvement of the House & utensils used in such coinage, which are the property of the Commonwealth — (C)

"Sent down for concurrence        Sam.ˡ Phillips Jun.ʳ Presd.ᵗ "

"In the House of Representatives Feb.ʸ 16. 1789

"Read and concurred with amendment at A & M.ʳ Mason of Boston & M.ʳ Breck are joined

                              " W Heath Speaker Pro Tem

"At A insert 'or with any other person who shall offer more advantageous terms' "

"In Senate Feb.ʸ 17.ᵗʰ 1789 —

"Read & concurred        Sam.ˡ Phillips j.ʳ Presid.ᵗ "

"In Senate Feb.ʸ 17.ᵗʰ 1789 — Read again and reconsidered & the Senate concur with the Hon.ᵇˡᵉ House with amendments at B & C

"Sent down for concurrence        Sam.ˡ Phillips j.ʳ Presid.ᵗ

"B dele 'with the said May'  C ins.ᵗ and the contract so made by the said Committee shall be binding on the part of this Commonwealth "

The conclusion of this phase of the business is thus recorded in the Journal of the House of Representatives:—

"Tuesday Feb 17 1789

"Amendment of the Hon Senate in the order appointing a committee to contract for the coinage of copper Read & ordered that the consideration of the whole subject be referred to the next session of the General Court"

As we find in the records no later reference to this project, it is presumed that it was abandoned on account of the article in the Constitution, mentioned by May, in his petition, (see page 265,) which provides that:— "The Congress shall have the power * * * To coin money, regulate the value thereof, and of foreign coin; and fix the standard of weights and measures: * * * No state shall enter into any treaty, alliance or confederation; grant letters of marque and reprisal; coin money; emit bills of credit; make any thing but gold and silver coin a tender in payment of debts; pass any bill of attainder, *ex post facto* law, or law impairing the obligation of contracts, or grant any title of nobility."

"Thursday January 22$^d$ 1789

"By a resolve of the General Court of the twenty second day of November last, The Governor & Council were requested to cause all the copper on hand to be coined as soon as possible & when compleated to discharge all the persons employed in the Mint until the further order of the General Court — By the accounts this day exhibited it appears that the expences of the Mint since the thirty first of October last amounts to one hundred thirty nine pounds one shilling & eleven pence $\frac{3}{4}$; — That the moneys coined since amounts to one hundred & nine pounds two shillings & seven pence — By the representation of M$^r$ Wetherle, Master Workman of the Mint, it appears also that all the stock of copper suitable for this business is now expended: — It is therefore the opinion of the Council that in compliance with the above order of the Court, the Master, Inspector & all others now employed in the Mint should be discharged until the farther order of the General Court ; & that measures should be immediately adopted for speedy settlement of the accounts —

"Ordered that Nathan Cushing & Artemas Ward esq$^{rs}$ be a Committee to examine the accounts of Joshua Wetherle, Master Workman of the Mint exhibited this day, together with the accounts heretofore exhibited & report —"

The following draughts of the letters discharging the officers and employees of the mint, are found in the Council files at date.

"Sir                                              "Boston January 23ᵈ 1789

"Agreeably to the directions of the Governour & Council you are hereby discharged from your employment in the Buisness of coinage of Copper and you are also directed to discharge all the persons now employed in that Business untill the further of the General Court —

"I am Sir with great Estee

"Your hum Servᵗ

"J. A"

"Sir                                              "Boston Janʸ 23. 1789

"Agreeably to the directions of the Gov. & Council you are hereby directed to discharge all the persons now employed in the Buisness of the Mint and you are hereby to consider yourself also discharged from this Business untill the further order of the Court —

"I am Sir your hum Sevᵗ"

"Sir                                              "Boston January 23. 1789

"Agreeably to the directions of the Governour & Council you are hereby discharged from your employ as Inspector of the Mint untill the further order of the Gen Court

"I am Sir with great Este

"Your hum Sevᵗ

"Ebenezer Hancock Esq                                        "J. A"

In the House of Representatives, Friday, January 23, 1789 : —

"The Secretary brought down the following message, from His Excellency the Governour viz.

"Gentlemen of the Senate & Gentlemen of the House of Representatives—

"In compliance with a Resolve of the General Court of the 22ᵈ of November last all the copper suitable for making cents, has been worked. In Consequence thereof the Master workman, the Inspector, and all others employed in the mint are discharged, untill the further order of the General Court, and measures are adopted for the most speedy settlement of all the accounts ; which I shall cause to be laid before you

"The building and tools necessary to carry on the business of the mint have been built and procured at the expense of the Commonwealth. You will give such directions concerning them, and the remaining stock unsuitable for the business as shall best promote the interest of the State.

Signed   John Hancock"

" Boston Jany, 23ᵈ 1789.

On Tuesday, January 27th 1789, we find a "Warrant drawn on the Treasury for Two hundred ninety eight pounds two shillings & seven pence in favor of Capt Joshua Wetherle Master Workman of the Mint — to be paid in Cents & to be accountable for the same — "

Before presenting the final statement of the accounts of the mint-master, we will give an abstract of his statements of "Expenses of Erecting, Compleating and Carrying on the Business of the Massachusetts Mint."

| | Expence of Erecting &c | Expence of Carrying on the Business | Amount of Stock | Amount of the whole accoᵗᵗˢ given in | Quantity of Coin Struck. |
|---|---|---|---|---|---|
| 1787 Novʳ 3 .. | £391 8 11¾ | £ 19 12 4 | | £411 1 3¾ | |
| 1788 May 31 .. | 83 1 1 | 108 15 9 | | 191 16 10 | |
| July 31 .. | 188 16 9½ | 135 19 6 | £265 2 0 | 589 18 3½ | ⎰ 2700 Dollʳˢ is |
| Augˢᵗ 30 .. | 11 14 4 | 113 4 6 | | 40 3 10 | ⎱ £810 0 0 |
| Octʳ 31 .. | 2 10 0 | 54 3 2¼ | 35 13 6 | 92 6 8¼ | 129 0 0 |
| 1789 Janʸ 21 .. | | 45 13 3¾ | 131 3 6 | 139 1 11¾ | 109 2 7 |
| | 677 11 2¼ | 477 8 7 | 431 19 0 | 1464 8 11¼ | £1048 2 7 |

Witherle's accounts were next presented in Council ; we give the record in full : —

" Wednesday January 28ᵗʰ 1789 Present in Council

" His Honor Benjamin Lincoln Esqʳ Lieut. Governor

Honble Nathan Cushing Azor Orne Jonathan Greenleaf Edward Cutts Esqʳˢ

Honble Samuel Adams John Frost William Phillips Artemas Ward Esqʳˢ

" The Committee appointed the twelfth instant to whom was referred the examination of the accounts of Mʳ Joshua Wetherle for the erecting, carrying on & purchase of copper for the Mint from the third of November 1787 to this day, reported a statement of said Accounts with the allowances made the Master Workman & the Inspector of said Mint & find a balance of one thousand & seventy pounds ten shillings and three pence½ due to Mʳ Joshua Wetherle late Master Workman which were read & thereupon Advised that

His Excellency be requested to lay the same before the General Court with the annexed inventory of those articles in his hands belonging to the Commonwealth —

"D.ʳ.    M.ʳ Joshua Wetherle in account with The Commonwealth of Massachusetts    C.ʳ.

| | | | 1789 | | |
|---|---|---|---|---|---|
| "1789  To 3498ˡᵇ of Copper from the Commissary General at 9ᵈ pr lb . . . | £131 | 3 6 | Jan 21 By amount of Account for the expences of erecting, carrying on & purchase of copper for the Mint from the 3.ᵈ of November 1787 to this day. | £1595 | 16 4¼ |
| "Janʸ 21 To amount of copper coined at the Mint to this day, paid into the Treasury & received out again & sundry warrants from the Governor & Council . . . | 1048 | 2 7 | By your salary from June 1. 1787 to 21 January 1789 is 19 months & 20 days at £300 p.ʳ Annum | 491 | 13 4 |
| Balance due to Joshua Wetherle . . . | 1070 | 10 3¼ | By Ebenezer Hancock esq.ʳ inspector of the Mint for his pay from the 13.ᵗʰ of September 1787 to January 21.ˢᵗ 1789 is 16 months & 7 days at £120 p.ʳ Annum . . | 162 | 6 8 |
| . . . . . . . | £2249 | 16 4¼ | | £2249 | 16 4¼ |

" Inventory of the buildings, implements &c for coining of Copper, now on hand the property of the Commonwealth of Massachusetts —

"2 Buildings on Boston neck viz.ᵗ N.º 1 containing 1 Machine for cutting Cents &c
1 D.º for stamping        D.º
1 Cast iron frame for cutting Machine
1 iron stove & funnel
537ˡᵇ Copper scraps —
N.º 2 containing 1 Air furnace with grates & doors
2 iron bars . . 2 D.º Ladles
1 D.º Shovel . . 1 D.º Rake
21 D.º Moulds  2 rolling machines
300 White bricks

"2 Buildings at Dedham Viz.ᵗ.
N.º 1 containing 1 Plating Machine — 1 Trip hammer & stake
4 tongs . . 2 iron rollers — 1 sett iron bed pieces
1 Forge . . 1 Nealing furnace
50 white bricks. —
N.º 2 a small coal house containing about 50 bushels Charcoal

"Joshua Witherle"

" Boston 21.ᵗ January 1789 —

"Commonwealth of Massachusetts In Senate June 9ᵗʰ 1789

"Resolved that there be allowed & paid out of the Treasury of this Commonwealth the sum of Ten hundred & seventy pounds ten shillings & 3¼ from the first money which shall come into the treasury from Tax Nº 6. not already appropriated to Joshua Wetherle in full for the balance of an account due to him for erecting sundry buildings and for carrying on the business of coining cents.

"Resolved further that the said Wetherle be & he is hereby impowered & requested to take charge' till the further order of this Court of the aforesaid building utensils &c the property of this Commonwealth remaining, as by an Inventory exhibited & annexed to his account beforementioned."

"Thursday June 11ᵗʰ 1789

"Warrant drawn on the Treasury for One thousand & seventy pounds ten shillings & three pence¼ in favor of Capt Joshua Wetherle in full for the balance of his account for erecting buildings & carrying on the business of coining cents — to be paid from the first money that shall come into the Treasury from tax Nº 6 not already appropriated — agreeable to a resolve of the ninth instant —"

"Commonwealth of Massachusetts      In Council June 17ᵗʰ 1789

"His Excellency communicated a Resolve of the General Court in favor of Joshua Wetherlee late Master workman of the Copper Mint, passed June 9ᵗʰ 1789, respecting the settlement of his account, — and mentioned, that Mr Wetherlee was desirous that the bonds he gave upon his introduction to the said business of coinage might be cancelled — and asked the advice of Council : The Council thereupon Advised, that the bonds of Joshua Wetherlee be cancelled, and that his Excellency give order to the Treasurer to cancell said Bonds accordingly —

"A true copy from the Minutes of Council      John Avery junr Secʸ"

"You are hereby directed to cancell the bonds of Joshua Wetherlee agreeable to the above advice of Council—

"To Alexander Hodgdon Esqr
                                                                      John Hancock"

Joshua Wetherle's bond is next presented : —

"Know all Men by these presents that We Joshua Witherly of Boston in the County of Suffolk in the Commonwealth of Massachusetts Esqr as Principal in the full and just Sum of one thousand pounds and Caleb Davis of Boston

Esq. and M.ʳ Benjamen Cobb of said Boston and of the said County of Suffolk Merchant — in the sum of five hundred pounds each as Sureties are held, and stand firmly bound and obliged to Alexander Hodgdon Esq.ʳ Treasurer and receivir General of this Commonwealth or to his Successor in said Office — To which Payment well and truly to be made We bind ourselves, our Heirs, Executors, and administrators jointly and severally firmly by these presents sealed with our Seals and dated this sixteenth day of May in the year of our Lord one thousand, seven hundred and Eighty seven, and in the Eleventh year of the Independence of the United States of America —

"The Condition of this obligation is such, that whereas the said Joshua Witherly Esq is appointed by his Excellency the Governour and the Council to carry on the buisness of coinage of copper, procure the materials for the purpose of erecting a Furnace, and doing every thing necessary for the carrying on said coinage; if therefore the said Joshua Witherly shall truly, and faithfully discharge the duty of his trust, according to Law, and agreeable to such Rules and regulations respecting the well ordering and managing the buisniss of the said Mint, as shall be established by the Governour and Council and render an Account of his proceedings as often as shall be required by the Governour and Council and shall appropriate the Copper that he may be furnished with by the Governour and Council to the buisness of coinage of Copper, and defraying the Expence of the same, then the above written obligation to be void and of none Effect, but in default there of to remain in full force —

"Signed, sealed & delivered
    in presence of us —
"John Avery jun
"W Harris

Josh.ª Witherle  [ L. S. ]
Caleb Davis  [ L. S. ]
Benj Cobb  [ L. S. ]"

"Treasury Office Boston 17 June 1789

"By Virtue of and Order from His Excellency the Governor with Advice of Council dated this day this Bond is cancel'd by me —

Alex.ʳ Hodgdon Treas.ʳ "

The following petition relates to the further use of the mint buildings: —

"To the Hon.ᵇˡᵉ Senate & House of Representatives of the Common Wealth of Massachusetts

"The Petition of Joshua Witherle of Boston humbly Sheweth,

"That your petitioner being informed that your Hon.ʳˢ have been pleased to request or direct him to take charge of the Buildings & apparatus of the Mint until the further Orders of Government, which your petitioner has no objection to — And begs leave to inform your Hon[rs] That He, in order to save expences to Government, erected those buildings on his own land, for which he has not charg'd any Rent — Except the land & Stream at Dedham, where the plating Mill stands, which land & stream is leased to your petitioner for a number of years, with a design of carrying on a particular Manufacture[1] which he concieves may be benefic[l] to the public as well as to himself — Your Petitioner therefore prays your Hon[rs] for liberty of making use of s[d] Mill, until Government shall see fit to dispose of it otherways, in consideration of which your petitioner is willing to relinquish the rent of s[d] land & Stream & to take care of the buildings & Apparatus of the Mint without any expence to Government — Which will enable your petitioner to prosecute the afores[d] business.  And your Petitioner as in duty bound shall pray

" Boston 10 June 1789                                        Josh[a] Witherle "

" Comm of Massachusetts   In Senate 26th June 1789

" On the petition of Joshua Witherle — Resolved that the said Witherle until the further order of the General Court, have liberty to make use of the mill at Dedham, with the house, appurtenances, and utensils to the same belonging, which were erected and provided for the service of the mint, he keeping the same in good repair, & returning them when required, according to an inventory which has been exhibited by said Witherle without any charge or expence to the government — "

A Resolve of June 10, 1790, relates to the disposal of the copper coin in the State Treasury.

" *Resolved*, That the Treasurer, be, and he hereby is directed to pay out the *copper cents* now in the treasury, in discharge of the debts due from the Commonwealth, at the rate of *one hundred* and *eight cents* for *six shillings* lawful money, subject however to such appropriations as have been or may be made by the Legislature, of the other public monies in the treasury, and that the Treasurer receive the same in payments at the same rate, any law or resolve to the contrary notwithstanding."

Joshua Witherle's house stood upon the site now occupied by dwelling houses numbered from 1132 to 1144 Washington Street, East Waltham Street dividing the estate near its southerly line.   Bushnell in his manuscript Numis-

---

[1] Probably the working of copper.  The Boston Directory of 1789 says, " Witherle Joshua & Co. copper-smiths, house Washington-street, shop in Kilby-street."

matic Notes says of it, "The mint house stood directly in the rear of Joshua Witherle's house, now three stories high, of wood, numbered 910 Washington street, and has been occupied for several years as a lying-in hospital at Boston Neck. The building used as a mint house was a wooden one, one story in height, of high stud, about twenty feet wide by forty feet in length. Mr. Witherle had probably occupied the building previous to the period of the State coinage. He was a copper smith by trade, and was commonly known among the boys of Boston, by the appellation of 'The Cent Maker.'"

"Some years ago there was a report that silver coins were struck at the Mass. mint, 1787–88, bearing the devices of the cents and half cents. The following letter written by the late Judge Savage, who was high authority upon Mass. history, is in reply to a query upon the truth of the above report:

"'Dear Sir,                                                    "'Boston 5 Novr. 1853.

"'To the several questions in your note of the 2ᵈ inst. relative to our mint in Boston, I can make no answer, except to the last. No SILVER coins were struck.

"'How vexatious is our ignorance; but the blessed advent of the Constitution of the Union so *soon* putting an end to our copper shop, will explain it.

Yours,                  Jas. Savage.'"

The copper for the coins of Massachusetts, (excepting a small quantity which was drawn at Newton,) after being cast into ingots at the mint at Boston, was carted to the mill at Dedham, where it was drawn under a trip-hammer, and rolled into sheets, when it was returned to the mint, where the blanks were prepared and the coin stamped.

The carting to and from Dedham is said to have been done by Rufus Whiting, who appears to have been a primitive expressman, taking orders from the inhabitants of Dedham for such articles as they desired, purchasing them in Boston and delivering them at their homes. Taking payment for his services for the mint in cents, he made his payments in the same until they became so plentiful as to cause some difficulty in making his larger purchases; after which, if he wished fifty pounds of sugar, or merchandise of similar amount he was compelled to obtain part at one store, and part at another, until his order was completed. Why tradition should have selected Rufus, from among the many Whitings, is uncertain, but the mint accounts which are preserved in the archives, (Vol. 140,) contain bills from Joseph and Paul, Richard, William, Rufus, Moses, and Edward Whiting, all having charges for carting copper.

# NEW JERSEY.

An earlier date is found upon many of the coins issued under the authority of New Jersey, than upon those of Massachusetts; but we have given precedence to the State last named, because her consideration of the subject of a coinage of copper preceded that of New Jersey, though only by a short time; the act authorizing a coinage in this State was, however, passed some months earlier than was that of Massachusetts.

It is probable that the undertakers of this coinage, having already had some experience in the business, (as it is said that Mould had followed a similar occupation in England, and brought to this country his entire apparatus, prepared to continue it,) found fewer, and less serious obstacles to overcome in the establishment of their mint, than did Witherle; and although they soon disagreed and established separate mints, they were able to issue their coins much more speedily, and to a greater amount than he found it possible to do.

The first introduction of the project of coining in this State is recorded in the "Votes and Proceedings of the tenth General Assembly", on Tuesday, May 23d, 1786, when :—

"The Speaker laid before the House proposals made by Walter Mould, Thomas Goadsby and albion Cox for striking a Copper Coin for the State of New-Jersey which was read Whereupon Ordered, That Mess^rs A Clark, R S Smith, Sheppard, Marsh and Nicoll be a Committee to Confer with the said Walter Mould Thomas Goadsby and Albion Cox on the Subject of the said proposals and report to the House the Terms they may agree upon "

"Wednesday May 24. 1786. M$^r$ A Clark from the Committee Appointed to Confer with Walter Mould Thomas Goadsby and Albion Cox on the Subject of their proposals for striking a Copper Coin in the State of New-Jersey reported as follows :

"That they have held the conference for which they were appointed and have agreed with M$^r$ Mould in behalf of himself and Associates on either of the Conditions following, as may be most agreeable to the Legislature

"First That said Persons if authorized to Coin a sum in Coppers not to exceed ten thousand pounds will engage to Coin that sum and no more and to pay one eleventh part thereof to the State

"Secondly If they shall be permitted to Coin any greater sum than the ten thousand pounds limitted by persons authorized for that purpose who may stop such Coinage whenever a sum shall be Coined to as large an amount as will pass current without Depreciation they will engage to Coin at least ten thousand Pounds and to pay to the State one tenth part of all the sums they may Coin which several Conditions are Submitted to the House

"By order of the Committee,

"Ab$^m_?$ Clark"

"The House having taken the above report into Consideration Ordered, That M$^r$ Mould and his Associates have leave to bring in a Bill agreeably to the Last mentioned Condition * * * * *

"M$^r$ Marsh agreeably to leave given and in behalf of the Petitioners presented the draught of a Bill intituled 'An Act for the Establishment of a Coinage of Copper in this State' which Bill was read and ordered a second reading."

"Thursday, May 25. 1786. A Petition from William Leddle Esq. Accompanied with proposals for Coining of Copper was read. Whereupon

"The Bill intituled 'An Act for the establishment of a Coinage of Copper in this State' was a second time debated and Ordered to be engrossed."

Who William Leddle, or Leddel as he writes it, was, we know not ; but he seems to have received rather cool treatment, not even "Leave to withdraw" being recorded upon his petition. This paper we have been so fortunate as to obtain, but that of Mould, Goadsby and Cox, cannot now be found.

### The Petition of William Leddel.

"To the Honourable the Legislature of the State of New jersey now Sitting at New Brunswick.—

"The Memorial and Petition of William Leddel humbly Sheweth,—

"That your Memorialist, being at present possest, of a considerable quantity of Copper, the Production of this State, suitable in quality for a copper Coin, and in possesion of sundry Iron Factories, in which the Coinage of Coppers would be, by Him, easily performed, and without any very considerable expence, and having for some Time past, considered a copper coinage, to be carried on in this State, subject to the controul of proper Commissioners appointed by the Legislature of the Same, as a circulating Medium, for small Change, and Export, as an eligable Expedient,—The evident Utility thereof,—

"hath induced, your Memorialist, to beleive and Pray, that your Honors would grant him the Privillidge, of coining a sum of Money in Coppers as large as the Commissioners appointed by your Honors, to regulate Said Coinage, should See, expedient and necessary,—

"To induce your Honors, to grant the Prayer of your Memorialist, he humbly Offers, for your Consideration the following Proposals, viz$^t$ —

"That the Coppers, when coined shall be eaqual in weight, and in quality to the best, Coppers that ever hath circulated in this State,—

"That the Legislature shall have the Privillidge, to give the Divise or impression to be made on the Coppers so to be coined.—and

"That in consideration of such Permission, your Memorialist will pay into, and render unto the Treasury of this State every Ninth Copper, and that your Memorialist, will at any Time, at the Desire of the Treasurer, or the Commissioners Afforesaid, receive any Paper Money emitted by this State and taken in Payment for Taxes, in exchange for Coppers so made and Coined.—

"Should your Honors, doubt the Skill and abillity, of your Memorialist, to compleat the, said Coinage he prayeth that he may have five Days, to convince your Honors, by producing an Ensample of his own Performance your Honors at the same Time giving the impression and Weight, . —

"New Brunswick.—
"25$^{th}$ May 1786.

"And your Petitioner as in Duty
Bound Shall ever Pray

W$^m$ Leddel "

We copy the act of June 1st, 1786, from the Pamphlet Laws of New Jersey.

### Chapter CLIV.

"An Act for the Establishment of a Coinage of Copper in this State.

"Whereas the Copper Coin now current and passing in this State consists mostly of base Metal, and of Coppers so small and light as to be of very little real Value, whereby the Citizens of this State are subjected to manifest Loss and Inconvenience, and are liable to be greatly defrauded; for Remedy whereof,

"Sect. 1. Be it Enacted *by the Council and General Assembly of this State, and it is hereby Enacted by the Authority of the same,* That Walter Mould, Thomas Goadsby and Albion Cox, and the Survivors and Survivor of them, are hereby authorized and empowered, from and after the Publication of this Act, to strike and coin in Copper, for this State, a Sum equal in Value to Ten Thousand Pounds at fifteen Coppers to the Shilling.

"2. *And be it further Enacted by the Authority aforesaid,* That the Coppers so to be coined shall be of pure Copper, and of the Weight of six Pennyweight and six Grains; that they shall be manufactured and coined within this State, and shall have such Marks and Inscriptions as shall be directed by the Justices of the Supreme Court, or any one of them.

"3. *And be it further Enacted by the Authority aforesaid,* That the said Coppers so to be struck and coined, shall be of the Value aforesaid, unless the United States in Congress assembled shall, by a publick Act, alter the Valuation thereof, to which Alteration the Value thereof shall at all Times be subject.

"4. *And be it further Enacted by the Authority aforesaid,* That the said Walter Mould, Thomas Goadsby and Albion Cox, before they shall enter on or begin the Coinage aforesaid, shall enter into Bond to the Governor or Commander in Chief of this State, to the Use of the State, with at least two sufficient Sureties, in the Sum of Ten Thousand Pounds, conditioned that the said Walter Mould, Thomas Goadsby and Albion Cox, or one or more of them, shall, within two Years after the Publication of this Act, strike and coin, within this State, the full Sum of Ten Thousand Pounds in Coppers as aforesaid; and that they shall faithfully and honestly demean themselves in coining said Coppers; and that they will deliver to the Treasurer of this State, or his Order, for the Use of the State, one Tenth Part of the full Sum they shall strike and coin as aforesaid, which said Tenth Part shall be paid quarterly unto the Treasurer, as aforesaid, by the said Walter Mould, Thomas Goadsby and Albion Cox, from the Time they shall begin to coin as aforesaid during the Time they may carry on said Business ; which Bond the Treasurer is authorized and empowered to take, and the same to file in the Auditor's Office : And the said Walter Mould, Thomas Goadsby and Albion Cox, shall, at the Time of giving said Bond, respectively take an Oath or Affirmation that they will well and truly account to the Legislature for the Tenth Part of all the Coppers they may coin as aforesaid, and that they will truly and faithfully execute the said Coinage agreeably to the true Intent and Meaning of this Act.

"5. *And be it further Enacted,* That if any Person or Persons whatsoever shall strike or coin any Coppers within this State, without Leave being first had and obtained from the Legislature to do the same, shall forfeit and pay, for each Day he or they may be so employed in striking or coining Coppers contrary to the true Intent and Meaning of this Act, the Sum of Twelve Pounds, to be recovered by the Collector of the County in an Action of Debt in any Court where the same may be cognizable, with Costs of Suit, to be paid into the Treasury of the State for the Time being for the Use of the State.

" Passed at New Brunswick, June 1, 1786."

In the General Assembly, Friday, November 17th, 1786 : —

" A Petition from Thomas Goadsby and Albion Cox was read, praying a Supplement may be made to the Act intituled, ' An Act for the establishment of a Coinage of Copper in this State;' which may enable them independant of Walter Mould, in said Act named, to proceed to the Coinage of two thirds of the sum limited by the Aforesaid Act :

" Ordered, That the said Thomas Goadsby and Albion Cox have leave to present a Bill agreeably to the prayer of their Petition. A Petition from M^r Mould was read, and ordered to be read a second time when the said Bill shall be presented to the House."

" Saturday November 18. 1786 * * * * * M^r Dayton agreeably to leave given, presented the draught of a Bill intituled ' A Supplementary Act to the Act intituled, An Act for the Establishment of a Coinage of Copper in this State ; which was read and ordered a second reading."

The following is a copy of the original manuscript of this bill : —
" State of New Jersey
" A Supplementary Act to the Act intituled ' An Act for the establishment

of a Coinage of Copper in this State.'   Whereas by An Act passed at Brunswick the first day of June last intituled 'An Act for the establishment of a Coinage of Copper in this State,' Walter Mould Thomas Goadsby and Albion Cox were jointly nominated to execute the said business subject to certain conditions restrictions and penalties and whereas it appears that delays have been occasioned and the good intentions of the before mentioned Act is likely to be defeated by the Circumstances of the parties being jointly bound to execute the Contract therefore in order to facilitate and forward the business agreeably to and on the Terms prescribed by said act

"Be it enacted by the Council and General Assembly of this State, and it is hereby enacted by the Authority of the same

"That it shall and may be lawful for the said Thomas Goadsby and Albion Cox from and after the publication of this Act to proceed in the Coinage of two third parts of the sum Authorised in the Act intituled 'An Act for the establishment of a Coinage of Coper in this State, to wit, of six thousand six hundred and sixty six pounds thirteen shillings and four pence in as full and Ample a manner as they might have done under the former Act had the said Walter Mould joined himself to and subscribed the Conditions and penalties enjoined by said Act

"Provided Nevertheless and it is hereby understood and required that previous to the entering upon the business aforesaid they the said Thomas Goadsby and Albion Cox give and enter into like Bonds and take the same Oath as is prescribed by the before mentioned Act excepting only so far as relates to the joining of the said Walter Mould to the said Thomas Goadsby and Albion Cox and also that they be subject to the like limitations and restrictions with those pointed out in the said Act ;

"And be it further enacted by the Authority Aforesaid that the said Walter Mould be and he is hereby Authorised and empowered to begin and enter upon the Coinage of the remaining third part, to wit, three thousand three hundred and thirty-three pounds six shillings and eight pence upon his previously taking the like Oath and giving a separate Bond in his own name with two sufficient sureties for the same sum and under the same restrictions Conditions and penalties with those required from the said Walter Mould Thomas Goadsby and Albion Cox in the before recited Act Provided always that in case of neglect refusal or falure on the part of the said Walter Mould to comply with the above Conditions and enter upon the Coinage of the above mentioned one third within two months from the date hereof it shall and may in that Case be lawful for the said Thomas Goadsby and Albion Cox to take upon themselves solely the whole coinage of the sum of ten thousand pounds as fully and amply and under the same exclusion Conditions and restrictions as Walter Mould Thomas Goadsby and Albion Cox were by the former Act empowered jointly to do

"And be it further enacted by the Authority Aforesaid that if they or either of them neglect to give bond as aforesaid he or they so neglecting shall be made liable to forfeit and pay the same sum to be recovered in the same manner that other persons are made liable to pay for striking or Coining Coppers by the before recited Act.

"Council Chamber Nov<sup>r</sup> 22<sup>d</sup> 1786. This Re-engrossed Bill having been read and compared Resolved — That the same do pass. By Order of the House

Wil. Livingston Presdt."

"House of Assembly November 22<sup>d</sup> 1786

"This re-engrossed Bill having been read and Compared Resolved That the same do pass By order of the House Benj<sup>a</sup> Van Cleve Sp<sup>r</sup>."

On Tuesday, May 29th, 1787, "Mr. Kitchel, with Leave of the House, brought in a Bill, intitled, 'An Act to prevent the Circulation of bad and light Coppers in this State;' which was read, and ordered a second reading."

This bill, after the usual references from Council to Assembly, and from Assembly to Council, and undergoing several amendments, was passed June 4th, 1787.

## Chapter CXCVII.

"An Act to prevent the Circulation of bad and light Coppers in this State.

"Whereas the Circulation of Coppers which are of base Metal and below the proper Standard, must be productive of great Evils to the commercial Part of this State, if not timely prevented ; therefore,

"Be it Enacted *by the Council and General Assembly of this State, and it is hereby Enacted by the Authority of the same,* That if any Person or Persons, from and after the twentieth Day of July next, shall pass or offer to pass in Payment, or in Exchange within this State, any Coppers other than those made within the same, agreable to Permission given by a Law passed the first Day of June, One Thousand Seven Hundred and Eighty-six, and the Supplement thereto, passed the twenty-second Day of November, in the same Year, each and every Person or Persons, so offending, shall forfeit and pay ten Times the nominal Value of the Sum or Sums so offered in Payment, or in Exchange, to be recovered by Action of Debt, by any Person that will sue for and recover the same, with Cost of Suit, to and for his own Use : *Provided*, That Nothing in this Act contained shall be construed to extend to any Copper Coin that shall be struck by the United States of America in Congress assembled.

"Passed at Burlington, June 4, 1787."

Mr. Bushnell furnishes the following, from his manuscript Numismatic Notes.

Extract from a letter from W. C. Baker, to Charles I. Bushnell, dated Morristown, Aug. 8, 1855.

"There were two mint-houses in this State, one located in Morristown, and the other in Elizabethtown. The mint-house in the former place, which is still standing, was the residence of John Cleve Symmes, Chief Justice of the State of New Jersey, uncle to John Cleve Symmes, author of 'The Hole at the North Pole', and father-in-law of Gen. Wm. H. Harrison, President of the United States. The residence was called 'Solitude.' It was at one time occupied by a Mr. Holloway, and is known by some as the 'Holloway House.' The mint here was carried on by Walter Mould, an Englishman, who previous to his coming to America, had been employed in a similar way, in Birmingham. In the coinage of the New Jersey coppers, a screw with a long lever was employed. This information is vouched for by Mr. Lewis Condict, of Morristown, who saw the mint in operation.

"The building in Elizabethtown, used as a mint-house, is near to the house formerly occupied by Col. Francis Barber, of the Revolutionary army, and is known as the 'Old Armstrong House.' It is still standing, and is situated in Water Street, and the coins were made in a shed back of the main building. The coining here was carried on by a man named Gilbert Rindle, probably for account of Messrs. Goadsby and Cox. I have this from Mrs. ——, of Elizabethtown, who remembers the circumstance."

Mr. Bushnell further says:

"Mr. J. R. Halsted informed me some [20] years ago that an acquaintance of his knew a Mr. Hatfield, who claimed to have made dies and coined New Jersey coppers, in a barn, (Mr. Halsted thought) below Elizabethtown, in striking which he was assisted by a negro."

We are indebted to Mr. Bushnell for a copy of an affidavit of John Bailey, who, it seems, also made New Jersey Coppers.

"'City of New York, ss.

"'Personally appeared before me, Jeremiah Wool, one of the Aldermen of the said City, John Bailey, of the said City of New York, cutler, who being duly sworn, deposeth and saith, That since the fifteenth day of April, 1788, he hath not, either by himself or others, made or struck any coppers bearing the impression of those circulated by the state of New Jersey, commonly called Jersey coppers : and that what he so made previous to the said fifteenth of April, was in conformity to, and by authority derived from an Act of the State of New Jersey, entitled, "An Act for the establishment of a Coinage of Copper in that State, passed June the first, 1786."

"'John Bailey.

"'Sworn this first day of August 1789
"'Before me, Jeremiah Wool, Alderman.'"

The coins of New Jersey are of a single type, but many varieties : —

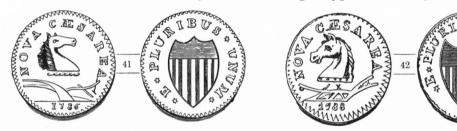

OBVERSE.

Device, — A horse's head, placed upon a wreath as in heraldry, beneath which is a plough.

Legend, — NOVA CÆSAREA

In exergue, — The date, — 1786, 1787 or 1788.

REVERSE.

Device, — A shield, argent, six pales gules, a chief azure.

Legend, — * E * PLURIBUS * UNUM *

Borders, — Serrated. Edges, — Plain. Size, — 16 to 19.

Some obverses have three leaves under the horse's head, and some reverses, two branches, or sprigs, crossed under the shield.

The weights of the coins of 1786, are from 137 to 178 grains ; 1787, 108 to 165 grains, and of 1788, 136 to 160 grains ; heavier specimens undoubtedly exist, as all the heaviest we have weighed were considerably worn, while the lightest were nearly uncirculated specimens.

Tables of the varieties will be found on the two pages following.

### 1786. OBVERSES.

| No. | Legend and Punctuation. | Handle Ends. | Beam. | | Dies. | With Reverses. | Rarity. |
|---|---|---|---|---|---|---|---|
| 1 | NOVA CÆSAREA · | Rounded. | Straight, | | 1 | A, B, F | R2 |
| 2 | NOVA CÆSAREA | Straight. | Straight. | | 3 | E, F | R1 |
| 3 | NOVA CÆSAREA | Straight. | End bent up, } With coulter. | | 2 | E, F | R4 |
| 4 | NOVA CÆSAREA | Straight. | Curved, | | 6 | C, D, H | C |
| 5 | NOVA CÆSAREA | Rounded. | Curved, | | 1 | C, G | R4 |
| 6 | NOVA CÆSAREA · | Straight. | Curved, } Without coulter. | | 2 | C, G | R4 |
| 7 | NOVA CÆSAREA | Pointed. | Curved, } Date under beam. | | 1 | G | R6 |
| 8 | NOVA CÆSAREA · | Pointed. | Curved, | | 1 | G | R6 |

### 1787. OBVERSES.

| No. | Legend and Punctuation. | Handle Ends. | Beam. | | Dies. | With Reverses. | Rarity. |
|---|---|---|---|---|---|---|---|
| 1 | NOVA CÆSAREA | Knobs, heavy. | Straight. | | 5 | B, D | R2 |
| 2 | NOVA CÆSAREA · | One knob, light. | Straight. | | 1 | B | R3 |
| 3 | NOVA CÆSAREA | Straight. | Straight. } No leaves under head. | | 5 | C, D, E, F | R |
| 4 | NOVA CÆSAREA | Straight. | Curved. | | 14 | A, B, C, D | C |
| 5 | NOVA CÆSAREA · | Straight. | Curved. | | 1 | E, F | R4 |
| 6 | NOVA CÆSAREA · | Rounded. | Curved. | | 1 | I | R4 |
| 7 | NOVA CÆSAREA | Rounded. | Curved. | | 2 | G, I | R |
| 8 | NOVA CÆSAREA | Straight. | Curved. | | 4 | A, D, K | R3 |
| 9 | NOVA CÆSAREA · | Light. | Curved. } Three leaves under head. | | 1 | I | R4 |
| 10 | NOVA CÆSAREA ✿ | Heavy, square. | Curved. | | 1 | H | R6 |
| 11 | NOVA✶CÆSAREA ✶ | Heavy, square. | Curved. | | 1 | H | R5 |

### 1788. OBVERSES.

| No. | Legend and Punctuation. | Facing | Beam. | | Dies. | With Reverses. | Rarlty. |
|---|---|---|---|---|---|---|---|
| 1 | NOVA ✶ CÆSAREA ✿ | Right. | Straight, no coulter or singletree. | | 1 | B | R6 |
| 2 | NOVA CÆSAREA | Right. | Straight, } Coulter and singletree. | | 1 | E | R4 |
| 3 | ✿ NOVA ✿ CÆSAREA ✿ | Right. | Straight, | | 2 | A, B | R4 |
| 4 | ✶ NOVA ✶ CÆSAREA ✶ | Right. | Slightly curved, | | 2 | C | R |
| 5 | NOVA CÆSAREA | Left. | Curved,          Coulter and ring. | | 3 | D | R4 |

### NOTES ON THE TABLES OF NEW JERSEY COINS.

The notes which follow may serve to elucidate some indefinite points.

#### 1786.

No. 1. The handle ends are not only rounded, but enlarged, though not sufficiently so as to be called with knobs.

No. 2, — E, is represented on Plate VI. No. 20.

No. 3. The beam is straight, but bent up at the end.

No. 4 — D is represented by Fig. 41, 4 — H, on Plate VI. No. 19.

No. 5. The handle ends are but slightly rounded. [Plate VI. No. 18.]

No. 6 closely resembles No. 5, but differs in punctuation.

Nos. 7 and 8. These have the date under the beam of the plough, and pointed ends to the handles. We have seen but one specimen of each, one of which, No. 7, [Plate VI. No. 17] is owned by A. S. Jenks, of Philadelphia: the owner of the other, No. 8, is unknown. All other varieties of this year

### 1786. REVERSES.

| No. | Legend and Punctuation. | Shield. | Pales of | Sprigs. | Dies. | With Obverses. | Rarity. |
|---|---|---|---|---|---|---|---|
| A | ✶ E ✶ PLURIBUS ✶ UNUM ✶ | Narrow. | Four. | Two. | 1 | 1 | R5 |
| B | ✶ E ✶ PLURIBUS ✶ UNUM ✶ | Narrow. | Three. | None. | 1 | 1 | R2 |
| C | ✶ E ✶ PLURIBUS ✶ UNUM ✶ | Narrow. | Four. | None. | 3 | 4, 5, 6 | R2 |
| D | ✶ E ✶ PLURIBUS ✶ UNUM ✶ | Narrow. | Four and five. | None. | 1 | 4 | R3 |
| E | ✶ E ✶ PLURIBUS ✶ UNUM ✶ | Medium. | Three. | None. | 4 | 2, 3 | C |
| F | ✶ E ✶ PLURIBUS ✶ UNUM ✶ | Wide. | Three. | None. | 1 | 1, 2, 3 | R3 |
| G | ✶ E ✶ PLURIBUS ✶ UNUM ✶ | Wide. | Five. | None. | 3 | 5, 6, 7, 8 | R4 |
| H | ✶ E ✶ PLURIBUS ✶ UNUM ✶ | Very wide. | Four. | None. | 3 | 4 | C |

### 1787. REVERSES.

| No. | Legend and Punctuation. | Shield. | Pales of | Sprigs. | Dies. | With Obverses. | Rarity. |
|---|---|---|---|---|---|---|---|
| A | ✶ E ✶ PLURIBUS ✶ UNUM ✶ | Narrow. | Four. | None, | 2 | 4, 8 | R5 |
| B | ✶ E ✶ PLURIBUS ✶ UNUM ✶ | Medium. | Three. | None. | 9 | 1, 2, 4 | C |
| C | ✶ E ✶ PLURIBUS ✶ UNUM ✶ | Medium. | Four. | None. | 3 | 3, 4 | R2 |
| D | ✶ E ✶ PLURIBUS ✶ UNUM ✶ | Wide. | Three. | None. | 8 | 1, 3, 4, 8 | C |
| E | ✶ E ✶ PLURIBUS ✶ UNUM ✶ | Wide. | Four. | None. | 2 | 3, 5 | R4 |
| F | ✶ E ✶ PLURIBUS ✶ UNUM ✶ | Wide. | Five and six. | None. | 2 | 3, 5 | R6 |
| G | ✶ E ✶ PLURIBUS ✶ UNUM ✶ | Narrow, | Four. | Two. | 1 | 7 | R6 |
| H | ✶ E ✶ PLURIBUS ✶ UNUM ✶ | Medium. | Four. | Two. | 1 | 10, 11 | R5 |
| I | ✶ E ✶ PLURIBUS ✶ UNUM ✶ | Medium. | Four. | Two. | 4 | 6, 7, 9 | R |
| K | ✶ E ✶ PLURIBS ✶ UNUM ✶ | Medium. | Four. | Two. | 1 | 8 | R3 |

### 1788. REVERSES.

| No. | Legend and Punctuation. | Shield. | Pales of | Sprigs. | Dies. | With Obverses. | Rarity. |
|---|---|---|---|---|---|---|---|
| A | ❖ ⚘ E ❖ PLURIBUS ❖ UNUM ❖ | Medium. | Four. | Two. | 1 | 3 | R4 |
| B | ⚘ ❖ E ❖ PLURIBUS ❖ UNUM ❖ | Wide. | Four. | Two. | 1 | 1, 3 | R4 |
| C | ✶ E ✶ PLURIBUS ✶ UNUM ✶ | Narrow. | Four. | Two. | 1 | 4 | R |
| D | ✶ E ✶ PLURIBUS ✶ UNUM ✶ | Medium. | Four. | None. | 2 | 5 | R4 |
| E | ✶ E ✶ PLURIBUS ✶ UNUM ✶ | Wide. | Five and six. | None, | 1 | 2 | R4 |

have the handles cut off straight. Reverse E of 1786, and B of 1787, are identical in two dies, and F of 1786, with D of 1787, in one die.

#### 1787.

No. 1. Both handles of these dies have heavy knobs.

No. 2. The lower handle is short, the upper, long with a very light knob: for 2—B, see Plate VI. No. 21.

No. 4. Most of these dies are much alike, differing mainly in the curves and positions of the plough-handles and beams; the specimen (4—B) on plate VI. No. 23, differs greatly from any other of this number.

No. 5. One of the most coarsely cut dies of the series. On plate VII. No. 20 is 5—E, and No. 19, 5—F; of the last we know but two specimens.

No. 8. The die of this variety found with reverse A, we have seen on but one specimen; that with D is also quite rare—Dr. Maris has one in brass: the two other dies are found with reverse K, the PLURIBS. [Plate VI. No. 22.]

No. 10.   The only die we know of this year punctuated with a quatrefoil, (✦) and only one specimen known; this belongs to Dr. Maris.

No. 11.   An extremely rare variety which we have always found double-struck, upon one specimen causing the R to resemble a K, whence it has been called the "PLUKIBUS" variety.   [Plate VI. No. 24.]

Reverse C of 1787, and D of 1788, are identical in two dies, F, with E in one die; the other die of F, is identical with the reverse of the IMMUNIS of 1786.

1788.

No. 1.   We are indebted to Dr. Maris for this variety.   It is punctuated with a star and a quatrefoil, and the plough has· neither coulter nor singletree; its reverse is the same with that of Plate VI. No. 25.

No. 2.   The horse's right ear, (at observer's left,) touches the letter C: we find none without cracks over NOVA and AREA, and across the plough handles, and beam : its reverse, E, is identical with one die of F of 1787.

No. 3.   This is called the "dog" or "fox" variety, from a small animal in the legend on the reverse, which on fine specimens is clearly seen to be a horse.   [Plate VI. Nos. 25 and 26.]

No. 4.   The beam is but slightly curved.   In one die the mane of the horse is long, hanging straight the length of his neck, and the plough equidistant from the stars; in the other, the mane is not as long, and the handles of the plough are much nearer to one star, than the beam is to the other.

No. 5, comprises the heads facing left.   That given on Plate VI. No. 27, is the smallest and most rare of the three : its reverse, D, is identical with one die of C, of 1787 : a curious fact concerning this reverse is, that while it is found on coins of 1787, with a heavy break across the shield, we have seen none of 1788, on which that break is visible.   For another die see Fig. 42.

For the purpose of imposing "rare varieties" upon collectors, some unprincipled person has altered New Jersey coins of 1786 and 1787, by engraving, or otherwise changing the facing of the horse's head, and in one instance, the plough also, from right to left.   No coin, having in its original condition the head to the left, and the date 1786, or 1787, has come to our knowledge.

The shields noted as· narrow, measure less than 9 ; medium, 9 to 10 ; wide, 10 to 11, and very wide, more than 11.

We are indebted to John H. Hickcox, Esq., of Albany, N. Y., for a copy of a letter from F. B. Chetwood of Elizabeth, N. J., dated March 19, 1858, who gives the following particulars : —

"My Mother, the daughter of Col. Francis Barber, is now seventy-six years old, and says that all of her recollection on the subject of your enquiry is that when she was a child ten or twelve years old, she used to go into the house on the adjoining premises to her father's residence in this place to see them make coppers — The business was carried on in a room behind the kitchen, by Gilbert Rindle and a person whose name she thinks was Cox — The *modus operandi* was as follows — In the middle of the room was a wooden box or pit sunk in the floor several feet deep, in the middle of which pit was placed an iron Die, the top of which was about level with the floor of the room — A workman sat on the floor, with his legs inside the pit — he placed the smooth coppers on the Die and when stamped, brushed them off the Die into the pit — The impression on the copper was made by a screw-press which was worked by two men, one at each end of an iron bar or horizontal lever, attached to the screw at the centre of its length, which was about nine or ten feet long.

"My mother thinks it was in operation only a year or two, but her recollection on this point is not very reliable.

"The copper was brought to that house, all finished, as she thinks, except the stamping — She has no recollection at all of any other branch of the business being carried on there — She recollects that the copper when coined was put into kegs and sent off somewhere, and that her mother used to purchase a bureau drawer nearly full at a time, and pay them out in daily use for household expenses."

An interesting study may be made of the varieties of the New Jersey coins, to some particulars of which we will direct attention. A careful examination of the letters reveals in many of these, some peculiarities of the punches by which the letters were impressed in the dies ; and as the same peculiar letters appear in several different dies, the natural inference is that all these dies were made by the same person.

The letter A upon many of them is broken near the top, as A, and when not broken, often shows an irregularity, the broken line being cut in. The N is irregular on the under side of the sloping line, as N; the P is imperfect at the left of its foot, the ceriph being broken from that side, as P. A general likeness may in many dies be traced in other letters, and also in the figures.

A comparison of these coins shows that No. 1 of 1786 differs in workmanship from any of the other varieties. Nos. 2, 3 and 4, are much alike.

Nos. 5, 7 and 8, (the last two have the date under the beam of the plough,) resemble each other in many points, and though in some respects they are much like Nos. 2, 3 and 4, yet in others they differ widely from them ; some of their reverses are among the finest dies of this State.

Nos. 1 and 2 of 1787, and some of Nos. 3 and 4, exhibit a style of workmanship much alike. No. 5 agrees closely with one die of No. 3, the PLURIBS, and Nos. 2 and 4 of 1788 ; in these the most marked letters are the N, (which in No. 5 is inverted) where the sloping line joins the right limb considerably above the foot, and the U, which is very broad : these two letters are sufficient for the identification of dies upon which they appear. No. 11 is of a style peculiar to itself, as also are some dies of No. 4 and 8 of 1787, and No. 5 of 1788, with the head to the left.

The reverses are not always of a style to correspond with their obverses, but often those widely differing in their workmanship are combined, sometimes a coarsely cut reverse appearing with a well executed obverse, and *vice versa,* as in the specimen shown on Plate VII, No. 19.

To extend this examination further, to the comparison of the issues of this State with those of Vermont and Connecticut, furnishes an interesting field for conjecture as to the business connection possibly existing between the parties conducting the several coinages ; for we find the letters A and N precisely as before described, upon many of the Vermont dies, and on some of those attributed to Connecticut. We therefore consider it certain that many of the dies of New Jersey and Vermont, and some of the AUCTORI CONNEC, (as well as some others yet to be treated of,) were the work of the same artist ; but whether the dies for the different mints were made at one place, or whether the artist followed an itinerant practice, and visited the mints as occasion required, which probably would be the more convenient method of conducting his business in the absence of the regular means of communication now in use, must be left to conjecture.

The opinion has been expressed, (p. 191,) that the dies upon which was a plough, cut by Atlee, were the Vermont coins with that device : it seems fully as probable, judging from the facts just stated, that, although Atlee may have cut some of those dies, (they do not all appear to have been the work of one artist,) he must have done many of these also, as they bear indisputable evidence of the same handiwork with most of the Vermont coins of 1787 and 1788, and also with that of the GEORGIVS · III · REX ·

# NEW YORK.

———▶•◀———

An attempt was made, as early as 1661, to establish a mint in New York, then known as New Amsterdam.

"The Burgomasters and Scepens of New Amsterdam, in pursuance of a previous resolution, made application on the twelfth day of October, 1661, to the Chamber of the Directors of the West India Company, at Amsterdam in Holland for authority to establish a mint in the colony for the coinage of silver. This application, however, did not meet with success."[1]

In 1672 an order was passed regulating the currency of silver coin in this State, regarding which we have the following memoranda : —

"Orders made and confirmed at yᵉ Geneᵃˡˡ Court of Assizes held in New York, beginning on yᵉ 2ᵈ and ending on yᵉ 7ᵗʰ day of October in yᵉ three and twentieth year of his Maᵗⁱᵉˢ Reigne Annoq Dom. 1672. * * * * *

"12. Whereas, it is thought expedient that a certaine regulacõn should be made upon yᵉ sylver Coyne which passeth to and fro in this Governmᵗ by yᵉ certainty of its value, It is Ordered That a Boston Shilling shall pass for one shilling, and a good piece of Eight Spanish Coine, whether of Mexico Sevill or a pillar piece shall be valued and go for six shillings in any payment either for debt and demands or purchasing goods or merchandize between man and man."[2]

The Massachusetts and New Hampshire Advertiser, of March 29, 1786, contains this announcement :[3] — "New York Connecticut and Vermont have authorized a person in each of those states to coin coppers ; numbers of them are now in circulation ; they are in general well made, and of good copper,

---

[1] Charles I. Bushnell.    [2] New York Records; C. I. B.    [3] Matthew A. Stickney.

those of New York in particular. Was a person authorized in this State for the same purpose, it would undoubtingly prevent the manufacture of those made of base metal."

What the New York coins were, to which the writer of the above paragraph refers, we are at a loss to determine, unless to the NON VIRTUTE VICI, (1786,) which may have made their appearance early in that year, and bearing the legend, NEO-EBORACENCIS, were taken to be coins authorized by the State, and thus considered as sufficient to warrant that statement.

It appears certain, however, that New York had not at that time authorized a coinage, and we have no proof that she did so subsequently ; indeed, whatever proof we have, is of a character to indicate that no such action was ever taken by that State.

We learn from Mr. Bushnell that petitions were presented Feb. 11th, 1787, by John Bailey, and Ephraim Brasher, for the privilege of coining coppers, which were followed, March 3d, 1787, by another to the same effect from Thomas Machin. These petitions cannot now be found and their terms are unknown to us, but the action of the authorities thereupon is thus recorded in the Journal of the Assembly : —

Feb. 12, 1787, "The several petitions of John Bailey and Ephraim Brasher, relative to the Coinage of Copper within this State, were read, and referred to Mr. Brooks, Mr. Galatian, and Mr. Duboys."

March 3, 1787, "A Petition of Thomas Machin, relative to the Coinage of Copper in this State, was read, and referred to Mr. Brooks, Mr. Duboys, Mr. Doughty, Mr. E. Clark, and Mr. Taylor."

We find no report referring particularly to these petitions; but under date of March 5th, 1787, is this statement of the action of the committee :—

"Mr. Brooks from the Committee appointed to bring in a bill to regulate the circulation of Copper Coin within this State, brought in the report of the said Committee, which he read in his place, and delivered in at the table, where the same was again read and is in the words following, viz.

"The Committee who were directed to bring in a bill to regulate the Copper Coin in this State, being at a loss to determine the extent of the intended regulation, whether it was only to ascertain the value of the pieces now in circulation, or was meant to extend to a new coinage, do present to the House the result of their enquiries on this subject.

"They find that there are various sorts of copper coin circulating in this State, the principal whereof are,

"First. A few genuine British half-pence of George the Second, and some of an earlier date, the impressions of which are generally defaced.

"Secondly. A number of Irish half-pence, with a bust on the one side, and a harp on the other.

"Thirdly. A very great number of pieces in imitation of British half-pence, but much lighter, of inferior copper, and badly executed.—These are generally called by the name of Birmingham Coppers, as it is pretty well known that they are made there, and imported in casks, under the name of Hard Ware,[1] or wrought copper.

"Fourthly. There has lately been introduced into circulation, a very considerable number of coppers of the kind that are made in the State of New-Jersey. Many of these are below the proper weight of the Jersey coppers, and seem as if designed as a catch-penny for this market.

"The following calculations will tend to shew the difference between the *real* and *nominal* value of the several kinds of coppers that are circulating among us.

"The very best red copper in sheets may be bought by the quantity at the factories in England, for 11*d.* sterling per pound.—The expence of importation will be from 20 to 25 per cent.—This will bring the price to about two shillings New York currency per pound.—But copper in the mass, or old copper which may be melted down into ingots, and manufactured in the plating mills, so as to be fit for cutting into blanks, as the coppers are called before they are milled, will not cost the purchaser more than 20*d.* per pound.

"*Forty-eight* of the genuine British half-pence, when new, weigh one pound Averdupois. Of the Birmingham Coppers that circulate among us, *sixty* make one pound Averdupois.—The genuine Jersey coppers, weigh each *six* pennyweight, *six* grains, which gives *forty-six* and *two fifths* to the pound Averdupois.

"These all pass by consent without discrimination, at *fourteen* to the shilling.—Hence the following comparative values:

---

[1] It will be noticed that the name "Hard Ware" is here definitely applied to copper coin; here is a partial confirmation of the opinion expressed in regard to the use of the same term, (p. 192,) in the articles of agreement between Reuben Harmon, Thomas Machin and others. Among the coppers here referred to, were probably many of those evidently counterfeit half-pence of George III. bearing date from 1772, (perhaps earlier) to 1787, of which I find ten varieties in my own collection, without particular effort to procure such pieces.

"A pound of Copper, may, as before stated, be reckoned at .    .    £0 1 8
A pound of genuine British half-pence passes with us for  .    .    0 3 5
                                                                      ———
The difference is,    .    .    .    .    .    .    .    .    0 1 9
Which is a little more than *fifty-one* per cent loss.

"A pound of Birmingham coppers passes with us for    .    .    .    0 4 3
                                                                      ———
The difference is    .    .    .    .    .    .    .    .    £0 2 7
Which produces a loss of near *sixty-one* per cent.

"A pound of Jersey coppers passes with us for nearly    .    .    .    0 3 4
                                                                      ———
The difference is    .    .    .    .    .    .    .    .    0 1 8
Which is exactly *fifty* per cent loss.

"If the expence of Coinage be deducted from the losses respectively, as before stated, the difference will shew the neat loss the State sustains by the influx of the several copper coins that are current among us.

"What the real expence of Coinage may be, the Committee have not been able to ascertain with any degree of accuracy, as the persons who could give the best information on that subject, find it their interest to keep the secret to themselves. It may be presumed, however, that the expence of Coinage on a considerable sum, would not amount to more than 25 or at the most 30 per cent. Taking it at the highest estimation, the neat loss on the three several kinds of coppers specified in this statement, would be as follows:

"On the British half-pence .    .    .    .    .    .    .    .    36 per cent.
On the Birmingham half-pence .    .    .    .    .    .    .    49 per cent.
On the Jersey Coppers    .    .    .    .    .    .    .    .    35 per cent.

"The profits that will arise to the Coiners on the aforegoing principles, will be as follows:

"On the British half-pence .    .    .    .    .    .    .    .    57 per cent.
On the Birmingham ditto .    .    .    .    .    .    .    .    96 per cent.
On the Jersey coppers    .    .    .    .    .    .    .    .    54 per cent.

"From this statement it appears, that there are very great profits arising from this traffic, even if we admit, that the price of copper, and expence of coinage, should be considerably higher than the Committee have stated them."

"*Ordered*, That the further consideration of the said report be postponed."

We next give the action of the Assembly and Senate, as recorded in their respective journals, only that of April 18th being from that of the Senate.

March 15, 1787. "The House resolved into a Committee of the whole House, on the report of the Committee appointed to bring in a bill to regulate the circulation of Copper Coin in this State; the said report which is entered on the Journals of this House, on the third day of March instant, was read and considered; and after some time spent thereon Mr. Speaker reassumed the chair, and Mr. Patterson from the said Committee reported, that he was directed by the said Committee to report to the House, that the Committee had agreed to a resolution in the words following, viz.

" *Resolved,* That it is the opinion of this Committee, that a Committee be appointed to prepare and bring in a bill to establish a Coinage of Copper in this State, and to regulate the value of the Copper Coin now in circulation.

"Mr. Patterson read the said report in his place, and delivered the same in at the table, where it was again read, and agreed to by the House. Thereupon.

" *Resolved,* That a Committee be appointed to prepare and bring in a bill to establish a Coinage of Copper in this State, and to regulate the value of the Copper Coin now in circulation; and

" *Ordered,* That Mr. Hamilton, Mr. Brooks, and Mr. Lansing be a Committee for that purpose."

April 7, 1787. "Mr. Brooks from the Committee appointed to prepare and bring in a bill to regulate the copper coin, according to order, brought in the said bill entitled *An act for regulating the value of copper coin within this State,* which was read the first time and ordered a second reading."

April 9, 1787. "Mr. J. Smith, from the Committee of the whole House, on the bill entitled *An act for regulating the value of copper coin in this State,* reported that the Committee had made some progress therein, and had directed him to move for leave to sit again.

" *Ordered,* That the said Committee have leave to sit again."

April 12, 1787. "Mr. John Smith, from the Committee of the whole House, on the bill entitled *An act for regulating the value of copper coin in this State,* reported that the Committee had gone through the bill, made amendments, and altered the title; that the altered title is, *An act to regulate the circulation of copper coin in this State,* which he was directed to report to the House; and he read the report in his place, and delivered the bill and amendments in at the table, where the same were again read, and agreed to by the House.

" *Ordered,* That the bill and amendments be engrossed."

April 13, 1787. "The engrossed bill entitled *An act to regulate the circulation of copper coin*, was read a third time.

"*Resolved*, That the bill do pass."

Senate Journal, April 18, 1787. "Mr. Peter Schuyler, from the Committee of the Whole, on the bill entitled *An act to regulate the circulation of Copper Coin in this State*, reported that they had gone through the bill without amendment, which report he read in his place, and delivered the bill in at the table, where it was again read and agreed to by the Senate: Thereupon,

"*Resolved*, That the bill do pass.

"*Ordered*, That Mr. Parks deliver the bill to the Honorable the Assembly, and inform them that the Senate have passed the bill without amendment."

In the Assembly, April 20, 1787. "A Message from the Honorable the Council of Revision was delivered by the Honorable Mr. Justice Hobart, 'That it does not appear improper to the Council that the bill entitled *An act to regulate the circulation of copper coin in this State* should become a law of this State.'"

## Chapter XCVII.

"An Act to regulate the Circulation of copper coin. Passed April 20, 1787.

"Be it enacted by the people of the State of New York, represented in Senate and Assembly, and it is hereby enacted by the authority of the Same, that from and after the first day of August next, no coppers shall pass current in this State, except such as are of the Standard and weight of one third part of an Ounce averdupois, of pure copper, which coppers shall pass current at the rate of twenty to a Shilling of the lawful current Money of this State and not otherwise.

"And be it further enacted by the authority aforesaid, that if any person or persons, shall after the said first day of August next, offer in payment any copper coin, other than of the Standard and weight aforesaid, such copper coin shall be liable to be seized, and shall be forfeited to the use of the person or persons who shall seize the same. And it shall be lawful for any person or persons, to whom such * * * * offer of payment shall be, to seize and take such copper coin; and the person or persons making such Seizure, shall forthwith give information thereof, and shall deliver the Coppers so seized to some Justice of the peace of the City or County in which such seizure shall have been made ; and the said coppers shall remain in the Custody of such Justice of the peace, for the space of ten days ; and if not claimed within that time, shall be adjudged to be forfeited, and shall be returned to the person or persons who delivered the same to such Justice of the peace, and the person or persons seizing such coppers shall on the request of the person or persons offering the same in payment, give information of the Name of the Justice to whom they shall have been delivered. And in case the said Coppers should be Claimed, and the legality of the seizure Controverted, it shall be lawful for such Justice to hear and determine the Same, in a summary manner ; provided the sum for which such coppers shall have been offered in payment, do not exceed the sum of forty shillings ; but if the same shall exceed the Sum of forty Shillings, then the said Justice of the Peace, if either of the parties require it, shall take to his assistance two able and sufficient freeholders, who, under Oath, shall with said Justice summarily hear and determine the said claim and controversy, and their Judgment in the case shall be final between the parties. And the said Justice shall, after such determination, deliver the coppers deposited with him, to such of the said parties as shall be adjudged to be intitled to the same, according to the true intent and meaning of this act.

"Provided that nothing in this act contained, shall be construed to extend to any copper coin to be struck by the United States of America in Congress assembled.

"And be it further enacted by the authority aforesaid, that if any person or persons shall pass or offer to pass in payment, any coppers of base metal, or of a standard or weight different from that which is hereby permitted to pass, knowing the same to be of such Base metal, or of such different standard or weight, such person or persons shall forfeit five times the Value of the Sum for which such coppers shall be so offered or passed in payment, to be recovered with costs of suit, before any Justice of the peace, by any person that will sue for the same ; which Justice is hereby fully empowered and required summarily, to hear and determine the same, and to award execution thereupon, if the said forfeiture shall not amount to more than six pounds current money of this State ; but if such forfeiture shall amount to more than that sum, then to be recovered with costs of suit, in any court of record within this State, by action of debt, bill or information, in either case, to the use of the person or persons who will sue for the same."

On the 7th of February, 1788, it was enacted, "That if any Person shall

counterfeit, or cause or procure to be counterfeited, or act or assist in counterfeiting, any of the Species of Gold or Silver Coins, now current or hereafter to be current in this State, or shall pass or give in Payment, or offer
to pass or give in Payment, any such Counterfeit, knowing the same to be
counterfeit ; then every such Person, being thereof convicted, according to
the due Course of Law, shall be deemed guilty of Felony, and shall suffer
Death as a Felon."

From the foregoing, it appears certain that, although a committee was
appointed to bring in a bill to establish a coinage of copper in this State, yet
no such bill was presented, neither was a coinage authorized.

Most of the specimens in our cabinets known as New York coppers, are
of English origin, and entitled to that name, if at all, only from the fact that
they bear devices or legends apparently indicating that they were struck for
circulation in that State, but under no authority, other than that of an act
which countenanced all copper coins of a specified quality and weight, irre-
spective of their legends, devices, or origin; while others we think might be
more properly classed under the head of Patterns.   All these will be considered on later pages.

Samuel Davis in a "Journal of a Tour to Connecticut," in 1789, printed
in the Massachusetts Historical Society Collections, April, 1869, refers to
the copper coinage of the States.  Of New Haven he says, "We find some
difficulty in making change in this place.  Coppers pass at six the penny.
Even those graced with the legend 'Auctori Conn.' are included.  Feel
chagrined that old Massachusetts, with his bow and arrow, should be under-
valued.  New York regulates their trade.  The crown passes there, and here
now, at 6s. 9d."

# THE FUGIOS.

These were the earliest coins issued by the authority of the United States. The records relating to them are very meagre, and the papers therein referred to cannot now be found. The ensuing copies of the entries in the Journal of Congress contain all the information that can now be procured regarding the proceedings of the authorities in relation to this coinage: these we copy according to their dates.

"Saturday, April 21, 1787 * * * * * The Committee, consisting of Mr. Johnson, Mr. King, Mr. Pierce, Mr. Clark, and Mr. Pettit, to whom was referred a report of the Board of Treasury on certain proposals for coining copper have reported,

"That the board of treasury be authorized to contract for three hundred tons of copper coin of the federal standard, agreeably to the proposition of Mr. James Jarvis, provided that the premium to be allowed to the United States on the amount of copper coin contracted for be not less than fifteen per cent. That it be coined at the expense of the contractor, but under the inspection of an officer appointed and paid by the United States; that the obligations to be given for the payment of the copper coin to be delivered under such contract be redeemable within          years after the date thereof, with an option of discharging the same at an earlier period; that they bear an interest not exceeding six per cent per annum, and that the principal and interest accruing thereon be payable within the United States; that the whole of the monies arising from the said contract shall be sacredly appropriated and applied to the reduction of the domestic debt.

"A motion was made by Mr. Madison, seconded by Mr. Few, to strike out the last clause, and on the question, shall the last clause stand, viz that the whole of the monies &c, the yeas & nays being required by Mr. Pettit, the question was lost, and the clause was struck out."

After the clause was stricken out, the original article was amended by inserting in the blank the word "twenty," and instead of the rejected clause, the following was inserted ;

"That the whole of the aforesaid loan shall be sacredly appropriated and applied to the reduction of the domestic debt of the United States, and the premium thereon towards the payment of the interest on the foreign debt."

In this form it was passed, and is so entered in the printed Journal of Congress.

The subsequent action relating to this coinage follows :

"Tuesday, May 8, 1787. On motion of Mr. King

"*Resolved*, That the board of treasury be and hereby are authorized to dispose of the public copper on hand, either by sale or contract for the coinage of the same, as they shall judge most for the interests of the United States."

"Friday, July 6, 1787 * * * * * On the report of a committee, consisting of Mr. Pierce, Mr. Kean, and Mr. Holten, to whom was referred a letter of the 11th May from the board of treasury :

"*Resolved*, That the board of treasury direct the contractor for the copper coinage to stamp on one side of each piece the following device, viz : thirteen circles linked together, a small circle in the middle, with the words 'United States,' round it ; and in the centre, the words 'We are one ;' on the other side of the same piece the following device, viz : a dial with the hours expressed on the face of it ; a meridian sun above, on one side of which is to be the word 'Fugio,' and on the other the year in figures '1787' below the dial, the words 'Mind your Business.'"

September 30, 1788. A committee, consisting of Mr. Clark, Mr. Dane, Mr. Carrington, Mr. Bingham, and Mr. Williamson, having been appointed to inquire into the department of finance, they reported, Sept. 30, 1788. Their report upon this subject was as follows : —

"There are two contracts made by the board of treasury with James Jarvis, the one for coining three hundred tons of copper of the federal standard, to be loaned to the United States, together with an additional quantity of forty-five tons, which he was to pay as a premium to the United States for the privilege of coining ; no part of the contract hath·been fulfilled. A particular statement of this business, so far as relates to the three hundred

# PLATE VII.

tons, has lately been reported to Congress. It does not appear to your committee that the board were authorized to contract for the privilege of coining forty-five tons as a premium, exclusive of the three hundred mentioned in the act of Congress.

"The other contract with said Jarvis is for the sale of a quantity of copper, amounting, as per account, to 71,174 pounds ; this the said Jarvis has received at the stipulated price of eleven pence farthing, sterling, per pound, which he contracted to pay in copper coin, of the federal standard, on or before the last day of August 1788, now past ; of which but a small part has been received. The remainder it is presumed, the board of treasury will take effectual measures to recover as soon as possible."

The last sentence of the foregoing report leads us to expect some further mention of the subject in the records : no such mention is to be found, and we are left in ignorance as to the quantity of coin struck, and the date and manner of settlement with the contractor. If, however, we may judge from the number of dies, and the plentiful supply of specimens still found, a large quantity must have been issued, and it may be that the whole of the contracts were fulfilled.

The design of the coins is as ordered in the resolve of July sixth :

OBVERSE.

Device, — Thirteen rings linked regularly, forming an endless chain.

Legend, — UNITED * STATES * on a small circular label around the centre.

Centre, — WE ARE ONE

REVERSE.

Device, — A sun-dial, the sun shining upon it from above.

Legend, — * FUGIO. * * 1787 *

In exergue, — MIND YOUR BUSINESS

Borders, — Milled. Edge, — Plain.

Size, — 17½ to 18. Weight, — 126 to 178 grains.

[Plate VII. Nos. 4, 5 and 6, and Figs. 43 and 44.]

We find impressions from no less than twenty-seven obverse, and twenty-four reverse dies, which differ, in most instances, very slightly. The most prominent points of variation in the obverses are to be found in the order of the words UNITED STATES, which are often transposed to STATES UNITED. In one die, from which we know of but three impressions, UNITED is above, and STATES below, (see plate VII, No. 4,) and in another, (plate VII, No. 5,) these words are separated by two stars of eight. The words WE ARE ONE also vary considerably in position, and in the spacing of the letters.

The principal differences of the reverses are in the different punctuations of the legend seen in Nos. 3 and 4, of plate VII, in the punctuation of the motto, MIND YOUR BUSINESS, (which on some specimens has five diamond-shaped dashes, on others, four, and on others, none, while one die, (plate VII, No. 3,) has two light dashes, and a point ;) and in the sun's rays, which in some dies, (see plate VII, No. 6,) are very heavy, and are known as "club rays." Fig. 43, shows the rings struck through from the obverse : this is often seen, and on some, the impression of the reverse is visible on the obverse.

There are, besides the regular issue of these coins, other pieces of the same general character, supposed to be patterns, which will next be described.

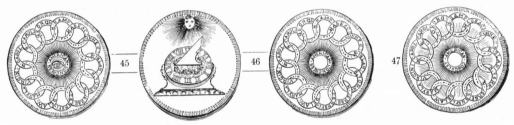

OBVERSE, NO. 1.

Device, — Thirteen rings linked alternately, a mullet within each.

Legend, — UNITED * STATES *  The label bearing this legend is on a large, open star, of thirteen triangular points.

Centre, — WE ARE ONE

OBVERSE NO. 2.

Device, — Thirteen rings linked regularly, each bearing the name of a State.

Legend, — AMERICAN · CONGRESS · on a small circular label.

Centre, — An eye.

A glory fills the space between the legend and the thirteen rings. [Fig. 45].

OBVERSE NO. 3.

This is apparently the same die with the last, but without the eye in the centre. We can learn of but two impressions of each of these obverses: those of 1 and 2, one each in silver and copper, are owned by Mr. Bushnell, those of 3, both in copper, by Mr. Appleton, and Mr. Brevoort.

[Plate VII. No. 2, and Fig. 46.]

### OBVERSE NO. 4.

We are informed by Mr. Bushnell that a variety exists with reverse similar to that last described, but differing in the obverse, the rays of the glory extending into the thirteen rings: this obverse is represented by Fig. 47.

Obverses 1, 2, 3, and 4, are found with reverse A.

### REVERSE A.

Device, — A sun-dial, the sun shining upon it from above.

Field, — Plain.

### REVERSE B.

Device, — A sun-dial, the sun shining upon it from above.

Legend, — ❀ FUGIO. ❀      ❀ 1787 ❀

In exergue, —   ❀MIND❀YOUR❀ BUSINESS

### OBVERSE NO. 5.

Device, — Thirteen rings linked alternately, a mullet within each: within the chain of rings, a large star of thirteen points, with an open centre.

We have seen reverse B, combined with obverse No. 1, only in the cabinet of Mr. Bushnell, who has a specimen in silver, and one in brass: with obverse No. 5, only in silver, in the cabinet of Mr. Brevoort.   [Plate VII. No. 1.]

### OBVERSE NO. 6.

Device, — Thirteen rings linked regularly, each bearing the name of a State.

Legend, — AMERICAN · CONGRESS ·   on a small circular label.

Centre, — WE ARE ONE

A glory fills the space between the legend and the thirteen rings.

### REVERSE C.

Device, — A sun-dial, the sun shining upon it from above.

Legend, — FUGIO .      1787 ❀

In exergue, —   MIND_YOUR_ BUSINESS.

[Plate VII. No. 3.]

Reverse C is found with obverse No. 6 upon three specimens in copper, two of which are owned by Mr. Brevoort, the other by Mr. Bushnell: it is also found, both with the UNITED❀STATES❀, and STATES❀UNITED❀ obverses, upon coins taken from circulation. All these pieces are of the usual size.

Upon the coins found in circulation, with perhaps one exception, the rings on the obverse are laid as seen in Nos. 2 to 6, of plate VII., which is the order we have termed "regular;" in those we have described as linked "alternately," they are arranged as in No. 1, of the plate. The re-strikes frequently seen, are of the latter style, and are from dies found in a store at New Haven, Connecticut, formerly occupied by Messrs. Broome and Platt.

These coins have been known by various names, as "Franklin," "Sun Dial," "Ring," and "Mind your business" cents, as well as by the name at the head of this chapter. Another name is proposed for them by Mr. Bushnell, in the annexed paragraph:

"This coin was issued by authority of Congress in 1787. It is generally known as the Franklin Cent, but should properly be called the Rittenhouse Cent, if named after any individual.[1] * * * It was first coined in the city of New York. A number of sets of dies were made, and the piece was subsequently coined not merely in New York, but also in New Haven, Connecticut, Rupert, Vermont, and other places. The dies were made by Abel Buel, of New Haven, and the coins were struck by means of a drop press."

The ensuing notice of these coins was circulated in the papers of that time:

"The coinage of federal CENTS, coppers, at New York, we are told, is carrying on, and we may expect soon to see them in circulation among us — these will free us from the impositions to which we are now exposed from the floods of light half-coined British half-pence, introduced among us — and as, from the excellent monitorial caution, 'MIND YOUR BUSINESS,' impressed on each of these, they may prove an antidote to insurgency, they will doubtless be held in high estimation."

---

[1] "In the year 1756, he (Rittenhouse,) made an eight-day clock, for his brother in-law, Mr. Barton; over the dial-plate of which, was engraven this mementory motto — *Tempus fugit;* and underneath, this blunt but too often necessary precept — *Go about your business.*

"On one description of the continental bills of credit, issued by congress during the American war, were represented a sun-dial and a meridian sun over it: above, the word 'Fugio;' and beneath, these words — 'Mind your Business.' And on the reverse of a copper one cent piece, struck in the year 1787, in pursuance of a resolve of congress of the 6th of July in that year, are impressed the same device and mottoes as those last mentioned; corresponding with those adopted by our Philosopher, when only twenty-four years of age: a circumstance that shews, how early in life he had formed a just estimate of the value of time.

"It may not be improper here to observe, that the various devices affixed to the continental money, as it was called, were much admired for their appropriate significancy; and that they were generally supposed to be the production of the late ingenious Judge Hopkinson, an intimate friend of Mr. Rittenhouse."—*Barton's Memoirs of David Rittenhouse*, p. 467.

# PATTERNS AND TOKENS.

In this chapter we shall describe a variety of pieces, some of which were of American manufacture, while others were struck in Europe, with reference to, and for circulation in, America; separating them into classes according to their purpose or origin.

As many of these were probably designed as patterns for either Federal or State coins, although no actual proof exists that all were so intended, we shall place them under the head of

## FEDERAL AND STATE PATTERNS.

First in this class should be placed the Massachusetts Pine Tree Copper, and Halfpenny, both dated 1776. Of neither of these have we any reliable history, antedating their comparatively recent discovery.

MASSACHUSETTS PINE TREE COPPER.

OBVERSE.

Device, — A Pine Tree, its trunk dividing the characters 1C LM

Legend, — MASSACHUSET  TS STATE

REVERSE.

Device, — The goddess of liberty, seated upon a globe, facing left, supporting with her left hand the staff of liberty, and holding the cap extended in her right. At her feet sits a dog.

Legend, — LIBERTY AND VIRTUE

In exergue, — 1776

Borders, — Milled.   Edge, — Plain.   Size, — 20.   Weight 198 grains.

[Plate VII. No. 7, and Fig. 48.]

This probably unique piece, now in the collection of Mr. William S. Appleton, was formerly owned by Mr. J. Colburn, of Boston, who obtained it about 1852, from Mr. Edward W. Hooper, then a school-boy collector of coins. Mr. Hooper purchased it from a grocer at the northerly part of the city, who found it many years before while excavating on his premises, in the vicinity of Hull, or Charter Street, for the purpose of making an addition to his dwelling. He had long preserved it as a curiosity.

We take this to be the first pattern for a Massachusetts Cent, and the characters upon the obverse to be abbreviations for " One Cent Lawful Money."

## MASSACHUSETTS HALFPENNY.

### OBVERSE.

Device, — Three heads combined, facing left, front, and right.

Legend, — STATE OF    MASSA: ½ D

### REVERSE.

Device, — The goddess of liberty, facing right, resting against a globe. Her right hand supports the staff of liberty, in her left she holds the cap, and at her feet sits a dog.

Legend, — GODDESS LIBERTY

In exergue, — 1776

Borders and edge plain.   Size, — 15.   Weight 81 grains.

[Plate VII. No. 8, and Fig. 49.]

This piece which has been known as the " Janus Copper," we think may more properly be called the Massachusetts Halfpenny. It has three heads combined, instead of two as in a Janus head. This device resembles the Brahma of Hindoo mythology, which represents the past, the present, and the future.

The only specimen known of this curious pattern is in the collection of Matthew A. Stickney, Esq., and was found with an engraved piece (see plate VII. No. 9,) and some proof impressions from plates for continental paper money engraved by Paul Revere ; from this circumstance Mr. Stickney is inclined to the opinion that they were the work of that engraver. However this may be, the Pine tree cent, and this Halfpenny sufficiently resemble each other in their workmanship, to be considered the work of the same artist. They were probably private enterprises, as no mention of them is found upon any records.

### CONTINENTAL CURRENCY.

#### OBVERSE.

Device, — Thirteen rings interlinked, each bearing the name of a State.

Legend, — AMERICAᴺ CONGRESS · on a small label around the centre.

Centre, — WE ARE ONE

A glory fills the space between the legend and the thirteen rings.

#### REVERSE.

Device, — A sun-dial, the sun shining upon it from the upper left.

In exergue, — MIND YOUR BUSINESS

Near the sun, in the same circle, the word FUGIO

Legend, — CONTINENTAL CURENCY 1776 around the whole.

Borders, — Beaded. Edge, — Ornamented with leaf-work. Size, — 25.

Weight, — Silver, 378 grains. Tin, 258 grains. Brass, 224 grains.

[Plate VIII. No. 15.]

One specimen of this variety, found in the cabinet of Mr. Parmelee, is struck in silver : this has probably done service as a dollar, as it bears evidence of considerable wear from circulation. Impressions from these dies are usually found in tin. A specimen in the cabinet of Mr. Brevoort, struck in brass, (size 23,) has the same reverse with that just described, but the rings upon the obverse are beaded, instead of plain as in all the others : Mr. Appleton has another, in brass, from the same dies, with the beads partly cut into lines ; both these have a comma under the ᴺ. This die was afterwards further altered, into the more common style described above.

Another reverse similar to the above, has the legend CONTINENTAL CUR-RENCY Its obverse is the same with that of the preceding. [Plate VIII. No. 16.]

The third obverse has the legend AMERICAN CONGRESS In this, "N. HAMP'S" precedes "MASSACHS" in the rings, thus differing from the other dies. Its reverse has the sun more nearly above the dial, and E G FECIT (E G probably the initials of the die cutter,) in the inner circle, above the date.

These pieces are not of extreme rarity, neither are they very common : the one most difficult to obtain, excepting those in silver and brass, (only one specimen of each of which is known,) is that last described.

In Watson's Chemical Essays, (Dublin, 1791,) we find this mention of these pieces : "The *Congress in America* had recourse to the same expedient ; [the coinage of tin,] they coined several pieces of about an inch and half in diameter, and of 240 grains in weight ; on one side of which was inscribed in a circular ring near the edge — *Continental Currency*, 1776 — and within the ring a rising sun, with — *fugio* — at the side of it, shining upon a dial, under which was — *Mind your business.* — On the reverse were thirteen small circles joined together like the rings of a chain, on each of which was inscribed the name of some one of the thirteen states ; on another circular ring, within these, was inscribed — *American Congress* — and in the central space — *we are one.* — I have been particular in the mention of this piece of money, because like the leaden money which was struck at *Vienna*, when that city was besieged by the Turks in 1529, it will soon become a great curiosity. I estimated the weight of a cubic foot of this Continental currency, it was equal to 7440 ounces : this exceeds the weight of our best sort of pewter, and falls short of that of our worst ; I conjecture that the metal of the continental currency consisted of 12 parts of tin and one of lead."

A fine specimen of an engraved pattern is the

NON · DEPENDENS · STATUS

OBVERSE.

Device, — A head facing right, with hair falling to the shoulder, where upon an oval shield are emblazoned a staff with flag, and a sword crossing ; in each angle, a fleur de lis. Upon the breast is a winged head.

Legend, — NON · DEPEN – DENS · STATUS

REVERSE.

Device, — An Indian, clad only with a tunic of feathers, facing left, seated upon a globe. In his right hand he holds extended a bunch of tobacco; his left rests upon a shield bearing the same emblems with that upon the obverse.

Legend, — AMER ICA

In exergue, — 1778

Borders and edge plain. Size, — 19. [Fig. 50.]

Nothing is known of the origin or history of this piece.

### THE NOVA CONSTELLATIO PATTERNS.

### THE "MARK."
#### OBVERSE.

Device, — An eye, forming the centre of a glory of thirteen points, the points intersecting a circle of thirteen stars.

Legend, — NOVA CONSTELLATIO ✱

Border, — A wreath of leaves.

#### REVERSE.

Device, — A wreath, enclosing the letters U. S and the figures 1.000

Legend, — LIBERTAS · JUSTITIA · 1783 ·

Border, — A wreath of leaves.   Edge, — Ornamented with leaf-work.

Size, — 21.   Weight, — 270 grains = eleven pennyweights, six grains.

[Plate VIII. No. 1, and Fig. 51.]

### THE "QUINT."
#### OBVERSE NO. 1.

Device, — An eye on a plain field within a glory of thirteen points, the points intersecting a circle of thirteen stars.

Legend, — NOVA CONSTELLATIO ♈

Size, — 16½.   Weight, — 135 grains = five pennyweights, fifteen grains.

[Plate VIII. No. 2, and Fig. 52.]

#### OBVERSE NO. 2.

Device, — An eye, forming the centre of a glory of thirteen points, the points intersecting a circle of thirteen stars.

In place of a legend this has a plain raised ring.

Size, — 16.   Weight, — 110 grains.

[Plate VIII. No. 3.]

#### REVERSE.

Device, — A wreath enclosing the letters U. S and the figures 500

Legend, — LIBERTAS · JUSTITIA · 1783 ·

Borders of both, beaded, and edges ornamented with leaf-work.

This reverse is upon both specimens of the Quint.

These are undoubtedly the first patterns for a coinage for the United States, and command an interest exceeding that of any others of this class : fortunately the early records supply some information definitely referring to them.

The financier, Robert Morris, reported, January 15, 1782, a system of coinage devised by Gouverneur Morris. We quote the portions most important in this connection, from Sparks's Life of Gouverneur Morris.

"The various coins, which have circulated in America, have undergone different changes in their value, so that there is hardly any which can be considered as a general standard, unless it be Spanish dollars. These pass in Georgia at five shillings, in North Carolina and New York at eight shillings, in Virginia and the four Eastern States at six shillings, and in all the other States, excepting South Carolina, at seven shillings and sixpence, and in South Carolina at thirty-two shillings and sixpence. The money unit of a new coin to agree, without a fraction, with all these different values of a dollar, excepting the last, will be the fourteen hundred and fortieth part of a dollar, equal to the sixteenth hundredth part of a crown. Of these units, twenty-four will be a penny of Georgia, fifteen will be a penny of North Carolina or New York, twenty will be a penny of Virginia and the four Eastern States, sixteen will be a penny of all the other States, excepting South Carolina, and forty-eight will be thirteen pence of South Carolina.

"It has already been observed, that, to have the money unit very small, is advantageous to commerce ; but there is no necessity that this money unit be exactly represented in coin ; it is sufficient that its value be precisely known. On the present occasion, two copper coins will be proper, the one of eight units, and the other of five. These may be called an Eight and a Five. Two of the former will make a penny, proclamation or Pennsylvania money, and three a penny Georgia money. Of the latter, three will make a penny New York money, and four a penny lawful, or Virginia money. The money unit will be equal to a quarter of a grain of fine silver in coined money. Proceeding thence in a decimal ratio, one hundred would be the lowest silver coin, and might be called a *Cent*. It would contain twenty-five grains of fine silver, to which may be added two grains of copper, and the whole would weigh one pennyweight and three grains. Five of these would make a *Quint*, or five hundred units, weighing five pennyweight and fifteen grains ; and ten would make a *Mark*, or one thousand units, weighing eleven pennyweight and six grains."

Here we have the name, value, and weight of these two patterns, which, probably with others, were submitted to Congress for their approval; but for some unknown reason, no immediate action was taken thereupon.

Jefferson, after consultation with Morris, remarks, "he seems to concur with me, in thinking his smallest fractional division too minute for a Unit, and, therefore, proposes to transfer that denomination to his largest silver coin, containing 1000 of the units first proposed, and worth about 4s. 2d. lawful, or $\frac{25}{36}$ of a dollar. The only question then remaining between us is, whether the Dollar, or this coin, be best for the Unit. We both agree that *the ease of adoption with the people*, is the thing to be aimed at."

One system of coins proposed by Morris was as follows : —

"One crown, or ten dollars, equal to . . . . . . 10,000
One dollar, or ten bills, equal to . . . . . . . 1,000
One bill, or ten pence, equal to . . . . . . 100
One penny, or ten quarters, equal to . . . . . 10
One quarter, equal to . . . . . . . . 1 "

(The term "bills," probably should be "bits," as in the official report.)

"The value of the *quarter* is equal to a quarter of a grain of pure silver, or one fourteen hundred and fortieth part of a Spanish dollar.

"This was his first plan of a new coinage, founded on the principle of decimals and a *money unit*. The largest piece, or crown, was to be of gold ; the next, or dollar, of silver. He proposed, also, that for convenience there should be other coins struck, besides those here designated, but that each should contain a precise number of the money unit. * * * * *

"Lastly, as to the names above chosen, they, like all other names, are arbitrary, and perhaps better may be substituted. The word *crown* occurred, from the following idea of an impression for a gold coin ; viz. An Indian, with his bow in his left hand, and in his right hand thirteen arrows, and his right foot on a crown ; the inscription, *manus inimica tyrannis*."

Morris subsequently remodelled his plan, and "assumed for his *Unit* an amount equal to twelve shillings and six pence sterling, which he called a pound, making this divisable by ten, and giving the names of pounds, shillings, pence, and doits to the several divisions ; thus,

"One pound is equal to . . . . . . . . . 1,000
One shilling equal to . . . . . . . . . 100
One penny equal to . . . . . . . . . 10
One doit equal to . . . . . . . . . 1
* * * * * * *

"The table of coins proposed in connection with this system of reckoning was as follows.

| | |
|---|---|
| "Crown, of gold . . . . . . . . . | value 1,200 doits. |
| Half crown . . . . . . . . . . | 600 |
| Dollar, of silver . . . . . . . . . | 300 |
| Shilling . . . . . . . . . . | 100 |
| Groat . . . . . . . . . . . | 20 |
| Doit, of copper . . . . . . . . . | 1" |

A still different system of coins upon the same basis, is given in the American State Papers ; this is as follows :

| | | | | | Penn. currency. | Virginia currency. |
|---|---|---|---|---|---|---|
| "Of gold, | weighing 188 qrs. | Expression 1,0000 | Value | £2 12 0 | £2 1 8 |
| " | " 94 " | " .5000 | " | 1 6 0½ | 1 0 10 |
| Of silver, | " 260 " | " .1000 | " | 0 5 2½ | 0 4 2 |
| " | " 104 " | " .400 | " | 0 2 1 | 0 1 8 |
| " | " 52 " | " .200 | " | 0 1 0½ | 0 0 10 |
| " | " 26 " | " .100 | " | 0 0 6¼ | 0 0 5 |
| Of copper, | " 00 " | " .5 | " | 0 0 0 | 0 0 0¼ |
| " | " 00 " | " .4 | " | 0 0 0¼ | 0 0 0 " |

In a statement of the accounts of the United States, we find among the "Expenditures for Contingencies," between January and July, 1783, the following items referring to the preparations for coining ; and there is no reason to doubt that these patterns are the results of those preparations.

| | Dollars. | 90ths. |
|---|---|---|
| "February 8. Jacob Eckfield, for Dies for the Mint of North America, | 5 | 18 |
| March 21. Benjamin Dudley employed in preparing a Mint, . . | 75 | 24 |
| April 17. John Swanwick, for Dies for the Public Mint, . . . | 22 | 42 |
| May 5. A. Dubois, for sinking, casehardening, &c. four Pair of Dies for the Public Mint, . . . . . . . . . . | 72 | |
| June 30. Benjamin Dudley employed in preparing a Mint, . . . | 77 | 60 " |

Some further particulars are furnished by Robert Morris, in his diary :

"1783. April 2ᵈ I sent for Mr Dudley who delivered me a piece of Silver Coin, being the first that has been struck as an American Coin.

"April 16ᵗʰ Sent for Mr Dudley and urged him to produce the Coins to lay before Congress to establish a Mint.

"April 17ᵗʰ Sent for Mr Dudley to urge the preparing of Coins &ᶜ for Establishing a Mint.

"April 22ᵈ Mr Dudley sent in several Pieces of Money as patterns of the intended American Coins."

"July 5th Mr Benjn Dudley * * * * * also informs of a Minting Press being in New York for sale, and urges me to purchase it for the use of the American Mint.

"July 7th Mr Dudley respecting the Minting Press, but I had not time to see him.

"August 19th I sent for Mr Benjamin Dudley, and informed him of my doubts about the establishment of a Mint and desired him to think of some employment in private service, in which I am willing to assist him all in my power. I told him to make out an account for the services he had performed for the public, and submit at the Treasury office for inspection and settlement.

"August 30th Mr Dudley brought the dies for Coining in the American Mint."

The dies for the larger piece, or Mark, differed materially from those for the smaller pieces, or Quint, as they were apparently cut by hand, while the latter were made in the more usual method, by the use of punches. The edges of all the coins were finished alike.

But three specimens from these dies are known, all of which are now in the cabinet of the writer. The ownership of two of them is traced to the Hon. Charles Thomson, the Secretary of the first Congress, in the following letter received with them from Mr. Henry S. Adams, by whom they were purchased from Mr. Haseltine :

"John W. Haseltine, Esqr.                    Philadelphia, May 28, 1872.

"Dear Sir  The history of the two coins which you obtained from me, viz. Nova Constellatio 1783, U. S. 1000, Nova Constellatio, 1783 U. S. 500 is as follows.

"They were the property of the Hon. Charles Thomson, Secretary of the first Congress. At his death his property was left by Will to his nephew, John Thomson, of Newark, State of Delaware. These two coins were found in the desk of the said deceased Charles Thomson, and preserved by his nephew during his life ; at his death they came into the possession of his son Samuel E. Thomson of Newark, Delaware, from whom I received them. So you will perceive that their genuineness cannot be questioned ; as they were never out of the possession of the Thomson family, until I received them.

"Yours respectfully,                    Rathmell Wilson."

The pedigree of the third we are unable to trace ; but it bears upon its reverse evidence of its genuineness, as it is from the same die that impressed the other of the same value — a Quint.

Samuel Curwen, in his diary, under the date of May 15, 1784, gives the following description of what he calls a medal : —

"Mr. Bartlet presented me with a medal struck in Philadelphia ; — in a round compartment stands, 'U.S......5....1783 ;' — round, '*Libertas et Justitia ;*' on the other side, in the centre, an eye surrounded by a glory ; the whole encompassed by *thirteen stars,* — with the legend, '*Nova Constellatio.*'"

This was evidently another of the patterns referred to by Morris, probably that called a "Five." If all the dies mentioned were for coin, and if impressions were taken from all, it remains for some fortunate investigator to discover the pieces still wanting to exhibit the designs of the dies as yet unrepresented in the cabinets of our numismatists. It is not improbable, however, that the item to Swanwick was for the dies in the rough, as that to Dubois so particularly specifies the work he performed. If this supposition be correct, and if the piece described by Curwen was the "Five," as we believe, we have descriptions of seven out of the eight dies mentioned.

Jefferson's modification of Morris's system ultimately prevailed, which probably accounts for the scarcity of the patterns of Morris's proposed coins : owing to the disadvantages under which they were produced, it is probable that very few of these were struck ; perhaps, indeed, and it is not unlikely, but a single specimen of each, to submit to Congress.

## THE IMMUNE COLUMBIAS.

OBVERSE, NO. 1.

Device, — An eye on a plain field, within a glory of thirteen points, the points intersecting a circle of thirteen stars.

Legend, — NOVA CONSTELLATIO

Border, — Serrated.

## OBVERSE NO. 2.

Device, — An eye on a plain field, within a glory of thirteen points, the points intersecting a circle of thirteen stars.

Legend, — NOVA · CONSTELLATIO *

Border, — Serrated.

### REVERSE.

Device, — The goddess of liberty, seated, facing right, with the scales of justice extended in her left hand, the staff, with liberty cap and flag, in her right.

Legend, — IMMUNE COLUMBIA ·

In exergue, — 1785.

Border, — Serrated.   Edges, — Plain, or Milled.   Size, — 17.

Weight, — Gold, 128.8 grains.   Silver, 92 grains.   Copper, 148 grains.

[Plate VII. Nos. 30 and 31, and Figs. 53 and 54.]

The following dies were muled with the Immune Columbia:

### VERMON AUCTORI.

Device, — A head, laureated, facing right, with mailed bust.

Legend, — VERMON AUCTORI

Border, — Serrated.   Edge, — Plain.   Size, — 16.   Weight, — 106 grains.

### CEORCIVS * III · REX.

Device, — A head, laureated, facing right, with mailed bust.

Legend, — CEORCIVS * III · REX.

Borders, — Serrated.   Edge, — Plain.   Size, — 16.   Weight, — 129 grains.

[Fig. 36, p. 186, and Plate VII. No. 32.]

The legend of the last, "CEORCIVS" is peculiar.   The same punches used on the dies for the New Jersey and Vermont coins, as well as on several other pieces, were used on this die.   In none of the dies referred to was a G required, except in another CEORCIVS, (muled with the Liber Natus,) and the GEORGE CLINTON ; and in the last, the same C punch was used, and cut into a G, in the die.   These must have been the latest impressions from the Immune die, as many of them have quite an uneven surface, proving the die to have yielded, and become concave.   The last two are found in copper only.

These pieces are all extremely rare, and as they were struck in gold, silver, and copper, it is presumed that they were intended as patterns for a coin in the metal for which they might be considered the most appropriate.

The only known specimen in gold, is that in the Mint at Philadelphia : its obverse is No. 2.  Mr. W. E. Du Bois, the Assayer of the Mint, sends us the following particulars: "The gold 'Immune' weighs 128.8 grains, near the full weight of the guinea (129.5) and therefore struck on a good piece. The guinea legend, of one of the Georges, can be seen beneath ; a golden 'palimpsest,' we may say.  The edge is milled or notched ; the whole coin very thin, as the guinea was.  The bullion value is $5.05."  Of those in silver we have seen but five, all with obverse No. 1, and with milled edges; and with this obverse, in copper, only one.  Of the copper with obverse No. 2, the number is probably about eight, all with plain edges.

The three dies first described, were probably the work of Thomas Wyon, of Birmingham, England ; and the obverses are both to be found on the copper NOVA CONSTELLATIO series.

Both of the muled pieces bear evidence of the same handiwork, probably that of James F. Atlee, of Machin's Mills.  These are found only in copper, and are as rare as the others in the same metal,— the VERMON AUCTORI more so.

## CONFEDERATIOS AND EXCELSIORS.

An interesting series of pieces is next presented, which are curiously connected, and extensively muled.  The Confederatios form the principal portion of this group, which is illustrated on Plate VII. Nos. 10 to 24 inclusive.

Most of the members of this group, the Confederatios excepted, have not been supposed to bear any relation to each other, or to any other series : but if it is allowable to judge of the origin of these pieces by marked peculiarities common to most of them, proving conclusively the use of the same punches in making the dies, and by the muling of these dies with others, the origin of which is believed to be known, and which exhibit the same marked peculiarities, we may fairly infer that all of these were produced by the same artist, or under his direction.

The group thus formed comprises the Confederatios, which include among their reverses a Libertas et Justitia of 1785, a Washington and the Immunis Columbia, of 1786, and the "New York Excelsiors."  It numbers in all, (excluding the two New Jerseys connected with it on the plate,) thirteen dies, which are struck in fourteen combinations.

It is very probable that some of these dies were designed as patterns for the coins of New Jersey, while others were intended for those of New York;

and some, perhaps, sprung from the more ambitious motive of furnishing a coin for National adoption, the Washington pieces of this group being not inappropriate, in respect to the ideas expressed upon them, for such a purpose.

The dies for these patterns we believe to have been made by Thomas Wyon, of Birmingham, England, and it is supposed that most of the impressions from them were struck there ; but it appears certain that one of the dies was brought to America, and used here, as it forms the reverse of one of the New Jersey coins.

The fact that the date of the obverse with which this reverse die first appeared, is that of the earliest coins of New Jersey, suggests that this die was the pattern adopted for the coin of that State, and was procured, and preserved as a model for other dies until the year following, when it was brought into use, but to a very limited extent, as we find but two specimens bearing its impress.

Implicit reliance as to the common origin of two dies cannot be reposed in a judgment based upon their presence upon the same planchet : but when this evidence is supported by a marked similarity in the workmanship of the dies, it may be taken as conclusive.

Thus in the case of the IMMUNE COLUMBIA · muled with the VERMON AUCTORI and the CEORCIVS*III· REX. ; the first is a finely executed die, probably by Wyon, while both the others are of a very inferior style of workmanship, probably by Atlee : we cannot account for their presence in the same hands in order to effect these combinations, unless the IMMUNE die was procured by Atlee, as it is probable that the shield die was, either by him, or by the undertakers of the coinage for New Jersey.

The same remarks will apply to the workmanship of the obverse of the New Jersey coin which is coupled with the reverse die of the IMMUNIS of 1786. This reverse we attribute to Wyon ; but we are not of the opinion that the New Jersey obverse came from the same hand, neither does it resemble in any respect, any die of the group now under consideration.

The INIMICA TYRANNIS · AMERICA · furnishes an interesting instance of a narrow escape from the loss of an important specimen. It was found in digging up an old drain, in Berlin, Connecticut, in 1861. How many varieties of coins have been thus lost, but not so fortunately recovered, it is impossible to estimate.

OBVERSE NO. 1.

Device, — A cluster of thirteen large stars, upon a central field of size 8, within a glory of twenty-four groups of fine rays.

Legend, — CONFEDERATIO · 1785 ·

Border, — Serrated.

OBVERSE NO. 2.

Device, — A cluster of thirteen small stars upon a central field of size 6, within a glory of sixteen groups of fine rays.

Legend, — CONFEDERATIO · 1785 ·

Border, — Serrated.

REVERSE A.

Device, — An Indian standing beside an altar, with his right foot upon a crown. In his right hand is an arrow, in his left, a bow, and at his back, a quiver full of arrows.

Legend, — INIMICA      TYRANNIS · AMERICA ·

Border, — Serrated. Edge, — Plain. Size, — 18. Weight, — 112 grains.

REVERSE B.

Device, — An Indian standing beside an altar, with his right foot upon a crown. In his right hand is an arrow, in his left, a bow, and at his back, a quiver full of arrows.

Legend, — INIMICA TYRANNIS · AMERICANA ·

Border, — Serrated. Edge, — Plain. Size, — 18. Weight, — 147 to 153 grains.

The two preceding reverses we take to be those designed for the foregoing obverses. Reverse A is found only with the first obverse ; reverse B, with both.

[Plate VII. Nos. 11, 12, and 13, and Figs. 56 and 57.]

REVERSE C.

Device, — U S in monogram, within a wreath of thirty pairs of leaves.

Legend, — LIBERTAS ET JUSTITIA · 1785 ·

Border, — (worn). Edge, — Plain. Size, — 17. Weight, — 103 grains.

[Plate VII. No. 10.]

REVERSE D.

Device, — Head of Washington facing right.

Legend, — GEN . WASHINGTON .

Border and edge, — Plain. Size, — 18½. Weight, — 134 grains.

[Plate VII. No. 14.]

REVERSE E.

Device, — An eagle displayed ; on his breast a shield argent, six pales gules, a chief azure. A bundle of arrows is in his right talon, and in his left, an olive branch with thirteen leaves. About his head are thirteen stars.

Legend, — * E · PLURIBUS    UNUM · 1786

Border and edge, — Plain. Size, — 18½. Weight, — 134 grains.

[Plate VII. No. 15.]

REVERSE F.

Device, — The goddess of liberty seated upon a globe, facing right ; the scales of justice extended in her left hand, the staff of liberty, with cap and flag, supported by her right.

Legend, — IMMUNIS COLUMBIA ·

In exergue, — 1786

Border, — Serrated. Edge, — Plain. Size, — 18. Weight, — 160 grains.

[Plate VII. No. 16, and Figs. 55 and 58.]

REVERSE G.

Device, — A shield argent, six pales gules, a chief azure.

Legend, — * E * PLURIBUS * UNUM *

Border, — Serrated. Edge, — Plain. Size, — 18.

[Plate VII. No. 17, and Fig. 58.]

REVERSE H.

Device, — An eagle displayed, on his breast a shield argent, six pales gules, a chief azure. In his right talon is an olive branch with thirteen leaves, in his left, a bundle of arrows. About his head are thirteen stars.

Legend, — E · PLURIBUS    UNUM *   ✦ 1787 *

Border, — Milled. Edge, — Plain. Size, — 18. Weight, — 114 grains.

The weights are of those with the Confederatio obverses.

[Plate VII. No. 21, and Fig. 59.]

Of these obverses, No. 1, is found with reverses A, B, C, D, E and F, No. 2, with reverses B and H.

No. 1 – F, and 1 – B, (Figs. 55 and 56,) we have not seen, but are assured upon good authority that they exist. The absence of these combinations would not, however, release from the group any one of the dies, as the connection of all is established independently of them. All the other combinations are known to us: they are all of extreme rarity, the only piece which we have seen duplicated being No. 2–B, (Fig. 57.) Upon one specimen, owned by Mr. Appleton, reverse D is muled with E (plate VII. No. 15–a) and in Mr. Stickney's collection is a mule of reverses E and G (plate VII. No. 18) : reverse F is also found, but very rarely, combined with G, (plate VII. No. 17, and Fig. 58) this is known as the New Jersey Immunis. The weights of these are respectively 117, 133, and 132 grains. Of the varieties represented on plate VII. No. 10, is owned by Mr. Hiram S. Shurtleff ; Nos. 12, 13, 15, 17, 21 and 24, by Mr. Lorin G. Parmelee ; Nos. 12, 18, and 24, by Mr. Matthew A. Stickney, and Nos. 12, 14, and 15a, by Mr. Wm. S. Appleton. No. 16, we are informed, was owned by the late Mr. J. G. Morris, of Philadelphia, but its present owner is not known, and a No. 17 and 19, are in the cabinet of the writer. The other pieces are found in most good collections.

Reverse H, is from the die forming the reverse of the pieces called the New York Excelsior cents ; this being muled with a Confederatio, connects them with this group. We shall therefore, in describing these, continue the numbers and letters.

OBVERSE NO. 3.

Device, — The State arms of New York. Upon an oval shield, the sun rising from behind hills, the sea in the foreground ; at the left of the shield stands Liberty, with staff and cap, and at the right, Justice, with sword and scales. Upon a section of a globe above the shield, stands an eagle with outspread wings, facing left.

In exergue, — EXCELSIOR

Border, — Serrated. Edge, — Plain. Size, — 18. Weight, — 141 grains.

[Plate VII. No. 22.]

OBVERSE NO. 4.

Like the last, except that the eagle faces the right.

[Plate VII. No. 23, and Fig. 59.]

REVERSE I.

Device, — A large eagle, displayed ; on his breast a shield argent, six pales gules, a chief azure : a bundle of arrows is in his right talon, an olive branch of thirteen leaves in his left, and thirteen stars about his head.

Legend, — * E * PLURIBUS UNUM 1787 *

Border, — Serrated. Edge, — Plain. Size, — 18½. Weight, 123 grains.

[Plate VII. No. 24.]

In the die last described, the eagle is large, his wings reaching nearly to the legend : his beak is widely open and his crest long and slender. We have seen but two specimens of this variety ; they are in the collections of Messrs. Stickney, of Salem, and Parmelee, of Boston.

Obverse No. 3, is found with reverse H. No. 4, with both H and I. These are all quite rare.

[Plate VII. Nos. 22, 23, and 24.]

In following the clues which we pointed out in our remarks upon the coins of New Jersey, (p. 287,) we have been compelled to change opinions we had formed as to the origin of some pieces, which, although in doubt, had previously been regarded as of English manufacture ; thus as we find upon the Non Vi Virtute Vici (1786,) and the Immunis Columbia (1787,) as well as on the Liber Natus Libertatem Defendo, and the George Clinton (1787,) letters and figures precisely the same with those there described, we consider them also the work of the same artist that cut the dies before referred to. It is probable that they were designed as patterns.

It will be remembered that Maj. Eli Leavenworth stated to the committee that he "Made blank Coppers the Last fall had them Stamped in New york With Various Impressions — Some few of them With an Impression Similar to the Impresion of the Coppers Coined by the Aforementioned Comp.ᵞ—" We have long believed that the Liber Natus Libertatem Defendo, and the George Clinton, were among the pieces struck for Leavenworth, probably at Machin's Mills, and must now class with them the Non Vi Virtute Vici, and the Immunis of 1787 : it is not unlikely that the Connecticuts of similar workmanship were also part of the same enterprise. The Non Vi Virtute Vici may have been a pattern of Atlee's, made before the beginning of operations at Machin's Mills, or, as is not unlikely, while he may have been engaged in making experimental pieces, previous to his association with partners.

## THE NON VI VIRTUTE VICI

### OBVERSE.

Device, — A bust in military costume, facing right.

Legend, — NON VI VIRTUTE VICI

### REVERSE.

Device, — The goddess of liberty seated, facing right, with scales of justice extended in her left hand, the staff, with liberty cap, supported by her right.

Legend, — NEO-EBORACENSIS ·

In exergue, — 1786

Borders, — Serrated. Edge, — Plain. Size, — 19. Weight, — 117 grains. Of this we have seen six or eight specimens.

This piece is sometimes classed among the Washingtons, because of the resemblance of the head to that upon some of the Washington medals.

[Plate VIII. No. 4, and Fig. 60.]

## THE IMMUNIS COLUMBIA OF 1787.

### OBVERSE.

Device, — The goddess of liberty, seated upon a globe, facing right, the scales of justice extended in her left hand, the staff with cap and flag, supported by her right.

Legend, — IMMUNIS COLUMBIA

In exergue, — 1787

### REVERSE.

Device, — An eagle, displayed, holding in his right talon an olive branch of thirteen leaves, and in his left, thirteen arrows.

Legend, — * E * PLURIBUS * UNUM *

Borders, — Serrated. Edge, — Plain. Size, — 16½. Weight, — 135 grains. This piece though not common, is not of extreme rarity.

[Plate VIII. No. 8, and Fig. 61.]

### THE GEORGE * CLINTON *

#### OBVERSE.

Device, — Bust of George Clinton, facing right.

Legend, — GEORGE * CLINTON *

#### REVERSE.

Device, — The State arms of New York. Upon an oval shield, the sun rising from behind hills, the sea in the foreground ; at the left of the shield stands Justice, with sword and scales, and at the right, Liberty, with staff and cap. Upon a section of a globe above the shield, stands an eagle with outspread wings, facing right.

In exergue, — 1787 EXCELSIOR

Borders, — Serrated. Edge, — Plain. Size, — 17. Weight, — 157 grains.

The letter G, on the obverse, was first stamped in with a C punch, and altered in the die, to a G.

We know of not more than five specimens of the George Clinton, the two finest of which are owned by Mr. Appleton, and Mr. Parmelee.

[Plate VIII. No. 5, and Fig. 62.]

### THE LIBER NATUS LIBERTATEM DEFENDO *

#### OBVERSE.

Device, — An Indian, standing, facing left, a tomahawk in his right hand, a bow in his left, and a quiver of arrows at his back.

Legend, — LIBER NATUS LIBERTATEM DEFENDO *

#### REVERSE A.

Device, — The State arms of New York. Upon an oval shield, the sun rising from behind hills, the sea in the foreground; at the left of the shield stands Justice, with sword and scales, and at the right, Liberty, with staff and cap. Upon a section of a globe above the shield, stands an eagle with outspread wings, facing right.

In exergue, — 1787 EXCELSIOR

The same die with the reverse of the George Clinton.

Borders, — Serrated. Edge, — Plain. Size, — 17. Weight, — 127 grains.

REVERSE B.

Device, — An eagle standing upon the section of a globe.

Legend, — NEO-EBORACUS 1787  EXCELSIOR

Border, — Serrated.  Edge, — Plain.  Size, — 17.  Weight, — 153 grains.

The dash in the legend is very light, and does not appear upon the plate.

[Plate VIII. Nos. 6 and 7, and Figs. 63 and 64.]

REVERSE C.

Device, — A bust of George III. facing right.

Legend, — CEORCIVS III REX

The last die much resembles in style of lettering that described on p. 313.

All these pieces are very rare ; that with reverse A is most easily procured; we can call to mind but three with reverse B, but can place only those of Mr. Appleton and Mr. Bushnell.  That with reverse C, is considered unique.

BRASHER'S DOUBLOON.

OBVERSE.

Device, — The sun rising from behind a range of mountains; at their foot, in the foreground is the sea; BRASHER underneath, a beaded circle around.

Legend, — NOVA ❖ EBORACA ❖ COLUMBIA ❖ EXCELSIOR ❖

REVERSE.

Device, — An eagle, displayed, on his breast a shield argent, seven pales gules, a chief azure ; in his right talon is an olive branch, and in his left, a bundle of arrows ; about his head are thirteen stars, and on his right wing is an oval punch-mark with the letters E B.  The device is encircled by a wreath of leaves.

Legend, — UNUM ＊ E ＊ PLURIBUS ❖      1787 ❖

Borders and edge, — Plain.  Size, — 19.  Weight, — 408 grains, gold.

Four of these doubloons have come to our knowledge ; they are owned by Mr. Bushnell, Mr. Parmelee, Mr. Stickney, and the United States Mint at Philadelphia ; the first has the punch-mark on the breast of the eagle.

[Plate IX. No. 24, and Fig. 65.]

# PLATE VIII.

HELIOTYPE PATENT.

# AMERICAN TOKENS.

Under the head of American Tokens we place those pieces struck in America, and also those struck in England by order of American merchants for circulation in this country, for purposes either of change or advertisement, arranging them, in most instances, according to their dates.

## THE GLOVCESTER TOKEN.

Of the history of the earliest of these, called the Gloucester Token, nothing is known. It appears to have been intended as a pattern for a shilling of a private coinage, by Richard Dawson of Gloucester [county ?] Virginia. It is probable that no tokens of this intended issue were actually put in circulation, as we find no specimen in silver. But two specimens of this are known, both struck in brass. A full description cannot be given of it, as both impressions are very imperfect, and together they do not supply the entire legends with certainty. The following description is as nearly complete as can be obtained.

OBVERSE.

Device, — A large mullet, voided at centre and points.

Legend, — RIC[HARD?] DAWSON · ANNO · DOM · 1714 ·

REVERSE.

Device, — A house.

Legend, — GLOVCESTER · CO · [ ? ] VIRGINIA ·

In exergue, — XII

Borders, — Beaded.   Edge, — Plain.   Size, — 14.   Weight, — 62 grains.

[Plate IX. No. 4.]

These pieces are owned by George W. Cram, of Norwalk, Conn., and L. G. Parmelee, of Boston, Mass.

The house upon this token may have been designed to represent a warehouse, but it is of a style corresponding more closely to that of some of the public buildings of olden times. Possibly it may have represented the court house of Gloucester county, and the legend, should any specimen fortunately be discovered to supply the missing portions, may prove to be, GLOVCESTER · CO · HOUSE · VIRGINIA · in accordance with the favorite method, (still continued,) of naming settlements in the Southern States, where many an insignificant hamlet is dignified by the appellation of "Court House," or "County House."

## THE GRANBY OR HIGLEY TOKENS.

The Granby or Higley Tokens are supposed to have been struck by John Higley of Granby, from metal obtained from the mines at "Copper Hill" in that town, then part of Simsbury, in the State of Connecticut. The authorities appear to have taken no notice of his issues of coin, which seem to have continued for about three years, — from 1737 to 1739 inclusive, — specimens being extant bearing these dates, though we know of none dated 1738.

### TYPE NO. 1. OBVERSE.

Device, — A deer, standing, facing left.

Legend, — · ☞ THE · VALVE · OF · THREE · PENCE.

### REVERSE A.

Device, — Three hammers, each bearing a crown.

Legend, — ✩ CONNECTICVT . 1737 . ›

Of this type there are two obverse dies, which are shown on plate VIII. Nos. 17 and 18. The principal differences in these may be seen in the positions of the ground lines on which the deer stands, and of the word "THREE," which in No. 18, rests upon the curved line below: Bolen's is a copy of this variety. Both obverse dies are found with reverse A; we have heard of four specimens of this type, but can place only those of Messrs. Appleton and Parmelee.

### TYPE NO. 2.  OBVERSE.

Device, — A deer, standing, facing left.

Legend, — ☞ VALVE . ME . AS . YOU . PLEASE . ✩

In exergue, — The Roman numerals III within scroll work; a crescent beneath.

### REVERSE B.

Device, — Three hammers, each bearing a crown.

Legend, — · ☞ . I . AM . GOOD . COPPER . ▧ ⁙ ⧆ 1737 ·

Of this reverse there are two dies, shown on plate VIII. Nos. 19 and 20. The principal difference is in the spacing of the characters. One die of the obverse first described is found upon two specimens, with one of these reverse dies, (plate VIII. No. 19,) one of which belongs to C. I. Bushnell, Esq., the other, to the writer. The other die of reverse B is found only with the obverse last described, and upon but one specimen, which is owned by L. G. Parmelee. [Plate VIII. No. 20 and Fig. 66.] We recollect no other instance where both forms of the U are used in the same legend.

### TYPE NO. 3. OBVERSE.

Device, — A deer, standing, facing left, a crescent above.

Legend, — ☞ VALUE . ME . AS . YOU . PLEASE ✩

In exergue, — The Roman numerals III within scroll work; a crescent beneath.

Of this obverse there are three dies, differing principally in the word "PLEASE," and in the positions of the numerals. In one, (plate VIII. No. 23, of which we find no well preserved specimen,) the letters P L are near together, the L low, and leaning to the left: the top of none of the numerals join the ground line. In another, (No. 24,) the letters are evenly spaced, and the tops of the first and third numerals join the line. In the third, (No. 25,) the letters PLEA, are widely spaced, and the tops of the second and third numerals join the line. The two obverse dies first described, are found with one die of reverse B, (plate VIII. Nos. 21 and 22,) of which, perhaps three of each are known: specimens of these varieties are owned by Messrs. Appleton, Brevoort, Parmelee, and by the writer. All three dies are found with the most common reverse, (C) that with a broad axe but no date, (plate VIII. Nos. 23, 24 and 25 and Fig. 67,) and the third, with the reverse of 1739.

### REVERSE C.

Device, — A broad axe.

Legend, — ☞ J . CUT . MY . WAY . THROUGH .

## 1739.

### OBVERSE.

Device, — A deer, standing, facing left, a crescent above.

Legend, — ☞ VALUE . ME . AS . YOU . PLEASE ✩

In exergue, — The Roman numerals III within scroll work; a crescent beneath.

REVERSE D.

Device, — A broad axe.

Legend, — J . CUT . MY . WAY . THROUGH . 1739 .

The borders of all are beaded, or milled, and the edges plain; in size they vary from 18 to 19, and their weight varies from 122 to 170 grains: the heaviest specimen is one of 1739, owned by Mr. Appleton. Two other impressions from these dies are known, one belonging to Mr. Bushnell, the other to the present writer.

Several of these tokens are double struck, apparently by accident, as the second impression is often visible only at one edge; this in one instance causes the first letter of the obverse legend to resemble a W, thus reading "WALUE," which it certainly was never intended to do. Mr. Parmelee has the piece here referred to.

It has been said that these were the work of Dr. Samuel Higley, a physician and blacksmith : as he was not living in 1737, this must be an error.

It is stated by Phelps, in his History of the Copper Mines at Granby, that "this coin is said to have passed for two and six pence, (forty-two cents,) in paper currency it is presumed, though composed chiefly, if not entirely, of copper."

These coppers, owing to the fine quality of the metal of which they were composed, were much in favor as an alloy for gold, and it is probably due in part to this cause that they are now so extremely rare. We are informed of an old goldsmith, aged about seventy-five years, that during his apprenticeship, his master excused himself for not having finished a string of gold beads at the time appointed, as he was unable to find a Higley copper with which to alloy the gold; thus indicating that they were not easily obtained sixty years ago.

We have heard it related of Higley, that being a frequent visitant at the public house, where at that time liquors were a common and unprohibited article of traffic, he was accustomed to pay his "scot" in his own coin, and the coffers of the dram-seller soon became overburdened with this kind of cash, (an experience not at all likely to cause trouble to collectors of the present day,) of the type which proclaims its own value to be equal to what was then the price of a "potation," — three pence.

When complaint was made to Higley, upon his next application for entertainment, which was after a somewhat longer absence than was usual with him, he presented coppers bearing the words, "Value me as you please" "I am good copper".

Whether this "change of base" facilitated the financial designs of the ancient coiner, or not, we have never been informed : sure we are however, that should he be aware of the immense appreciation in the value of his coppers, since that day, it would amply reward him for the insulting conduct of the publican.

We cannot vouch for the truth of this "legend," but we believe those first issued bore the words, "The value of three pence," and, whatever the cause, subsequent issues more modestly requested the public to value them according to their own ideas of propriety, although they did not refrain from afterwards proclaiming their own merits.

We extract the following information relating to the place where the metal for these coppers was obtained, from Phelps's History of the Copper Mines and Newgate Prison at Granby, Conn:—"After 1721, when a division of the mining lands took place among the lessees, each company worked at separate mines, all situated upon copper-hill, and (excepting Higley's) within the compass of less than one mile. * * * At Higley's mine, which lies about a mile and a half south of this, extensive old workings exist, though commenced at a later period than the others. Mr. Edmund Quincy, of Boston, had a company of miners working at this place at the breaking out of the war of the revolution; soon after which the works were abandoned."

At the session of the General Assembly in October, 1773, "an Act was passed 'constituting the subterraneous caverns and buildings in the copper mines in Simsbury, a public gaol and workhouse for the use of the Colony;' to which was given the name of *Newgate Prison*. The prisoners were to be employed in mining. The crimes, which by the Act subjected offenders to confinement and labor in the prison, were burglary, horse stealing, and counterfeiting the public bills or coins, or making instruments or dies therefor."

As a prison, this locality appears to have been no less a failure than it was as a mining speculation. The buildings were three times destroyed by fire, and revolts, violence, and escapes were of frequent occurrence up to the time of its abandonment, in 1827, when it had been in use as a prison for upwards of fifty years.

## CHALMERS' ANNAPOLIS TOKENS.

IN 1783 a goldsmith of Annapolis, Maryland, issued silver tokens as a speculative venture of his own. They consisted of shillings, sixpences and threepences, and are all now very rare, the two smaller pieces especially so. The shilling first to be described is supposed to be unique.

### THE CHALMERS SHILLING.

#### OBVERSE.

Centre, — *Equal to One Shi*   Above is a branch, below, two hands clasped.

Legend, — I. CHALMERS * ANNAPOLIS * 1783 ❀

Border, — Finely milled.

#### REVERSE.

Device, — A chain of twelve rings linked regularly, another ring interlinked with the three lower rings, the middle one supporting a staff with liberty cap, above which is an eye: eleven of the rings enclose each a mullet, and at each side of the liberty cap is a mullet.

Border, — Beaded.  Size, — 13.  See Figure 68.

The centre of the obverse is very indistinct, but faintly shows the inscription, in three lines, "Equal to One Shi"  At the sale of the Mickley collection, (No. 2527,) it brought fifty dollars: as its present owner is unknown to us, no further particulars regarding it can be given.  The following are descriptions of the more common varieties of these tokens.

#### OBVERSE.

Device, — Two hands clasped, within a wreath.

Legend, — I. CHALMERS, ANNAPOLIS. *

#### REVERSE.

Device, — Within a beaded and lined circle is a field divided by a horizontal bar.  On the superior portion of the field is a serpent, and on the inferior, two doves holding in their beaks a branch.

Legend, — ❀ ONE * SHILLING ❀ 1783.

Borders and edge, — Milled.  Size, — 14½.  Weight, — 57 grains.

[Plate IX. Nos. 5 and 6, and Fig. 69.]

There are two dies of this reverse, not greatly differing: in the more common, (plate IX. No. 5,) the bar lies between N and N, and in the rarer variety, (plate IX. No. 6,) between N and I: the character following "ONE" also differs from that of the other, being here a group of eight points.

## THE CHALMERS SIXPENCE.

### OBVERSE.

Device, — A mullet, within a wreath.

Legend, — ⁻I · CHALMERS . ANNAPOLIS .

### REVERSE.

Device, — A cross with hands clasped on the centre, two arms terminating in crescents and two in stars.  In each angle of the cross is a leaf.

Legend, — I. C. SIX PENCE 1783.

Borders and edge, — Milled.  Size, — 11.  Weight, — 28 grains.

We find also two dies of this reverse, differing principally in the size of the letters, but only a single die of either of the obverses.

[Plate IX. Nos. 7 and 8, and Fig. 70.]

## THE CHALMERS THREEPENCE.

### OBVERSE.

Device, — Two hands clasped.

Legend, — I. CHALMERS . ANNAP'S ★

### REVERSE.

Device, — A branch encircled by a wreath.

Legend, —  · THREE ✳ PENCE · 1783 .

Borders and edge, — Milled.  Size, — 8.  Weight, — 12 grains.

[Plate IX. No. 9, and Fig. 71.]

It may be that the edges were not intentionally milled, and that this appearance arises from the manner of cutting the planchets.

We are indebted to Mr. Joseph J. Mickley of Philadelphia, for the following translation from the German, of an account of the Chalmers coinage, by Doctor John David Schöpf, who travelled in this country in 1783 and 1784.

"In the United States, Annapolis has the honor of having furnished the first silver money for small change. A goldsmith of this place coins on his own account, though with the consent of the Government. After the depreciation of the paper money it became customary, and necessary, throughout America, to cut the Spanish dollars in two, four, and more pieces for change. This dividing became soon a profitable business in the hands of expert cutters, who knew how to cut five quarters, or nine and ten eighths, out of a round dollar, so that shortly every one refused to take this kind of money otherwise than by weight, or at discretion. To get over this embarrassment the said goldsmith assists in getting these angular pieces out of circulation, by taking them in exchange, with a considerable advantage to himself, for pieces of his own coinage." The work from which the above account is taken is considered as reliable, but we find no proof that this coinage was issued by consent of the Government, and perhaps the author intended no more than to convey the idea that the Government tacitly allowed it.

## THE BALTIMORE TOWN THREEPENCE.

A curious little silver token, of which we have no history, is supposed to have made its appearance in Baltimore, Maryland, in 1790. It is apparently a private issue, by Standish Barry, and represents the value of three pence. A curious feature in this token is the preciseness of its date — July 4 90·; Whether any especial celebration of the anniversary of American independence was observed in 1790, is unknown to us: if there was, this silver token was probably issued in commemoration of that event.

OBVERSE.

Device, — A head, facing left, within a plain circle.
Legend, — BALTIMORE . TOWN · JULY · 4 · 90 ·

REVERSE.
Inscription, — THREE PENCE within a plain circle.
Legend, — STANDISH · BARRY . entwined in a beaded network.
Borders and edge, — Milled.   Size, — 9.   Weight, — 13 grains.
[Plate X. No. 23, and Fig. 72.]

## THE NOVA CONSTELLATIO COPPERS.

This is a series of tokens struck in England for use in America. It comprises several varieties, specimens of most of which are often found, though some of them are very rare.

But little is known of the history of these tokens. The most that can be learned in relation to them is contained in the following extract from Bushnell's Numismatic Notes in manuscript:—" The Nova Constellatios were made in Birmingham, in England, and the dies were cut by Wyon, of that place. Over forty tons were issued from one die alone, and many more from another. They were manufactured by order of a gentleman of New York, who is believed to have been Gouverneur Morris."

We shall give a description of only one of these pieces for each year, 1783, 1785, and 1786, leaving the dies to be described in the tables of varieties.

### 1783.

#### OBVERSE.

Device, — An eye on a plain field, within a glory of thirteen points, the points intersecting a circle of thirteen stars.

Legend. — NOVA · CONSTELLATIO ✴

#### REVERSE.

Device, — U · S in large Roman capitals, encircled by a wreath.

Legend, — LIBERTAS ✴ JUSTITIA · 1783 ·

Borders, — Usually milled, sometimes serrated.  Edges, — Plain.

Size, — 16½ to 18.  Weight, — 117, to 138 grains.

[Plate VII. Nos. 25, 26, and 27, and Figs. 73 and 74.]

### 1785.

#### OBVERSE.

Device, — An eye on a plain field, within a glory of thirteen points, the points intersecting a circle of thirteen stars.

Legend, — NOVA CONSTELLATIO

1783.  OBVERSES.

| Legend. | Long Rays of Glory | Two Rays point | No. | With Reverse. | Rarity. |
|---|---|---|---|---|---|
| NOVA · CONSTELLATIO ✿ | Heavy, points fine. | Just left of N, and right of A. | 1. | A. | R3. |
| NOVA · CONSTELLATIO ✿ | Light, points fine. | Just left of N, and at right foot of A. | 2. | B. | C. |
| NOVA · CONSTELATIO ✧ | Heavy, cuneiform. | At N, and just to right of A. | 3. | C. | R. |

1785.

| Legend. | Long Rays of Glory | Two Rays point | No. | With Reverse. | Rarity. |
|---|---|---|---|---|---|
| NOVA · CONSTELATIO ✧ | Same die with last. | At N, and just to right of A. | 1. | B. | R3. |
| NOVA  CONSTELLATIO | Points blunt. | At left foot of N, and right foot of A. | 2. | A. | R4. |
| NOVA  CONSTELLATIO | Points fine. | At left foot of N, and right foot of A. | 3. | B. | C. |
| NOVA  CONSTELLATIO | Points blunt. | Just left of N, and at right foot of A. | 4. | { C. D. | R5. R6. |
| NOVA  CONSTELLATIO | Points blunt. | At O, and at left foot of A. | 5. | E. | R4. |

1786.

| Legend. | Long Rays of Glory | Two Rays point | No. | With Reverse. | Rarity. |
|---|---|---|---|---|---|
| NOVA  CONSTELLATIO | Points blunt. | Just left of N, and right of A. | 1. | A. | R5. |

REVERSE.

Device, — U S in script monogram, encircled by a wreath.

Legend, — LIBERTAS ET JUSTITIA · 1785 ·

Borders, — Usually milled, but on some serrated.   Edges, — Plain.

Size, — 16½ to 18.   Weight, — From 108, to 127 grains.

[Plate VII. Nos. 28, and 29, and Figs. 75, 76 and 77.]

One die, which is used in both No. 3, of 1783, and No. 1, of 1785, (see Figs. 74 and 75,) has the legend spelled NOVA · CONSTELATIO ✧

## 1783.  REVERSES.

| Legend and Date. | Wreath of | U S | No. | With Obverse. | Rarity. |
|---|---|---|---|---|---|
| LIBERTAS ✦ JUSTITIA  · 1783 · | 24 pairs. | Large. | A. | 1. | R3. |
| LIBERTAS ✦ JUSTITIA  · 1783 · | 24 pairs. | Smaller. | B. | 2. | C. |
| LIBERTAS ✧ JUSTITIA  · 1783 · | 23 pairs. | Same as last. | C. | 3. | R. |

## 1785.

| Legend and Date. | Wreath of | Leaves of Wreath | No. | With Obverse. | Rarity. |
|---|---|---|---|---|---|
| LIBERTAS  ET  JUSTITIA   1785 | 30 pairs. | All separate at points. | A. | 2. | R4. |
| LIBERTAS  ET  JUSTITIA  · 1785 · | 30 pairs. | Four to six joined by a break. | B. | { 1. 3. | R3. C. |
| LIBERTAS  ET  JUSTITIA  · 1785 · | 30 pairs. | Two over U join. | C. | 4. | R5. |
| LIBERTAS  ET  JUSTITIA  · 1785 · | 29 pairs. | Two over U and three over S, join. | D. | 4. | R6. |
| LIBERTAS  ET  JUSTITIA  · 1785 · | 26 pairs. | Five at left of U, close. | E. | 5. | R4. |

## 1786.

| Legend and Date. | Wreath of | Leaves of Wreath | No. | With Obverse. | Rarity. |
|---|---|---|---|---|---|
| LIBERTAS  ET  JUSTITIA  · 1786 · | 23 pairs. | All separate. | A. | 1. | R5. |

A marked difference exists between the LIBERTAS ET JUSTITIA die found with the Confederatio obverse, (Plate VII. No. 10,) and these dies. In the former the curve of the U coils around the body of the S, which we have seen in no other die. This piece is now in the cabinet of the writer.

### 1786.  OBVERSE.

Device, — An eye on a plain field, within a glory of thirteen points, the points intersecting a circle of thirteen stars.

Legend, — NOVA CONSTELLATIO

### REVERSE.

Device, — U · S in large Roman capitals, encircled by a wreath.

Legend, — LIBERTAS ET JUSTITIA · 1786 ·

Borders, — Milled.  Edge, — Plain.  Weight, — 123 grains.

[Plate VII. No. 33.]

But two impressions from the dies of 1786 have come to our knowledge: one of these is owned by Mr. Appleton, the other by Mr. Bushnell.


## THE BAR CENT, OR U S A COPPER.

This is another piece about which little is known. Bushnell says of it, "This copper was coined in Birmingham, in England, in the year 1785, and was probably the work of Wyon. The obverse U S A is the same as the device of the old Continental Buttons, having been copied from them. This novel

piece was put into circulation in the city of New York, and made its first
appearance there in the month of November, of the above mentioned year.
On account of its light weight, as well as its device, it was not received with
favor, and was not extensively circulated."

OBVERSE.

Device, — U S A in large Roman monogram, on a plain field.

REVERSE.

Device, — Thirteen horizontal bars.

Borders, — Serrated.   Edge, — Plain.   Size, — 15½.   Weight, — 85 grains.

[Plate IX. No. 25, and Fig. 78.]

There were two pairs of dies for this token: that given on the plate is
the rarest variety.  A piece somewhat smaller than that last described, was
gotten up a few years since, and has by some been believed to be designed
for a half cent of the same type: we have, however, good reason to suppose
that it is of quite recent manufacture; it is represented by Fig. 79.

THE MOTT TOKENS.

A copper token, issued in the year 1789, by the Messrs. Mott, of the city
of New York, dealers in watches, clocks and jewelry, is generally conceded
to have been the first tradesman's token issued in America; it was manufactured in England, and is of the following description:

OBVERSE.

Device, — An old style of clock, with an eagle perched upon its top.

Legend, — MOTTS, N. Y. IMPORTERS, DEALERS, MANUFACTURERS, OF GOLD
& SILVER WARES.

REVERSE.

Device, — An eagle with wings expanded, facing left. In his right talon he holds an olive branch of seven leaves and four berries, aud in his left, three arrows. On his breast is a shield argent, six pales gules, a chief azure: above his head, the date, — 1789

Legend, — CHRONOMETERS, CLOCKS, WATCHES, JEWELRY, SILVERWARE,

Borders, — Milled. Edge, — Usually plain, but on some, milled.

Size, — 17. Weight, — 108 to 171 grains.

[Plate IX. No. 17, and Fig. 80.]

From the upper left hand corner of the clock, a heavy break is seen upon most impressions, though some are found without the break.

Bushnell, in his "Early New York Tokens," states regarding the firm that issued this token, "The firm of Motts was composed of William and John Mott, and their place of business was at No. 240 Water street, a location at which they continued for a number of years, and which was at the time a most fashionable business part of the city."

## TALBOT, ALLUM & LEE.

The next enterprise of the same character with that of the Motts' token, appears to have been the tokens issued by Talbot, Allum and Lee, merchants in the India trade, also of New York city. This firm put into circulation a large quantity of coppers comprising several varieties, and of the dates of 1794 and 1795. These also were of English manufacture.

1794. OBVERSE.

Device, — A ship sailing toward the right. Above the ship, NEW YORK

Legend, — TALBOT ALLUM & LEE. ONE CENT

REVERSE.

Device, — The goddess of liberty standing beside a bale of merchandise, supporting the liberty staff with cap, with her right hand, her left resting upon a rudder.

Legend, — LIBERTY & COMMERCE.

In exergue, — 1794

Edge, — PAYABLE AT THE STORE OF  —:—  —:—  —:—  —:—

Borders, — Milled.

### 1795. OBVERSE.

Device, — A ship under full sail toward the right.

Legend, — AT THE STORE OF TALBOT ALLUM & LEE NEW YORK. *

### REVERSE.

Device, — The goddess of liberty standing beside a bale of merchandise, supporting the liberty staff with cap, with her right hand, her left resting upon a rudder.

Legend, — LIBERTY & COMMERCE

In exergue, — 1795

Edge, — WE PROMISE TO PAY THE BEARER ONE CENT ·

Borders, — Milled.   Size, — 18.   Weight, — 153 grains.

[Plate IX. Nos. 18, 19 and 20, and Figs. 81 and 82.]

Of these tokens for 1794, there were four obverse, and two reverse dies. The rarest variety may be distinguished by the large & in both legends, and the absence of the words New York, from the reverse. One variety has a large & in the legend on the obverse only, and the bowsprit of the ship points just forward of the last E. Both the other obverses have a small & in the legend: in one the bowsprit points at the last E, and in the other more nearly at the period. The reverse found with the last three, has a small &.

Of 1795 we have found but one pair of dies.

Bushnell, in his "Early New York Tokens," says of these: — "The dies of the two latter tokens [those of 1794 and 1795,] were cut at Birmingham, in England, and the variety bearing the date of 1795 is by far the rarest, fewer of that die having been struck."

"The names of the individuals composing the firm of Talbot, Allum & Lee were William Talbot, William Allum and James Lee, and their place of business was at No. 241 Pearl street. They were extensively engaged in the India trade —at that time, as well as now, a very lucrative branch of mercantile pursuit."

"The firm of Talbot, Allum & Lee was formed in 1794, and continued until the year 1796, when Mr. Lee retired from the concern. The remaining partners carried on the business, under the name of Talbot & Allum, until the year 1798, when the firm was dissolved."

Six "mules" with reverses of these tokens are described in Bushnell's work, but as they bear no evidence of being intended for America, we omit them.

## ANGLO-AMERICAN TOKENS.

The tokens thus classed, are supposed to have originated in England, as speculative ventures of some of the engravers of that country, who looked upon America as a favorable market for the products of their enterprise.

### THE CAROLINA AND NEW ENGLAND TOKENS.

The pieces first to be described in this chapter are two which were perhaps not intended for circulation as currency, but are introduced here, as no more appropriate place offers for their insertion. These were issued in 1694, probably in London, and are now known as the Carolina, and the New England, Elephant tokens.

They were struck upon copper planchets of very unequal weight, the New England token in Mr. Appleton's collection weighing 236 grains, while the only other known, Mr. Parmelee's, (which is somewhat worn,) is much thinner, and weighs but 133 grains ; the Carolinas are more regular in this respect, their weight ranging from 130 to 162 grains.

It is not known whether these tokens were intended to serve as coins, or were struck only as medals, to increase or perpetuate the interest in the American Plantation; the latter seems much the more reasonable view of their purpose.

Snelling, writing in 1769, makes no mention of the New England tokens, but says of the Carolina, " We cannot ourselves conceive the intent of striking it, or for what purpose it was intended ; however, we think it has no claim to be admitted as a piece of money, but rather is of the ticket kind, and we are of the same opinion in regard to another piece, which is certainly of the same class with this; be it what it will, it is what we call the London Halfpenny, one side of both, that is the Elephant, we apprehend was struck from the same dye, which is still remaining in the Tower, and appears to be the work of Rotiers ; on the other side instead of GOD PRESERVE CAROLINA AND THE LORDS PROPRIETORS 1694, as upon this; there is upon that, round the city arms, GOD PRESERVE LONDON; we have heard two or three opinions concerning the intent of uttering this piece, as that it was for the London Workhouse; also, that its inscription alludes to the plague, and was struck whilst it raged in London; and we have likewise heard it was intended to be made current at Tangier in Africa, but never took place."

## CAROLINA.

### OBVERSE.

Device, — An elephant standing, facing the left.

### REVERSE.

Inscription, — GOD : PRESERVE : CAROLINA : AND THE : LORDS : PROPRIE-
TERS · 1694

Borders, — Milled.   Edge, — Plain.   Size, — 18½.   Weight, — 143 grains.
[Plate IX. No. 1.]

The above is the rarest of the Carolina tokens ; the two specimens we
know of are in the collections already named as containing the New England
Elephant tokens.   In the more common variety of this token, the obverse
closely resembles the last, but the elephant's tusks nearly touch the milling,
and his right legs are more smoothly cut.   A more marked difference is found
on the reverse, where, though the same die is used, the inscription has been
altered to GOD : PRESERVE : CAROLINA : AND THE : LORDS : PROPRIETORS · 1694
the last E is still to be seen under the O.   These were struck on copper
planchets of from 17 to 18½, weighing from 130 to 162 grains.   It is said that
they were struck also in brass, but we have seen none in that composition.
[Plate IX. No. 2.]

## NEW ENGLAND.

### OBVERSE.

Device, — An elephant standing, facing the left.

### REVERSE.

Inscription, — GOD : PRESERVE : NEW : ENGLAND : 1694 :

Borders, — Milled.   Edge, — Plain.   Size, — 18½.   Weight, — 133 and 236
grains.

The obverses of the New England Elephant token and of the Carolina
last described, are from the same die with that of the London tokens.
[Plate IX. No. 3.]

## THE VIRGINIA HALFPENNIES.

Under the heading of "Coins for the Colonies," Ruding describes the
pieces we call Virginia half-pennies.   There is so much uncertainty as to
whether, or not, these were authorized coins, that we place them in this chapter,
considering it altogether likely that they were an unauthorized issue.   It seems
probable that had there been a coin legally struck and issued for Virginia,

# PLATE IX.

COPIES

HELIOTYPE PATENT.

Jefferson would have been cognizant of the fact; but he writes in 1782, (Jefferson's Works, Vol. 1, p. 136,) "In Virginia, coppers have never been in use." From this it would appear that whatever their origin, and notwithstanding the considerable number of dies represented by them, their use in that State must have been very limited.

#### OBVERSE.

Device, — A bust of George III. laureated, facing right.

Legend, — GEORGIVS · III · REX ·

#### REVERSE.

Device, — An ornamental and crowned shield, emblazoned quarterly : — 1, England impaling Scotland; 2, France; 3, Ireland; 4, the Electoral dominions.

Legend, — VIRGI  NIA ·      The shield divides the legend.

Date, — 17  73 ·         The crown divides the date.

Border, — Milled.   Edge, — Plain.   Size, — 15½ to 17.   Weight, 110 to 123 grains.

[Plate IX. Nos. 10, 11 and 12, and Fig. 83.]

In one variety of this, the legend of the obverse is found without the point after GEORGIVS. Several dies are found of both varieties, and we should judge that about twenty pairs of dies must have been used upon them: the differences, however, are so slight, as to render it useless to attempt a table of dies, as they consist principally of different spacings in the legends, and slight differences in the position of the points.

The largest piece is quite rare, and is sometimes, we think without good reason, called a penny. It weighs 131 grains.

The pieces described above are struck in copper; but specimens of a similar design, dated 1774, exist in silver.

These may have been issued as patterns for a silver coin for this State. They are extremely rare, but three specimens being known to us : these are owned by Messrs. Henry S. Adams, Chas. I. Bushnell, and L. G. Parmelee.

OBVERSE.

Device, — A bust of George III. laureated, facing right.

Legend, — GEORGIVS · III     DEI · GRATIA ·

REVERSE.

Device, — An ornamental and crowned shield, emblazoned quarterly: — 1, England impaling Scotland; 2, France; 3, Ireland; 4, the Electoral dominions.

Legend, — VIRGI  NIA ·     The shield divides the legend.

Date, — 17  74     The crown divides the date.

Borders and edge, — Plain.   Size, — 16.   Weight, — 84 grains.

[Plate IX. No. 13, and Fig. 84.]

## THE NOVA EBORACS.

The tokens next to be described are commonly known as New York coppers.  They were not issued by authority of that State, but have probably derived their name only from the legends and shield upon them.

OBVERSE NO. 1.

Device, — A bust facing right, laureated, and mailed.

Legend, — ♣ NOVA ♣     EBORAC ♣

REVERSE A.

Device, — The goddess of liberty seated upon a globe, facing right, with the New York shield beside her, holding in her left hand an olive branch, and supporting the staff of liberty with her right.

Legend, — ♣ VIRT     ET · LIB ♣

In exergue, — 1787

Of these tokens there are four varieties, all having the New York shield on the reverse beside the goddess, who, on all that follow, faces the left : that described above is the most common: the legends of the others are given below, in the order of their rarity.

NO. 2.

Obverse No. 1, — ❖ NOVA ❖ EBORAC ❖ (The same die with the first.)

Reverse B, — ❖ VIRT . ET LIB ❖ Liberty faces the left.

NO. 3.

Obverse No. 2, — ❖ ❖ NOVA EBORAC ❖

Reverse C, — ❖ VIRT . ET LIB. ❖ Liberty faces the left.

NO. 4.

Obverse No. 3, — ∗ NOVA ∗ EBORAC ∗

Reverse D, — ❖ VIRT . ET . LIB ❖ Liberty faces the left.

The four varieties are represented on Plate VIII. by Nos. 10, 11, 9 and 12, respectively: the first three by Figs. 85, 86, and 87.

The borders of Nos. 1 and 2, are usually found plain, but sometimes show a slight milling; the reverse of No. 3, and both sides of No. 4, have milled borders. The edges of all are plain. The weight of Nos. 1 and 2 is about 112 grains, No. 3, 120 grains, and No. 4, from 120 to 142 grains.

Of No. 4 we have seen but three specimens, owned by Messrs. Appleton, Bushnell, and Parmelee.

All of these tokens are supposed to be of English origin, but we have no authentic information regarding their issue ; they probably were a private speculation of some English merchant.

## THE GEORGIVS TRIUMPHO.

### OBVERSE.

Device, — A head, laureated, facing right.

Legend, — GEORGIVS · TRIUMPHO ·

### REVERSE.

Device, — The goddess of liberty facing left, behind a framework of thirteen bars with a fleur-de-lis at each corner. In her right hand she holds an olive branch, and her left supports the staff of liberty.

Legend, — VOCE POPOLI

In exergue, — 1783

Borders, — Milled. Edge, — Plain. Size, — 18. Weight, — 117 grains.

[Plate IX. No. 14.]

Great differences of opinion have been occasioned by this token, most collectors considering it as having reference to George Washington, as the Triumphant George, and some have, on that account, placed it among the Washington pieces, while others insist that George the Third was the person referred to, and in proof of their position they adduce the resemblance of the head to that upon some of his coins. It is true that the head bears a strong resemblance to that upon some coins of George III., but it is not probable that this resemblance was intentional. It is more likely that the die was cut by an artist, who, having a hub of the head of King George, used it in making this die, regardless of the want of correspondence between the head and the legends: or it may have been left with an ambiguous character, in order to obtain for it a more extensive circulation.

We know of no occasion at the date of this token, to claim any triumph for King George, but a triumph may justly be claimed for Washington, in the successful termination of the Revolutionary war, by which the independence of the United States was secured.

We consequently consider the Georgivs Triumpho a token intended to commemorate this result, and designed for circulation in this country.

## THE AUCTORI PLEBIS.

The Auctori Plebis is a token of English origin, which from its resemblance to the coins of Connecticut, is by many classed with the issues of that State. We are in ignorance as to its maker, but as the piece is represented in a book of engravings of English tokens, entitled "The Virtuoso's Companion," published in England in 1796, we consider the place of its origin satisfactorily established, and it was probably struck for use in America.

OBVERSE.

Device, — A bust, facing left, laureated and draped.

Legend, — • AUCTORI: • • PLEBIS: •

REVERSE.

Device, — A female seated, her left arm resting upon an anchor, her right hand upon a globe; at her feet is a lion.

Legend, — ○ INDEP:  ET · LIBER ○

In exergue, — 1787

Borders, — Milled.  Edge, — Plain.  Size, — 17.  Weight, — 116 grains.

[Plate IX. No. 15.]

The device of this reverse is found upon three other English tokens.

We have seen two pieces with the head facing right, bearing the same legend with the obverse of this, but as their reverses bear a harp, and the legend and date, HISPANIOLA · 1736 we of course do not class them, as some have done, with tokens intended for America. This mention of them is inserted, as we have heard of two impressions from the obverse dies, the reverses of which have been obliterated, probably by attrition, and which from the legend have been considered rare varieties of the piece just described.

## THE KENTUCKY TOKENS.

The first of these, which is known as the Kentucky "Triangle," or "Pyramid token," is also represented in "The Virtuoso's Companion," and is supposed to have originated in Lancaster, England. The name of this State is applied to it from the circumstance that the initial K appears upon the star at the top of the pyramid.

### OBVERSE.

Device, — A hand holding a scroll inscribed, OUR CAUSE IS JUST

Legend, — UNANIMITY IS THE STRENGTH OF SOCIETY +

### REVERSE.

Device, — A radiant triangular pyramid of fifteen stars united by rings, each star bearing the initial of a State, that of Kentucky at the top.

Legend, — E PLURIBUS UNUM *

Borders, — Milled. Size, — 18 to 19½. Weight, — 155 to 192 grains.

[Plate IX. No. 26.]

The edges of some of these are plain, others are lettered, "PAYABLE IN LANCASTER LONDON OR BRISTOL" and we have heard of different lettering, but can of our own knowledge give no other than the above. The Clay Catalogue, Nos. 298 and 299, designates different edges, — viz: "Payable *at* Bedworth, etc." and "engrailed."

## THE MYDDELTON TOKENS.

These two most beautifully executed tokens relating to Kentucky, were from the establishment of Boulton and Watt, near Birmingham, England. Of their history we know nothing, and can therefore give only a description of them.

### OBVERSE.

Device, — Hope, beside an anchor, presenting two children to a female whose right hand is extended to receive them, while her left supports the staff with liberty cap: before her is an olive branch and wreath, and behind her a cornucopia.

Legend, — BRITISH SETTLEMENT KENTUCKY.

In exergue, — 1796.

### REVERSE A.

Device, — Britannia, with head bowed, her spear inverted; a bundle of fasces, the scales of justice, and a broken sword at her feet, while before her the cap of liberty rises from the earth.

Legend, — PAYABLE BY P · P · P · MYDDELTON.

Borders, — Milled.  Edge, — Plain.  Size, — 18.  Weight, — silver, 175 grains; copper, 177 grains

### REVERSE B.

Inscription, — COPPER COMPANY OF UPPER CANADA within a plain circle.

Legend, — ONE HALF PENNY ·

Borders and edge as preceding.  Size, — 18.  Weight, — 166 grains.

[Plate IX. Nos. 22 and 23, and Figs. 88 and 89.]

The reverse last described is that which properly belongs upon another token, apparently intended for Canadian circulation, the obverse of which has for a device, — a figure of Neptune reclining against a water conduit; legend, — FERTILITATEM DIVITIAS QUE CIRCUMFERREMUS · and the date, — 1794  It is a very rare token, and we have seen it only in Mr. Parmelee's collection.

The obverse die is found with reverse A, both in silver and copper, but with reverse B, in copper only.  They are all very rare.

From the legends of the reverses it would appear that these were designed to serve as a token currency; but what value those in silver were intended to represent, is uncertain.  In beauty of design and execution, these tokens are unsurpassed by any piece issued for American circulation.

## THE FRANKLIN PRESS.

This may, perhaps, be more properly ranked as an English token, but as it has so evident an allusion to an eminent American, and has so long been accorded a place in collections of American coins, we shall here describe it.

OBVERSE.

Device, — A printing press, of old style.

Legend, — SIC ORITUR DOCTRINA SURGETQUE LIBERTAS ·

In exergue, — 1794

REVERSE.

The inscription, — PAYABLE AT THE FRANKLIN PRESS LONDON ·

Borders, — Milled.  Edge, — Plain.  Size, — 17½.  Weight, — 120 grains.

[Plate IX. No. 16.]


## TOKENS OF UNCERTAIN DATE, ORIGIN AND PURPOSE.

The tokens next to be considered are two about which nothing can be written, not founded entirely upon conjecture.  Both appear to be of Dutch origin, are quite rude in their design and workmanship, and were probably struck late in the seventeenth, or early in the eighteenth century.

### THE NEW YORKE TOKEN.

The first of these is called the New Yorke Token, and has until quite recently been considered unique, but within three years, three new specimens have been discovered ; two of these are owned in Boston, Mr. Appleton having one in lead, and Mr. Parmelee one in brass.  The other specimen is in lead, but its present ownership is unknown to us.  The only specimen in lead accessible to us is so much corroded as to furnish no satisfactory basis for ascertaining its original weight.

OBVERSE.

Device, — An eagle displayed, resting upon a branch with a leaf at each end.

Legend, — ✱ NEW · YORKE · IN · AMERICA ⁙ ⁓

In the centre a group of five palm trees ; at the right stands a female (Venus?) with flowing robes.  At the left is a Cupid with his bow in his left hand, his right extended toward the female, to whom he is running.

Borders, — Milled.    Edge, — Plain.    Size, — 13.    Weight, — brass,  55 grains.

[Plate VIII. No. 14, and Fig. 90.]

The only account we have found of this piece, is in the Historical Magazine for 1861, from which we make the following extracts: "The style in which it is executed is more Dutch than English; and as the only existing specimen has been preserved in Holland, it is probable that the dies were originally cut there. * * * There is no date upon the token; but it evidently belongs to the period between 1664, when the name NEW YORKE was first adopted, and 1710, after which it was rarely spelled with an *e*.  It should probably be referred to the latter part of this period, for the currency of the colonies was then in a very unsettled state, and the amount in circulation was not adequate to the wants of trade.  In Massachusetts, early in 1701, 'not a few individuals stamped pieces of brass and tin, and palmed them on community at a penny each.' * * * It is not unlikely then, that at some time between 1700 and 1706, there was in New York, as we know there was in other American colonies, a deficiency of cash, to supply which and perhaps somewhat to regulate the unsettled currency, the dies of our coin were prepared in Holland (possibly at the instance of some Dutch inhabitant of New York), but were used to strike nothing more offensive to the sovereign's right of coining than this harmless trial-piece in soft metal.

"Many conjectures may be offered as to why the half-penny was not brought into circulation after the dies were ready.  The wants of the market may have been relieved by an importation like that proposed in Massachusetts, or the proclamation of Queen Anne may have made the New Yorkers afraid of trespassing on the royal prerogative.

"Without venturing to claim that this coin contains the earliest display of the American eagle, we think it unquestionably deserves to be considered THE EARLIEST NEW YORK TOKEN."

In regard to the *e* in Yorke, we would call attention to the fact that it is thus used upon the reverses of the Continental Currency pieces of 1776.

### THE "NEW ENGLAND STIVER."

The second token is known as the "New England Stiver," a small copper piece presumed to have originated in Holland, to furnish small change for some of the Dutch merchants of that day in New Amsterdam.

#### OBVERSE.

Two Lions, the upper facing the left, the lower inverted, and facing the right. At the left of the lions $\frac{i}{v}$ and at the right $\frac{s}{c}$ A circle of dashes surrounds this device, forming a deeply milled border.

#### REVERSE.

In four lines, the inscription, NEW ENGLA ND M The Ns all reversed, the M inverted.

Edge, — Plain. Size, 12. Weight, 37 grains.

[Plate VIII. No. 13.]

The letters on the obverse have been supposed to signify, "1 Stiver Von Connecticut": we think it more probable that they were the initials of some Dutch trader, as I. S. Van C. It probably was not very extensively circulated, only one specimen, that in the collection of L. G. Parmelee, being now known. We have no clue to the date of its issue, except in the style of its workmanship, which we should judge to be that of the seventeenth century.

### ENGRAVED PATTERN.

The engraved piece mentioned on page 304, having inadvertently been omitted from a more appropriate place, will next be described. Whether this was intended as a pattern, is impossible to decide, as it has neither legend or date: but if so, it was probably designed as a pattern for some coin of the United Colonies.

#### OBVERSE.

An Eagle resting upon a crown, with five stars at his left, and five at his right.

#### REVERSE.

A shield bearing a cross and a fleur-de-lis impaled by dimidiation. At the left of the shield are five stars, three above, and five at the right.

Borders, — Beaded. Edge, — Plain. Weight, — 87 grains. Size. — 15.

[Plate VII. No. 9.]

Having omitted from this work some pieces usually considered as belonging to America, our reasons for so doing may be expected.

The "Colonies Francoises," of 1721, 1722 and 1767 were omitted, as they are supposed to have been coined with no especial reference to America, but, as the inscriptions indicate, for the French Colonies in general.

The tin piece of James II, has been, we think without reason, considered as intended for Florida: we have not described it, as we see no ground for such an opinion: another "Florida piece," with the legend JVAN ESTEVAN DE PENA FLORIDA has recently been decided to be a Spanish medal, and the legend, the name of an individual.

The "Dansk Americ" pieces we have not included, as they are obviously outside of our contemplated limits.

Among the Tokens, we have included some which have but a very slight claim to recognition among American numismatists, while we have excluded others which have been supposed to have reference to this country, being satisfied that no such reference was intended.

It may be also, that some Washington medals we have not described will here be sought ; but we are conscious of including in our list some which should not be considered as coins, rather than of omitting any that can properly be so described, as we have intended, under the general head of Washington pieces, to include all which can reasonably be supposed to have served the purposes of coins, and also the medals produced by muling one die of a coin with one of a medal. And in this department, as well as in that of the tokens, we have intended to describe all such pieces as were struck in the eighteenth century, for use in this country.

# THE WASHINGTON PIECES.

———◦—◦———

The early Washington pieces form a most interesting department in the collection of coins, and, if the interest be extended to the collection of all pieces graced with the likeness, or bearing the name of Washington, it forms also a very extensive field for research : our intention is, however, to describe only those struck in the eighteenth century, which may have been intended as patterns, or used as coins.

Tradition furnishes a reasonable excuse for the refusal of any pattern bearing the head of the first President, if indeed they were actually presented as patterns as has been supposed, in the repugnance of Washington to the adoption of a style of coinage so closely resembling that of a monarchy, and in his personal feeling against appearing so conspicuously upon the coins of the country.

The pieces first to be described are not considered as intended for patterns, and are supposed to have been issued by private persons for speculative purposes, but nothing is actually known in regard to their origin or intention.

## WASHINGTON & INDEPENDENCE.

The first of the pieces bearing this legend is usually known, from the legend upon the reverse, as the Unity States Cent.

### OBVERSE NO. 1.

Device,— A large bust of Washington, laureated and draped, facing left.
Legend, — WASHINGTON & INDEPENDENCE  1783

REVERSE A.

Device, — Two olive branches forming a wreath, which encloses the words ONE CENT

Legend, — UNITY STATES OF AMERICA

Under the bow which fastens the ends of the branches is the fraction $\frac{1}{100}$

Borders, — Milled.   Edge, — Plain.   Size, — 17½.   Weight, — 114 grains.

[Fig. 91.]

The piece just described is supposed to be of French origin; the error in the legend upon the reverse may be owing to an ignorance of the English language in the designer of it.   These planchets are usually quite rough.

OBVERSE NO. 2.

Device, — A large bust of Washington, laureated and draped, facing left.

Legend, — WASHINGTON & INDEPENDENCE · 1783 ·

REVERSE B.

Device, — A female figure facing left, seated upon a rock: in her right hand she holds an olive branch, and her left supports the staff of liberty, with cap.

Legend, — UNITED STATES

Borders, — Beaded.   Edge, — Usually plain.   Size, — 17½.   Weight, — 128 grains.

Of the above obverse we find impressions from two dies, one of which has a button on the drapery, and of the reverse, also two dies, one of which resembles the reverse next to be described, having the letters T. W. I.     E. S. in the exergue.   These are found both in copper and brass, and sometimes with edges engrailed.

OBVERSE NO. 3.

Device, — A small bust of Washington, in military dress, laureated, facing left, with hair tied in a queue.

Legend, — WASHINGTON & INDEPENDENCE · 1783 ·

Device,—A female figure, facing left, seated upon a rock: in her right hand she holds an olive branch, and her left supports the staff of liberty, with cap.

Legend,— UNITED STATES

In exergue,— T. W. I.    E. S.

Borders,—Beaded.  Edge,—Plain.  Size,—17½.  Weight,—120 grains.

Of the obverse last described we find two dies, and of the reverse, three.

[Plate X. Nos. 1 and 2.]

## THE DOUBLE HEAD WASHINGTON CENT.

### OBVERSE.

Device, — A bust of Washington, in military dress, laureated, facing left, with hair tied in a queue.

Legend, — WASHINGTON

### REVERSE.

Device, — A bust of Washington, in military dress, laureated, facing left, with hair tied in a queue.

Legend, — ONE CENT

Borders, — Beaded.  Edge, — Plain.  Size, — 17.  Weight, — 124 grains.

On each side is an elongated star under the bust.

[Fig. 92.]

None of the Washington pieces yet described are very rare, except one die of the Washington & Independence with the smaller head.  In that die the face has less prominent features, and the expression is very different from the others.  A modern restrike of one of those with the larger head is frequently found, and appears in silver, brass, and copper: its edge is engrailed.

## WASHINGTON · THE · GREAT · D · G .

### OBVERSE.

Device, — A very ugly head, facing right.

Legend, — WASHINGTON · THE · GREAT · D · G ·

Border, — Serrated.

### REVERSE.

Device, — A chain of thirteen rings, each bearing the name of a State, and on the central space, — 84

Border and edge, — Plain.  Size, — 16½.  Weight, — 102 grains.

[Plate X. No. 3.]

The 84, may be the last two figures of the date, and it is possible that the figures 17 may have been above them, as the two now visible occupy only the lower half of the central field.

But two specimens of this, the ugliest of all pieces bearing the name of Washington, are known : neither of them is sufficiently well preserved to give the full particulars of the reverse. One is in the cabinet of Mr. Appleton, the other, in the Mint at Philadelphia.

A new, and probably unique Washington piece, of 1785 or 1786, (judging from the dies with which its obverse is combined, for it has no date,) has recently come into the possession of the writer : its obverse die is identical with reverse D, and its reverse, with reverse G, of the Confederatios (p. 317) : it was probably designed as a pattern. A line drawn on plate VII. between those two reverses will represent this piece, and may be numbered 14a.

### THE WASHINGTON TRIAL-PIECES.

The most important of these was procured from the widow of Hancock, a die cutter of Birmingham, England, and is an impression of the unfinished obverse die of one of the Washington cents of 1791—which of them, it is difficult to determine, so much alike are the busts upon both. It has a head of Washington, facing left, but there are no buttons on the coat, the epaulettes and the queue are unfinished, and there is no legend.

It is struck on a copper planchet apparently prepared for a Macclesfield halfpenny, as it has upon the edge, PAYABLE AT MACCLESFIELD LIVERPOOL OR CONGLETON · × · as on the edge of those tokens. Its reverse is plain, showing only the roughness of the anvil upon which it was supported in striking. Its size is 19, and its weight, 194 grains.

This interesting trial piece was procured by the writer at the sale of the Clay collection: the catalogue says of it, " It was obtained of the widow of Hancock, the medallist, of Birmingham, and proves the origin of the Washington Cents, beyond a doubt."

Two other trial-pieces, struck only upon one side, are described in the catalogue of W. E. Woodward's sale of April, 1863, (Nos. 2270 and 2271.) One of these is of the large eagle reverse, A, soon to be described, with the edge lettered, BERSHAM BRADLEY WILLEY SNEDSHILL; the other is from reverse B, with edge, PAYABLE AT THE WAREHOUSE OF THOS . & ALEX . HUTCHINSON. We know not where these now are, but they were imported in a package of English tokens which afterwards came into the possession of Mr. Jeremiah Colburn, and were sold with his collection.

## THE WASHINGTON CENTS OF 1791.

The Washington cents of 1791, and the Washington tokens having a ship on the reverse, are all from the two obverse dies which have a bust identical with that upon the trial piece first described, and must have sprung from the same origin. A considerable number of the large and small eagle cents, and of the token of 1793, must have been issued, as so many specimens of all of them are now known. The other token, that struck with the reverse die of the Liverpool halfpenny, is much more rare than either of the others, only four specimens of this having come to our knowledge.

As the obverses of these pieces are from the same dies, we shall describe them all in this section, although one of the reverses has the date of 1793.

### OBVERSE NO. 1.

Device, — A bust of Washington in military costume, facing left, with hair tied in a queue.

Legend, — WASHINGTON PRESIDENT 1791

### REVERSE A.

Device, — A large eagle, displayed; on his breast a shield argent, six pales gules. In his beak is a scroll inscribed UNUM E PLURIBUS In his right talon he grasps an olive branch of thirteen leaves, and in his left, a bundle of thirteen arrows. Above his head are the words ONE CENT

Edge, — UNITED STATES OF AMERICA · × ·

Borders, — Milled. Size, — 19. Weight, — 194 grains.

[Plate X. No. 5, and Fig. 93.]

### REVERSE B.

Device, — A ship sailing to the right, a break like a liberty cap on the top of the mainmast.

Legend, — LIVERPOOL HALFPENNY

Edge, — PAYABLE IN ANGLESEY LONDON OR LIVERPOOL · × ·

Border, — Milled. Size, — 18. Weight, — 138 grains.

[Plate X. No. 6, and Fig. 95.]

Obverse No. 1, with reverse A, known as the Large Eagle Cent, is the most common of the Washington cents of date subsequent to 1783. This obverse is found with reverse B, on four specimens, of which but three are now known to us; these are in the cabinets of Messrs. Appleton, Parmelee, and that of the writer, and are called the Washington Liverpool Halfpenny.

### OBVERSE NO. 2.

Device, — A bust of Washington, in military costume, facing left, with hair tied in a queue.

Legend, — WASHINGTON PRESIDENT .

### REVERSE C.

Device, — A small eagle, displayed, with upraised wings : on his breast a shield argent, six pales gules, a chief azure. In his right talon he holds an olive branch with eight leaves and three berries, and in his left, six arrows. About his head are eight mullets, above the stars a cloud reaching from wing to wing, and above the cloud the words ONE CENT  Under the eagle is the date 1791

Edge, — UNITED STATES OF AMERICA · × ·

Borders, — Milled.  Size, — 19.  Weight, — 190 grains.

[Plate X. No. 7, and Fig. 94.]

### REVERSE D.

Device, — A ship sailing toward the right.

Legend, — HALFPENNY

On a panel under the ship, the date, 1793

Edge, — PAYABLE IN ANGLESEY LONDON OR LIVERPOOL · × ·

Border, — Milled.  Size, — 19.  Weight, — 163 grains.

[Plate X. No. 14, and Fig. 96.]

Obverse No. 2 is found with reverses C and D.  That with reverse C is called the Small Eagle Cent, and is rather more rare than that with the large eagle reverse (A); while the token with reverse D, the Ship Halfpenny, is of about the same degree of rarity with that last named.

A curious and probably unique medal with reverse A, is in the collection of Mr. James E. Root, of Boston: its obverse is a bust of George III.

# PLATE X.

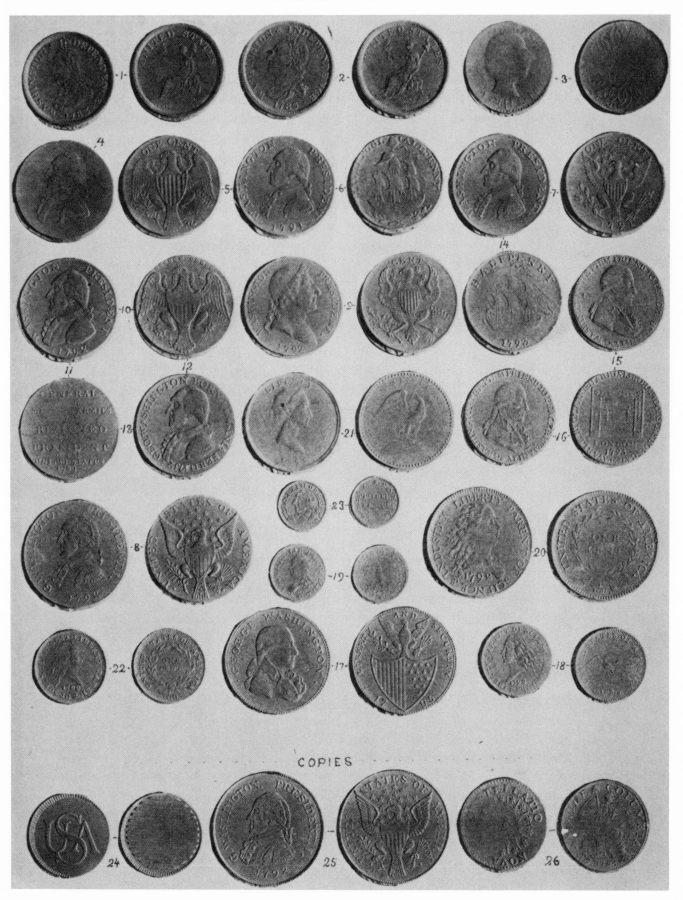

COPIES

HELIOTYPE PATENT.

facing left, with the legend GEORGIVS III  DEI GRATIA  It is struck in copper, size 20, and has a beaded border and engrailed edge: this obverse is illustrated in the Clay catalogue, at the upper left of the second plate.

## THE WASHINGTON PIECES OF 1792.

### OBVERSE NO. 1.

Device, — An undraped bust of Washington, facing right, the hair confined by a fillet which is tied in a bow with long ends.

Legend, — WASHINGTON PRESIDENT . 1792

### REVERSE A.

Device, — A small eagle, displayed, with upraised wings, on his breast a shield argent, six pales gules.  In his right talon he holds an olive branch of fourteen leaves and six berries; in his left, thirteen arrows; about his head are six mullets, and above it is the word, CENT

Edge, — Plain, or lettered UNITED STATES OF AMERICA · × · × · × ·

Borders, — Milled.  Size, — 19.  Weight, — 198 grains.

Of obverse No. 1, reverse A, usually known as the " Naked bust," but sometimes called the "Roman head," Washington, we have heard of six or eight specimens, three of which are in the same cabinets with the three having the Liverpool Halfpenny reverses; another is owned by Mr. Bushnell.

[Plate X. No. 9, and Fig. 97.]

### OBVERSE NO. 2.

Device, — A bust of Washington, in military costume, facing left, with hair tied in a queue.

Legend, — WASHINGTON PRESIDENT  1792

### REVERSE B.

Device, — A large eagle, displayed; on his breast a shield argent, six pales gules, a chief azure.  In his beak he holds a scroll inscribed UNUM E PLURIBUS  In his right talon is an olive branch with thirteen leaves and one

berry, and in his left, thirteen arrows.  Over his head is a single voided star,
above which twelve similar stars form a curve reaching from wing to wing.

Edge, — Plain, or lettered UNITED STATES OF AMERICA • ×

Borders, — Milled.    Size, — 19.    Weight, — Copper, 180; silver, 187;
gold, 252 grains.

[Plate X. No. 10, and Fig. 98.]

Obverse No. 2, with reverse B, is also an extremely rare variety, but the
number known we cannot specify: the only specimens we have seen in copper,
are found in the cabinets of Messrs. Appleton, Bushnell, Cohen, Parmelee, and
the writer.  We have seen about the same number of impressions from these
dies in silver, as in copper, of which specimens are owned by Messrs. Appleton,
Bushnell, Parmelee, and  A. S. Jenks of Philadelphia.  One impression in
gold is known, owned by Col. M. I. Cohen, of Baltimore.

The fact that impressions are found in gold, silver, and copper, gives us
reason to believe that they were intended as patterns for a coin in that
metal for which they might be considered most appropriate.

OBVERSE NO. 3.

Device, — A  bust of Washington, in military costume, facing left, with
hair tied in a queue.

Legend, — GEO. WASHINGTON BORN VIRGINIA FEB. 11. 1732 ·

REVERSE C.

Inscription, — ⁘ GENERAL OF THE AMERICAN ARMIES 1775  RESIGNED
1783  PRESIDENT OF THE UNITED STATES 1789  ——

The foregoing inscription is in ten lines, with the star above, and dash
below.

Borders, — Milled.    Edge, — Plain.    Size, — 19.    Weight, — 178 grains.

Obverses 2 and 3 with reverse C, (Plate X, Nos. 11 and 13,) were evidently designed for medals, but are so connected by muling, with the dies of
the Washington piece last preceding, that they properly follow that in our
descriptions.  Neither of these is very rare, though the first is by no means
common.

These are usually struck in copper and with plain edge; but Mr. Appleton
has one with obverse No. 2 and reverse C, with edge lettered UNITED STATES
OF AMERICA  These are usually struck in copper.  Impressions are found in
silver of obverse No. 3 and reverse C, but they are extremely rare.  A single
impression is known of obverse 3 combined with reverse B.  It is in copper,

and is found in the collection of Col. Cohen. Its size is 20, weight, 173 grains. It is illustrated on plate X. by No. 12.

Of reverse C, we find two dies, in one of which the words OF THE are directly over the letters ICAN, while in the other they are over the letters CAN A

### OBVERSE NO. 4.

Device, — A bust of Washington, in military costume, facing left, with hair tied in a queue.

Legend, — G . WASHINGTON . PRESIDENT . I .   1792

### REVERSE D.

Device, — An eagle, displayed, on his breast a shield argent, six pales gules, a chief azure; in his right talon is an olive branch of thirteen leaves, and in his left, thirteen arrows.

Legend, — UNITED STATES OF AMERICA

[Fig. 99.]

This die does not appear to have been approved, as it was defaced by a chisel mark; probably a mark of condemnation by its maker.

### REVERSE E.

Device, — An eagle, displayed, with upraised wings; on his breast is a shield argent, seven pales gules, a chief azure; in his right talon is an olive branch of fifteen leaves, and in his left, a bunch of six arrows. About his head are fifteen mullets.

Legend, — . UNITED STATES OF AMERICA .

Borders, — Milled. Edge, — Plain. Size, — 20 to 22. Weight, — copper, 220 to 273 grains; silver, 193 to 234 grains.

[Plate X. No. 8, and Fig. 100.]

The only impression of obverse No. 4 with reverse D, is in silver, and as its present owner is unknown we can give no further particulars in regard to it. The same obverse is found with reverse E in silver and copper; and though both are very rare, in silver it is much more so than in copper.

We have seen one specimen in copper, now owned by Jules Fonrobert, of Berlin, Prussia, the edge of which is ornamented in circles and squares.

It is believed that the three dies last described were the work of Peter Getz, of Lancaster, Pa: a self-taught, but skillful mechanic and engraver. He was of German descent, the original name being Götz, and was born near Lancaster about the year 1768. He is said to have constructed the first fire-engine ever made in the United States, and there is, (or was,) at the Mint in Philadelphia, a pair of scales made by him, for weighing gold, which were highly valued for their great accuracy. He belonged to the Masonic order, and made the jewels for the Lodge in Lancaster, (of which he was a craftsman,) which are still preserved by the Lodge. It is related of him, that upon one occasion an English engineer visited Lancaster to survey some lands, and had the misfortune to break one of his most valuable instruments, which at that time it was impossible to replace in this country. While lamenting that he would be obliged to lay idle for many months, until he could replace it from England, he was told that Getz could repair the damage. The Englishman laughed incredulously, but concluded to let the "Dutchman" try his hand at the job. It was done to the perfect satisfaction, and agreeable surprise of the engineer, who, (as the story goes,) rewarded Peter's skill by "pouring his hands full of gold." Getz died from the effect of an accident, at the early age of thirty-six years.

The foregoing information was obtained from a letter to Mr. J. J. Mickley, from J. Lawrence Getz, of Reading, Pennsylvania, a grandson of Peter Getz.

We shall here describe a piece we have not been fortunate enough to see, referring to Snowden's "Washington and National Medals," plate XI, No. 43, for an illustration of the one specimen then known.

OBVERSE.

Device, — A bust of Washington in military costume, facing left, with hair tied in a queue.

Legend, — WASHINGTON PRESIDENT 1796

Border, — A beaded circle surrounded by a glory.

REVERSE.

Probably identical with reverse D last described, but altered at the border, the rays of the glory upon the obverse apparently extending over and turned in on the reverse, as if to convey the idea of glory shed upon the United States, by Washington. Its diameter is represented as nearly 24.

A search in the Mint cabinet for this piece being unsuccessful, we are obliged to rely upon the illustration referred to above, for our description.

### THE "GRATE" TOKEN.

##### OBVERSE.

Device, — A bust of Washington, in military costume, facing right, with hair tied in a queue.

Legend — G. WASHINGTON. THE FIRM FRIEND TO PEACE & HUMANITY ❀

##### REVERSE.

Device, — An open fire-place, with a grate.

Legend, — PAYABLE BY CLARK & HARRIS . 13 . WORMWOOD S$^T$ BISHOPSGATE. In exergue, — LONDON 1795

Borders, — Milled.  Edge, — Engrailed.  Size, — 17½.  Weight, — 144 grains.  [Plate X. Nos. 15 and 16.]

Of the obverse of this token we have found two dies, (in one of which the space between the two ends of the legend is much larger than in the other,) and of the reverse, but one. The planchets upon which they were struck were usually so small as to leave but very little space outside of the legend, in consequence of which the impression of the borders is very seldom to be seen. The legend on the reverse proves this to be an English token.

### LIBERTY AND SECURITY.

Whether the three pieces bearing the above motto as a legend, were intended to be circulated as penny and halfpenny tokens, or were designed merely as medals, is uncertain; but whatever their intent, we consider them not out of place in this chapter.

OBVERSE NO. 1.

Device, — A bust of Washington, in military costume, facing the left, with hair tied in a queue.

Legend, — GEORGE WASHINGTON.

### REVERSE A.

Device, — A shield, argent, seven pales gules, impaling argent, fifteen mullets, five, four, three, two, one.

Above the shield an eagle, displayed, grasping in his right talon an olive branch of nine leaves, and two berries, (or stems,) and in his left, three arrows.

Legend, — LIBERTY AND SECURITY

Edge, — AN ASYLUM FOR THE OPPRESS'D OF ALL NATIONS ∷ ⁝ ∷

Border, — A plain, double ring.  Size, — 21.  Weight, — 300 grains.

[Fig. 101.]

### OBVERSE NO. 2.

Device, — A bust of Washington, in military costume, facing the right, with hair tied in a queue.

Legend, — · GEORGE WASHINGTON ·

### REVERSE B.

Device, — A shield, paly of sixteen argent and gules, impaling argent, fifteen mullets, five, four, three, two, one.

Above the shield an eagle, displayed, grasping in his right talon an olive branch of eight leaves and four berries, and in his left, six arrows.

Legend, — . LIBERTY AND SECURITY .  The date 17  95 is divided by the shield.

Edge, — AN ASYLUM FOR THE OPPRESS'D OF ALL NATIONS ∷ ⁝ ∷

Border, — A plain circle, with milling around it.

Size, — 20½.  Weight, — 310 grains.

[Plate X. No. 17, and Fig. 102.]

### OBVERSE NO. 3.

Device, — A bust of Washington, in military costume, facing the right, with hair tied in a queue.

Legend, — GEORGE WASHINGTON

Border, — A plain circle, with milling around it.

REVERSE.

Device, — A shield, argent, seven pales gules, impaling azure, fifteen mullets, five, four, three, two, one.

Above the shield, an eagle, displayed, grasping in his right talon an olive branch of eight leaves and three berries, and in his left, six arrows.

Legend, — LIBERTY AND SECURITY  The date 17  95 is divided by the shield.

Edge, — Usually — PAYABLE AT LONDON LIVERPOOL OR BRISTOL · (See below.)

Border, — Milled.  Size, — 18,  Weight, — 139 grains.

[Fig. 103.]

A specimen in the collection of Mr. Appleton, has the edge lettered, BIRMINGHAM REDRUTH & SWANSEA and one in the writer's collection has the edge, AN ASYLUM FOR THE OPPRESS'D OF ALL NATIONS · × · We have seen no duplicate of the last, and the other is very rarely found.

The large piece, without date, (that first described,) cannot be called rare; but the other, having a date, is extremely so, only two specimens being known.  Mr. Appleton is the owner of one, and the writer, of the other.  The smaller piece, though much more rare than that without date, is not of extreme rarity.

A mule of the reverse last described, with a die of the · IRISH HALFPENNY · is sometimes found, but is considered of very little importance.  It is probable that all of these were of English origin, and the two more common varieties are illustrated in "The Virtuoso's Companion."

The pales upon the shields have all been described as "gules," — they being evidently so intended, — although not all so engraved, several of them having the pales plain instead of composed of fine perpendicular lines, which properly represent gules, or red.

## NORTH WALES.

Device, — A bust of Washington, in military costume, facing left, with hair tied in a queue.

Legend, — GEORGEIVS WASHINGTON

### REVERSE.

Device, — A harp, crowned.

Legend, — NORTH WALES

Borders, — Plain.    Edge, — Usually plain, (see below.)    Size, — 17. Weight, — 111 grains.

[Fig. 104.]

The more common variety of reverse has at each side of the base of the harp, a star of six.   Another reverse, known on only a single specimen, has two smaller stars at each side of the harp, and a fleur de lis on top of the crown, in place of the star found in the more common die: one other specimen, on a thick planchet weighing 143 grains, has on the edge, PAYABLE IN LANCASTER LONDON OR BRISTOL  Both of these are owned by the writer. Most of the North Wales pieces are in a brassy composition, but the two last mentioned are in copper.

A curious Washington piece is owned by Mr. Stickney, which he believes to have been intended as a pattern for a dollar, and the work of Jacob Perkins.  It is struck as an incused shell, and, (we speak from recollection only, it being now impossible for us to obtain an exact description of it,) has in the centre, a bust of Washington, facing left, and closely resembling those upon the small funeral medals of Washington, the dies of which were cut by Perkins.  Around the field surrounding the bust, is fine engine-work of intricate pattern, which covers the rest of the surface of the planchet, the size of which is about 21.

It is not improbable that Jacob Perkins made this, and for a pattern ; but it seems scarcely possible that it could have been intended to issue it upon so thin a planchet, this being hardly one fifth of the thickness of a dollar.

Mr. Stickney refers to this piece, in a communication to the Journal of Numismatics, (Vol. III. No. 5,) as, " a Silver pattern for the first coinage of United States Dollars, beautifully executed by Jacob Perkins of New-buryport, and obtained by me from his nephew, which last was not accepted by the government, because it bore the medallion head of Washington, a too aristocratic design for a period governed by French influence."

# THE EARLY PATTERNS OF THE UNITED STATES MINT.

On Wednesday, July 6, 1785, Congress took into consideration the report of a grand committee on the subject of a money unit, and resolved:

"That the money unit of the United States of America, be one dollar.

"That the smallest coin be of copper, of which 200 shall pass for one dollar.

"That the several pieces shall increase in a decimal ratio."

On the 8th of August, 1786, further action was taken, the names and weights of coins specified, and the board of treasury ordered to report a draft of an ordinance for the establishment of a Mint.

The draft was therefore presented, and on the 16th of October, 1786, an "ordinance for the establishment of the Mint of the United States of America, and for regulating the value and alloy of coins," was passed.

The form of the ordinance, and the action relating thereto, may be found in the Journals of Congress between the dates specified above.

The Mint was not in readiness for coining until late in the year 1792, when a small amount of silver was coined, and in 1793, the regular coinage of copper was commenced.

It appears from a paragraph in the Newburyport Herald, of July 18, 1792, that the opinion then prevailed that Jacob Perkins was to be the superintendent of the United States Mint. We know that he was employed in making dies for the Mint of Massachusetts, and it may be that he was concerned in the preparation of some of the patterns described in this chapter; but of this we have no proof. The following is the article alluded to: —

"Several newspapers of the past and present week have prematurely mentioned Mr. PERKINS of this town being sent for to Philadelphia, for the purpose of superintending the coinage there. Mr. PERKINS' abilities in that line are fully adequate to such an appointment, as the specimens he has exhibited in that line amply testify. — Instead of the former method of performing the business he has invented a new machine, which cuts the metal into such circular pieces as are wanted, and gives the impression at the same time — its motion is accelerated by a balance wheel, and more than one third of the time and labor thereby saved. He has also constructed another machine, of his own invention, for milling or lettering the edge, by which a boy can mill sixty each minute."

Washington, in his fourth annual address, November 6, 1792, says: — "In execution of the authority given by the legislature, measures have been taken for engaging some artists from abroad to aid in the establishment of our Mint. Others have been employed at home. Provisions have been made for the requisite buildings, and these are now putting into proper condition for the purposes of the establishment. There has been a small beginning in the coinage of half dismes, the want of small coins in circulation calling the first attention to them."

The half dismes here referred to were issued before the Mint was completely organized ; and tradition reports, that, owing to the scarcity of silver, Washington caused some of his own private plate to be melted to supply the deficiency, and that it was from that supply that these patterns were coined. It is said that the value of about one hundred dollars was coined into half dismes.

## THE DISME.

OBVERSE.

Device, — A head with flowing hair, facing the left.

Legend, — LIBERTY PARENT OF SCIENCE & INDUS.

Date, — 1792 under the head.

REVERSE.

Device, — A small eagle, flying toward the left.

Legend, — UNITED STATES OF AMERICA

Beneath the eagle, the word DISME

Borders, — Milled. Edge, — Milled. Size, — 14. Weight, — Silver, 40 to 57 ; copper, 58 grains.

[Plate X. No. 18, and Fig. 105.]

### THE HALF DISME.

#### OBVERSE.

Device, — A head with flowing hair, facing the left.

Legend, — LIB · PAR · OF SCIENCE & INDUSTRY ·

Date, — 1792 under the head.

#### REVERSE.

Device, — A small eagle, flying toward the left.

Legend, — UNI · STATES OF AMERICA

Beneath the eagle HALF DISME

Borders and edge, — Milled.  Size, — 10½.  Weight, — 21 grains.

[Plate X. No. 19, and Fig. 106.]

### THE LARGE PATTERN CENT.

#### OBVERSE.

Device, — A head with flowing hair, facing the right.

Legend, — LIBERTY PARENT OF SCIENCE & INDUSTRY *

Date, — 1792 under the head.

The name BIRCH is on the shoulder of the bust.

#### REVERSE.

Device, — A wreath formed of two laurel branches tied by a ribbon below, enclosing a plain circle, within which are the words ONE CENT

Legend, — UNITED STATES OF AMERICA.

Under the bow in the ribbon is the fraction $\frac{1}{100}$

Edge, — Differing in each of the three specimens we have examined, one being plain ; one reading, TO BE ESTEEMED * BE USEFUL * while on the third, the first mullet is omitted, and at each side of the one remaining, is a small leaf.

Borders, — Milled.  Size, — 21.  Weight, — 217 to 286 grains.

[Plate X. No. 20, and Fig. 107.]

It has been said that the head upon this pattern, as well as those upon the disme and half disme, was intended for a likeness of Martha Washington.

## THE EAGLE PATTERN CENT.

### OBVERSE.

Device, — A head facing the right, the hair confined by a band and knot.

Legend, — LIBERTY.

Date, — 1792 under the head.

Border, — A slightly raised rim.

### REVERSE.

Device, — An eagle with upraised wings, standing upon the section of a globe, facing the right.

Legend, — UNITED STATES OF AMERICA.

Border, — A circle of 87 small stars.

Edge, — Milled. Size, — 18. Weight, — 175½ grains.

[Plate X. No. 21, and Fig. 108.]

## THE SMALL PATTERN CENT.

### OBVERSE.

Device, — A head with flowing hair, facing right.

Legend, — LIBERTY PARENT OF SCIENCE & INDUST:

Date, — 1792 under the head.

### REVERSE.

Device, — A wreath formed of two olive branches, tied below, enclosing the words ONE CENT

Legend, — UNITED STATES OF AMERICA

Under the bow in the ribbon is the fraction $\frac{1}{100}$

Borders and edge, — Milled. Size, — 14. Weight, — 65 grains.

[Plate X. No. 22, and Fig. 109.]

The " Silver Centre Cent " is from the same dies with that last described, but it has a small plug of silver inserted in the centre, as indicated by its name. The weight of one in Mr. Parmelee's collection is 59 grains.

The Eagle pattern cent is in the cabinet of the Mint at Philadelphia, and we have heard of but one other. The collections of Messrs. Appleton and Parmelee supply specimens of all the other pieces, all of which are extremely rare.

# SOUTH CAROLINA.

The following, relating to the proposed coinage for South Carolina, was received from Mr. Bushnell, but not in season to be given in its proper place ; we therefore present it in an additional chapter.

"In the year 1785, Mr. Charles Borrell made a proposal to the Legislature of South Carolina to coin 20,000 pounds in silver, and 10,000 pounds in copper for the use of the State, the petitioner agreeing to receive and accept the paper money of the State in exchange. This proposal being accepted, an ordinance was passed on the twenty-second day of March, 1786, granting the privilege to Mr. Borrell, and the Governor of the State was authorized to designate the device and legend for the coins. Mr. Borrell thereupon proceeded to Europe, and made a contract in Switzerland for the amount, and in a letter to Mr. Lewis Newhouse, of Charleston, dated July 21, 1786, he says, 'Be pleased to assure His Excellency, the Governor, that when you receive this, there will be on the way to Charleston, from One Thousand to Fifteen Hundred Louis d'ors, to be presented to the Treasury, and, after examination, a certificate, in due form, must be obtained, approving and declaring these monies to be just and conformable to the ordinance, and that in consequence, the State will receive the surplus.'

"A Louis d'or is 24 livres, equal to about \$4.444. * * * * * This is all I have been able to learn respecting this coinage, the authority for which is given below.

"'An Ordinance respecting Silver and Copper Coins.

"'Whereas a proposal has been made by Mr. Charles Borrell, for coining a quantity of silver and copper money, and paying the same into the Treasury in exchange for the paper medium of this State ;

"'Be it therefore ordained by the Honorable, the Senate and the House of Representatives, now met and sitting in General Assembly, and by authority of the same, That if the said Charles Borrell shall, within Fifteen Months next ensuing, import into this State, copper coin, to the amount in value, of ten thousand pounds sterling, one moiety, in pieces of the value of one penny each, and the other moiety in pieces of the value of half a penny each, according to the standard of British half-pence, and silver coin to the value of Twenty Thousand pounds sterling, that is to say, Three fourths in pieces to the value of one shilling each, and the other fourth in pieces of the value of six pence each, which pieces shall be of the same weight as English shillings and sixpences, and contain an alloy proportioned to that of the French Crowns, and shall be impressed, stamped, and made with the figures, words, and devices, and in such way and manner as the Governor shall direct, and shall be respectively called a penny, a half-penny, a shilling and a sixpence ; and if the said coin shall on being assayed in the presence of the Treasurer be found to be of the value above mentioned, according to the standard aforesaid, which the Governor, on a certificate thereof from the Treasurers shall cause to be notified by proclamation, the Treasurers shall and may receive the same in exchange for the paper medium of this State and give the said medium in exchange for the said coin; and that the said coin shall be the lawful money of this State, receivable and issuable as such, at the value aforesaid, in all payments at and from the Treasury, and a tender in law according to the rates and value aforesaid, in satisfaction of all private contracts, and that the counterfeiting, clipping, defacing, or debasing the same, shall be felony, without the benefit of clergy.

"'In the Senate House, the twenty-second day of March, in the year of our Lord, One Thousand Seven Hundred and Eighty Six.

"'John Lloyd,
"'President of the Senate.
"'John Fauchereaud,
"'Speaker of the House of Representatives.'"

We will conclude with a paragraph already printed on page 144 : —

"Charleston, S. C. Sept. 29.

"Government has received information that Mr. Borel has compleated his contract of coinage for this State, in Switzerland, and may be soon expected here by the way of London. The stipulation was for 30,000 l. in silver and copper, to be exchanged for the paper medium."

# CONCLUSION.

Since the tables of varieties were printed, several new dies, and some new combinations, have been discovered, which will here be described: an omission, also, may here be supplied, by copying Ruding's description of one of Lord Baltimore's coins. He says: "One shilling has the arms of his wife, a cross botony, quartered on the reverse. This coin, which is supposed to be unique, was in the possession of the late Sir Frederick Morton Eden, bart." We have no knowledge of this piece, having never found any other mention of it.

Mr. H. S. Adams has an impression upon copper, from Pine Tree Shilling dies, and having an engraving made of it, kindly presents an opportunity for its illustration. We copy the comments upon the piece, made in the report of the Boston Numismatic Society, at one of the meetings of which it was exhibited. "It is struck over a half-penny of George I., part of the date of which is discernable, and is supposed to be 1723. The piece has been in various collections during the past twelve or fifteen years, and from the owners it is traced back to the discoverer, Charles Payson, Esq., of Portland, Me. Mr. Payson purchased it of an old gentleman, who said it had been in his possession some forty years. Mr. P.'s *theory* about it is, that the die was rejected on account of the last N being left out of the word England; this accounts for not finding Shillings of the same die. * * * * * That this die should have been in existence at the period of the issue of the half-pennies of George I., is not strange, as a die of a similar character, used here one hundred and twenty years ago, was shown at the November meeting."

Mr. Stickney also has a similar piece in copper, but from different dies, and of larger size.

As connected with the Continental Currency pieces, (by having for a reverse a similar obverse die,) though evidently a medal, may be described a piece, specimens of which are owned by Mr. Appleton, and Mr. Henry W. Holland, of Cambridge.

#### OBVERSE.

Device, — At the left, and in the back ground, the city of London. In the centre, an Indian with bow and quiver, standing before Britannia, who is seated at the right; between them is a dove, flying toward the Indian.

Legend, — FELICITAS : BRITANNIA : ET : AMERICA

In exergue, — MDCCLXXXIII SEP.ᵗ 4

#### REVERSE.

Device, — Thirteen rings interlinked, each bearing the name of a State.

Legend, — AMERICAN·: CONGRESS *

Centre, — WE ARE ONE

A glory fills the space between the legend and the thirteen rings.

Border, — Beaded.  Edge, — Ornamented with leaf-work.  Size, — 25.

Descriptions of two pieces were purposely omitted from the last chapter, as they are evidently modern impressions, although the obverse dies may have been cut at the date claimed for them.

#### OBVERSE NO. 1.

Device, — An eagle facing left, resting upon a rock.

Field, — Plain.

#### OBVERSE NO. 2.

Device, — An eagle, with wings displayed, resting upon a shield.

Field, — Plain.

#### REVERSE.

Inscription, — Trial piece. Designed for United States Cent.  1792

Borders, — Raised.  Edges, — Plain.  Size, 19.

## COPIES.

We have placed at the foot of most of our plates, (but in a few instances on other plates,) copies of some pieces there illustrated, that comparisons might be readily made, and the counterfeits recognized when met with. We will here give a list of these copies, not all of which were originally intended as counterfeits, but which are sometimes offered as genuine pieces.

Plate I. No. 18, — Sommer Island Shilling, — issued by A. S. Robinson.

Plate I. Nos. 19 to 25, Plate II. Nos. 25 to 28, and Plate III. Nos. 17 and 18, — Wyatt's Counterfeit New England Silver money.

Plate III. Nos. 19, — W. Idler's Lord Baltimore Penny. No. 20 represents one with the name and address removed.

Plate IV. No. 20, — A. S. Robinson's Rosa Americana Twopence of 1733.

Plate VII. Nos. 34 and 35, — J. A. Bolen's Confederatios.

Plate VIII. Nos. 27 to 30, — The George Clinton, Liber Natus, and Higley Copper, by J. A. Bolen.

Plate IX. Nos. 27 and 29, — New York Doubloon, and New England Elephant, issued by A. S. Robinson, and No. 28, — The Carolina Elephant, by J. A. Bolen.

Plate X. No. 24, Bolen's Bar Cent, 25, — Idler's Washington Half Dollar, and 27, — Edwards's Immune Columbia.

We have endeavored to make our descriptions, measurements, and weights, as complete as possible, but it will often be found that planchets were used greatly differing in thickness, size and weight ; therefore, where a range of weight is not specified, the weight of the heaviest specimen found is given. An apparent difference may also be noticed where some dies when struck on a small planchet appear to be milled at the border, while when struck on a large planchet the border will be beaded ; this appears among the Rosa Americanas, the Vermonts, and perhaps elsewhere.

The following pieces have come to our knowledge since the chapters in which they belong were printed.

A new obverse die of the larger Saint Patrick piece ···FLORE AT REX· with the letters of the legend much larger than that before described : its reverse does not differ from that of the other variety.

The smaller St. Patrick piece FLOREAT : REX: · noted as in silver, is an error, as the piece supposed to be in silver proves to be copper, plated.

A new obverse die of the Rosa Americana Twopence, the reverse of which has no label and is shown on plate III. No. 14.

A specimen in brass, of the Wood's Pattern, with reverse No. 2, (p. 147,) is in Mr. Appleton's collection, thus making two specimens in brass.

A Vermont coin of 1788, with legend VERMON AUOTORI the C inverted : it is found with reverse A, and is owned by Dr. Maris.

Nos. 3 and 4 of Connecticut coins of 1785 are found with reverse A.

A new head, mailed bust, probably of 1786, No. 2, but so worn as to render a description impossible. It belongs to Dr. Maris.

A new reverse of 1786, punctuated, INDE ⚬ ET · LIB: with obverse No. 5.

Reverse B of 1786, should have the legend INDE ⚬ ET LIB an impression from that die, owned by Dr. Maris, showing this singular punctuation. The impressions previously found were imperfect, and the punctuation illegible.

A new reverse of 1787, with legend *INDE:** * ET·I IB:* is found with obverses 35 and 37. Both specimens are owned by Dr. Maris.

Reverse N, of 1787, draped busts, should have a period instead of a dash between ET LIB

Among New Jerseys a new die of No. 3, of 1786, with reverse F.

Dr. Maris sends us a new die of No. 6 of 1786, which has the cross-bar of the singletree parallel with the beam of the plough.

A new die of reverse B of 1787, with obverse 1. In this die the second U shows that an s was first put in its place, and the U stamped over it.

Two new dies of No. 4 of 1787, with reverse D. Both belong to Dr. Maris.

A Washington piece like Fig. 106, on a thin planchet, owned by Mr. Parmelee, has an edge ornamented in circles and squares like a thick one before described, and weighs but 180 grains.

# INDEX.

☞ For references to particular pieces and plates, see legends and inscriptions. The pieces not represented on the plates are indicated by a cipher (0), but no references are made to the cuts, which will be readily found. The figures refer to pages, and the Roman numerals to the plates.